DISCARD

DUEL for the MIDDLE KINGDOM

DUEL for the MIDDLE KINGDOM

The Struggle Between *Chiang Kai-shek* and *Mao Tse-tung* for Control of China

William Morwood

EVEREST HOUSE
Publishers   New York

Maps by Rafael Palacios

The author is grateful to Lois Wheeler Snow and Grove Press, Inc. for permission to quote excerpts from the first revised and enlarged edition of *Red Star Over China* by Edgar Snow. Copyright 1938, 1944 by Random House, Inc. Copyright © 1968 by Edgar Snow.

The author is also grateful to Han Suyin and her publishers, Little, Brown and Company for permission to quote excerpts from *The Morning Deluge: Mao Tse-tung and the Chinese Revolution 1893-1954.*

Copyright © 1980 by William Morwood
All Rights Reserved
ISBN: 0-89696-047-1
Library of Congress Catalog Card Number: 79-51193
Published simultaneously in Canada by
Beaverbooks, Pickering, Ontario
Manufactured in the United States of America by
American Book-Stratford Press, Inc.
Saddle Brook, New Jersey
Designed by Sam Gantt
First Edition

*For Joel
with love and admiration.*

Contents

1. Reunion in Chungking — 5
2. Son of the Tiger Gentry — 17
3. The Rebel of Shaoshan — 36
4. The Bungled Bomb at Wuhan — 46
5. Revolutionaries in Limbo — 57
6. Cross Currents — 74
7. The Tsungli Passes — 87
8. Claimants to the Mantle — 105
9. The Aborted Crusade — 115
10. Massacre at Shanghai — 128
11. Thunder on the Plains, Fire in the Mountains — 144
12. The Fat Days of the Kuomintang — 156
13. Years of the Ram and the Rooster — 172
14. Flight of the Hundred Thousand — 193
15. Eve of a Great Change — 213
16. Collision in Sian — 227
17. The Devil Is our Leader — 244
18. Typhoon from the North — 254
19. One Divides into Two — 264
20. Kill All, Burn All — 274
21. The Will to Fight — 287
22. Squatting on Mount Omei — 302
23. Shall We Dare to Win? — 319
24. Circles within Circles — 334
25. Amid Fire and thunder — 348
26. Transformations Utterly Inconceivable — 373
    Afterword — 388
    Bibliography — 397
    Notes — 403
    Index — 417

Maps

1. China Under the Manchus and Kuomintang — *2*
2. Red Bases 1927-1934 — *149*
3. The Long March (Oct. 1934 to Oct. 1935) — *194*
4. Stilwell in Burma 1942-1944 — *288*
5. North China and Manchuria 1945-1949 — *335*

The Occident called the vigorous nation "Chinese," presumably after the Chin dynasty that created the empire, but in their own language they call themselves "men of the Middle Kingdom (*Chung Kuo Jen*)."

—O. Edmund Clubb in *20th Century China*

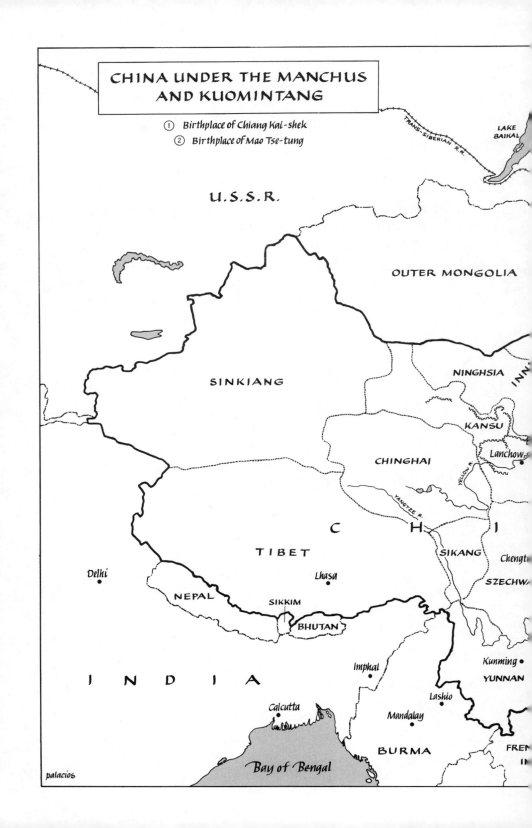

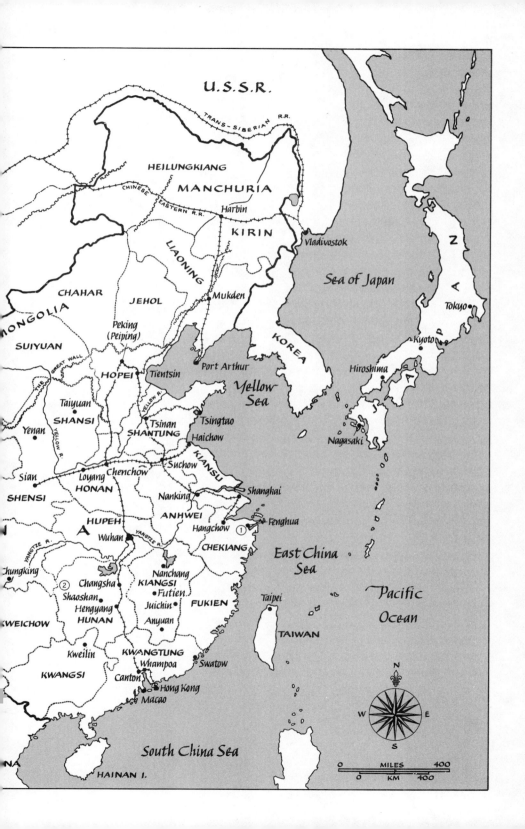

1

Reunion in Chungking

THE C–47 LET DOWN, LOSING ALTITUDE FAST WEST OF the mountains. It circled the river, taking bearings, then slid in between the hills for a landing on the airstrip. August 28, 1945 and it was hot. Hot with a soupy viscosity dreaded by foreigners and which had led Chungking to be called before the war the hell-hole of China. The all-pervading humidity would last into October, to be replaced as winter came on with a clammy chill no less persistent.

The notables gathered to meet the plane—National Government officials in long silk gowns, Chinese and U.S. army officers in dark brown or suntan uniforms—were sweating. Fans fluttered and brows were mopped as the aircraft swung around, then taxied across the infield and braked, wheels kicking rocks from the macadamized surface. A door was wrested open from the inside and landing steps were pushed up.

First to emerge was Major General Patrick J. Hurley, U.S. Ambassador to China. An energetic, uninhibited man in his early sixties, Hurley had played a vital role in promoting the negotiations about to take place between the National Government of China and the Communist dissidents. He looked dapper in a double-breasted suit, bow tie, and gray fedora. He removed the hat and waved it triumphantly at the scrambling photographers.

Next down the steps was Mao Tse-tung, chairman of a regime known as the Border Region government, leader of a radical movement which had exploded in North China with the force of Christianity under the Roman empire. Mao was garbed in a creased cotton uniform. He held an umbrella, and his head was half lost under a pith helmet. Why the helmet—a solar topee, a type of headgear more associated with foreign taipans (Englishmen who went out in the midday sun) than with Marxist intellectuals—was never explained.

Mao Tse-tung was fifty-one, six feet tall—unusually tall for a Chinese—with a frame once worn lean from evading pursuit but now filled out, chubby, after ten years of directing a revolution from a cave in his capital at Yenan. Mao, usually calm and imperturbable, described a few years earlier as a "plain man of the people, the queer mixture of peasant and intellectual, the unusual combination of great political shrewdness and earthy common sense," appeared uncertain today, ill at ease. He stood shifting from one foot to another, blinking as though dazed by the sudden attention after eighteen years of obscurity. Other members of his party—Chou En-lai, chief diplomat of the Red regime and Wang Jo-fei, prominent in the secretariat—seemed composed by comparison.

The reception committee—officials of the Nationalist Party, called the Kuomintang—closed in to offer greetings. Many of them were known to Mao. He had been their comrade in the old days in Canton, working with them to prepare the crusade that was to sweep China under the leadership of Sun Yat-sen, Founding Father of the revolution. But then Sun had died and paths had divided. Mao had been driven from the ranks of the respectable, decreed a bandit with a price of $250,000 on his head.

Next it was the turn of the newsmen, foreign and domestic. They crowded around with questions. "What did you think of your first plane ride?" Mao was asked. He pondered as though exploring political implications before answering, "Very efficient." He might have added that the trip had been an easy passage compared with the last time he had passed this way—give or take a few hundred miles to the west. That had been during the Long March when his hosts of today had tried to exterminate him and his ragged army at every river crossing and crook in the mountains. But he hadn't come to Chungking to brood about the past. As he told the reporters, peace was the only important matter now. The victory over the Japanese must not be lost; it was of "the utmost urgency" to unite China and avert a civil war. That is what he had come to negotiate.

Greetings and interviews over, movement began toward the waiting cars. Ambassador Hurley, ignoring the vehicle provided by the National Government, pressed Mao Tse-tung into his own black limousine. The cavalcade started back for town, past the rice paddies and the malodorous cabbage fields of Szechwan Province, the road lifting as it approached the narrow plateau between the Yangtze and Chialing rivers where Chungking, the wartime capital of China, was jammed. Throughout the twenty-mile drive the ditches were lined with people standing silently. Peasants who had been known to till their fields impassively while Japanese bombs dropped all around during air raids had downed tools to catch a glimpse of the visitor from the North. Mao Tse-tung was used to veneration in his own region, a territory straddling three provinces with a population of a hundred million. There he was often affectionately called Laotse, or the "Old Boy," a name harking back in inference to the sixth century B.C. founder of Taoism, the cult of simplicity and oneness with nature. But now Mao was far from home and the wonder was that word about him had spread. Few of the bystanders on the road to Chungking could have known much about communism but all were ready for change, any change, and perhaps the moon-faced man in the speeding American automobile was the instrument to bring it about.

Crowds grew thicker on the outskirts of the city. Without any official posting of time or route, somehow the people had heard and were congregated on the streets. Ambassador Hurley had meant to whisk the distinguished visitor across the river to his own summer residence, but by now Mao Tse-tung was firm in what he wanted. He would lodge with the rest of the Communist delegation in quarters provided by the National Government. Accordingly the limousine crept up narrow lanes to the settlement known as Red Cliff while Mao stared out the windows amazed at the commotion he was causing. It was the first time he had even seen a city of any size since 1930 when his peasant armies had been beaten back from the walls of Changsha.

All afternoon throngs milled about the building where the delegation from Yenan was housed, pressing against police cordons, calling for Mao to appear. He remained out of sight, but privileged persons who were admitted to his presence brought out news of "his every gesture, his habits, what he ate, what he said." It became known that Mao had written a poem on his flight to Chungking and the residence was soon deluged with reciprocal verse.

Actually Mao, never a man to waste time, was hard at work discussing strategy with his Communist colleagues. The prospect of changing enmity to friendship with the Nationalists after so many years of bitterness and bloodshed was a thorny matter. And in between talks, no doubt, he luxuriated in eating rice again. For a decade he had been limited to a diet of millet in impoverished Northwest China, and Mao came from Hunan, a province of rice and notably spicy cuisine. He used to say that it was a combination of Karl Marx and Hunan hot pepper that had made him a Communist, equating fiery food with revolutionary ardor.

That night a state banquet was held. Present were the leading officials of the Kuomintang, the political party that alone held legal status in the land, along with a full-dress turnout of army officers, financiers, and scholars. Present too were high ranking foreigners—American, British, French, Russian—heads of embassies and military missions. It was a gathering of eagles but inevitably interest narrowed down to the chief protagonists of the evening—Mao Tse-tung and his implacable enemy for twenty years, Generalissimo Chiang Kai-shek. President of the National Republic of China.

In August 1945 Chiang Kai-shek was fifty-seven. He was five-foot-ten, erect, lean, soldierlike, his dark eyes piercing, his cheeks still unlined, showing age only in that he had shaved off his hair and mustache to conceal encroaching gray. For eighteen years he had been the acknowledged strong man of China, for the last fifteen its unofficial dictator. In the minds of his followers he had become the indispensable leader of his country, a legend to which Chiang himself wholeheartedly subscribed. Seven years before, when driven from his capital at Nanking by the Japanese, he had faced retreat without qualms. "Wherever I go, there goes the government," he had said, and he meant it, not as a boast but as a sober matter of fact.

Like Mao Tse-tung, Chiang was a mixture of elements—part ascetic, part scholar, part resourceful politician, part determined, if not always successful, military commander. It was the Confucian side of his nature that appealed most to his conservative contemporaries. Drilled in the ancient texts—the *Four Books* and *Five Classics*—he had throughout his career modeled himself on a Confucian ideal, the superior man who is at all times "stern, high-minded, unyielding in his sense of propriety, ruthless and incorruptible." His success in this respect was much admired, but because of his lofty principles Chiang had always found it hard to compromise, and compromise was essential if peace negotiations with the Communists were to come to anything.

At the banquet Chiang Kai-shek offered a toast. Leaning across a table decked with white iris—symbols of peace—he raised his glass to Mao Tse-tung and expressed the hope that "we can now go back to the days of 1924." The toast was described as the "sole political remark" of the evening but its significance was not lost on the assembly.

In 1924 Sun Yat-sen had invited the Communists to join his Kuomintang Party. They were not permitted to enter *en bloc* but individual Reds might retain previous affiliations while promising to be loyal to the Kuomintang and subject to its discipline. Chiang Kai-shek was now clearly inviting Mao and his followers back on the same terms.

It was a doomed expectation. Too much had changed since the glory days when Sun Yat-sen was alive. Mao and Chiang had changed in outlook, personality, and stature, changed beyond recognition. In 1924 Mao Tse-tung had been a rather complacent young politico climbing the ladder of success. Eloquent and persuasive, he had by the age of thirty-one risen to prominence in the youthful Communist Party and to position and office in the mature Kuomintang where he served as a director of propaganda and sat on the august Central Executive Committee. Chiang Kai-shek's career had lagged by comparison. Doggedly devoted to Sun Yat-sen but without evident flair, he had been relegated to background duties. At thirty-seven the best post that could be found for him was commandant of Whampoa Military Academy, training cadets for the forthcoming revolution.

Three years later the positions were radically reversed. Sun Yat-sen was dead and the coalition he had forged died with him. The forces of the Right turned on the Left with a vengeance. Mao Tse-tung was out of office, out of orthodox politics, hunted as an outlaw along with all other Communists. Chiang Kai-shek, making good use of the troops he had trained at Whampoa, had risen to power through an anti-Red purge and was well on his way to capturing control of the nation.

At the banquet in Chungking Chiang Kai-shek offered his toast to the days of 1924 and Mao Tse-tung responded politely. The men smiled at each other as the flashbulbs exploded and the cameras clicked. Considering everything that had happened, the wonder was that they could smile. For in the years of devastation and slaughter between 1927 and 1936 Mao had lost a wife, two children, a sister, a brother, and a host of close comrades to Chiang and his relentless legions; the Generalissimo, frustrated again and again in his efforts to eradicate the Reds, had suffered defeat and humiliation at the hands of Mao and his insolent guerrillas. So the men smiled but few were deceived as to what they really felt. As Mao once put it in another connection, smiles can have a "murderous intent behind [them]."

Some saw the banquet as a revival of an old Chinese tradition—the meeting of generals before battle to size each other up. If so, what weaknesses were uncovered? Perhaps Chiang, watching Mao shovel in food with a coolie's gusto and chain-smoke cigarettes between courses, came to the conclusion that he was flabby. Or Mao, offended by the Generalissimo's aloofness once the opening ceremonies were over, might have been confirmed in his opinion that his foe was arrogant. In either case the estimates would have been off the mark. For before the duel was over, before the fury of combat had reached its height—or, as the Chinese say, before the tree had fallen and the monkeys had scattered—it was Chiang who turned flabby and Mao who swelled up as arrogant as they come.

With the banquet over and festivities out of the way, the delegates settled down for talks that were to last forty-two days. There were strong pressures for a quick adjustment of differences. After eight years of the Japanese war the country was prostrated, farm lands ruined, populations dispersed, towns and cities looted and bankrupt, communications in shambles, and everywhere the living were mourning the dead. The threat of further agony, a civil war, was not to be tolerated. The demand was for peace, a time for recovery and reconstruction.

And there were outside pressures. In the United States, President Harry S. Truman, alarmed that World War II had opened the door for revolutionary overthrows, demanded an end to civil strife in China and promised generous American loans and assistance once a democratic coalition government was established. And in Russia, Joseph Stalin, also intent on supporting the status quo for his own reasons, exerted what little influence he had left with the Chinese Communist Party by strongly advising Mao Tse-tung to make and be satisfied with the best deal he could get in Chungking.

So prospects for a successful negotiation looked good, though they didn't take into account the peculiarities of the situation. Sitting across the conference table were two parties on different levels. One, the Kuomintang, claimed to be the sole legitimate government in the land; the other, the Communist Party, was without status, outlawed in fact, its members subject to arrest and imprisonment if not summary execution. It was as if the convicts were negotiating with the wardens not only for better conditions but, audaciously, for equal rights. Of course, this distinction was politely ignored by all concerned. Nobody was going to arrest anybody because of one overriding consideration. The Communists possessed a formidable army—a million men,

600,000 regulars and some 400,000 auxiliaries and partisans—and unless some way could be found to neutralize this force the talks were doomed to failure.

In the early stages of the conference the delegates deftly skirted around this central issue, concentrating instead on broad declarations of democratic principles. Considering that none present had ever lived under a democracy, they made an excellent job of it. It was agreed that an effective coalition government must depend on the consent of a free and enlightened electorate, so a bill of rights was drawn up guaranteeing freedom of person, belief, speech, press, assembly, and other liberties "as enjoyed by the people in all democratic countries." From this it was only a small leap to cross the first hurdle; legalizing all patriotic political parties, including the Communist Party, thus terminating the Kuomintang's long monopoly of government by exclusive rule.

Here, though, Chiang Kai-shek entered an exception. Full democracy, he claimed, could not yet be applied to Mao Tse-tung's Border Region. That regime had been set up illegitimately by rebels, and free elections there at the present time could only compound lawlessness. He proposed postponing democracy in that area until other political adjustments had been worked out.

Mao Tse-tung lodged vigorous objections but agreed to table the matter while the delegates moved on to an even more prickly problem: unifying and nationalizing the rival Kuomintang and Communist armies.

Mao proposed that all parties join in creating a Military Council which would reduce the armies to a standing militia, troops to be drawn pro rata from either side. Again the Generalissimo intervened. He saw no need for a new Military Council since the Kuomintang had a perfectly serviceable one already in existence. If the Communists wanted to show good faith, they should hand over their soldiers to this body to be absorbed into the Nationalist forces. The proposal was tantamount to asking for the surrender of an army in advance of battle. Or, as an exasperated Mao Tse-tung put it, killing off the watchdogs, then turning the chickens over to the guardianship of the foxes.

There was much to exasperate Mao as time went on. It was

galling that he had to sit through the stifling heat of September in the conference room while the Generalissimo remained aloof, cooling himself in his hilltop mansion known as the Eagle's Nest. Every evening detailed minutes of the meetings were carried up to Chiang for criticisms, revisions or, often, rejections, necessitating further grueling sessions on matters already thought disposed of. Later Mao was to say that Chiang Kai-shek had treated him like a peasant while he was in Chungking, and no doubt the Generalissimo's Olympian attitude contributed to the complaint.

Another cause for irritation was the dubious role played by Patrick J. Hurley, the American ambassador. Hurley had gone out of his way to win Mao's confidence before the negotiations, representing himself as strictly impartial between the Kuomintang and Communists, not wedded to the philosophy of either side and wanting only what was good for China to result from the conference. But it became evident as talks continued that Hurley was growing impatient at what he considered Communist stubbornness and Mao suspected, not without reason, that he was urging the Generalissimo to stand firm and make no unnecessary concessions because, no matter what happened, the support of the United States government would remain solidly behind him.

No doubt Chiang was gratified by Hurley's reassurances, but he didn't really need them. As always he was playing his own game and American winds, blowing alternately hot and cold, were merely barometric readings. He was pleased by the attention the Chungking talks were getting. The world press was depicting him as an enlightened statesman meeting rebels more than halfway, forgetting bygones in the national interest. That was what was important at the moment—rebuilding his image, which had suffered in recent years. The negotiations themselves were inconsequential. He had agreed to nothing that couldn't be rescinded if the necessity arose. Meanwhile he was gaining time, and a cover, to prepare his own solutions for China's ills.

For by now Chiang Kai-shek had lost all interest in the coalition government that U.S. President Harry S. Truman was trying to force on him. He had never been sanguine that he could come to an accommodation with the Communists on the only terms acceptable to him as China's unchalleged leader. Now he knew there was no chance whatever. But his conscience was clear; he had tried. At the opening banquet he had given the Reds a last opportunity. He had invited them, if somewhat elliptically, to join his government on the same conditions under which they had entered Sun Yat-sen's government in 1924. That meant as individuals, without an army, owing their first allegiance to the Kuomintang, loyal to its policies and subject to its discipline.

According to Chiang's view, the conditions had been rejected, and that ended the matter. He had no intention of entering into a coalition with armed rebels who had defied him for eighteen years and would continue to make trouble. There was only one way to deal with insurrection and that was to crush it. Even if he had had little success in that enterprise in the past, the circumstances were now radically different. In his own mind, he calculated that he had the power to eradicate the Communist conspiracy in from eight to ten months, or at most a year.

The Generalissimo had planned his strategy carefully. He had an army of five million men to pit against the poorly equipped Red bandits, odds of five to one. Many of his troops had been trained by American officers and were provisioned with the latest weapons and machines of war. And American military aid was also flowing in to him in other ways despite President Truman's demand that peace be found at the conference table. Even as the Chungking talks dragged on, American ships and planes were transporting Chiang's troops to designated battlefronts with no questions asked as to what they would do when they got there. The Generalissimo didn't need Ambassador Hurley's assurances that United States policy would stand behind him no matter what he did; he was already obtaining the proof. And he was confident that as time went on, America would be drawn even closer into alliance.

By late September the movement of Chiang's troops and the Communists' efforts to impede or counteract them had introduced a new atmosphere into the Chungking conference room. Armed clashes were taking place throughout North China and Manchuria and the negotiations were constantly broken into by accusations of treachery and bad faith.

In early October the meetings, deteriorating from parliamentary differences to dogfights, formally adjourned. As a face-saving measure a document called the October 10th Agreement was drawn up. But there was very little agreement in it: all substantive issues had been tabled or left in deadlock. Mao Tse-tung subsequently characterized the document as "words on paper."

His mission over, Mao prepared to fly home. He was depressed by the turn of events. Despite his years of conflict with the Kuomingtang—half of them spent fighting in the open, half feuding behind the scenes during the uneasy pretense of a united front—he had genuinely believed that an accord might be reached at Chungking. He believed that the times and conditions were ripe for it. Cautiously optimistic, he had told his followers before leaving Yenan that a coalition government "would bring about a new stage of cooperation" between the Communist and Kuomintang parties, requiring changed attitudes and different "methods of legal struggle."

He had never put much faith in Chiang Kai-shek. At various times he had called him a liar, a butcher, and a very treacherous fellow, but he had hoped that "domestic and foreign pressures"—especially President Truman's personal interest in a coalition government—would force the Generalissimo into a change of policy. Chiang had shown once before that he was capable of change—at Sian, nine years earlier, when astonishing events had liberalized his inflexible will—and surely he could change again when the alternative was a civil war that would convulse China for years to come. Even the Generalissimo, steeped in Confucianism and conservative to the core, must realize that a new spirit of liberation was abroad in the Middle Kingdom and, unless he helped to direct and guide it, other hands would do it for him.

But Mao Tse-tung had been wrong. In Marxist terms, he had applied concrete analysis to concrete conditions, and misjudged the result. He knew now that there was to be no coalition government and he was returning home to announce his failure. He could anticipate a bitter fight within his own party, perhaps a break-up into factions that could never be drawn together again. Then there was the Red army, exhausted after years of struggle, desperate for new weapons and time for recuperation. And there were the people of North China—Mao's people, almost one-third of the nation's population. How would they react when told that civil war, not peace, lay ahead?

Months later Mao Tse-tung was to be asked the question, "Can you dare to win?" On that plane ride back to Yenan his only answer could have been, "Can we hope to survive?"

But underground currents were at work. The sleeping giant of China was at last awakening from hibernation and, in the end, Mao's analysis of concrete conditions was to prove correct. Change there was because change there had to be.

Exactly four years less ten days after Mao Tse-tung's departure from Chungking, he was to stand in Tien An Men Square in Peking announcing the founding of the People's Republic of China while Chiang Kai-shek, defeated by forces he could no longer understand, let alone control, had fled for refuge to Taiwan.

2

Son of the Tiger Gentry

WHERE A MAN IS BORN IS OF GREAT IMPORTANCE IN China. Each province, as with some states in the United States, carries connotations, real or imagined, concerning the character of its inhabitants. Thus the residents of Kwangtung Province are supposed to be belligerent and argumentative and those of Hupeh artful and tricky, just as Texans are clichéd as loud and bragging and Vermonters as taciturn and shrewd. Chiang Kai-shek was born in Chekiang, a province noted for its silk industry, mountain scenery, the beauty of its women, and the irascibility of its men.

He was born on October 31, 1887 in the village of Chikow in the hsien or county of Fenghua. Like many people coming from insignificant rural locations he preferred to connect himself with his county rather than his native hamlet. So also Irishmen who claim to be from County Clare or County Cork rather than from Bally-this or Carrick-that.

The Chiangs were comparative newcomers to Fenghua as such things go in China. Supporters of the Ming Dynasty, they had fled to the highlands of the Southeast when the Manchus, or Ching Dynasty, conquered the nation in 1644, twenty-four years after the Pilgrims landed on Plymouth Rock. The Chiangs were farmers and in time became prosperous landlords in a region of terraced rice paddies, bamboo groves, and gurgling brooks, a landscape suggestive of Chinese prints. It was a paradise to grow up in for a small boy called Chou-tai, the infant or "little" name of the man who was to become Chiang Kai-shek.

The patriarch of the Chiang clan during the boy's childhood was his grandfather, an austere dignitary who had once lived an adventurous life. As a young man, in the 1850s, Chiang Yu-piao had been driven from his home by the wild-haired Taiping rebels and forced to travel for safety to Shanghai a hundred miles away, a considerable journey in those days. But energetic and able even in adversity, he seems to have done well in the fabulous city built by foreigners on the mudflats at the mouth of the Yangtze River. At least he came home after the tide of rebellion had subsided with enough money to buy additional land and set up as a tea and salt merchant. The salt suggests political influence since it was an imperial monopoly.

Chou-tai learned much in his walks about the village with his long-gowned grandfather. He became familiar with the local hierarchy, noting the gradations between the depths of bows to his distinguished relative and those accorded lesser mortals. He listened while peasants were admonished for being behind in rent payments, and sometimes saw persistent delinquents beaten with bamboo canes or dispossessed. At the clan temple he heard his grandfather lecture on the Confucian verities to a congregation of Chiangs ranging from the well off to the wretchedly poor. A man's lot in life must be accepted, the patriarch told them; it was fate that determined wealth or poverty. Fate and, of course, the aid and advice offered by the spirits of ancestors. Though here again there were inequalities that could not be overcome. An ancestor interred in a ditch was not likely to provide as much benevolent assistance to the living as one laid away in a choice lot situated with due regard to wind and water and other geomantic considerations. It was a pity but *mei-yu fa-tze*, nothing could be done about it. Of course, members of the clan who were Buddhists might hope for better fortune in their next reincarnation.

Little by little the boy Chou-tai gained experience in the precepts, written and unwritten, of Confucian society. Born to the elite of the rural gentry—the "tiger" gentry it was called, as distinct from the "sedan chair" gentry of towns and cities—he learned the authority of status, of education and wealth, particularly landed wealth, and the submissions to be exacted. Most of all he learned to cherish the old, traditional, immemorial ways and to hate and fear change and disorder.

The Taiping rebels had been disorderly, as the grandfather never tired of pointing out. Even their wild hair, allowed to flow without restraint, was a travesty of the neatly braided queues of decent people. They had been nothing but a horde of riotous peasants disrupting the calm and order of everyday life. Not that riots in themselves were so unusual; at times of crop failure or flood and general starvation they were common enough. In fact, there was an old saying that every thirty years there was, somewhere in China, a small upheaval, every one hundred a great tumult. What had made the Taipings different and obnoxious were the airs they put on, their claims to grandeur through divine mission.

Their leader had been a man called Hung Hsiu-chuan, a failed schoolteacher who had become a Christian, converted by a foreign missionary in Canton. Hung had dreamed of a white-haired man seated on a throne who had adopted him as a son and presented him with a great sword of vengeance. Later Hung realized that the white-haired patriarch was the Christian God, so in effect he had been anointed the younger brother of Jesus Christ and charged with the mission of establishing on earth a kingdom of Taiping or Great Peace. All hocus-pocus, Chou-tai's grandfather scoffed; window dressing to conceal the fact that the Taipings were no more than common bandits.

Still, there was no denying that the movement had caught on. Thousands flocked to join Hung Hsiu-chuan, now calling himself the Heavenly King, in the hills outside Canton. The Christianized community numbered a million or more when it organized into a crusade and headed north to conquer China. Nothing could stop the fanatical fighting men, deploying swords and spears and later captured muskets. Provincial levies and imperial banner troops alike gave way before them. The forces of the Heavenly Kingdom swept up to the Yangtze, capturing Nanking in 1853 and establishing a capital and government there that was to last for eleven years.

There were those who said that the Taipings had done good things, that they had divided up the land equally among all, that they had put a stop to foot-binding and raised women to equal status with men, that they had prohibited opium smoking and the sale of children, but—and Chou-tai's grandfather was stern in warning—such fables were not to be believed. The Taipings hadn't shared land equally with him, had they? They'd dispossessed him and run him off his property just because as a landlord and money lender he was unpopular with riffraff. Let Chou-tai remember that no good ever came of upsetting the social order. As Confucius himself had said, propriety serves as a dike against excesses, and the Taipings were proof of what could happen when wild, foreign ideas circulated among the ignorant.

If little Chou-tai wanted to pick a hero from the sorry mess of the Taiping period, let it be Tseng Kuo-fan, the Confucian-scholar official who had turned soldier to save his country. Entrusted by the Manchu emperor to crush the rebellion, and appointed governor of Hunan Province to finance* his campaigns, Tseng Kuo-fan had trained a disciplined army which, with foreign help, had turned the tide and defeated the Taipings. Their capital at Nanking was captured and sacked July 19, 1864, just three months and thirteen days after General Ulysses S. Grant took Richmond and effectively ended another rebellion.

The grandfather's character-building role ended with his death in 1894. Chou-tai was then seven and other drastic changes were taking place in his life. He had passed through what the Chinese call the "golden years"—from birth to the beginning of school—when children are pampered by parental attention and overt affection.

School days brought an abrupt halt to permissive routines.

---

*A common imperial practice. The governor was expected to squeeze military funds out of his province through taxes, thus sparing the royal purse.

Discipline took over in the form of stern, often harsh, treatment from teachers, parents, and senior members of the clan. The objective was to suppress individuality and self-assertiveness in the youngster. From now on he was to be taught that in all things the interests of the family came first. Personal ambitions and aspirations, even the freedom to think and act according to conscience, were to be sacrificed when they clashed with the consensus or welfare of the group.

Since the village of Chikow was too small to boast a school, Chou-tai began his formal education in a neighboring town, boarding with relatives while he was meshed into a pedagogic system that hadn't changed in two thousand years. The teacher enunciated texts and his pupils yelled them back at him until they were indelibly committed to memory. Later came introduction to written characters or ideographs that stood for words, the complicated strokes copied from the blackboard with errors smartly criticized by means of the teacher's rod.

The curriculum was progressive, from easier to harder, from the *Hundred Names** to the *Four Books* and *Five Classics* of Confucius, and then on to more obscure philosophic essays of the ancients. Maxims, proverbs, and moral precepts were learned by rote with little effort made to explain their meaning. It was though unnecessary; life would explain them when students matured.

Chou-tai's father died when he was nine, so home training during his formative years devolved on his mother. She was not a first or "great" wife; her husband had been married and bereaved twice before, thus her status in the Chiang clan was low. Widowhood depressed it even more. Left with five children, not all her own, she was hard put to it to support her brood on scanty means. In time-honored fashion, her husband's assets had been divided among all the family units with no allowance made for her special needs. However, she seems to have accepted the situation stoically, raising pigs and chickens and taking in sewing to make ends meet.

---

*The clan surnames of China put to verse. Traditionally there were only a hundred names, though more crept in through the centuries. Most populous families were the Wangs, Changs, and Lis—the Smiths, Browns, and Joneses of the nation.

From all accounts she was a determined woman, a devout Buddhist and a strict disciplinarian, who was no doubt ambitious for her first-born son. Though there is perhaps some exaggeration in Chiang Kai-shek's later claims of how much he owed her—he raised a tablet in her memory inscribed "Greater than my mother there is none"—we may give her credit for encouraging the methodical work habits and persistency in action that were always the hallmarks of his career.

Childhood anecdotes about Chiang Kai-shek are few, partly because intimacy is alien to the culture and partly because he was not blessed with a biographer like Parson Weems to invent cherry trees for him. But one tale survives that has a ring of authenticity.

During mother Chiang's absence one night, the house was surrounded by village pranksters, moaning as though ghosts risen from tombs in a vengeful mood. Chiang's younger brothers and sisters were paralyzed by fear, but our hero, divining what was going on, determined to retaliate in kind. Grabbing a sheet, he ran for a big tree which the mischievous boys must pass on their way home. Suddenly emerging from behind the trunk, draped in the sheet and howling like a Chinese banshee, he frightened the pranksters into hysterics, some even falling insensible to the ground. Chiang calmly returned home and later didn't even bother to report the incident to his mother.

The anecdote illustrates several characteristics of the man who was one day to lead China: his imperturbability, his tactical imagination, and his talent for swooping down suddenly on unsuspecting enemies.

Chou-tai left school at eighteen, his head stuffed with classical learning. He was drilled in the Eight Virtues (loyalty, filial piety, benevolence, love, sincerity, righteousness, harmony, and peace), thoroughly familiar with the Five Obligations (duties as between ruler and subject, father and son, husband and wife, brother and brother, friend and friend), expert on the Four Social Bonds (decorum, propriety, integrity, and sense of shame), and word perfect on the Three Moral Qualities (wisdom, thoughtfulness, and courage). This curriculum undoubtedly seems to Western eyes overloaded on the moral side, with glaring omissions in mathematics, languages, and science, but such studies were thought irrelevant to the times and the society. A Confucian education was designed to turn out right-thinking gentlemen and generalists. It was assumed that any specialized knowledge later required would be supplied by underlings or otherwise picked up on the job. And in this elitist thinking the Chinese were not so different from the British who believed, until very recently, that governments and complex industries could be adequately run by men with no specialized training except in Greek and Latin verse.

Along with an education, Chou-tai had acquired a wife—picked out for him by his mother when he was fifteen—and two new names, also a maternal gift. He was to answer to Chung-cheng throughout his adulthood, with the alternative cognomen of Chieh-shih* for ceremonial occasions. It was his misfortune that Chieh-shih was transformed by the barbaric dialect of Canton into Kai-shek. And as it was in Canton that he first rose to fame, Chiang Kai-shek it has been to the world ever since.

The year in which Chiang Kai-shek emerged from the classrooms and began looking around for a career was 1905. Had the date been earlier, there would have been no hesitation as to his course of action. Inevitably he would have sat for the provincial examinations in the hope of obtaining a *hsiu tsai*, equivalent to a B.A. degree and the necessary qualification for official appointment. For by tradition, only through the imperial civil service, through tenure and advancement in the bureaucracy, could a youth without powerful family connections rise to distinction and wealth.

Unfortunately for young Chiang the times were out of joint. The Empress Dowager in Peking, harassed by debts, bullied by foreigners, and pressed by her own officials to at least go through the motions of reforming and modernizing her government, had suspended the imperial examinations which had been held unin-

---

*He had also had the baby or "milk" name of Jui-yuan. If this seems a plethora in nomenclature for a single individual, consider the plight of a Western youth as articulated by a jingle: "My mother calls me William/ My father calls me Will/ My sister calls me Willie/But the gang all call me Bill."

terruptedly since the seventh century A.D. The year of suspension was 1905, the year of Chiang Kai-shek's eligibility.

There were anxious meetings of the Chiang clan to decide what to do about the young man. His future was of conern to them all, for should he fulfill the promise of his stalwart personality he could bring distinction to the family and all would rise by, as the Chinese say, clinging to the hair of the dragon.

It was decided that a legal career was the best prospect available and money was raised to send him to Hangchow, the provincial capital, to train as a lawyer. Or perhaps more accurately, to train as an advocate for litigants, since there was in China no written code or body of laws in the Western sense except for the punishment of criminals. Civil cases were decided on their individual merits, or on the disposition of the magistrate which, more often than not, could be influenced by bribes and special favors. It was believed that in this shadowy world of dicker and deal young Chiang might do well once he learned his way about.

But the youth himself had another idea. It must have been difficult, a traumatic experience, for him to express it. The self-assertion involved, the opposition to the wisdom of family and clan, went against everything he had been taught or had absorbed by instinct. Yet somehow he found the courage to make known his ambition. He wanted to become a professional soldier.

The news must have been received with profound shock because no Chiang had ever before set his sights so low. Soldiers had no status in Chinese society. They were lumped at the bottom with vagrants, prostitutes, actors, and bandits, and it was a common saying that good iron is not used for nails nor good men for soldiers. Had the youth taken leave of his senses? What other explanation could there be for deliberately choosing an ignoble profession and bringing dishonor on his family?

But Chiang persisted. He had been developing his willpower by standing rigid for fifteen minutes a day with his jaws clenched, and now the exercise paid off. He delved into history, geography, and legend to add force to his arguments as he eloquently presented his case.

China had suffered unprecedented humiliation for more than

sixty years, he told his elders. The British had begun the reign of insults with the Opium War of 1840-42, forcing the Manchu emperor to accept an ever increasing traffic in the drug. The French had added further injury by grabbing off the possession now called French Indo-China in 1882-83. Afterward the Russians, Germans, and Japanese had crowded in for thefts of territory, either outright or under the guise of "spheres of influence." And when the Chinese had protested, as the common people had during the uprising known as the Boxer Rebellion in 1900, the foreign powers had combined to humiliate the nation further. They had marched together on Peking, sacking the city and then demanding an enormous indemnity to repay them for their trouble.

Such disgraces were not to be borne, but there would be no disposing of them until China made herself strong enough to drive out the foreign devils. A new race of heroes must arise, like Yo Fei or Wen Tien-hsiang of ancient times celebrated in the classics. Yet to be effective these new heroes must learn to fight in modern ways. And what better place for learning than in Japan, a nation that had been rising in power as China declined? Even as young Chiang spoke, Japan was astonishing the world by military victories on land and sea over mighty czarist Russia. The secret of Japan's strength and adaptation to the modern world must be found and brought back to revive China.

The youth's enthusiasm and appeals to patriotism carried the day. The funds collected to start him on a law career were turned over to take him to Japan. Chiang traveled to Shanghai and boarded ship for Tokyo. Then on the voyage he did an extraordinary thing—he cut off his queue.

The queue, a lifetime's growth of hair braided into a pigtail and worn down the back, was a badge of servitude and inferiority imposed on all Chinese by the conquering Manchus three centuries before. Actually it fitted neatly into a Confucian concept of filial piety—nothing inherited from parents was to be destroyed, the reason why some literal-minded cranks also wore foot-long fingernails—and in due course people forgot the humiliating origin of the practice and took pride in their ropy coiffures. Which was just as well, because disposing of them was still a serious offense, especially when radicals and revolutionaries took to cutting off their queues as symbols of liberation and protest against the oppressive Manchu regime.

That Chiang Kai-shek, fresh from the provinces, traditionally educated and conservative to the bone, could have separated himself from his pigtail for political reasons seems inconceivable. Yet cut it off he did, and boasted about it in later years without ever really making his motives clear. Biographers have tried to suggest that it was the Chiang clan's ancient grudge against the Manchus, the invaders who had driven the family from its ancestral acres generations ago, finding expression in its boldest member. But there could be a less complicated answer. It is possible that Chiang on shipboard, surrounded by the short hair of the Japanese and his own liberated countrymen, applied the knife to prevent looking like a country bumpkin when he reached Tokyo.

He had troubles enough as it was when he disembarked. He found he was ineligible for a Japanese military education because only advanced courses were offered foreigners. He was told to go home for basic training and return sponsored by the Chinese government. Cast adrift in an alien city, unable to speak the language or order food except by gestures, he was gloomily contemplating an ignominious return home when he was rescued by friendly Chinese students. There were thousands of them in Japan in that year of 1906, drawn by the same curiosity as Chiang, though most were studying literature, art, politics, and industrial techniques. They welcomed the exile from Fenghua into their company and in due course introduced him to another compatriot named Chen Chi-mei.

Chen Chi-mei, breezy, confident, about thirty years of age, was the secretary of a flourishing political organization known as the Tung Meng Hui or United League. The founder and president of the league, a dynamic man called Sun Yat-sen, was off traveling at the time, so Secretary Chen had leisure to devote to the frustrated young man seeking to be a soldier.

Chiang Kai-shek must have been startled to learn that the United League was a secret society run by revolutionaries. He knew from the classic texts that first among the Five Obligations comes a subject's loyalty to his ruler. Yet here were men plotting in a foreign country to overthrow the Chinese imperial system and substitute something called a republic in its place. The shock doesn't seem to have lasted long, however, possibly because of his growing attachment to Secretary Chen, a fellow provincial, born in Chekiang to a rich and influential silk manufacturing family. At any rate Chiang stayed on in Tokyo for several months, attending league meetings and making himself useful in its activities, while Chen wangled an appointment for him at Paoting Military Academy outside Peking.

Establishing a modern military academy was something else the Manchus had been forced into against their wills. But finally it was borne in on the Empress Dowager Tzu Hsi, also known as the Old Buddha and the current incumbent on the dragon throne, that sandaled troops armed with spears and bows were no longer adequate in the era of the Gatling gun and high explosives. Reluctantly she had commissioned Yuan Shih-kai, her most distinguished general, to found an up-to-date training school for officer cadets. And typically she had financed it in the imperial fashion, on the cheap, appointing Yuan governor of a province to sweat out what revenues he needed.

Chiang Kai-shek returned to China and entered Paoting Academy at the end of 1906. He was relieved to find that his missing queue excited no comment. Many of the cadets had cut theirs off too, since pigtails got in the way of martial equipment. Shearing was permitted but it was mandatory off the post to wear false queues. These were pinned inside the hat but rarely deceived sharp-eyed youngsters who gleefully followed the cadets around mocking them as "imitation foreign devils."

Chiang, hard-working, conscientious, physically fearless, soon made a reputation for himself. His capacity for command was also recognized and by 1907 he was back in Japan for advanced training, this time sponsored and supported by the Chinese government.

He enrolled at Shinbo Gokyo, a staff college near Tokyo, where he was to remain for two years. Apart from his military education, which continued proficiently, it seems to have been an unhappy period. He was isolated from Japanese cadets by the language barrier and found little in common with his Chinese classmates. Most of these were from the sedan-chair gentry, sons of Peking mandarins who had little serious interest in a military career. They smiled at Chiang's zeal, snickered at his high-pitched Chekiang accent and excluded him from their mah jong and drinking parties. Vacations must have come as a relief to the young soldier-in-training. He must have returned home to Fenghua at least once during this period, because his first son was born in 1909.

Little is known about Chiang's wife, the girl his mother had carefully selected for him in his fifteenth year. No doubt she was a few years older than her groom, which was both conventional and useful in that it put a stronger back immediately to work. She seems to have been obedient, dutiful, and uncomplaining, with small understanding of her husband's goals and ambitions. Of course, she came from without the clan as established by convention and, oddly enough in the light of subsequent history, her maiden surname was Mao.

During school terms in Tokyo, Chiang was inevitably drawn back to Secretary Chen and his colleagues at the United League. And soon there was another attraction. For Sun Yat-sen, leader of the plot to overthrow the Manchus, described as a man who "impressed not only by [his] fervor and sincerity . . . . but also by his intellectual powers," had returned from his travels to galvanize all around him. Sun Yat-sen, energetic, inspiring, charismatic, was a man to capture the imagination, as he did Chiang Kai-shek's for the rest of his life.

Sun Yat-sen, born in 1866 in a Kwangtung village under humble circumstances, remained to the end proud of his origins. He frequently boasted, "I am a coolie and the son of a coolie," though perhaps he was exaggerating a little. His father seems to have had some education, though he was sunk in poverty when his son arrived and the boy was early inured to hardships.

The struggle to exist combined with a sensitive nature inculcated in Sun Yat-sen a lifelong sympathy for the oppressed. He too had learned about the Taiping Rebellion in his childhood, but whereas to Chiang Kai-shek, echoing the sentiments of his grandfather, the wild-haired Taipings had been monsters, to Sun Yat-sen they had been much maligned patriots striving for justice.

From veterans of the Heavenly Kingdom crusade—Sun had been born just two years after the uprising had been crushed—he heard about the Great Peace as a time of sharing and equality and brotherhood never before known in China. He always considered the Taiping movement as the forerunner of the revolution he himself was trying to bring about, and prophesied that his success would be proof that the Taipings had not failed.

Perhaps it was the Taiping precedent of destroying old values, or perhaps it was the rebelliousness of Sun's own nature coming out, but Yat-sen, not yet a schoolboy, took to defacing Confucian tablets in the village temples. This quickly brought him to the attention of the authorities and the prognosis for the boy's future looked poor until he was rescued from further trouble by an older brother who had migrated to Hawaii and was doing well as a merchant. In the line of filial piety, Elder Brother Ah-mi sent for obstreperous Younger Brother Yat-sen to feed, clothe, and educate him until sense entered his head.

The education took place at a British missionary school where the boy not only acquired excellent English but also, as a teenager, developed a new and dangerous aberration. Rebellious again, expressing his independence of thought and personality, he announced that he meant to become a Christian. Confucian Ah-mi was appalled and shipped the reprobate back to his parents in China for reconditioning.

The young Yat-sen was lectured, threatened, and even married off to a suitable bride to tie him down by family responsibilities. But he wasn't to be diverted. He escaped to Hong Kong, received Christian baptism, and enrolled in a missionary medical school. He graduated as an M.D. in 1888 and set up in private practice, only to run afoul of Treaty Port prejudices. Westerners would have nothing to do with a "King's Chinaman," while his own compatriots who could afford medical services preferred European doctors for prestige reasons.

Again Yat-sen reacted, as he did all his life, to slights, insults, and injustices. He formed an organization to combat foreign arrogance and native sycophancy, thus beginning his struggle to restore national pride and rescue China from what he called a semi-feudal, semi-colonial status. His first secret society, founded in 1894, went under the name of the Hsing Chung Hui or Revive China Club. It was a reform group, aimed at awakening the Dowager Empress at Peking to the plight of her people, and to dramatize his program Sun Yat-sen staged a putsch at Canton.

The putsch failed. Plans were betrayed, gun deliveries went awry, supporters fell away, and the police had no trouble rounding up and executing conspirators caught on the spot. Similar mishaps and treachery were to plague all Sun's attempts at insurrection for the next fifteen years. But he kept trying. Even as he ran from local authorities and the Manchus' overseas agents, he continued to plot and organize uprisings. He believed in what he called the "propaganda of the deed," that heroic action in itself was contagious. In later years he used to say that he had tried and failed to mount revolutions ten times, and had succeeded on the eleventh attempt only by accident.

As time progressed, Sun Yat-sen's program changed. He was no longer content with mere reform, he wanted the Manchu Dynasty and its corrupt bureaucracy swept away, to be replaced by a republican form of government. In between putsches he traveled tirelessly around the world soliciting funds from the ten million overseas Chinese and appealing, with little success, for the support of democratic nations.

In 1896 Sun Yat-sen caused a stir. He was kidnapped by Manchu secret agents, in London of all places. Returning to his lodgings one day, he was set upon and hustled into the Chinese Embassy in broad daylight. He was held captive in an upstairs room while a ship was chartered to carry him home for death by the slicing sword.

Sun wrote messages and dropped them to the street until the ruse was discovered and the windows were sealed. But he did succeed in bribing an embassy servant to carry a note to his old chief at the Hong Kong medical college, now living in retirement a few blocks away. Dr. James Cantlie went to the British Foreign Office and Scotland Yard and Sun was rescued just in time.

From being a nobody, a fugitive conspirator, Sun Yat-sen was transformed overnight into an international celebrity of sorts. The rescue, with its overtones of honest virtue pitted against the sinister machinations of the East, appealed to the public imagination and the episode became a ten-day sensation in the world press. Sun got ample opportunity to explain his cause and the democratic struggle he was leading. But his efforts to exploit the situation with responsible statesman met with no better success than before. The Great Powers, he learned, were primarily concerned with maintaining the status quo in China and wherever else their commercial interests were at stake.

But Sun's newly won prestige did benefit him in another respect. It marked him as the outstanding patriotic leader of the Orient. His Hsing Chung Hui was by no means the only secret society aimed at the overthrow of the Manchu Dynasty. By the turn of the century there were at least a dozen, some operating precariously on the mainland but most headquartered in Japan where the Nipponese government, pursuing a policy of keeping China weak through dissension, offered them a wary hospitality.

It was in Tokyo in 1905—the year prior to the young Chiang Kai-shek's futile trip to the city—that Sun Yat-sen had combined many of these splinter groups, including his own Revive China Club, into the single organization called the Tung Meng Hui. He also provided the new society with a political program, a set of doctrines that were to become famous as the San Min Chu I or Three People's Principles—nationalism, democracy, and the people's livelihood.

Sun Yat-sen, an admirer of American institutions, said that he derived the principles from Abraham Lincoln's "of the people, by the people, and for the people." But of greater interest is what his followers made of the terms. For they were political innocents, venturing out from under the roof of patriarchal monarchy for the first time, completely unversed in the practical realities of self-government.

The first principle—nationalism—presented no problems. It was taken to mean getting rid of the Manchus and few looked for a further significance. Toppling the dynasty was a complete and cogent end in itself.

The second principle—democracy—was harder to grasp. In a culture where the closest definition of liberty was "running wild without a bridle," concepts of free elections and delegated responsibility tended to be vague. It was generally assumed that democracy meant carrying out in practice the Confucian virtues of righteousness and benevolence, which was acceptable enough to all concerned.

It was the third principle—the people's livelihood—that was the real stumper because it involved consideration for the underprivileged. Members of the league, intellectuals coming from the gentry class, were vitally concerned with the welfare of clan and family, but simply could not conceive of obligations to outsiders, especially contemptible peasants. Sun Yat-sen, with broader experience, knew that unless the land problem, which affected some 80 percent of China's population, was solved, there was little hope that a truly democratic government could succeed. But even he was so close to age-old traditions and prejudices that he had trouble finding a valid solution. The best he could come up with was a theory of "equalization of the land" by which "excess" acreage of big landlords would be purchased by the government for distribution to dispossessed farmers. The staggering cost and socialistic implications of the policy always disturbed him but he could see no other way out.

In 1905, however, the interpretation of the last two principles didn't really matter. Nationalism was the order of the day and "Down with the Manchus!" the battle cry. With that slogan the United League could and did advance. Members were sent back to China to organize clandestine chapters of the society. Within a year cells were established in seventeen of the eighteen provinces of China Proper. By 1907 membership was 10,000, recruits drawn mainly from schools and colleges, traditional secret societies, and army garrisons. By 1911, a year of destiny, enrollment had swelled to 300,000.

Sun Yat-sen in Tokyo in 1907—his forty-first year—was charged with vision and purpose. We have an eyewitness account of him from an earlier time—"of average height, thin and wiry, [possessing] a reckless bravery of the kind which alone can make a national regeneration"—which no doubt still held good. His enthusiasm was what most people remembered. His eyes gleamed as he talked revolution, which he could by the hour, riveting his listeners with an almost hypnotic spell.

He was, besides, a man of the world. He had seen more countries than the average Chinese had villages, and he could talk with a cosmopolitan charm and humor that set him apart from the classics-bound intellectuals of his day. Sun Yat-sen was a unique personality, and certainly the impressionable young Chiang Kai-shek had never met anyone like him.

It must have seemed to the awed young man, listening to the master lecture, or pulling close to him at informal meetings, that he had been singularly blessed. Chance had first guided his blundering footsteps to the United League's headquarters, pure accident had determined that Secretary Chen Chi-mei should be a fellow provincial from Chekiang and hence a surrogate elder brother, and only that astonishing sequence of events could have led to his meeting with Sun Yat-sen. The diffident, awkward youth could never have accomplished the meeting on his own. Somewhere the hand of fate must have been involved.

It was as if Chiang Kai-shek could never quite believe his luck. He could never take it for granted, then or later, when he achieved a relationship with Sun that approached intimacy. Through the rest of his life he never failed in respect and veneration for the great man, usually referring to him as the Tsungli (supreme leader) or the "father of our nation," or by his scholar's title Sun Wen, never by the name known to the rest of the world without deferentially preceding it with "Doctor." After Sun's death, when Chiang had succeeded him as the country's leader, he made the reading of the Tsungli's last will and testament compulsory on Monday mornings at all government offices and as part of the opening ceremonies at official party meetings. And he was jealous in his devotion. He once dismissed from office a veteran colleague for implying that he knew more about the dead Sun's purposes and intentions than Chiang did. He never seems to have recovered from the impact of those first years in Tokyo.

And what about Sun? What were his impressions of the youthful Chiang? One biographer of the Generalissimo tells us that there was immediate recognition of potential and quotes Sun as saying "that man will be the hero of our revolution." But this need not be taken too seriously. That the young man was training as a professional soldier was no doubt a recommendation to Sun. His movement was overloaded with intellectuals and the time might come when a man of action would be worth a dozen of them. But nothing in the record suggests that his interest went further than that.

Inevitably, sometime between 1907 and 1909, Chiang Kai-shek officially joined the United League. A struggle of will and conscience must have preceded the decision. He was, after all, an officer of the imperial army, drawing pay from the Manchu Dynasty and sworn to uphold the dragon throne with his life. Then there was the danger of his connection with revolutionaries becoming known—not unlikely in a Tokyo riddled with Manchu agents. At best he would be promptly dismissed from the army, at worst shipped home for punishment, in either case bringing disgrace on his family. And he would have deserved whatever penalties were imposed, for the Confucian texts were clear upon the point: among the Ten Unpardonable Crimes of a subject was conspiracy against the emperor.

But whatever the inner turmoil and misgivings, devotion to Sun Yat-sen and his cause won out. Chiang Kai-shek drank from the cup mingling his blood with that of his new brothers and took the oath of membership: "I swear unto heaven that I will do my utmost to work for the overthrow of the dynasty, the establishment of the Republic and the solution of the agrarian question by the equitable distribution of the land. I solemnly swear to be faithful to these principles. If I ever betray my trust may I be submitted to the severest possible penalties."

In 1909 Chiang graduated from Shinbo Gokyo and was given a choice of returning home to assume a command in China or staying on in Japan for practical field training. He chose the latter, perhaps partly to remain close to the United League and its charismatic leader and partly to assuage his conscience for dereliction of loyalty to the emperor by accepting the hardships he knew to be in store.

And indeed life in the Japanese artillery, to which Chiang was assigned as a private second class, was rigorous. Even as a foreign cadet and officer in training, he was spared no duty of his menial rank. He currycombed horses, pitched manure, cleaned officers' boots, and turned out in rain and snow to polish artillery pieces, with ferocious beatings the penalty for less than perfect performance. Chiang nevertheless seems to have delighted in the harsh discipline. Years later he was to tell his own cadets that it had helped mold his character, instilling patience and a deeper appreciation of simple things, such as the bowl of rice garnished with raw fish that constituted his daily meal.

In October 1911 the young soldier's career in the Japanese artillery came to an abrupt end. Receiving a startling message, he applied for a weekend furlough from which he never returned. Disguised as a workman, he was hustled aboard a ship and dispatched back to China where his services were more urgently needed.

For the long-awaited revolution had begun, an upheaval that was to disrupt the lives of millions of Chinese and start the career not only of Chiang Kai-shek but also that of an insignificant Middle School student called Mao Tse-tung.

3

The Rebel of Shaoshan

CONFUCIAN CULTURE, STRETCHING OVER THE NATION like a caul, stifled the genius of its people. Few Chinese were noted for independence of thought, initiative, or action, or cared to be. The whole system, which put its main emphasis on obedience to family and clan and loyalty to ancestral ways, was against it. Even the fifth century B.C. founder of the philosophy, the great Confucius himself, had hidden behind the pretense of collecting and passing on the wisdom of still earlier days rather than admit his role as a creator and innovator, and his example was slavishly followed. The land was full of imitators and reproducers, carbon copies of each other in the image of the past. Even men born to originate and lead were reluctant to develop their talents unless forced to it by dire necessity.

Yet every now and again there were exceptions, individuals of innate confidence who refused to quell their self-assertive natures, and among them was a boy called Mao Tse-tung, born December 26, 1893 in the village of Shaoshan in Hunan Province. From all accounts, he early knew his own mind and insisted on his personal rights within an all-encompassing authoritarian society. There seems no other explanation but that he was born a rebel and never changed character to the end of his life.

His childhood was replete with instances of revolt. In 1902, at the age of nine, indignant at an undeserved whipping at school, he spoke his piece to the teacher and walked out of the classroom. Afraid to go home to a beating from his father, he decided to run away. He had heard of a wonderful city beyond the hills and set out to find it. He tramped for three days, begging food and sleeping in ditches, only to wind up virtually on the doorstep of his distracted parents. The boy had confused directions and traveled in a circle.

Mao Tse-tung learned two things from the episode: it's better to know where you're going and, since both teacher and father treated him better on his return, militant action has value. Throughout his career it was his habit to submit experience to analysis and extract practical conclusions.

Mao's father, Jen-shen, came from rugged peasant stock. As a young man, escaping from the debts that were ruining his family, he joined the provincial army and apparently became adept in the tricks of extortion and squeeze that gave soldiering a bad name in China. At any rate, when he returned to his native village he had enough money to redeem the family property and honor. By the time Tse-tung, the oldest of three sons, was born the father was in comfortable circumstances, owning two and a half acres of prime rice land. Later he added to his holdings and also became a merchant in grains, moving into the category of "rich peasant."

It isn't often that a father's class status is defined for him by his son, but in this as in other respects Mao Tse-tung was exceptional. His classic description formulated later in life, fits his father into an exact category: "The rich peasant . . . engages in labor himself, but also relies on exploitation for part or even the major part of his income. His main form of exploitation is the hiring of labor . . . " And sure enough the Maos had hired hands, one on a full-time basis and another taken on during the rice processing season. The employees worked for their keep and wages of one Chinese dollar a month, the equivalent of about 35 cents U.S. In addition they got an egg with their rice once a month—a sore point with young Tse-tung who claimed he worked just as hard in the fields but never got the egg bonus from his parsimonious parent.

We see Jen-shen, the father, as harsh and austere, made stingy by the realities of peasant life where only the ruthless could survive. He was a traditional Confucian husband and father, authoritative and domineering, working his wife as he did his water buffalo and putting his sons to labor at the age of six. Though comparatively well off, he never failed to hear the wolf at the door and each day's toil was insurance against being devoured. It was through no yearning for culture or better things that Tse-tung was sent to school between the ages of eight and thirteen. The boy was clearly bright and what he learned from books might be of commercial benefit to the family. Tse-tung gained no indulgence as a scholar; after school and on holidays he worked in the fields, and at night he kept the ledgers up to date.

Mao père was literate enough for basic reading and writing but his foot-bound wife was totally uneducated. She was a devout Buddhist and often took her oldest son up the hill to burn incense at a monastery. It was a source of sorrow that her husband refused to have truck with religion, though after being frightened by a tiger on a lonely road* Jen-shen's attitude toward salvation seems to have changed. He began lighting joss sticks just about the time his son turned antireligious.

Buddhism in its Chinese version was very different from the original Indian concept of an endlessly revolving wheel of fate, from which the only escape was into nirvana, the extinction of all earthly passions and desires. Chinese Buddhism was more hopeful. It offered the prospect of existence after death through the

---

*This account comes from Edgar Snow's classic work *Red Star Over China*, p. 134. Most of what we know about Mao Tse-tung's early history begins and ends with that book. Snow, an American journalist, was the first Westerner to recognize the potential of the Communist movement. In 1936 he traveled into the hinterland to meet Mao and found him in a mood to talk. Even today, most of what the Chinese know about their late chairman's background and origins comes from translations of Snow's biography in *Red Star.*

intercession of deities, the most famous being Kuan Yin, Goddess of Mercy, a gender that made her particularly appealing to women. And not only joy in heaven was promised but a return to earth hereafter in some form of life, human or animal. This encouraged both charity and vegetarianism. A bowl of rice handed a beggar might feed a reincarnated ancestor, while meatless and fishless days could prevent cannibalizing a family spirit returned as a hog or a carp.

Buddhism was largely the religion of rural folk, though not exclusively so. A person, whether from a town or the countryside, could be a Buddhist, Confucian, or Taoist at will, or all three simultaneously if he so wished. Confucianism—more precisely a code of ethics than a religion—was the overall ruling system of the nation, beloved by scholars, officials, and the gentry in whose favor it was weighted. Buddhism brought comfort to simpler hearts while Taoism, or The Way, with its derision of human striving and calls for a return to nature, was a creed for poets, cynics, and vagabonds. It was said that a bureaucrat in power was always a Confucian, when dismissed from office a Taoist, and when nearing death a Buddhist. One of the perplexing things about Christianity to the Chinese was the dogmatic insistence on exclusivity. Few saw why they couldn't at least be Buddhists as well, a doctrine not unlike Christianity in many of its aspects.

Mao Tse-tung, finishing with primary school at thirteen, was put to work full time farming and merchandising, though he was expected to continue his classical studies at night. Mao père, who had once been involved in a law suit in which he had lost the verdict owing to an apt Confucian quote by the opposition, was determined that his clever son would be prepared with the *mot juste* the next time. The boy, already bored with the moral maxims of the sacred texts, took to reading romances in the privacy allowed him. These were literary works in a popular vein, novels called *The Water Margin, Revolt Against the Tang*, and the *Three Kingdoms*, stirring tales of derring-do drawn from China's historic past. Though imaginatively written and fascinating to the young, romances were poorly regarded by serious-minded elders and stormy scenes ensued when Mao Jen-shen discovered that his son was wasting valuable time on trash.

Conflicts between father and son continued throughout the boy's adolescence. Mao Tse-tung was later to give a humorous account of the dialectics of the situation:

> There were two "parties" in the family. One was my father, the Ruling Power. The Opposition was made up of myself, my mother, my brother, and sometimes even the laborer. In the "united front" of the Opposition, however, there was a difference of opinion. My mother advocated a policy of indirect attack. She criticized my overt display of emotion and attempts at open rebellion against the Ruling Power. She said it was not the Chinese way.

During those years of friction the boy developed his debating skills. When his father accused him of unfilial conduct, Tse-tung, quoting from the classics, pointed out shortcomings in affection and kindness due a son. When charged with laziness, the youngster rebutted by making an issue of age: the father was three times as old as the son but he certainly didn't do three times the work. The retorts must have been doubly galling. Not only was there the impertinence; the elder Mao must also have realized that the chip was flying farther and farther from the authority of the old block.

A couple of years of bickering and boredom served to convince Tse-tung that he wasn't cut out for farming and merchandising. School might be dull but bending over books was better than stooping over rice paddies and he began to think about resuming his formal education. The father, reluctant to lose the boy's labor, tried to head him off through marriage. It was high time; the youth was fifteen, nearing six feet in height, rangy and strong, perfectly capable of fathering the children that would tie him down with family responsibilities and end his nonsense.

A bride was bartered for, a girl close to twenty, mature enough to know her place and be put to work immediately in the Mao household. She arrived in the traditional bridal chair, coolies following behind with trousseau boxes and articles of furniture. Tse-tung, apparently making a last effort to satisfy convention and his father's wishes, dutifully went through the wedding ceremony but afterward reneged. He refused to have anything more to do with his bride, no consummation or cohabitation, though she could stay on as his mother's servant if the arrangement was agreeable.

There was consternation all around, wailings and explosions of anger. Finally the girl was sent home, bag and baggage. The record is silent on what happened to her afterward, though it is likely that she tried to redeem her honor, Confucian style, by remaining a grass widow for the rest of her life. We do not even know the unfortunate girl's name. It was obliterated from memory to spare her family further disgrace.

As a result of rows following his failed marriage, Mao Tse-tung left home. He later said that he ran away, traveling to a distant village to study with a law student. But as he was gone for almost a year and also enrolled at a secondary school, it is likely that his father knew of his whereabouts and sent funds to sustain him. Probably the absence was arranged to allow time for the scandal, which also involved the Mao family, to subside.

While away from home Tse-tung underwent a formative experience. There was a famine in Hunan Province that year and a peasant delegation petitioned the governor for relief. When an insulting reply was sent back, the peasants staged a demonstration. Soldiers moved in, beating and arresting the demonstrators and executing several of the leaders. Mao Tse-tung's schoolmates sympathized with the peasants and were indignant at the governor's brutality, but they felt that such age-old wrongs were beyond correction because, as Confucius had said, "Courtesy is not extended to commoners nor punishment to lords." Tse-tung saw it differently. He had no solutions yet, but his emotional involvement was keen: "I felt that there with the rebels were ordinary people like my own family and I deeply resented the injustice of the treatment given to them."

When Tse-tung returned to his native village of Shaoshan at the end of the year there were more civil disturbances. Hungry peasants roamed the countryside with such slogans as "Let's eat at the Big House," implying raids on landlords' storage bins. During the troubles a shipment of Mao père's grain was seized and the old man was livid with rage. We can imagine that Tse-tung didn't make himself popular by arguing hungry men's rights, though he later admitted, "I thought the [marauding] villagers' method was wrong also." He was beginning to puzzle about the inequities of production and distribution with as yet no idea that they had anything to do with politics.

Still in his sixteenth year, Tse-tung learned of a modern school where natural science and other Western subjects were taught. Nothing would do but he must enter it, precipitating further wrangles with his father. But in the end Mao père, convinced by elders of the clan that a modern education might be helpful in expanding the family business, let his son go.

So in 1910 Mao Tse-tung set out on a notable journey of eight miles, farther than he had ever traveled from home before, to enroll in the Tungshan Higher Primary School. He arrived wearing the rural uniform of tunic and pants, shuffling along in felt slippers, his pigtail dangling beneath a cone straw hat, carrying his books and possessions at the ends of a bamboo shoulder pole. At first the school doorkeeper, mistaking the newcomer for a peasant delivery boy, refused to allow him in. But the headmaster, summoned to deal with the situation, was impressed by the youth's sharp mind and polite address. Besides, Mao had the 1,400 coppers necessary for tuition in advance, so admittance was arranged.

Schooldays at the Tungshan Higher Primary were not altogether comfortable. For one thing, there was Mao's age and size. He was sixteen and six feet tall in an institution that catered to children between eleven and thirteen. His rice-seed look and country manners caused snickers among the diminutive sons of merchants and the gentry, neatly turned out in scholars' gowns. The snickers were subdued in his presence, however, because no one wanted to tangle with the giant.

Then there was the strange curriculum and the even stranger teachers. Many were returned students from Japan who wore the false queues of imitation foreign devils and were impatient with the backwardness of their own country. From them Mao learned astonishing things. He learned that there was a new emperor in Peking—a boy of five named Pu Yi who had ascended the dragon throne two years before, though word had not yet penetrated to Mao's village. He discovered too that all was not well under the Manchu regime. Reform movements were afoot—no one dared call them revolutionary movements—such as had taken place in many foreign countries.

As the teachers responded to Mao Tse-tung's awakening mind, they fed him books and the wonders grew. Years later he could recall the excitement: "In a book called *Great Heroes of the World*, I read ... of Napoleon, Catherine of Russia, Peter the Great, Wellington, Gladstone, Rousseau, Montesquieu, and Lincoln." He learned a smattering of mathematics and the sciences, and formed an acquaintance with foreign languages and geography. He had never seen a map or heard of a compass before he entered the Tungshan school.

By traveling eight miles he had moved from the feudal past into the hodgepodge Chinese present. He was still politically naive. In his own words: "I considered the Emperor as well as most officials to be honest, good, and clever men. They only needed the help of [reformers]." Reform was the immediate goal; if people's hearts could be changed, governments would change, bringing into being Confucius's Great Commonwealth of righteousness and benevolence. All it took was to make others see the light.

Though when Tse-tung went home over the New Year holidays, he found spreading the light in his own family an uphill task. The countryside was still suffering from famine and when his father sent him out to collect rents he couldn't endure the misery he saw. He returned emptyhanded, even giving away his overcoat to a beggar he passed on the way. His father's rage supplied an additional political lesson. The youth was no longer dealing with abstract ideals of behavior but with the very real fury of a landlord bilked of his pittances. How could benevolence change a heart like that? And if not benevolence, what other methods were available?

Before the end of his first year at the Tungshan school, Mao Tse-tung grew understandably restless. He had been overage and lagging in education on entry, but by now he had outstripped all the curriculum had to offer and was eager to move on to more advanced instruction. Encouraged by his teachers, he took the entrance examinations for the Middle School at Changsha, the provincial capital, and passed with honors.

He arrived in Changsha in September 1911, a tall, serious, impressionable youth of seventeen with "kindly eyes [looking out] from a face that suggested the dreamer." He might well have been dazed by the sights and sounds of the first city he had ever seen and subdued by the humility that, in one form or another, characterized a side of his nature for the rest of his life. A half century later, as a celebrated and aging sage in Peking, he was to say that essentially he was a very simple man, a lone monk who had done nothing more than walk the world with a leaky umbrella.

But the sense of strangeness and isolation couldn't have lasted. There was too much to do—classes to attend, societies to join, and exciting new literature to read. In Changsha Mao saw and read his first newspaper, starting a lifelong addiction. All around him new currents were stirring. The students talked and organized and endlessly debated revolution. Mao learned about Sun Yat-sen and his dynamic party called the United League. He thrilled to accounts of the insurrections staged. So far the uprisings had been suppressed, but the time would come when Sun Yat-sen would succeed in driving out the Manchus and liberating the nation.

Carried away by the ferment, Mao wrote a tract which he pasted on a wall—"my first expression of a political opinion" he afterward noted, though he admitted that his thinking was somewhat "muddled." He advocated calling Sun Yat-sen home from Japan to appoint him president of a reform government with a couple of arch-conservatives as his premier and minister of foreign affairs. Still unversed in practical realities, the young politician was proposing a coalition between cats and dogs.

Strangely, Mao seems to have been unaware that an active cell of Sun Yat-sen's United League existed in Changsha. Perhaps he was too busy to scout it out. He had enough to do deciding on his own political affiliation, whether he was a reformer or something more radical. At least he showed his heart was in the right place by participating in street demonstrations and cutting off his queue. There is no doubt in his case—as there was with Chiang Kai-shek—as to why he sacrificed his pigtail. Spiritually he was well on his way to becoming a revolutionary.

And just in time. Mao had arrived in Changsha early in September, so had little more than a month to adjust to the turmoil going on in and about him. For on October 9, 1911 a bomb exploded in Wuhan, a hundred miles to the north, that was to change the course of history in China.

4

The Bungled Bomb at Wuhan

EACH GREAT TURNING POINT OF HISTORY COMES DOWN to us with a distinctive dramatic value. Thus the resistance of the Minutemen at Lexington and Concord was heroic; the defeat of the Persians at Salamis and Marathon majestic; the destruction of Napoleon's armies in the snows of Russia epic; but the prevailing tone of the Chinese Revolution of 1911 was ineluctably comic. The action, the characters, the sequence of events were so haphazard, so unexpected and improvised, that the whole drama seems to have been played out in the theater of the absurd.

The year 1911 began grimly enough. In March, Sun Yat-sen staged his tenth abortive attempt at insurrection. The scene naturally was Canton, a city with an apparently inexhaustible appetite for belligerency. The plan was to seize the yamen,* the official seat of government, and from there fan out proclaiming the monarchy defunct and a republic arisen.

---

*Literally "flag gate," indicating the headquarters of an imperial "banner" regiment. The yamen was also City Hall and the center of law and administration. Often it was the location of the arsenal and a storage depot for grains and goods collected in taxes.

The Bungled Bomb at Wuhan

For six months arms and ammunition were smuggled into Canton, often ingeniously in funeral coffins or in the boxes and baggage of bridal processions. But chief reliance was put on homemade bombs, simple if tricky mechanisms, their construction taught by anarchists on the run from the Russian police. All looked well until, as was usual with Sun Yat-sen's uprisings, things began to go wrong. One of the conspirators took it into his head to test out a bomb on a local tyrant in advance of schedule, thus alerting the authorities that something was afoot. Preventive arrests were made and stores of bombs and ordnance uncovered. When the insurrection took place anyway, it was easily suppressed. Captured rebels were executed on the spot, adding seventy-two more martyrs to the United League's roll of honor.

Sun Yat-sen, still undaunted by failure, sailed to America to collect money for the next time, while other leaders of the league returned gloomily to exile in Japan. But they needn't have been downhearted. Sun's theory of the propaganda of the deed was to pay off handsomely. The Seventy-two Heroes were widely mourned and memorial demonstrations were staged throughout the country. In one of them, in Changsha that autumn, Middle School student Mao Tse-tung marched with thousands of others in protest. Revolutionary zeal reached a new high. Enrollment in the United League swelled to 300,000 members, all dedicated to the next revolt, though none could guess how soon it would come.

The spark was struck, literally struck, on October 9, 1911. That night a group of amateurs—students, workers, soldiers from a nearby garrison—were manufacturing homemade bombs in a Hankow warehouse when one exploded by accident. The damage seems to have been limited—at least there was no general detonation of ammunition and the building held up—but the roar and smoke attracted the police. The bomb makers managed to escape and fled across the river to the United League's headquarters in Wuchang*. Then someone remembered that they had left behind

---

*The three cities of Hankow, Wuchang, and Hanyang, which straddle the confluence of the Han and Yangtze rivers, are called collectively Wuhan.

incriminating lists of members, including the names of sympathetic government officials and officers in the imperial army.

At a hasty conference it was decided that the only hope of preventing discovery of the fatal documents was to stage a diversionary action. Accordingly league members rushed out into the streets, carrying torches and shouting revolutionary slogans. To their astonishment people poured out of their homes to join them. Wuhan, an industrial center known as the Pittsburgh of China, was in a slump just then and workers out of jobs welcomed the chance to demonstrate. It was also a warm night, always conducive to street activity, and many people turned out just for the excitement.

Before long the impromptu sortie in Wuchang developed bulk, cohesion, and purpose. It transformed into a spontaneous crusade against the establishment. The yamen was attacked and seized, the police were disarmed and locked up. And the crowds were not yet ready to call it quits. Thousands of them, armed with rifles from the raided arsenals, crossed the rivers to capture Hanyang and Hankow. What became of the incriminating lists was now academic because most of the men named were out participating in the insurrection.

By midnight the tri-cities of Wuhan were in the insurgents' hands and a new dilemma faced the United League chieftains. They had accidentally touched off a successful uprising by inciting hordes of disgruntled men who still roamed the streets without leadership. Something must be done to forge the mobs into a revolutionary army before the night's gains were lost. A commander must be found, a soldier of experience and reputation capable of organizing effective resistance to the Manchu troops sure to be sent to crush the revolt. But who?

Army officers dedicated to the revolutionary cause were considered one after the other, but none seemed suitable. Then someone remembered Colonel Li Huan-hung, commander of the imperial garrison in Wuchang. Throughout the disturbances Colonel Li had kept a low profile, suggesting that his sympathies were with the rebels. Clutching at this hope, the league sent a delegation posthaste to the colonel's house. However, it wasn't sympathy that had kept Li quiet but fright. The delegation, bursting in, found him hiding under his wife's bed. When he was dragged to light, boots first, he clearly thought that his end had come. It was a reprieve to learn that he had been appointed commander of the revolutionary forces in Wuhan and he gratefully took the oath of office.

That was on the morning of October 10, 1911, the tenth day of the tenth month, or Ten-ten Day as it was called under the Republic and still is on Taiwan. It became the day from which independence was dated, the Chinese Fourth of July.

For the revolution, spontaneously begun in Wuhan, spread rapidly throughout the country. Within weeks the provinces of Hunan and Shensi revolted against imperial rule. In Shansi, mobs assassinated the governor and burned his yamen in his capital of Taiyuan. In the North, the populations of Tientsin and Tsinan staged uprisings. In far off Szechwan Province a professional army officer called Chu Teh, one day to be the most famous of all Red generals, participated in a takeover of government. And at the Changsha Middle School, Mao Tse-tung put down his books and joined the revolution.

Chiang Kai-shek, after hurrying home from Japan, found that his old patron, Elder Brother Chen Chi-mei, had preceded him and was directing operations from Shanghai. The twenty-four-year-old Chiang was given his first command assignment—to seize his native province of Chekiang for the revolution. This meant in effect capturing the capital, Hangchow, a city of stout walls where Marco Polo had once ruled as governor under the Mongol emperors.

Chiang, accompanied by a picked band of insurrectionists known as "dare-to-dies" in those heroic times, traveled down the coast by sampan. Reconnoitering carefully, a practice he didn't always follow in later days, Chiang entered Hangchow in disguise to determine the disposition of the imperial troops. An attack was launched in late October and carried through with complete success. The governor fled, the yamen fell, and the city was liberated for the Republic. Chiang reorganized the administration, then returned to Shanghai having made his mark as a reliable and effective subordinate.

By mid-November virtually all of central and south China was in insurgent hands. The Manchu reaction to the rebellion had been curiously delayed, the well-equipped troops of the imperial "model" army, commanded by Yuan Shih-kai, remaining frozen in and around Peking. But it was a situation that wasn't likely to last. The revolution desperately needed leadership to discipline its tumultuous ranks and provide direction and a program for the future. But Sun Yat-sen, the Tsungli, the leader of leaders, the architect of the upheaval that was convulsing China, was nowhere to be found. From the earliest hours of the insurrection frantic cables had been dispatched urging him to hurry home and assume his rightful place at the head of his triumphant legions. But his answers had been evasive and unsatisfactory. Nobody knew what had gotten into him.

Sun Yat-sen was in San Francisco on October 9 (actually October 8 in the United States because of the time differential), the night the faulty bomb exploded in the Hankow warehouse. His mind was on collecting money for his next attempt to overthrow the Manchus; he had no inkling that the "next" could be *now*. In fact he had thought so little of the prospect of revolutionary activity that he had sent his code books on to Denver with his luggage, so was unable to interpret the first urgent cables he received.

He hurried after his code books but before his train pulled into Denver he had learned the story from the American newspapers: Wuhan was captured, a republic was proclaimed, China was in turmoil.

Sun Yat-sen appears to have been stunned by the news. It was as if it were the last thing he could have expected, as if he had spent his career gnawing like a termite at the foundations of the imperial dynasty without ever really believing that the structure could collapse. He seemed dazed, needing time to adjust to the situation, to absorb the overwhelming responsibilities that were now his, to develop and cultivate the attitudes of a statesman and ruler.

At any rate he sent excuses for not returning immediately to China and resolutely continued in the opposite direction, adhering to his money-collecting route and schedule. Perhaps, as a salesman, he couldn't resist the financial lure of his new position. For years he had been painfully peddling bonds for his uncertain future republic, certificates in denominations of tens, twenties, and hundreds, redeemable come the revolution at two to one. Now with a sure thing in hand, with the republic a virtual certainty, the bonds sold like hot cakes. Traveling incognito—he knew better than to expose himself to swarms of American reporters—he is said to have collected $400,000 before he reached New York.

From New York, still unprepared to go directly home, he sailed for England. He dropped his incognito on British soil and a big fuss was made over the man who had first risen to fame by escaping Manchu kidnappers on the streets of London. Cashing in on his celebrity, Sun visited the Foreign Office to demand that a loan floated to assist the Manchus be transferred to his republic instead. The ministry demurred on that point but readily agreed to lift the ban on the future President of China that had made Sun, the revolutionary, persona non grata in Hong Kong and other British possessions since 1895.

Still without haste, traveling as if on an extended vacation, Sun crossed to Paris where he obtained an interview with Georges Clemenceau, the Tiger of France, then out of office and no doubt envious of Sun who was about to assume it. From Paris, the Tsungli traveled on to Marseilles. He booked passage third class as always to preserve funds, passed through the Mediterranean and Suez Canal, and sailed out into the Indian Ocean. He stopped off at Singapore to be feasted and collect more money, finally arriving in Shanghai on December 24. He had long ago selected Nanking, the ancient stronghold of the Ming Dynasty, to serve as his capital, and to Nanking he was hurried to be sworn in as the provisional President of the Republic of China on January 1, 1912.

Meanwhile there had been developments to the north. The Manchus, frightened by the revolutionary upheaval, turned for protection to their commander-in-chief, Yuan Shih-kai, creator of their "model" army and founder of Paoting Military Academy from which Chiang Kai-shek had graduated.

Yuan Shih-kai, in his early fifties, handsome, suave, unscrupulous, had always been a wily politician. Sixteen years before, acting as Chinese military adviser to the Korean court, he had sold out the armies of the Korean queen to win favor with the attacking Japanese, then just beginning their dream of world conquest. Later he had participated in a palace coup d'état in Peking, imprisoning the legitimate ruler in order to restore the Empress Dowager Tzu Hsi (the Old Buddha) to the throne. He had won honors and riches by these betrayals, but nothing in the past offered the staggering possibilities of the insurrection of 1911. Always a gambler, especially when the cards were stacked to his advantage, Yuan bided his time, waiting for the draw that would fill out his royal flush.

At any time after the disturbances began in Wuhan, Yuan could have moved in with his superior forces to crush the rebellion. But he found excuses—the disposition of his troops, the gout from which he suffered—to delay action until the insurgents were well established in central China. Then he moved a couple of regiments to inflict bloody blows, warning the rebels that he had the whiphand any time he cared to use it.

Next Yuan Shih-kai went to the Imperial Palace. Stretching himself in the kowtow position as required by eitquette, he informed the current emperor, the seven-year-old boy Henry Pu Yi, that the military situation was precarious. The rebels were growing stronger every day and the empire was on the verge of toppling. This was not what the court wished to hear and questions were raised as to Yuan's fitness to command. But the crafty general persisted, exaggerating accounts of the enemy's strength, shamelessly playing on the timidity of the royal family while he recalled, with tears in his eyes, what had happened during the French Revolution when another monarchy had been a bit slow in yielding power.

Besides, Yuan insinuated, abdication need not be unmitigated disaster. A comfortable future might be assured the Manchus if power passed into the right hands, meaning *his* hands. Prince Chun, the boy emperor's father and regent of the realm, took the hint and opened negotiations. In return for abdication, he demanded for the royal family perpetual possession of the palace and its grounds, together with all rights and privileges as enjoyed in the past, including the services of some four thousand eunuchs, slaves, and concubines necessary for the regal comfort, the whole to be financed by a stipend of $4 million paid annually. When the conditions were met, a decree was issued under the emperor's name authorizing his benevolent subject Yuan Shih-kai to form a republican government with royal consent.

His bargaining chips assembled, Yuan made his final move at the end of January 1912. He duly notified Sun Yat-sen at Nanking that the Manchus had bowed out and the revolution was all but completed. The sole remaining question was who was to be president of the new republic. It was true that Sun Yat-sen had worked for years to bring about the present happy state of affairs; on the other hand it was he, Yuan, who had been authorized by the emperor to form a government—a legitimate transfer of power that would win immediate recognition from the Chinese people and the world outside. Surely Sun would be big enough to step aside for the good of the nation and yield the title of president he had assumed.

There was indignation in Nanking at the outrageous request. Yuan Shih-kai was well known as a schemer but he had outdone himself in the way he had manipulated the Manchus. Few objected to the royal family staying on in Peking as paid guests in perpetuity. That disposed of what to do with them, an accommodation entirely within the Chinese scheme of things. But Yuan's gall in trying to filch the presidency from Sun Yat-sen by a pretense of legitimacy aroused the fury of the Tsungli's followers. The revolution had been won by dedication and sacrifice, and finally by force of arms, and in no other way.

Hotheads were for sending an expedition north to teach Yuan Shih-kai a lesson. But Sun promptly squelched such talk. And it wasn't only Yuan's "model" army of forty thousand battle-ready men that prompted caution, though Chiang Kai-shek could have warned, and probably did, that Nanking's levies of half-trained provincial troops and enthusiastic amateurs didn't stand a chance against them. Other considerations gave Sun pause and forced him to consider seriously Yuan's proposal.

For the truth was that, after barely a month in office, Sun's administration was in a mess. Neither he nor any of his followers was experienced in running a government and they were finding the strategies developed to tear down a regime were of little help in making a fresh one work. W.H. Donald, an Australian journalist and friend of China, then acting as an adviser in Nanking, has described scenes of incredible confusion. Officials snarled at each other over jurisdictions and privileges, corridors were jammed with office seekers, and the chickens Sun Yat-sen had been selling for years in the form of provisional bonds came home to roost: overseas Chinese crowded into town by the thousands to redeem their certificates at the rate of two to one.

Money was needed—to pay off bonds, soldiers, officials, and keep the services of the country running—but no one knew how to get it in quantity. When appeals to foreign governments and banks failed, harebrained schemes took over. There was a proposal to work the treasury printing presses overtime turning out bills of large denomination, and another to call in all the silver tea services in China and melt them down for bullion. But nothing practical developed.

It was a bewildering and dismaying time. Sun Yat-sen, essentially an idealist and man of goodwill, felt deeply his own inadequacy. In contrast, Yuan Shih-kai had much to offer. As the governor of a province, he was an experienced administrator. As commander of a modern army, he possessed the force to insure order during the growing pains of the republic. He also had prestige with foreigners who were already tilting in his direction because of his claims to legitimacy. No doubt the Great Powers would advance badly needed loans and credits to Yuan when they wouldn't to Sun.

The main objection to Yuan Shih-kai was his shifty character. He had built a career on deceit and double-dealing, and what was to prevent him from betraying for his own selfish ends Sun Yat-sen's hard-won republic? Unless—and on this Sun banked his hopes—he could be circumvented, hemmed in by constitutional restrictions so as to force him to play straight for once in his life.

To Sun's surprise, Yuan Shih-kai seemed perfectly willing to accept any and all restrictions imposed on him. He agreed to call a National Assembly and elect a parliament. He undertook as president to be bound in all important measures by parliamentary consent, even forgoing the right of veto. All this was to be written into a constitution drawn up by the assembly with iron-clad provisions.

Sun Yat-sen was satisfied by these guarantees which seemed to assure both Yuan Shih-kai's good behavior and his own undiminished influence. For United League representatives were sure to provide a majority in parliament and dominate the legislation. Thus, while Yuan might sit in Nanking as president of the Republic, Sun Yat-sen would continue to run the country from behind the scenes. Or, as the Chinese put it, Yuan would have *yu ming wu shih*, the name without the reality, while Sun would possess *yu shih wu ming*, the reality without the name.

It was important to Sun that Nanking, the "Southern Capital" of the Ming Dynasty, continue as the seat of government. The city had historic importance (the Mings were the last native Chinese rulers), it was closer to the center of the country, and it was removed from the atmosphere of intrigue that surrounded Peking. On this issue alone Yuan Shih-kai hemmed and hawed. Finding Sun adamant, he finally gave in, though within days he began maneuvers that should have given ample warning that his character hadn't changed. His "model" army mysteriously revolted and Yuan rushed from place to place "restoring order." He used this mutiny as an excuse for retaining the capital in Peking—his power base—and Sun, still confident that he had Yuan in a political straitjacket, overgenerously conceded the point.

The transfer of office took place on February 13, 1912. After an incumbency of forty-four days, Sun Yat-sen resigned as President of the Republic of China—a republic that his will and persistence almost singlehandedly had brought about. There was a good deal of second-guessing and disappointment within his party. Many felt that he had given up too easily, that he should have taken a stronger stand on his rights even at the risk of precipitating civil war.

But Sun seemed to have no misgivings. He appeared if anything relieved to be rid of the burdens of administration and proud that he'd arranged for a peaceful, orderly future. On the day of his resignation he visited the tombs of the Mings whose last emperor had hanged himself from an apple tree when the invading Manchus reached the gates of his palace. In an eloquent address, he informed the suicide and other phantoms of his distinguished family that their spirits could now rest easy. The usurpers had been humbled and the nation was once more back in Chinese hands.

Sun Yat-sen was a paradox typical of his place and times. He might be a revolutionary, a cosmopolitan, a Christian convert, and an M.D. Western style, but he remained at heart a Confucian. He might have engineered eleven bloody uprisings, advocated the "propaganda of the deed" and have tolerated political assassinations, but he still yearned for the ancient virtues of harmony, righteousness, and benevolence.

Or at least he did until, outraged by Yuan Shih-kai's conduct, his attitudes changed.

5

Revolutionaries in Limbo

POLITICAL EXPLOSIONS REVERBERATE WIDELY IN A STRUC-tured society. The gray-haired are shaken as much, if not more than youths, though in a different way. They must reexamine traditional formulas and beliefs to demonstrate yet again that the old has anticipated the new and there is nothing novel under the sun. This is especially true of classroom situations where fresh ideas must be released if only to be recaptured and put back in the bottle. Above all, educators must not fail in a show of open-mindedness.

It was a sign of the times that, within days of the Wuhan uprising, the principal of the Changsha Middle School invited a spokesman from the outlawed United League to address his pupils. Mao Tse-tung listened breathless along with the rest: "Not a sound was heard as the orator of the revolution . . . spoke before the excited students." Any hopes the principal may have entertained of orderly debate afterward collapsed in the wild enthusiasm. Resolutions were passed denouncing the Manchus and calling for the establishment of a republic.

And it didn't end there. The bolder students resolved to go to Wuhan and join in the revolutionary action. Mao Tse-tung sold his books and borrowed extra money to finance his trip, but the revolution was moving faster than he was. He had hardly left town when he met a republican army marching to liberate Changsha.

He climbed a hill and had an excellent view of the subsequent battle. The imperial garrison was no match for the ardent revolutionaries who breached the gates and took possession of the city. Mao waited until the republican flag was hoisted, then meekly returned to school to await further events.

He soon received an education in the changing tides of revolution. The republicans reorganized the provincial administration, appointing a new governor and vice-governor. "They were not bad men," according to Mao, "and had some revolutionary intentions, but they were poor and represented the interests of the oppressed [so] the landlords and merchants were dissatisfied with them." The dissatisfaction took a violent form once the republican army had left town. The new governor and vice-governor were decapitated. Mao Tse-tung was witness to "their corpses lying in the street."

It was still October and the outcome of the revolution was far from certain, so a student group was organized to assist in the fighting. Mao Tse-tung refused to join this contingent, considering it elitist. Instead, he searched for a unit of the republican army and joined it as a common soldier.

Unfortunately his company was assigned to garrison duty, so for four months Mao drilled spasmodically and otherwise hung around camp. But his time wasn't totally wasted; he read newspapers and books and first learned about socialism. He also found a congenial companion with whom to discuss the subject, a fellow recruit and ex-coalminer who appears to have been an early Chinese Marxist. Socialism, though, didn't seem to have ignited Mao's imagination at the time; his circumstances lacked the friction necessary to strike a spark. In February 1912 Sun Yat-sen turned the republic over to Yuan Shih-kai, the revolution seemed won, and the volunteer armies were disbanded.

Mao Tse-tung returned to Changsha but not to the Middle

School. He was eighteen, a veteran, and considered that he had outgrown classroom disciplines. He was in that in-between stage known the world over as "idling away his time." What was he going to do for a living?

He describes some of the moves he made:

> An advertisement for a police school caught my eye and I registered for entrance to it. Before I was examined, however, I read an advertisement of a soap-making "school." No tuition was required, board was furnished and a small salary was promised. It was an attractive and inspiring advertisement. It told of the great social benefits of soap making, how it would enrich the country and enrich the people. I changed my mind about the police school and decided to become a soap maker. I paid my dollar registration fee here also.

But the soap making impulse didn't last long. Mao was diverted by the prospect of becoming a lawyer, seeing himself as "a jurist and mandarin." But once again his mind was swept in another direction.

> Fate again intervened in the form of an advertisement for a commercial school . . . . I . . . paid my dollar and registered, then wrote my father . . . He was pleased. My father readily appreciated the advantages of commercial cleverness. I entered the school and remained—for one month.

The trouble was that classes were conducted in English, of which Mao knew little and never learned much. After a vain attempt to keep up, he withdrew and returned to the advertisements. He enrolled in a school that offered an advanced liberal education but, finding the curriculum unsatisfactory, he decided to study on his own in the Hunan Provincial Library. "I was very regular and conscientious about it, and the half-year I spent in this way I consider to have been extremely valuable to me. I went to the library in the morning when it opened [and] stayed . . . every day reading until it closed." He browsed through Chinese poetry and romances and investigated, in translation, the works of Adam Smith, Charles Darwin, John Stuart Mill, and Herbert Spencer. He also applied himself to the history and geography of Russia, America, England, France, and other countries.

Autodidacticism came to an end when Mao père discovered what his son had apparently failed to tell him—that he had withdrawn from commercial school. With financial support from home cut off, Tse-tung was forced back to the advertisements.

This time he hit the jackpot in the Hunan Normal (Teachers' Training) School. Because of a brilliant entrance examination he was accepted on a scholarship. He was to remain at the Normal School for five years, majoring in the social sciences. While he had the usual undergraduate complaints about compulsory courses—still-life drawing was his particular bugbear—the experience brought him to life intellectually. Exposed to new ideas and influences, he developed his powers of thought and expression through essays and poems and in strenuous argument at the debating clubs. For good measure he also built up his physique, taking prodigious walks around the countryside in all kinds of weather.

Even more important for his future, he started experimenting with his talent for organizing groups and challenging orthodox minds with fresh ideas. His approach was direct. Long a devotee of advertising, he placed an ad in a newspaper inviting persons interested in discussing politics to get in touch with him. The initial response was disappointing—only three and a half replies, the half being his description of a youth who showed up to ask questions but left without committing himself. But Mao persisted and in time organized the New People's Study Society (Hsin-min Hsueh-hui). The group grew to eighty members, many to become active in the still unborn Chinese Communist Party.

Mao graduated from the Normal School in 1918. He was to describe his political beliefs at the period as "a curious mixture... of liberalism, democratic reformism, and utopian socialism." Which was not a bad orientation for the teacher he was now convinced he wanted to be. Years later, as a venerated giant in Peking, he was to say that his current titles—Great Teacher, Great Leader, Great Supreme Commander, Great Helmsman—

were nuisances. Of them all, only Teacher would stand the test. He had begun his adult life as a teacher with no further ambition than to remain one. He wondered at the curious chance that had led him to become a Marxist and a founder of the Chinese Communist Party. He had learned, though, that volition had little to do with the working out of individual destinies.

In 1918 the middleaged Sun Yat-sen was as much at sea politically as the fledgling Mao Tse-tung. He was living in a back street of Shanghai's French Concession at the time, low in spirits, funds, and prospects, his faithful followers dispersed and his career all but moribund.

Troubles had piled up on him since he had yielded the presidency to Yuan Shih-kai six years earlier. At the beginning, all had seemed to go well. The National Assembly had drawn up a liberal constitution and a parliament had convened, substantially controlled by Sun's party though under a changed name. It was felt that Tung Meng Hui (United League) no longer reflected the aspirations of a triumphant legal and national party, so a new title, broader in scope, was invented—the Kuo-min-tang, or People's Party. Under the banner of the Kuomintang the fortunes of Sun Yat-sen and his successors were to rise, fall, and ossify during the thirty-seven years (1912-1949) of its existence on the mainland of China.

At the beginning, too, relations between the current president and his magnanimous predecessor had been harmonious. Yuan Shih-kai had offered Sun a lucrative post as Director of Railroads, charged with developing a transportation system worthy of the nation's needs. Sun had taken on the project with gusto, designing a network of trunk and auxiliary lines to expand trackage from the existing 8,000 miles to 75,000 at a calculated cost of three billion dollars gold.

From 1912 to 1913 Sun had toured the country in a special train, equipped with sleeping and dining cars, formerly owned by the Manchus, to drum up enthusiasm and extract rights-of-way from provincial chiefs. Among the notables aboard was Sun's wife, the bound-foot bride of his youth, now approaching fifty. She was along to act as chaperone for a winsome girl called

Ailing Soong, just back from schooling in America and now Sun's secretary. Also on hand was the Australian W.H. Donald, adviser to China's great. Donald's function, at least as he saw it, was to restrain Sun from making a fool of himself by exaggerated claims of what he was going to do in railroading. There wasn't a chance of 75,000 miles being built, or even 75, as long as money was as tight as it was in Peking.

It was money, or the need for it, that opened the breach between Sun and Yuan Shih-kai. Yuan, desperate for funds, began negotiating a $125 million loan with a consortium of foreign bankers. The terms were stiff—a lien on the government's salt monopoly in guarantee of repayment—but Yuan saw no alternative to meeting the demands.

When Sun Yat-sen found out about the secret negotiations he was incensed. He forgot, or chose not to remember, his own woes with financing and let fly at his successor. The assets of China were not to be mortgaged. That had been a Manchu crime—bartering away revenues and resources—and was not to be repeated by the Republic. Certainly not in stealth, without sanction of parliament. Sun was angry enough to order the Kuomintang members of the cabinet to resign in protest.

Yuan responded by appointing a new cabinet more amenable to his views and went right on negotiating. Sun rashly ordered a parliamentary vote forbidding further dealings with the consortium. The Kuomintang representatives, though reluctant to commit themselves beyond compromise, dutifully obeyed the Tsungli's wishes.

That ended Yuan Shih-kai's patience, such as it was. He had always detested the idea of democracy and now jumped at the chance to get rid of its encumbering institutions. He dissolved parliament and announced that from here on he would rule by fiat.

Sun Yat-sen declared war, proclaiming what he optimistically called a Second Revolution in defense of the constitution. Back in the thick of things, he directed operations with all his old zest and fervor. He ordered uprisings, allocating strong points to be seized and arsenals taken. Chiang Kai-shek was assigned the arsenal at Shanghai. He made a valiant effort to capture it but, without adequate troops and weapons, was defeated, as were most other attempts to carry out Sun's ambitious plans.

From the start it was no contest. Yuan Shih-kai's "model" army was everywhere at hand to suppress insurrection. The Kuomintang Party was outlawed, its members subject to arrest and arbitrary execution. By the turn of the year 1914 revolutionaries were running for cover throughout the country. Sun Yat-sen and a group of the faithful, including Chiang Kai-shek, were back in Tokyo trying to find the heart to begin all over again. China's first and, as it turned out, only experiment in republican democracy had lasted for less than two years.

It had been a discouraging period for Chiang Kai-shek even before the Republic ended in panic and confusion. He had returned from the capture of Hangchow in November 1911 eager for another combat assignment but his patron, Elder Brother Chen Chi-mei, had put him to work training the volunteers pouring in to join the revolution. And Chiang remained a drillmaster while the Manchus abdicated, the Republic was declared and its presidency fumbled from Sun Yat-Sen into the firm grasp of Yuan Shih-kai.

Even then Chiang had wanted to continue training a national army. He was well acquainted with Yuan Shih-kai through his attendance at the Paoting Military Academy, distrusted him thoroughly, and believed that a government-controlled militia might well be needed to keep his ambitions in check. But in those halcyon days of optimism he could find no one to share his suspicions and the volunteer units were disbanded. As a reward for services rendered, Sun Yat-sen offered to obtain a governmental post for Chiang. But the young soldier, unable yet to see himself as a politician, chose to retire to his home and family in Fenghua.

Biographers tell us that during his rustication Chiang studied books on warfare, with special emphasis on the campaigns of Napoleon. Perhaps too he found satisfaction in reunion with his mother and his three-year-old son Ching Kuo, but there could have been little else to engage his interest. He had seen too much and done too much to fit any longer into the mold of the rural gentry, yet his career in a larger world appeared to have come to an abrupt terminus at the age of twenty-five. His irritability grew, and he began acquiring his later reputation for a terrible temper. Failing other outlets for his frustrations, he took to beating his wife—not reprehensible in the culture, though not recommended.

Through it all his loyalty to Sun Yat-sen never wavered, and when the Second Revolution was proclaimed he hurried back for the Tsungli's orders. As noted, he was sent to seize the Shanghai arsenal and nearly lost his life in the attempt. During the confusions of the attack, Chiang was captured and marched off for execution. We should not really be surprised to learn that he escaped. One obvious thing historic characters have in common is the ability to survive until their work is done, so it was inevitable that when Chiang made a dash for freedom pursuing bullets missed their mark.

After the aborted uprising, Chiang traveled into exile with Sun Yat-sen, returning to familiar scenes in Tokyo where the Japanese government, as interested in keeping Yuan Shih-kai weak as the Manchus before him, offered an uneasy hospitality. But the atmosphere had changed from the glory days of the United League. The Kuomintang refugees, trying to set up revolutionary shop again, were a dispirited group, conscious of a missed destiny, grumbling at each other and even bitter, though covertly, at Sun Yat-sen. For inevitably Sun was blamed for the present predicament. He had pressed Yuan Shih-kai too hard; he had raised impossible standards of honesty in government that had led to the dissolution of parliament and, worse still, loss of jobs for the Kuomintang faithful.

For centuries the goal of an ambitious Chinese had been to become a public official, an ideal demonstrated by such maxims as *"sheng-kuan fa-tse,"* or "become an official and spread benefits." In imperial times, few of Sun's followers, disadvantaged by social position and education, would have been able to pass the state examinations or later obtain appointments to officialdom. But the revolution had changed all that. Quite ordinary people had been elevated to parliament on the strength of nothing more than party loyalty and, in Peking, had busily gone to work peddling influence. Naturally there was dismay that Sun's ill-timed crusade against Yuan Shih-kai's foreign loan manipulations had put an end to this promising traffic.

Sun Yat-sen tried to rally his forces by optimistic plans to overthrow Yuan's dictatorship. But it was noticed that the Tsungli himself seemed distracted during the winter and spring of 1914 owing to an unexpected development. At the age of forty-eight he had fallen in love with a girl of twenty, his charming secretary of the train trip the previous year, Ailing Soong.

Ailing was the daughter of Charlie Soong, an affluent Shanghai businessman. As a youth, Charlie had spent several years in Massachusetts and Tennessee and had come back to China a convert to Christianity and American methods. He had prospered as a comprador, the indispensable middle man between East and West in all commercial dealings, and had branched out into printing, for the most part manufacturing Bibles. He was a long-time friend and supporter of Sun Yat-sen; in fact, his prominence in the Kuomintang had led to his proscription by Yuan and his flight to Japan with the other party leaders. He brought with him his wife and eldest daughter Ailing, his other four children being then at school in the United States. Sun Yat-sen had sent his own wife back to Canton when the Second Revolution began.

That spring in Tokyo, perhaps stimulated by cherry blossoms, Sun pursued his interest in the attractive girl. We do not know her reaction but we do know her parents' when marriage was proposed. It was shock. The Soongs weren't impressed by Sun's offer to get a divorce; they were Christians, as indeed was he, and divorce was impermissible. Besides, Sun had grown children Ailing's age. The whole thing was thoroughly unsuitable.

There was in Tokyo at that time a youth called H. H. Kung, son of a prominent Chinese banking family. Young Kung, a graduate of Oberlin College, and now putting in a stint as a YMCA secretary, had also shown interest in Ailing. His suit met with a better reception from the parental Soongs. A marriage was hastily arranged between the young couple, whisking Ailing out of Sun Yat-sen's orbit.

The Tsungli was not left to grieve for long. Within months the

Soong's second daughter, Chingling, returned from America, just out of Wesleyan College, and Sun promptly transferred his affections to the newcomer. This time he was on firmer ground; Chingling was equally enamored and swept aside parental objections. Sun applied for a divorce though it was a difficult suit as his wife had fulfilled all the Confucian obligations: she had borne him a son, had always done his bidding, and had never been loud or objectionable. But somehow the divorce was arranged and in October 1915 Sun and Chingling were united as man and wife, though there is no telling what the first Madame Sun may have called her.

Loyal soldier Chiang Kai-shek had stood by patiently through all this, though perhaps chafing at his own inaction. Only twice that we know of had his capacities been utilized: when Sun Yat-sen sent him on clandestine missions to Shanghai and into Manchuria to investigate the climate of revolt. Each time Chiang had brought back a discouraging report; revolutionary fervor was either dead or in deep hibernation and there was little chance for uprisings in the foreseeable future.

By the end of 1915 Chiang had grown restless. Perhaps Sun's immersion in his new marriage made the young soldier feel superfluous, or possibly the Japanese police were beginning to catch up with him as a deserter from the imperial army. At any rate he left Tokyo to seek sanctuary in Shanghai's International Settlement, where Elder Brother Chen Chi-mei had preceded him to set up secret Kuomintang headquarters. Prospects for revolutionary activities had by then improved because, in Peking, President Yuan Shih-kai had begun to outreach himself.

Earlier in the year, desperate for money again, Yuan had opened negotiations with the Japanese for a loan. The Japanese proved less rapacious than the banking consortium in regard to security terms, but they were more ambitious politically. They advanced conditions of supervision and control over the nation that would have reduced China to a virtual colony. These provisions gained notoriety as the Twenty-One Demands when they were leaked to the press. The resulting howls of indignation were so loud that Yuan was forced temporarily to back off.

Ruminating over this defeat, Yuan Shih-kai came to the

conclusion that it was impossible to govern China without the all-embracing authority the emperors had enjoyed. He had a more or less legitimate emperor at hand in the abdicated ten-year-old boy in the Forbidden City, but Yuan's mind was working in another direction.

He prepared a careful campaign. He organized rallies, promoted petitions, and encouraged editorials, all demanding that Yuan ascend the dragon throne as the first monarch of a new dynasty. He even employed an American professor to argue learnedly that autocracy was the form of government best suited to the Chinese temperament. And when the time came, Yuan Shih-kai graciously acceded to the imagined clamor of the populace. He worshipped at the sacred tombs, chose a name for his dynasty, and announced the date for ascension.

It was too much. The Chinese people might be vague as to the kind of rule they wanted, but they were united in what they didn't want—Yuan Shih-kai as emperor. There was a general uproar—speeches, polemics, mass demonstrations—though in the end it was the threat of military action that decided the matter. When the governors of seven provinces threatened to march on Peking, Yuan threw in the towel. He renounced his imperial ambitions, resigned as President of the Republic and went home to die in bed on June 6, 1916. There were rumors that he was poisoned, but the uremia from which he had been suffering for years was cause enough for a natural death.

Yuan was succeeded in office by his vice president, Li Huan-hung, the colonel, now general, who had had greatness thrust upon him when pulled out from under his wife's bed during the Wuhan uprising. President Li lifted the ban on the Kuomintang Party. He could hardly evade this obligation because, after all, it had been the Kuomintang (then the United League) that had started him on his way to power. But he made it clear that he had no intention of restoring parliamentary government. He continued to rule in the pattern set by Yuan Shih-kai—by administrative decree with a secretariat to enforce his orders, a form of dictatorship that was to be followed by an assortment of generals who succeeded him to office.

It was a time for generals, the beginning of the warlord era, not only in Peking but throughout the provinces. Yuan Shih-kai had been responsible for that too by promoting a Tuchun or military governor system. Without the moral sanction of the emperors and lacking the troops to police the vast nation, Yuan had recognzied any authority, legitimate or not, that could enforce order and remit revenues to Peking. Thus he opened the doors to ambitious strongmen, adventurers, and bandits who were to plague China for the next thirty years.

Still, under Li Huan-hung's presidency a certain tranquillity was restored. Political persecutions ceased, permitting Sun Yat-sen and his entourage to return from Japan, though it was too late for Elder Brother Chen Chi-mei, who had preceded them to Shanghai when conditions were more hazardous. In May 1916, three weeks before the death of would-be emperor Yuan Shih-kai, Chen Chi-mei had been lured into a trap by Yuan's agents and assassinated.

Chiang Kai-shek was inconsolable in his grief. The guilt of a younger brother, and a soldier at that, who had failed to protect his senior lay heavily on him. He immediately adopted Chen Chi-mei's two nephews and forever after tried to make up in loyalty to them his failure with their uncle. Even when he became head of state and the Chen brothers took advantage of their favored position to form the C & C clique, notorious for its corruption, Chiang refused to listen to charges brought against them. They were loyal and obedient to him personally and that was all that counted.

As time went on, loyalty and obedience became ultimate tests in Chiang's mind. He who had been disloyal to the Manchu emperors and disobedient in his vows to uphold their dynasty, made allegiance a touchstone of faith. Anything short of it became treason.

Mao Tse-tung in 1916 had little concern for loyalty or obedience or anything else that smacked of established beliefs. Still a student at the Changsha Normal School, his mind was roving, trying to reconcile the difference between his ideals and the conditions he saw around him, searching for some unifying principle.

For some time a war—World War I—had been going on in Europe and by 1916 China became peripherally involved. The Allies sent out a call for help, not for soldiers but for laborers—porters, ditchdiggers, and unskilled factory workers. In 1916, 8,000 Chinese were assembled and sent overseas. By 1918 the figure had risen to 175,000, the majority bound for France and Belgium and, to a lesser extent, Britain. With the laborers went interpreters, teachers, and welfare workers, contingents known as Work-Study groups.

In Changsha, Mao Tse-tung's organization, the New People's Study Society, helped recruit for the program, and in the spring of 1918 Mao himself, a newly graduated and qualified teacher, accompanied a Work-Study unit to Peking. He tells us he just went along for the trip with no thought of embarking for Europe: "I felt that I did not know enough about my own country, and that my time could be more profitably spent in China." But it is at least possible that he would have continued on to France, the most popular of the destinations, if he could have passed the language test at the capital. If he was examined, he surely failed; Mao had no more ear for French than he had for English or any other foreign tongue. He was only to leave China twice in his lifetime and that was when, as head of state, he visited Russia. Though by that time travel wasn't really necessary because heads of state—notably American presidents—made it their business to visit him.

Once in Peking in that spring of 1918, Mao Tse-tung decided to stay for a while. He was impressed by the vast public squares and the imposing buildings with columns and carved panels, though he found living "very expensive." He obtained a job as an assistant librarian at the National University. The salary was $8 per month which bought him space in a room shared with seven others. Sleeping conditions were so tight that they all had to turn over in bed at the same time. And at work his situation wasn't much happier. He located books and documents for long-gowned scholars who twitched eyebrows at the shabby clerk with the Hunanese dialect. He was starved for intellectual companionship, though things improved when he was given permission to audit university courses in journalism.

He made friends in class, leading to introductions among the faculty. He met Chen Tu-hsiu, dean of the School of Letters, but more famous as the founder and editor of *New Youth*, the most influential magazine of the period.

New Youth was different in both content and style. It was radical and irreverent, mocking the Confucian verities as H. L. Mencken's *American Mercury* was later to mock the "booboisie" in the United States with an equally thrilling effect on students. *New Youth* was written in *pai hua*, or vernacular form, a departure from the age-old tradition of *wen yen*, or scholarly composition. This was a literary breakthrough that caused excitement, much as Ernest Hemingway's muscular syntax and staccato rhythms were to surprise and delight Western audiences within the next decade. Certainty Mao Tse-tung had never read anything like *New Youth* and in its pages he found ways of communicating ideas that were to help shape a revolution.

He tried his hand at writing for the magazine and at least one of his contributions was accepted. His attitude toward Editor Chen Tu-hsiu was at the time an understandable mixture of reverence and awe. Though inevitably, later, when the two were joined in political action and the many-sided, liberal editor was unable to live up to Mao Tse-tung's expectations, a change took place. Today in China *New Youth* is all but forgotten, but the name of Chen Tu-hsiu lives on in infamy as a Judas of the Communist movement.

In the ferment of ideas at National University, Mao Tse-tung, not surprisingly, renewed his acquaintanceship with Marxism. He joined a Marxist study group, though lightning did not as yet strike. As he himself put it: "I was still confused, looking for a road.... I read some pamphlets on anarchy, and was much influenced by them.... I often discussed anarchism and its possibilities in China. At the time I favored many of its proposals."

It was a stimulating year, but when the time came for Mao's Work-Study group to leave for Europe, he accompanied it to the docks at Shanghai, waved good-bye and returned to Changsha. He settled down as a teacher at a primary school, intent on establishing himself and saving money because, among other things, he had fallen in love in Peking and wanted to get married.

The girl was Yang Kai-hui, daughter of a professor at the university. Mao tried to save money by living on rice and beans and going without repairs to his shoes.

But it was a bad time to plan for personal happiness. Within weeks of Mao's return from the North a political explosion occurred that was to reverberate throughout the country. This was the May Fourth Movement of 1919, initiated by a mass rally of Peking students demonstrating against the Japanese.

Japan had been active during the 1914-18 European war. With Western foreigners busy killing each other on far-off battlefields, Japanese merchants had profited handsomely in China. Their trade through the Treaty Ports had jumped by 50 percent and investments in Chinese industries and enterprises had tripled.

Not content with economic gains, Japan also moved into China territorially. Joining the Allies in 1915 and declaring war on Germany, it promptly seized German possessions in the port of Tsingtao, then extended its control over the entire Shantung peninsula. Japan claimed it was doing all this as a trustee for China and that when the war was over the possessions would be returned. But Japanese diplomats played shrewd games behind the scenes and, at the Treaty of Versailles terminating World War I, wrung consent from the Great Powers for the retention of their Chinese holdings.

The reaction in China was violent, flaring first among the students of Peking. The purpose of the May Fourth demonstration was to force the warlord government of the Republic to renounce the Versailles Treaty and expel the Japanese from Shantung. When the government refused to budge, mass indignation translated into a boycott of Japanese goods. In Peking, Tientsin, Shanghai, and other Treaty Ports, all classes and ranks closed behind the movement. Merchants stopped stocking or selling products made in Japan, rickshaw coolies would not pull Japanese citizens and singsong girls refused to sing or otherwise entertain them. The lockout was remarkable as the first spontaneous, universally supported political action in Chinese history and has sometimes been called the real beginning of the Second Revolution, Sun Yat-sen to the contrary.

In Changsha, Mao Tse-tung could hardly be expected to go on calmly teaching first-graders in such a stirring time, and he didn't. He was soon in the thick of things, writing tracts, organizing rallies, and marching in support of the Japanese boycott. When the governor of Hunan decided that the demonstrations were getting out of hand and tried to put a stop to them, Mao organized resistance against him. This led to unpleasantness with the police and Mao was forced to leave town speedily.

He went back to Peking to visit his fiancée, but returned to Changsha when he learned that the governor had been driven out and replaced by a more liberal official. He found, however, that the change had made little difference in his own status; he was still marked as a troublemaker to be kept under surveillance and arrested at the first false move.

The recognition that administrations might change but policies remained the same preyed on Mao's mind. If demonstrations were to be interpreted as civil disturbances, how were reforms to be achieved? If spokesmen for the poor were treated as criminals and locked up, how were needs to be made known? If ever there was a single, precipitating factor that drove the young philosopher into radical ranks beyond recall, it was his discovery of the reactionary nature of constituted authority.

Or as he himself put it: "I became more and more convinced that only mass political power, secured through mass action, could guarantee the realization of dynamic reforms." And in the winter of 1920, despite the dangers, he took the only road he saw open to him. "I organized workers politically for the first time, and began to be guided in this by the influence of Marxist theory.... [O]nce I had accepted it as the correct interpretation of history, I did not afterwards waver."

He married that year, savings or no savings, and continued to teach school as a cover while he engaged in revolutionary activity. He had seen in the May Fourth Movement how the nation could arise and unite against the Japanese. He believed the time would come when it would arise again for its own liberation. Once Karl Marx's stirring challenge—"The philosophers have only interpreted the world; our business is to change it"—had lodged in Mao's mind, nothing could erase it.

Sun Yat-sen, too, gained new impetus from the May Fourth Movement. Living dispiritedly in Shanghai—especially downhearted because a recent attempt to foment revolution in Canton had ended in betrayal and failure—he saw in the anti-Japanese demonstrations the resurgence of a patriotic fire he had begun to believe extinct.

He dashed off telegrams to the warlord president in Peking and to all provincial governors, supporting the student leaders and demanding the release of activists thrown in jail. To the students themselves he sent a warm letter, carefully phrased to remind them that he was still in business as the nation's authentic democratic leader. "The success of the revolution which is carried on by [my] Party must depend on a change of thought in China.... Therefore [your] new ... movement is really a most valuable thing."

Only Chiang Kai-shek stood apart, apparently untouched by the rousing events. He too was living in Shanghai at the time—he hadn't had the heart to return to Fenghua except on visits—but his attitudes and mode of life had changed. He no longer thought of himself as a soldier. He was trying to fit into an existence for which he had little taste and no doubt less aptitude. At the age of thirty-two, frustrated in his military hopes, he was attempting to convert himself into a money-grubbing civilian.

Perhaps when he went through his morning exercise, standing at attention with his jaw locked to develop his character—if he still indulged in the ritual—his memory may have been stung by classical quotations. There was the promise of Mencius: "Heaven arranges suffering of body and mind to prepare a man for great things." And there was the equally encouraging dictum of Laotze, the philosopher of nature: "When the hour of the great man has struck he rises to leadership, but before his time has come he is hampered in all he attempts."

But what "great things" could be in preparation for a man piddling away his time in the Shanghai Stock Exchange? Or perhaps his hour had already struck and he hadn't heard the summons, or at least made the most of his opportunities. Chiang Kai-shek had reason to feel despondent. He was then in the depths of what have been called his "lost" or "mystery" years.

6

Cross Currents

SHANGHAI WAS AN INVENTION OF FOREIGNERS. THEY conceived it, built it, and developed it into one of the great cities of the world from virtually nothing, from a fishing village on mudflats at the mouth of the Yangtze River. The unlikely site was "opened up" for foreign commerce as a result of the Treaty of Nanking which terminated the Opium War of 1840–42. Several other flourishing and populous harbors also became available by that treaty and the Chinese looked on it as prime evidence of Western madness that the "big noses" decided to concentrate on desolate Shanghai. Even its name, meaning above the sea, was a kind of joke, for when the river was in flood it often wasn't.

But the foreigners had sharp eyes for trade and they saw the potential of locating at the mouth of a river navigable for a thousand miles inland, draining down commerce from the richest regions of the nation. They went to work, driving piles and dredging up mud as landfill while deepening the harbor. And on the built-up shores, they created a functional, polyglot city that became the wonder and curiosity of China.

By the turn of the twentieth century Shanghai was at a peak of power and prosperity. The hub of commerce was the Bund, the embarcadero along the river where ships of all nations docked or rode at anchor on the Whang-poo estuary. The architecture that fringed the Bund was varied, Georgian giving way to Victorian Gothic as the years advanced. Here was located the great commercial establishments, banks, insurance companies, and import-export houses—Jardine, Matheson of Britain (importing manufactured goods, exporting teas and silks), Standard Oil of America (importing kerosene for the lamps of China, exporting pig bristles, indigo, ceramics, and jade) and other less famous firms. In all, trading companies from fourteen nations maintained offices along the Bund.

Fanning out beyond the harbor were the residential and entertainment districts. Bubbling Well Road was where the taipans, the foreign trading chieftains, lived in ornate mansions crammed with servants. Kiangsi Road was the address for gambling houses and the plusher brothels, the most popular girls coming, for some reason, from San Francisco. Then there was the racetrack, originally planned for exercising horses and playing polo, but extended in function to accommodate the universal fever for gambling. And not to be forgotten was the exclusive Shanghai Club which boasted the longest bar in the world.

The administration of the city was divided. There was the International Settlement, eight and a half square miles governed by a Municipal Council composed of British, American and, later, Japanese members. Contiguous was the French Concession, smaller in area but in some ways more selective, ruled under the Napoleonic code. And surrounding the foreign quarters was the enormous "native" city, administered by whatever warlord happened to be in power.

The foreign precincts were separately policed and under consular jurisdiction, meaning that foreigners could be tried only in their own national courts and not by Chinese law—a concession wrung from the tottering Manchus and always a sore point for Sun Yat-sen and like patriots. But then Westerners in Shanghai never made a pretense at being democratic, at least as far as

Chinese were concerned. "Natives" of whatever rank were excluded from their best hotels, clubs, bars, brothels, and even public parks. The famous sign "No Dogs or Chinese Allowed" may have been apocryphal, as some old China hands claim, but its spirit was certainly everywhere. In 1919 the population of the city was some 1,500,000; of this number only 23,000 were Westerners, but there was no doubt about who was running the show.

This was the Shanghai that Chiang Kai-shek came to know intimately during most of a decade—from 1916 to 1923—but we are curiously blank on how he lived or what he did there.

From his birth until May 1916—or until Elder Brother Chen Chi-mei was assassinated—the record is reasonably filled in. Few facts of chronological importance have escaped the historians. Then suddenly Chiang Kai-shek disappears and—except for a couple of cameo resurrections—remains buried until 1923 when he is brought sharply back into focus to remain so for the rest of his long career. All that seems certain is that he passed his "lost" or "mystery" years in Shanghai. But doing what? We are left to speculate because he never cared to discuss the period himself.

Of course, conjectures are rife. There is a tradition that he was somehow connected with the Shanghai Stock Exchange. Some authorities claim he was a runner, a stockbroker's clerk, living off tips and handouts. Others are equally certain that he was a successful speculator, making a fortune that he afterward contributed to Sun Yat-sen's war chest. But neither version seems convincing. It's as difficult to imagine Chiang, the proud soldier and son of the gentry, running errands as to conceive of him as a frantic jobber. So let's hold the Stock Exchange connection for the moment.

Another tradition has it that drink and women figured prominently at this stage of his life. He is said to have gone on wild binges to release bottled-up frustrations. "He would fly into storms of temper before which few human beings can stand" one awed biographer tells us. And the picture is acceptable. Later on, even without alcohol, tantrums lurked beneath Chiang's impassive exterior. As a commanding officer he was given to launching vindictive tirades against subordinates, and his fury sometimes transgressed reason. Once, taking violent objection to a movie he was being shown, he ordered the projectionist thrashed.

But what about his reputation with women? He apparently found an expert guide to the "blue chambers" of the Kiangsi Road—such as Chinese were permitted to patronize—in Elder Brother Chen Chi-mei who turned out to be a womanizer when off duty. But what happened after Chen's assassination? The theory is that Chiang continued to bed hop in order to assuage his grief, until something startling happened. He met another Chen—a girl called Chen Chieh-ju—and was transformed. She was "a harlot who particularly captivated" the young soldier, we are told. Chiang was so enraptured that he obtained a divorce from his prosaic wife in Fenghua in order to marry Chen Chieh-ju.

Again we are stopped by the contradictions between this quixotic performance and what we know of Chiang's squirearchal character. The fascinating girl was real and Chiang married her, but perhaps under circumstances that strain credulity less.

The fact is that Chiang Kai-shek might not have led as aimless and dissolute a life as pictured. We have hints breaking through a welter of counterevidence that suggest a more ordered existence. And it is a logical surmise. Chiang's training and background would tend to keep him on an even keel, and besides he had a helpful friend in Shanghai in Sun Yat-sen.

Sun had returned from exile in Tokyo shortly after Chen Chi-mei's assassination. He must have been concerned by Chiang's disconsolate grief for his "elder brother" and looked around for someone who could act in a substitute relationship. And what better person than Chang Ching-chiang, an old colleague from United League days, now a power in the Shanghai Chinese community? Perhaps Chang, Sun's contemporary, was a little old to serve as a brother, but he was admirably suited as a father figure. Or, because fathers were austere and forbidding in the Confucian system, perhaps it's best to think of him as Chiang Kai-shek's sympathetic patron.

Chang Ching-Chiang, in his fifties, urbane, enigmatic, physically crippled but energetic and persuasive, was a remarkable personality in his own right. Described as "an almost mythical character," he came from a wealthy silk-trading family in Chekiang, Chiang Kai-shek's home province, thus providing an additional bond for the young man. Chang Ching-Chiang had early branched out into enterprises of his own, including the jewelry and curio trades, and he was a curio dealer in Paris when Sun Yat-sen first met him. Sun had been at the time on one of his round-the-world collecting tours and Chang had contributed generously to the revolutionary coffers.

Back in Shanghai, the curio dealer had turned financier, helping to found the Shanghai Stock Exchange. And here we begin to make the connection with Chiang Kai-shek, especially when we learn that his patron sat on the board of banks and shipping companies. Under such circumstances Chiang Kai-shek could easily have accepted dignified employment in the fiscal community.

Through the millionaire financier, if not through his own efforts, Chiang Kai-shek undoubtedly established contact with the Shanghai underworld at this period. It was imperative that he did, because no business could be transacted without the cooperation of the organized gangsters. There were several mobs—the Red, the Green, and the Blue—each with its own territory and rackets. Traffic in opium, gambling, and prostitution were routine, but many ingenious sidelines were developed. Notable was a kidnap gambit: rich Chinese were kidnapped for ransom and, after release, were required to pay "protection" fees to avoid going through the uncomfortable experience again.

As in Chicago a decade later, Shanghai gangster chiefs acquired colorful names. "Pock-marked" Huang was a feared killer, but more powerful was Dhu Yueh-sheng, who amalgamated the Green and Blue gangs and was known to foreigners as "Doughty Dhu." Dhu was so powerful, in fact, that he had gone semirespectable and sat on the boards of the very enterprises from which he drained illegal tribute. Chiang Kai-shek developed a friendship with him that was one day to pay off handsomely.

So it is safe to assume that the young soldier prospered during his "lost" years. Perhaps he wasn't following the path he believed fate had cut out for him, but he wasn't suffering hardships either.

And there is evidence that he accepted the situation and made an effort to improve it by binding himself closer to financier Chang Ching-Chiang by family ties. For we learn that at sometime during the period Chiang was married "to a member of his [patron's] household."

We aren't supplied with the girl's name but the Chen Chieh-ju of romantic legend will do. She was certainly no harlot; more likely a niece or adopted daughter of the financier, and she may have been related to deceased Elder Brother Chen Chi-mei, though Chen is too common a surname for more than speculative inference. At any rate she was a good enough match for Chiang to divorce the mother of his two sons (a second, Wei-kuo, had been born in 1916) and settle down for a civilian career.

But it wasn't a career that was to last long. Soon enough Sun Yat-sen, embattled again, put out a call for duty and Chiang Kai-shek obediently donned uniform.

Among the more dynamic warlords that rose to power after the fall of the empire was a tuchun (or self-imposed military governor) called Chen Chiung-ming, also known as the Hakka* general. By 1918 he had fought his way to uneasy control of several southern provinces and, looking about for a way to consolidate his gains, invited Sun Yat-sen to Canton to form a government. Sun, never loath to grasp at an opportunity, however unpromising, traveled south with a retinue, including Chiang Kai-shek, to act as his cabinet.

The Hakka general accepted Chiang as his chief of staff, though he sneered at his spit-and-polish approach to rabble troops. Chiang, in turn, thoroughly distrusted his commander-in-chief and privately warned Sun Yat-sen what was evident from the beginning—that the Hakka general had no intention of allowing the Tsungli to govern but wanted him only for the prestige of his name. How this three-way feud might have worked out is academic because the Hakka general suffered military reverses and was driven out of Canton. Within months Sun

---

*Hakka means "guest" or "stranger," polite euphemisms for aliens from outside the province. A family could be considered hakka for a hundred years or more.

Yat-sen was back in the French Concession and Chiang Kai-shek back in mufti.

There was a repeat performance three years later, in 1921. The Hakka general, triumphant over his warlord enemies, retook Canton, formed a regime he grandiloquently called the Southern Government of China and asked Sun Yat-sen to serve as its first president. This time Chiang Kai-shek didn't go along. His mother had died and he was in obligatory mourning, a ritual that could last for three years.

And it was just as well. The second time around was more disastrous than the first. Sun, trying to run an honest and efficient government, was continually at loggerheads with the Hakka general who wanted to milk his domain warlord style. The situation blew up in an order for Sun's arrest and imprisonment. The Tsungli escaped just in time—to a gunboat commanded by a loyal officer.

When the news reached Fenghua, Chiang Kai-shek broke off mourning and hurried to his chief. He found his way aboard the gunboat and for fifty days cruised the China Seas with the Tsungli, waiting for friendly forces to assemble and crush the Hakka general. Sun Yat-sen, oppressed by still another failure and the loss of all his books and possessions in the fire that swept his lodgings after his escape, was distraught and near collapse. Chiang soothed him, read to him, talked to him, cooked his meals, and cleaned his cabin during the trying days of waiting. And Sun was duly grateful.

Beyond doubt that period was the turning point in their relationship. Chiang was advanced from useful subordinate to close disciple and comrade of the man he revered. He was later to say that the two greatest influences in his life had been his mother and Sun Yat-sen. It was a happy coincidence that as the living presence of one passed from the scene, the other took him into intimacy.

When it became clear that the rescuing forces had failed to muster strength and that the Hakka general remained unchallenged in Canton, Chiang Kai-shek gave the order that headed the gunboat for Shanghai. The Tsungli was too despondent to care any longer about destinations.

He would have been cheered to know how soon his fortunes were to change. He had fought the good fight for a quarter of a century, standing for the most part alone, shunned by powerful capitalist governments which claimed to share his ideals of independence and self-determination of nations. None was ever to raise a finger for him, but help was to come from another source, a brand new socialist republic that had disposed of capitalism within its own boundaries and was willing, ready, and eager to export its successful revolutionary techniques.

The Soviet Union, following on the collapse of the czars and a short-lived bourgeois regime, had come into being in November 1917. A year and a half later the upstart state astonished the world by an unprecedented declaration. It proposed to abrogate unequal and secret treaties and return to China, without compensation, all territories, possessions, and rights seized by imperial Russia.

The announcement, called the Karakhan Declaration, had caused a sensation. But it had come during the excitements of the 1919 May Fourth Movement and too much was happening for a thorough investigation of its significance. The government at Peking, as well as Sun Yat-sen and others who should have been interested, were far too inclined to accept the explanation of the capitalist powers that it was all just Communist propaganda.

In 1920 the Soviets took steps to show that they were in earnest. Leo P. Karakhan, who as a Commissar for Foreign Affairs had issued the famous declaration, was sent as the Soviet diplomatic representative to Peking. He was sent, moreover, as an ambassador, thus upgrading the post from the mere ministers of other foreign powers. The compliment was not lost on the Chinese, though Red diplomacy continued to be regarded with suspicion.

More important for the future, Ambassador Karakhan brought with him delegates from the Comintern*, among them a Dutchman named Hendricus J. F. M. Sneevliet who went under

---

*An abbreviation for Communist International, the agency set up in Moscow to guide and perhaps foment revolutions in capitalist countries.

the nom de guerre "Maring." Maring soon made acquaintances within Marxist circles in Peking and Shanghai and suggested that the time had come to translate Marxist study into action by forming a Chinese Communist Party. He found an ardent backer in Chen Tu-hsiu, the professor of literature and editor of the pioneering magazine *New Youth*, who had lost his job at the National University because of radical activities and was ready to take a final step to the left.

Encouraged by this successful proselytizing, Maring traveled down to Canton to try his luck with Sun Yat-sen. Sun was then serving his stint as President of the Southern Government of China under the auspices of the Hakka general, with the blow-up yet to come. He listened politely to Maring's proposal—that he accept the aid and cooperation of the Soviet Union to further his political plans—and courteously turned it down. When it came to revolutions, Sun was a conservative and a Confucian and he feared the disorders that class warfare would entail. Besides, he believed he was making headway in his present collaboration with the Hakka general and saw no reason to change direction. It would be some time yet before, desperate for alternatives, he seized on Russian help as the only way to solve his and China's dilemma. So now he thanked Maring for his kind interest and sent him on his way.

Maring, perhaps sensing that events must inevitably drive Sun into the Soviet orbit, returned to Shanghai to prepare for the future. He consulted again with Editor Chen Tu-hsiu and together they drew up plans to found a Chinese Communist Party. Invitations for a convention were sent out to various Marxist groups, including the New People's Study Society in Changsha. Mao Tse-tung, organizer and dynamo of that society, was intrigued and decided to find out what was afoot. He records what he did with a sense of history: "In May of 1921 I went to Shanghai to attend the first meeting of the Communist Party."

It was a peculiar convention in many ways. For one thing, attendance seems to have been left entirely to chance. As it happened, twelve young men showed up, but it could just as easily have been six or none. For another, neither Editor Chen nor Maring put in an appearance at the meetings. Chen's absence is explainable; after the troubles he'd been having as a radical, he probably didn't wish to expose himself until there was a Communist Party already in existence. But Maring hiding behind the scenes is harder to understand, unless he was trying to conceal his Comintern connection. Undoubtedly some of the delegates were acting as agents of the absentee leaders and helped keep the agenda focused, but otherwise the young (average age twenty-six) and politically naïve enthusiasts were left alone to fight out issues it had taken Marx, Engels, and Lenin lifetimes to clarify.

The congress began on June 30 at a girls' school in Shanghai's French Concession where rooms were rented out during the summer vacation. The participants were headstrong and opinionated and soon began forming the factions that were to plague the party for years to come. Arguments raged so loud and long that after four days the attention of the police was attracted and a change of venue was deemed advisable.

The delegates repaired to a houseboat on a lake where they could shout at will out of earshot of the police and, incidentally, their surreptitious supervisors, Maring and Chen, who now had no idea what was going on. Which was perhaps just as well, for at one point a proposal to investigate both the German and the Russian Communist parties (equivalent to investigating both the twig and the tree) before deciding on which to join was only narrowly defeated, and a resolution that the newly formed Chinese Communist Party must have nothing to do with Sun Yat-sen's outmoded Kuomintang Party was actually passed.

During the last sessions officers were elected, and here influence from behind the scenes became evident. Editor Chen was chosen as Secretary General (it must have come as a surprise to some that he was even interested in the job) and an eight-man Central Committee (Mao Tse-tung not included) was installed as a governing body. The delegates then dispersed to establish Communist cells at home and begin recruiting workers. Industrial workers, that is; peasants were ruled out. A resolution by Mao-Tse-tung that a committee be formed to organize peasants had been soundly defeated. The delegates, word perfect in Marxist literature, knew that workers were the backbone of any socialist revolution and peasants, petit-bourgeoisie by class and nature, were auxiliaries at best. What did it matter if in China peasants comprised 80 percent of the population and industrial workers less than 4 percent? The canons of the code must be observed.

Maring was appalled to learn about the resolution forbidding cooperation with Sun Yat-sen and his Kuomintang Party, since his future strategy was based on such a collaboration. Eighteen months later, at the Second Congress of the Chinese Communist Party, he tried to get the ruling reversed. But he hadn't counted on the stubborness of minds as yet untuned to political realities and the ban remained. Getting desperate—for the time was ripe to approach Sun Yat-sen again—Maring and Editor Chen called a special meeting of the Central Committee and prevailed on that more amenable body to permit negotiations with the Kuomintang.

That was early in 1923 when Sun Yat-sen's situation had changed considerably for the better. He had assembled a coalition of Kwangtang warlords to drive the Hakka general out of Canton and was preparing to return there as president of the newly named Republic of South China. Meanwhile Maring had been busy. Unable to influence Sun on his own, he had applied to higher echelon and Adolph A. Joffe had been sent out from Moscow to help him.

Joffe was a forceful and experienced diplomat. He had been the chief Soviet negotiator at the Brest-Litovsk Treaty of 1918 which had taken Russia out of World War I and the prestige of that achievement still clung to him. Sun Yat-sen was flattered to receive a call from this eminent personage and was impressed by the message he brought. The Soviet Union, Sun was given to understand, had no interest in imposing communism on China but was vitally concerned about the nation's independence and freedom from foreign domination, and to achieve this end was willing to supply arms, money, and advisers as needed.

When Sun, still suspicious, asked if Joffe would put that in writing, the Soviet diplomat readily agreed and a famous joint statement was issued:

> Dr. Sun Yat-sen holds that the Communist order, or even the Soviet System, cannot actually be introduced into China because conditions do not exist here for the successful establishment of either Communism or Sovietism. This view is entirely shared by Mr. Joffe...

A giant step had been taken, especially as the Soviets soon began backing up their words with deeds. Ships arrived in Canton carrying weapons and supplies and promised technical and economic advisers, all reassuring Sun Yat-sen that, in one quarter of the world at least, he was a valued ally. And into this atmosphere of gemütlichkeit walked Comintern agent Maring with a bold proposal—that Sun take the Chinese Communist Party into partnership with his Kuomintang in a coalition government.

It probably came as a surprise to the Tsungli that there *was* a Chinese Communist Party; in any case he brushed the impertinent suggestion aside. His agreement with Adolph Joffe had guaranteed him independence of action and he had no intention of sharing power with political upstarts at this stage of the game. But to avoid offending the Soviet Union, he agreed to permit Chinese Communists to enter the Kuomintang as private individuals. He made it clear that there was to be no caucusing or voting en bloc, and that Communist members must abide by all Kuomintang Party rules and disciplines. Unable to get more out of the stubborn Tsungli, Maring had to be content with this slim concession.

With Soviet assistance rapidly arriving, revolution took on a new urgency in Canton. And yet Sun Yat-sen, benefiting as he was from his Russian alliance, seemed to have lingering doubts about the company he was keeping. The connection with an atheist dictatorship continued to trouble him.

As late as the spring of 1923 he approached Jacob Gould Schurman, the American Minister to China, with a proposition. Would the United States—singly or in concert with other capitalist nations—undertake an unprecedented act of generosity and international responsibility? Would it act as a benevolent power to take over the management of China for a period of, say, five years? During that time it was to introduce efficient methods of business and industry and, even more important, educate the people in democratic ideals and duties. When the period was up, when democracy had been established and elections held, the benevolent power was to withdraw from China, leaving behind the undying gratitude of 400 million people, then a quarter of the earth's population.

In 1923 the idea seemed not only brazen but absurd, and Sun Yat-sen was once more scoffed at as a dreamer. But in retrospect, considering the billions that have been squandered on corrupt and doomed regimes, the Tsungli's imaginative proposal has appeal. It was his misfortune that he was years ahead of lend-lease subsidies, of Truman Doctrines and Marshall Plans, of unlikely charities to Germany and Japan, not to mention the blood and treasure pumped into Vietnam. Had Sun Yat-sen lived fifty years later, he might have been hailed as a prophetic statesman. In 1923 he was dismissed as a clown.

Rejected by the West, Sun never again doubted his Soviet alliance. He went feverishly to work, organizing along the lines suggested by his Russian advisers. There was an army to be built—the Tsungli would no longer be dependent on fickle and self-serving warlords—and in Chiang Kai-shek he had just the man to recruit and train a crusading force dedicated to the Republic. And a new breed of officials had to be found, men of brains and energy like Mao Tse-tung—though Sun wasn't even aware of the name yet—who could bring an effective administration to a China conquered by force of arms.

So in Canton in 1923 the pieces were fitted together, Soviet machinery meshing with the driving force of Chinese personnel. Chiang Kai-shek left Shanghai and came to town, en route to becoming the most famous man of his generation. Mao Tse-tung arrived too—on the run, as it happens, pursued by the police—in transit to an eminence of his own. They met for the first time in Canton, comrades in a crusade that under Sun Yat-sen's idealistic leadership was to regenerate the nation.

7

The Tsungli Passes

CANTON HAS BEEN CALLED THE CRADLE OF REBELLIONS. Extend the city to include its province (Kwangtung) and the description is apt. The area's history of riot in the last two centuries alone has been impressive.

It was in Canton that the earliest demonstrations against the Western barbarians were staged, as far back as 1830. In the mountains outside the city the Taiping Heavenly Kingdom movement was nurtured, developing into the crusade that engulfed half of China for eleven years, from 1853 to 1864. Sun Yat-sen sprang his first uprising in Canton in 1895, and it was to remain his favorite site for repeat performances until the 1911 Revolution unexpectedly erupted in Wuhan. And it was invevitable that from 1917 on Sun was drawn back to Canton in frustrated efforts to establish a redoubt from which to unseat the dictatorship in Peking. He was born in a village close to Canton and that city represented the closest thing he had to a power base.

Canton literally translated means the City of Rams, no doubt an allegorical allusion to the temperament of its people. Westerners, coping with Cantonese bellicosity, took to calling the inhabitants the Irish of the Orient and thought to detect in the local dialect an Irish lilt. That dialect was in other ways remarkable because it differed so widely from the patois of neighboring provinces as to seem almost a foreign language. The Cantonese prided themselves on their unique tongue, claiming that it came down pure from ancient Chinese, uncorrupted by the Mongol and Manchu invasions. Outsiders weren't as complimentary. To many, the jargon sounded barbarous, in keeping with the character of the citizenry. Rumors spread that Cantonese were addicted to diets of newborn rats, raw monkeys' brains, and fried snake.

Canton, a port tucked into the southeast corner of the nation, was the first Chinese city to be exposed to Western influences. In the beginning, during the seventeenth and eighteenth centuries, the Western traders, mainly Portuguese and Dutch, were kept isolated, walled in on the island of Macao at the mouth of the Pearl River. But around 1800, with the advent of the more aggressive and better gunned British, the walls ruptured and Canton was inundated. The experience wasn't altogether dampening. Compradors grew rich acting as middlemen for Western merchants at Shameen, Canton's foreign concession area, and jobs multiplied for the less privileged. Population grew to 600,000 by 1908 and over a million in the 1920s.

Canton became the chief Chinese port of embarkation for a brisk trade in the export of coolies. By 1900, some 120,000 indentured laborers were being sent overseas annually to dig ditches and build railroads and, incidentally, establish Chinatowns and a taste for Cantonese cooking throughout Europe and America. About 90,000 of these emigrants returned each year, bringing back money for burial in China. They also brought back expanded horizons and at least a rudimentary knowledge of democratic processes. Canton was probably the one city in the land where references to "individual rights" and "representative government" could be even vaguely comprehended.

All in all, it was a fertile field for revolution, provided the right leadership and organization were supplied. And in 1923, with the Hakka general temporarily driven to cover and assistance from the Soviet Union at hand, Sun Yat-sen was ready to meet the challenge. Or he would be when an extraordinary man called Michael Borodin arrived from Russia to help him.

Through the summer, scenes of disorientation and confusion had reigned, reminiscent of Sun's short-lived government at Nanking in 1912. The Kuomintang faithful had come flocking into Canton along with the not-so-faithful, now that the Tsungli was back in power with jobs to hand out, which resulted in the old jealousies and the squabbling and the endless jockeying for administrative posts.

Only two appointments come clear from the mess. Sun Fo, the Tsungli's thirty-two-year-old son, was named mayor of Canton, and Chiang Kai-shek was confirmed as superintendent of the new Whampoa Military Academy which was to train the revolution's cadets. As the installation's barracks and parade grounds were still under construction, Chiang was dispatched to the Soviet Union on an interim diplomatic and educational mission, leaving in August via the Trans-Siberian Railway. Otherwise the picture of furious activity at cross-purposes remains constant until October, when Michael Borodin arrived with a group of Comintern advisers.

Borodin was an assumed name, the nom de guerre of a revolutionary. His real name seems to have been Grusenberg. He was born in Latvia in 1882 but was taken as a child to Chicago, U.S.A. He became a radical early and went to Russia to join in the abortive uprising against the czar in 1905. Escaping the subsequent bloodbath, he returned to Chicago, married a woman named Fannie Orluk and settled down as a teacher, rising to become a principal in the public school system. Then Lenin seized power in 1917 and Grusenberg/Borodin returned to Russia and to politics.

He joined the Comintern, the newly formed agency designed to guide and assist socialist revolutions, as Lafayette and other internationalists like him had once aided and abetted democratic revolutions. Borodin saw service in Scotland, Mexico, and Turkey. His activities caused his eviction from all three countries but he learned lessons of patience and perseverance that were to prove invaluable in China.

Borodin has been described as a large, quiet man "with the natural dignity of a lion or a panther." He wore a heavy mustache which seemed to go with his deep voice and his habit of rumination, weighing his words before he spoke. His deliberation and calm stemmed, according to one observer, from "a long view of history." It was agreed by all who knew him that he was a man of great charm and he was warmly welcomed by Sun Yat-sen when he reached Canton. The men had met before—in America during one of Sun's fund-raising tours—and of course there was no language barrier between them; each spoke impeccable English, even sharing an American accent.

Borodin was well aware of Sun's suspicions of communism and the class struggle, so he set about tutoring the Tsungli with infinite tact. Instead of lecturing, he listened, allowing Sun to explain the history and organization of his Kuomintang Party—its structure, aims, problems, and confusions—and in so doing reveal its abysmal weaknesses. In Borodin's own words, the Kuomintang stood exposed as "more akin to a clique than to a true Party."

Borodin deftly pointed the advantages of the Soviet governmental structure—working subcommittees reporting back to departmental committees, which in turn were responsible to an overall Central Executive Committee (CEC) under a chief of state. Sun was particularly won over by a provision that, as president and chief of state, he would have veto powers over all decisions made at a lower level, even by the august Central Executive Committee in plenary session.

Borodin next turned to the Three People's Principles, the collection of slogans and ideals that had served as Sun Yat-sen's platform ever since the founding of the United League but hadn't been reexamined in twenty years. Obviously the first principle, nationalism, no longer applied to getting rid of the long-gone Manchus. And disposing of the present dictators in Peking was too narrow an objective. Borodin proposed broadening the principle to put an end to the insults and injustices China had suffered at the hands of foreigners. "Extraterritoriality," the jaw-breaking word that covered rights and privileges Westerners had assumed for themselves, must go. Also "consular jurisdiction," which supported privilege by imposing foreign legal codes on Chinese soil, must be terminated. And finally the "unequal treaties," forced on the Manchus at gunpoint, must be renegotiated. If foreigners wanted to stay on in China for business reasons, let them conform to the laws of the land and not pose as visiting royalty.

Sun Yat-sen readily adopted this proposal. He had his own grievances against the outlanders who had turned a deaf ear to his appeals for help, and besides, as a publicist, he could see a slogan shaping up—"China for Chinese, not Foreigners!"

The second principle, democracy, was next submitted to scrutiny. Sun had been discouraged by the parliamentary experiment under the presidency of Yuan Shih-kai. Of course, that parliament hadn't been a truly democratic body. There had been no general election; representatives had been hand-picked from among the Kuomintang faithful and, without pressure from their constituencies, had behaved selfishly and irresponsibly. Still, the problem remained—how to educate an ignorant population into an enlightened electorate once power was again achieved. As Sun saw it, a temporary dictatorship for some five or six years—a "period of tutelage" he called it— was inevitable until the people could be taught the principles of democracy. He proposed to delegate education to local officials who would set up training courses and conduct exercises in electoral self-government at municipal and county levels.

Borodin concurred that a period of tutelage was necessary but he had a suggestion. Instead of trusting local officials, why not encourage the people to learn self-government through their own institutions? If trade unions in the cities and peasant associations in the countryside were fostered, ordinary citizens would quickly master the techniques of debating, running for office, and election via the ballot box through keen self-interest.

Sun Yat-sen thought the idea brilliant. We don't know what Borodin, under the name of Grusenberg, taught in the Chicago public schools, but it should have been revolutionary civics.

Now only the third principle, the people's livelihood, remained for review and as always it was a stickler. Agriculture was still the central problem. Sun Yat-sen had developed a slogan—

"Land for the tillers"—but otherwise he hadn't moved any closer to a solution than his vaguely socialistic* plan of buying, at staggering cost, "excess" holdings from landlords for distribution to impoverished peasants.

Not surprisingly Borodin had no contributions to make on the subject. He was content to let the question of the people's livelihood go unanswered for the moment, confident that when labor unions and peasant associations began to flourish they would find their own solutions.

Borodin, an orthodix Marxist, no doubt put his main faith in the labor unions. Industrial workers, the proletariat, were traditionally the storm troopers of revolution. But Borodin was new to China and did not yet understand all the peculiarities and difficulties. Whereas Mao Tse-tung, native born and fresh from organizing industrial workers in Hunan Province, was beginning to wonder what role if any the proletariat would play in a Chinese socialist upheaval, should one ever occur.

Mao Tse-tung had returned to Changsha after the founding congress of July 1921 intent on carrying out the new Communist Party's program. He would have much preferred to work among peasants. He was a peasant himself and understood their potentials better than anyone else in China, as was to be abundantly proved. But peasants had been ruled out by the Central Committee, so Mao dutifully applied himself to the organization of industrial workers.

Accompanied by his brother Tse-min, he traveled to the coal fields of south Hunan. Apparently the dedicated young men worked effectively because in September 1922 a strike was called to improve safety conditions and raise wages to $5 per month.

---

*It has often been pointed out that conditions in China were ripe for a thoroughgoing capitalist economy. There was ample "primary accumulation" among the compradors in the Treaty Ports, a plethora of labor and a vast potential internal market. Three factors conspired to prevent capitalist development: the conservatism of Chinese financiers who found foreign securities and native land speculation more profitable than industrial development; the opposition of foreign traders to capitalist competition within the country; and the traditional apathy of the culture. So Sun Yat-sen and those who followed him to power were forced to think in terms of socialism or no reform at all.

Inevitably troops were rushed to the scene, the strike was crushed, and the Mao brothers, exposed as agitators and troublemakers, were forced to beat a hasty retreat.

Mao returned to Changsha to become secretary of the provincial Communist chapter. He kept on organizing—municipal employees, printers, workers at the government mint—he calculated "more than twenty trade unions" in all. In the spring of 1923 solidarity was tested by a general strike throughout the province. The outcome was never in doubt; troops broke up the demonstrations and dispersed the marchers with gratuitous violence.

Mao Tse-tung had once more called himself to the attention of the Hunan governor who is supposed to have said: "This Mao . . . is dangerous . . . there is not enough place in Hunan for both of us." His arrest was ordered and Mao was on the run again.

As he fled from the police, Mao summed up the significance of his attempts and failures. Industrial workers in China were too few and hence too vulnerable. The forces of reaction surrounded them everywhere in the cities, ready to snuff out the first sparks of revolt. If the situation could somehow be reversed, if the reactionaries could themselves be surrounded—and here begins the famous imagery of the cities surrounded by the countryside—the workers might have a chance to organize and strike from within. And there was only one source for the overwhelming numbers necessary to bring about the conditions Mao envisioned—the peasantry.

Mao Tse-tung arrived in Canton in May 1923 in time for the Third Congress of the Chinese Communist Party. As has been noted, the Central Committee had authorized collaboration with the Kuomintang the previous year and already Communists had joined Sun Yat-sen's followers in working relationships. But there were still questions to be resolved and, at the Third Congress, one of particular importance was debated: Should the Communist Party permit cooperation with the Kuomintang in the sensitive area of labor organization?

Mao Tse-tung, a member of the Central Committee by now, thought not. He had found in Hunan that Kuomintang collaborators, torn by class interests, were unreliable at times of crisis, so he cast his vote in the negative. As it happened, his was the decisive vote in a closely contested issue. The Kuomintang was excluded from cooperation.

Immediately, and in private, pressure was brought to bear on Mao. The Secretary General, Editor Chen Tu-hsiu, and Maring, the adviser from the Comintern, urged him to rethink his position. What arguments they marshaled are unimportant now, but Mao gave in, submitting for the only time in his career, as far as is known, to moral suasion. When the issue was resubmitted to the Central Committee (the manipulation of procedures is a matter for wonder) the resolution carried by Mao's switched vote. Cooperation with the Kuomintang *was* permitted.

Rewards were immediate. Within his own party, Mao was appointed chief of the Organizational Bureau (ORGBURO) and was in addition promised an important post in the Kuomintang, though confirmation on that would have to wait until the Kuomintang convened its own congress.

The First National Congress of the Kuomintang Party was brought together in January 1924. It was to be a historic and stormy convention. From all over China, delegates and their retinues flocked into Canton: bankers and compradors from Shanghai; manufacturers from Wuhan; merchants from Tientsin, Sian, and Chungking; and officials, landlords, scholars, and students from everywhere. For the most part they were inheritors of a memory, survivors of the vast conspiratorial network of United League days, now grown prosperous and conservative with the passage of years. All eighteen provinces of China Proper were represented and there were delegates from Manchuria, Mongolia, Tibet, and from overseas branches as far off as New York and Sydney, Australia. Many had heard rumors of what was going on in Canton and few had liked what they heard.

From the opening session Sun Yat-sen, firm and commanding as he had rarely been before, made no bones about laying out the situation. The Kuomintang had adopted a new friend in the Soviet Union and that fact must be accepted. The supplies, money, and expertise necessary for a successful renewal of the revolution depended on the alliance. That didn't mean that either Sun or the party were moving toward communism—Sun's joint statement with Adolph A. Joffe was proof to the contrary—but it did mean that collaboration had been extended internally to the Chinese Communist Party. That fact too must be accepted. In the slate of candidates Sun was about to advance for the Kuomintang's Central Executive Committee, the names of nine Communists appeared, including that of an unknown young politician called Mao Tse-tung. The Tsungli invited debate on the names but there were to be no objections on principle or disruptive partisan arguments.

Of course there *were* objections and arguments, plenty of them; the wrangling went on for weeks. But in the end the assembly gave in. Sun Yat-sen was, after all, the indispensable leader. He had guided the party to one successful revolution and he could conquer the nation again, with all that meant in jobs and opportunities and influence at every level.

And in the final days of the congress Sun was helped by two events that occurred abroad. In England, Ramsay MacDonald was elected to office as the first Labor prime minister in British history and, in Russia, the great V. I. Lenin died after a lingering illness. Telegrams were dispatched in the name of the Republic of South China: congratulations to MacDonald, condolences to the Politburo in Moscow. A telegram of appreciation came back immediately from Russia but Ramsay MacDonald never troubled to reply—he wasn't wasting his new-won prestige on Orientals. His arrogance infuriated the congress, causing it to close ranks behind Sun and foreign imperialism as nothing else could have done. While the militant mood lasted, the rest of Sun's program was voted in, including the admission of Communists into the Kuomintang Party and the seating of Mao Tse-tung on the Central Executive Committee as an alternate member.

The congress adjourned and the delegates went home, some fired with enthusiasm, others no doubt disgruntled by the trend toward radicalism. With them, as disgruntled as any, went Chiang Kai-shek, though his discontent was not political. He was in the throes of his first and only quarrel with Sun Yat-sen and felt miserable about it. He returned to his birthplace at Fenghua, not Shanghai. Fenghua was nearer at hand should the Tsungli care to make up.

Good soldier Chiang Kai-shek had more than done his duty since his departure for the Soviet Union in August 1923 and he had reason to feel neglected on his return. He had spent some four months in Moscow, diligently studying ordnance, training techniques, methods of political indoctrination, and everything else to which his hosts introduced him. He had met and conversed with high Soviet officials, including Chicherin, Zinoviev and, of course, Trotsky, famous as the creator of the Red army and now Minister of War. He didn't meet Stalin, little known at the time outside his own country, nor Lenin who was already too ill to receive visitors.

Chiang wasn't impressed by the Soviet leaders nor the Soviet system. He suspected the regime of having designs on China, especially its outlying possessions, the Mongolias and Manchuria. To his mind Russian communism was simply "Tsarism by other names." This hostile opinion didn't apply to the Red army, however. He admired its efficiency and discipline and was much taken by its system of political commissars to propagandize the party's point of view and sustain morale.

When Chiang returned to Canton in December he found Sun Yat-sen, closeted with Borodin in preparation for the approaching National Congress, too busy to spare him much time. So Chiang wrote a long report on his impressions and observations in Russia, submitted it to the Tsungli and patiently awaited a reply. None was forthcoming. Deeply hurt, Chiang sat through the fireworks of the Kuomintang convention in January 1924, then stoically departed for Fenghua.

Sun Yat-sen let him cool his heels until construction on the new Whampoa Military Academy was near completion, then ordered him back to duty. Chiang was aggrieved by what he imagined to be a peremptory tone. He stalled, claiming that he had resumed mourning for his mother and couldn't leave yet. And indeed he had been busy. He had chosen a choice location for her grave, a site that commanded "a beautiful position with vistas all around" and was landscaping it with "violets . . . as big as daisies."

Sun soon tumbled to what was wrong. He wrote an affectionate and teasing letter, upbraiding Chiang for his terrible temper and reassuring him as to his importance to the revolution. Appeased and relieved, Chiang hurried back to Canton.

Whampoa Academy opened on June 16, 1924 and was a great success from the beginning. Three thousand candidates applied for admittance, from which 500 were selected for the first six-month course. Later the enrollment per class was doubled and tripled until, at the peak, 5,540 cadets stood in ranks on graduation day.

The instructing staff comprised both Chinese and Russian officers. The Soviet contingent was headed by General Vasili K. Bluecher, going under the nom de guerre "Galen," with thirty advisers under him. Chiang Kai-shek and Galen seem to have hit it off well; three years later, when the parting of the ways came, Galen was the only Russian for whom Chiang retained affection and respect. A corps of political commissars was also incorporated into the training program. Its deputy chief was a slender intellectual called Chou En-lai. Chou, then twenty-six, the grandson of a mandarin, was noted for a soft voice and courteous manner which seemed to contradict the communism he had embraced as a Work-Study teacher in France during World War I.

Chiang Kai-shek was in his element as superintendent and commanding general at Whampoa. Everything he had learned in Japan and Russia along with his experiences as a resourceful revolutionary soldier were put to use. He exhorted his cadets in mixed martial and Confucian harangues: "Do not fear death . . . When a man lives to see his own accomplishments as a revolutionary, we call this success. When . . . [he] sacrifices his life first, we call this the establishment of virtue."

Always loyal to Sun Yat-sen and his policies, no matter what his private feelings, he extolled the Soviet alliance: "If our . . . Russian comrades had not come to guide us and teach us the technique of revolution, I am afraid that our revolutionary army would not be where it is today."

Chiang Kai-shek was coming out from under wraps. Like other rigid, self-controlled people, he found in military command an authorized outlet for his aggressions. He had always had strength of character; now he was developing dash and charisma, the ability to impress men by words and deeds and bind them to him in loyalty.

And he was helped by peculiar outer circumstances. Training at Whampoa was no mere exercise in military theory; actual practice awaited not far afield. For the Hakka general and other warlords, alarmed at Sun Yat-sen's growing military power, had begun attacks on Canton. Time and again Chiang Kai-shek was forced to deploy his half-trained cadets in defense of the city, in fierce encounters where bullets flew and men were killed and wounded. Perhaps never before or since has a military academy engaged in field maneuvers under such grimly realistic conditions. The ever-present prospect of death insured discipline and hastened learning.

In some respects the Whampoa days were Chiang Kai-shek's finest. Certainly he always looked back on them with nostalgia. Moral values were simple and straightforward then, loyalties unmixed and duties direct. Compared to his later complexities, the Whampoa years were golden years.

If Chiang Kai-shek was having the time of his life in the first surge of Kuomintang–Communist collaboration, Mao Tse-tung was not. For him the period began in boredom and ended with disaster. In fact, before it was halfway through, Mao was out of government altogether, if only temporarily.

1924 began promisingly enough. Seated on the executive boards of both Kuomintang and Communist parties, Mao was considered an ideal man to act as a liaison officer, coordinating the activities of the groups. Accordingly he was sent to the propaganda bureau in Shanghai to join forces with two high-ranking Kuomintang officials, Hu Han-min and Wang Ching-wei, flatteringly called by Sun Yat-sen his right and left hands.

Righthand-man Hu Han-min had performed valuable services for the revolution as a theorist and writer back in the days of the United League. But since then conservatism had taken over and he was jaundiced about many things in the Tsungli's present program, including collaboration with the Communists.

Lefthand-man Wang Ching-wei was also a tried and true and tired revolutionary. He had once cut a dashing figure in the movement, second in fame only to the Tsungli himself. But again time had taken its toll. He had become a puritan in his habits and, sinking ever deeper into a Confucian mold, was inclined to shrink from crudities both in life and in politics. There was, too, an unstable streak in him which widened as he entered middle age. The fault was still partly concealed beneath a lacquered finish—he was called China's "perfect gentleman"—but one day it was to betray him into infamy.

Mao Tse-tung could hardly have found stimulation in such companionship. Mao was then thirty-one, eager and dedicated. We have a description of him at about this time from a former school chum which stresses his more evident characteristics: "First ... Mao is a person who takes great pains to plan very carefully whatever he undertakes.... Second, he can estimate quite accurately the power of his enemies. Third, he can hypnotize his audience. He's really got a terrific power of persuasion and there are very few people who are not carried away by his words."

It's probable that Hu Han-min and Wang Ching-wei remained among the few. There is no evidence that Mao's powers of persuasion put a dent in their cynical attitudes. They considered the whole committee idea ridiculous, an importation of the Soviets for their own ends. The less done to coordinate it the better.

Mao stuck it out for the rest of the year, but when he headed back to Canton in January 1925 for the Fourth Congress of the Chinese Communist Party he was resolved to ask for a new assignment. It came as a shock to find that he was in no position to ask for anything. The attitude of his party had suddenly changed toward him. He was no longer a rising young leader but under deep suspicion.

For there had been developments in Moscow. When the decision taken at the Third Congress of the Chinese Communist Party—to cooperate with the Kuomintang in labor organization—was reported back to headquarters, the Comintern, sitting in plenary session, was outraged. Communists must *never* collaborate with anyone in organizing workers. The party of Marx and Lenin was the vanguard of the proletariat and to share its responsibilities with others was tantamount to capitulationism. The resolution of the Chinese party was repudiated. Comintern adviser Maring, made the chief scapegoat of the error, was called back to Moscow for reeducation and rehabilitation. In addition, any Chinese party member promoted during Maring's regime was to be considered a deviationist and removed from office.

So Mao Tse-tung was relieved of his position on the Orgburo, dismissed from his party's Central Committee and forced to resign his posts in the Kuomintang. And like Maring, he too was sent away, but only to his home in Hunan Province for self-analysis and reappraisal.

Eleven years later Mao was to gloss over the episode, telling the American journalist Edgar Snow only that "I returned to Hunan for a rest—I had become ill in Shanghai." But the evasion seems to indicate, how much he had suffered from the humiliation. Even so, indignant as he may have been, he never considered doing what Maring did in protest at *his* treatment—withdrawing from the Comintern and returning to his native Holland to pursue revolution in his own way. Mao remained firm in his dedication. He had at one time said, "Once I had accepted [Marxism] as the correct interpretation of history, I did not afterwards waver"—and he meant it.

Twelve years later he was to write: "A Communist should have largeness of mind and he should be staunch and active, looking upon the interests of the revolution as his very life and subordinating his personal interests to those of the revolution." In the spring of 1925 he began living out this belief. Back in Hunan, with the help of his wife, two brothers, and adopted sister, all ardent Communists by now, he started on his own to organize peasant associations. At last he was doing something that he wanted to do, something that he was good at, and something that would in the end change the structure of China.

Sun Yat-sen and Michael Borodin, working together after the Kuomintang congress adjourned in 1924, organized Sun's party along lines of efficiency it had never known before. A network of committees was set up in preparation for the great crusade, the Northern Expedition that was to sweep from Canton to Peking to liberate the nation. There were committees for administrative and fiscal reform, for industrial and labor organization, for judicial and business codes, for youth, education, health, welfare, workers, peasants, and women. Few aspects of life under a democracy were left uncovered.

Sun, though a little dazed by it all, was grateful for Borodin's deft management and the very real assistance of the Soviet Union in personnel, supplies, and money. He showed his appreciation in a manifesto proclaiming Three Great Policies to go with his Three People's Principles. The three policies were alliance with the Soviet Union, cooperation with the Chinese Communist Party, and assistance to peasants and workers. The Three Great Policies lived as long as Sun did, then were quietly forgotten by all, it seemed, but Mao Tse-tung.

Things were going so well, in fact, that Sun Yat-sen, who had made a lifelong habit of tinkering and tampering with his political apparatus, was left with nothing to do. To keep him employed, Borodin put him to work lecturing. Through the spring and summer of 1924 Sun delivered a famous series of lectures clarifying the Three People's Principles, as close as he ever came to leaving behind a doctrine and writ for the faithful.

Sun was at his best as a public speaker and his San Min Chu I (Three People's Principles) addresses were triumphs. The spirit of the man, his idealism, his honesty, his dogged persistence, and, above all, his unquenchable patriotism, shone through his words. It didn't matter that he lagged a bit in scientific advancement, confusing the principle of the internal combustion engine with that of steam. ("Oil, called 'gas oil,' is ... highly volatile," he told his audience, "and as it vaporizes, drives the piston.") Or that he could misconstrue the Darwinian theory so lamentably as to state: "[T]he increase and decrease of population [has] played a large part in the rise and fall of nations; this is the Law of Natural Selection." Or that, despite his many visits to America, he was so unobservant as to believe that in the United States "all citizens have received military training in high school and college, so that the government can at any time add hosts of soldiers to the army."

What did matter was that he defined democracy as "the sovereignty of the people," that he insisted on the people's livelihood being at "the center of government, the center of economics, the center of all historical movements" and that he invented wonderful phrases, such as likening the Chinese people to "a sheet of loose sand" and describing the fate of the peasant masses as to be "born in a stupor and die in a dream." Important too was his persistent theme: "When the people share everything in the state, then will be truly reached the goal of the Min-sheng (livelihood) principle, which is Confucius's hope of a Great Commonwealth."

Despite his best efforts to keep up with the times, Sun Yat-sen remained a traditionalist to the end. He wrote in old-fashioned, stilted Chinese. The great literary movement of the 'teens, the revolution led by Editor Chen Tu-hsiu which had substituted the colloquial for the scholarly style, had passed him by. He even wrote English poorly, though he had learned it as a youth in a British school in Hawaii. But as a public speaker he had few equals. Standing at the edge of the platform, his slight figure bending forward for closer contact with his audience, he expressed his thoughts easily and naturally, his voice charged with a belief that made an indelible impression on his listeners. In the final months of his life Sun Yat-sen communicated an aura of inspiration that was never to be forgotten.

His time was growing short. During his last lectures of the summer it was noticed that he would sometimes pause and press his hand to his side in pain. By autumn his doctors told him that he was seriously ill and must receive attention. To Sun that only meant that his schedule of revolution must be hurried before his time ran out.

An opportunity offered when the warlord government in Peking, alarmed at what it heard about the developing Kuomintang army, invited Sun north for what was called a Rehabilitation Conference, meaning it was willing to work out a deal. Sun's advisers urged him not to go. Power-broking had been the curse of China since the Revolution of 1911 had been aborted and the

The Tsungli Passes

Tsungli mustn't stoop to such methods. Besides they were entirely unnecessary; the forces Chiang Kai-shek was training would be strong enough to crush the tuchuns for good in another year.

But Sun didn't have another year, and in December he left Canton for the North. In typical leisurely, indirect fashion, he took his time about the trip and turned it into a triumphant procession. He called in at Japan and at Osaka addressed a huge gathering. Then he crossed the Yellow Sea for another gala reception in Tientsin. Not surprisingly he overtaxed his strength; he was deathly sick when he reached Peking. He was hurried to the Western equipped and staffed Union Hospital for an exploratory operation. The surgeons found cancer of the liver, too far advanced to do anything about.

Sun was taken to the home of friends where he lingered on for two more months. Right and Left hands Hu Han-min and Wang Ching-wei went up to Peking to be with him, so did Borodin and other leaders from Canton. Sun's mind reverted to ancient ways and customs as the days moved on. Since the foreign doctors could do nothing for him, he—an M.D. with a Western diploma and a professed Christian—allowed Chinese herbalists and faith healers to be called in. But perhaps better than their treatments was the news Chiang Kai-shek telegraphed him: the Canton militia led by the Whampoa cadets had gone on the offensive and beaten Sun's old enemy, the Hakka general, in a decisive battle.

On March 11, 1925 Sun Yat-sen drew up his will, a document addressed to the Chinese people accounting for his forty years of struggle on their behalf and recommending what must be done to continue his work. He also wrote a letter to the Politburo of the Soviet Union in which he said: "Taking my leave of you, dear comrades, I want to express the hope that the day will soon come when the USSR will welcome a friend and ally in a mighty, free China. . . ."

Sun Yat-sen died at 3 A.M. March 12. His last words were "Peace . . . struggle . . . save China." Almost alone among the great men of his time he died in poverty; he had only his house and books to bequeath to his widow, and that in a country where officialdom meant riches if he had cared to avail himself of his opportunities. He was carried to rest in the Azure Cloud Temple outside of Peking, a temporary abode until the nation was unified and a suitable mausoleum could be provided.

He left behind three candidates to compete for the leadership of China—Right-hand Hu Han-min, Left-hand Wang Ching-wei, and another Kuomintang official of long service and reputation, Liao Chung-kai. No one ever considered Chiang Kai-shek an entrant in the sweepstakes; Sun Yat-sen's suspicion of strong-armed generals was reflected in the Kuomintang constitution, which prohibited militarists from rising to political power. And who in his right mind could have conceived that an obscure and troubled politician called Mao Tse-tung was even in the running?

8

Claimants to the Mantle

WHEN A GREAT LEADER DIES IT OFTEN SEEMS THAT AN epic era has ended. Glory is in eclipse; the future must necessarily be debased because power has passed from a giant to pygmies.

So it was in Canton during the months of mourning for Sun Yat-sen. The successors to his mantle—Hu, Wang, and Liao—apportioned the reins of government among them and conscientiously tried to perform their duties as the Tsungli might have wanted.

Only the Communist camp escaped the pervading gloom. Sun Yat-sen, after all, had not been specifically *their* leader, and their party was too new and too brash to cherish traditions and memories. There was perhaps no conscious effort to capitalize on the Kuomintang's period of mourning, but owing to the press of circumstances Communist activities stepped up.

There were strikes to be led and boycotts to be organized against foreign employers and goods. On May 30, 1925, a demonstration in the International Settlement in Shanghai was fired upon by the British police and a dozen paraders were killed. This led to further protest demonstrations and in Canton on June 23 the British again tried to silence chants and shouts with gunfire, killing fifty-six. Anger peaked throughout the country. In British-owned Hong Kong, 150,000 employees walked off their jobs and elsewhere 540,000 workers flocked into the newly organized All-China Labor Federation—a remarkable number considering that at most there were only four million industrial wage-earners in the nation.

The Communists grew in strength as a result of aggressive leadership. The party had slowly increased in numbers from the original 12 founders in 1921 to 342 in 1923 and 995 in January 1925. But the turmoil of that year provided all the recruiting incentive necessary to jump membership to 10,000 by November. Conservatives in the Kuomintang watched this growth with apprehension. Without Sun Yat-sen's influence to hold the collaboration together, sentiment for a break between Right and Left was growing.

Oddly, when the first split came, it was within the ranks of the Kuomintang Party. In August 1925 Liao Chung-kai, the third member of the triumvirate ruling the Republic of South China, was assassinated. In the subsequent investigation, Right-hand Hu Han-min's brother was revealed to have been implicated in the crime and Hu's political career was compromised. He withdrew from government, leaving Left-hand Wang Ching-wei as sole chief of state, supported by Chiang Kai-shek as commander of the republic's armed forces.

Both men, as yet limited in their ambitions, were dedicated to the ideals of Sun Yat-sen and determined to carry out the revolution in his image. Wang refused the title of President of the Republic; that office was retired in perpetuity in honor of Sun, and Wang was content to be called Chairman of the Central Executive Committee. Similarly Chiang refused the title Generalissimo, or general of generals, because it had been previously bestowed on the Tsungli. Commander-in-chief of the army was good enough for him.

But modesty in office was not what the conservatives wanted. They were looking for more drastic action. In November a group of bankers, compradors, and industrialists made a sentimental journey to Peking and held a meeting beside Sun Yat-sen's temporary crypt in the Western Hills. They were a powerful caucus and their demands—an end to the Communist collaboration and the eviction from the country of Borodin and the other Russian advisers—made an impression. The Western Hills Clique—as it came to be called—created more mischief by trying to promote a rift between Left-hand Wang and Chiang Kai-shek. A slogan was devised: "Ally with Chiang to overthrow Wang." The conservatives already saw a potential "Man on horseback" in the army commander even if he didn't.

The chief of state and the general were quick in their attempts to offset the troublemakers. They denied that there were any differences between them, they were still united in a common cause. Wang Ching-wei issued a statement declaring that, "We are taking you along the path of the Three People's Principles." Chiang Kai-shek went further: "The National Revolution cannot... neglect communism. We cannot deny that the Chinese Revolution is part of the World Revolution." And to give substance to his words, he sent his sixteen-year-old son, Ching-kuo, to Russia for his education.

But a breach had been opened. The substantial personages of the Western Hills Clique were widely respected, and their stand against radicalism and the Russian alliance gave impetus to other malcontents.

Already the winds of reaction had been felt in the countryside. They blew with particular force in Hunan Province where Mao Tse-tung and his family were busy promoting peasant associations. Landlords began organizing min-tuans, squads of armed bullies, to intimidate the villages. Peasant leaders were waylaid and manhandled and public meetings harassed. A special hunt was on for "outside agitators"; the Maos were driven to cover and forced to suspend activities for a while.

Mao Tse-tung reappeared in Canton in the late summer of 1925. He seems to have been taken back into the Communist fold, though apparently on probation. Kuomintang officialdom was more enthusiastic about his return and put him to work editing *Political Weekly*, the polemic government journal. And in October he was appointed director of the Peasant Institute, the training school for agrarian cadres.

In contrast to labor organization, the peasant program had lagged under Sun Yat-sen and Borodin. This was largely because there were few party members—either Communist or Kuomintang—who cared to lose caste by such distasteful work. The whole trend of the culture was to regard the agricultural masses as brute creatures without aims beyond their plots of land or minds capable of development. Even Sun Yat-sen, who had boasted of being a coolie and the son of a coolie, lost contact with his origins when he metaphorically donned a scholar's gown.

Mao Tse-tung changed that attitude, at least within the institute. He did it by hiring a new staff of instructors, men experienced in the field like his brother Tse-min, and encouraging them to recruit students whose enthusiasm matched their own. Before Mao took over, the school had graduated some 30 political workers. A year later 327 were enrolled, "representatives of 21 different provinces [including] students from Inner Mongolia." The consequences were to be far-reaching. By June 1926, despite landlord opposition and min-tuan threats, a million peasants had been organized throughout China; by June 1927, ten million.

In its way, Mao Tse-tung's Peasant Institute was as important to the revolution as Chiang Kai-shek's Whampoa Military Academy—more important if the pen, or ideas from the pen, are mightier than the sword. But it was to take time for ideas to seize solid hold; meanwhile the sword was in the ascendancy. And on March 20, 1926 Chiang Kai-shek dropped the blade in what has come to be called the "Canton Coup," a stroke that changed the immediate future.

Chiang Kai-shek had distinguished himself since the Tsungli's death. His victory over the Hakka general was followed by campaigns against other regional warlords until the entire Southwest was firmly under control of the Canton government. And he had been rewarded for his triumphs. His title as Supreme Commander of the Republican Armies had been officially confirmed and he had been elected to a seat on the Kuomintang Central Executive Committee.

Until then, Chiang had carefully kept clear of politics. He was fond of quoting the Confucian precept, "Those who do not occupy the seats of authority should not concern themselves with the government." In his Whampoa lectures he emphasized that it was a soldier's duty to fight, not politic—a rule he strictly adhered to, though his cadets were breaking up into factions of left and right. But after he was installed in political office, Chiang was willing enough to make his real views known. At the Second Kuomintang Congress in January 1926 he voted to limit Communist membership in any important committee to one-third of its total. This was to check aggressive, take-over tendencies; the Communists were given to understand that they were to play auxiliary, not principal, roles in the forthcoming revolution.

But in spite of his punctilious regard for the proprieties, there was much to distress Chiang in what was going on. The constant strikes and demonstrations staged by the Communists made him uneasy, dedicated as he was to civil obedience. He knew that the disturbances were discrediting his party and that his own reputation was suffering. In Shanghai and other Treaty Ports, the government at Canton was being called the Red Regime, with Borodin as its emperor and Chiang Kai-shek his complacent general. Nevertheless he bore these trials with what patience he could muster, confident that all would be set right with the commencement of the Northern Expedition—the great crusade that proposed to fight its way from Canton to Peking reestablishing the Republic of China—and to hasten matters, Chiang intensified preparations so that the march could begin sooner than scheduled.

By the beginning of spring 1926 Chiang judged that his forces were ready to move out and ordered his staff to draw up operational plans. Curious hitches developed: the Soviet advisers protested that the army was still short on supplies and training and nowhere near ready to being the northern march. The obstructionist tactics tied in with another occurrence—Borodin's mysterious disappearance from Canton. It was rumored that he had gone to the Northwest to negotiate with a warlord called Feng Yu-hsiang, also know as the "Christian General."

And indeed Comintern policy—or Soviet policy, depending on how much it was one and the same thing—had undergone a change. The death of Sun Yat-sen had made a difference. His successors to revolutionary leadership were viewed with skepticism—a tired politician, Left-hand Wang Ching-wei, as head of state, backed by a cabinet of nonentities, with an untried general in command of his military forces. Seeking an alternative instrument for power in China, the Comintern had begun dickering with the shrewd and experienced Feng Yu-hsiang.

Feng, rising from peasant origins, had remained resolutely a peasant in dress, habits, and style since becoming the dominant warlord of the Northwest. He had also added to his democratic veneer by adopting a trick or two from populist movements. He called his army the Kuominchun, or People's Army, and had himself, as a sign of progress, converted to Christianity. Later he converted his military forces by marching them into a river for mass baptism. Actually Feng was a deft politician who hoped to squeeze money and supplies out of the Soviets in return for a pretense of revolutionary zeal—a fact that Borodin, secretly negotiating with him in March 1926, was probably finding out.

In Canton, Chiang Kai-shek was shaken by these obstacles at home and rumors from abroad. He discussed matter with Left-hand Wang Ching-wei and received at least partial support for a line of action he proposed. Wang told him to go ahead and dismiss the Soviet military advisers if Chiang doubted their loyalty. But he wouldn't move on the rumor that Borodin was conducting negotiations with the Christian general, refusing to lodge a diplomatic protest without concrete evidence.

Chiang went away unsatisfied. In his opinion something had to be done, and at once, to shock the Soviets into realizing that they couldn't play fast and loose with their Chinese ally. And since Wang Ching-wei refused to act, the responsibility devolved on him.

It must have been an agonizing decision. To act on his own, to stage an insurrectionary act, meant a deliberate betrayal of his duty, since it was clearly established that all but routine military operations must have the sanction of the government. And beyond that there was the psychological barrier to be hurdled: to act on his own meant self-assertion, independent initiative without the consent of the group, a breach of the Confucian gentleman's code, the behavior of a pariah. But somehow he found the courage to strike. It was a necessity, as he saw it, in order to teach the Soviets, and incidentally the local Communists, a lesson.

The incident Chiang devised, the so-called Canton Coup, reflects his doubts and uncertainties. It gives every indication of having been hastily conceived, action for action's sake, the less thought out the better. Haphazard planning combined with erratic execution show up in every detail of the plot.

On March 20 the gunboat *Yung Feng* steamed upriver to dock at Whampoa Island. It was never clearly established who had given the sailing order though afterward the gunboat's captain claimed it had come from Chiang himself. More important was that the captain was a Communist, one of the few in the navy, recently and controversially appointed to his command.

Chiang, claiming that the docking was unauthorized and that it was, in reality, a ruse to kidnap him, ordered the gunboat boarded and the captain seized. Cashing in on the confusion of the moment, he declared a state of emergency and imposed martial law on Canton. He followed this up with arrests of all Soviet advisers, including the chief of the military mission, General Vasili K. Bluecher passing as "Galen." And for good measure he rounded up all the known local Communists, both in town and at Whampoa. Chou En-lai was caught in the net; Mao Tse-tung, in Shanghai on business, escaped.

Marital law and the detention of prisoners didn't last long. By evening Chiang seems to have been seized with panic for what he had done. He ordered amnesty and release of all captives, then went to Left-hand Wang Ching-wei to make a full confession and ask for punishment.

Wang received him in his sick room. Wang had been suffering in late years from an ailment, thought to be diabetes, and no doubt the news he had been receiving through the day further depressed his spirits. He coldly informed Chiang that he had ordered an investigation and that questions of punishment must wait until the findings were in. But he made no effort to conceal his indignation at the general's behavior, telling him that by a "single act [he had] destroyed the whole of his [Wang's] work, [and made] all [future] cooperation between [them] impossible."

Chiang Kai-shek might well have taken this to mean that his days as commander-in-chief of the Kuomintang armies were numbered. If so, he had failed to take into account Wang Ching-wei's instability of character which revealed itself at its worst in a crisis. This time, with all the cards apparently in his hands, with his moral position strong and his right to exert authority clear, Wang's qualities of will collapsed. The next morning the chief of state had disappeared from Canton. For several days his whereabouts were unknown; then it was learned that he had traveled to Hong Kong and was now on his way to Europe for treatment of his illness.

Without Wang present to press charges, the investigation into Chiang Kai-shek's misdeeds was quietly dropped. The government, left leaderless, gravitated toward him as the man of the hour. At least he had demonstrated the ability to take action, however mistaken, and that was enough to arouse admiration at a time of confusion and doubt.

The wonder was how completely Chiang's Canton Coup succeeded. It accomplished everything he had hoped from it, and more. Borodin came hurrying back from the Northwest to make his peace. He assured Chiang that the alliance between Kuomintang and Comintern had never been stronger, rumors and appearances to the contrary. Chiang retorted that he would be more convinced if Borodin could take steps to suppress the Communist disturbances that were giving the Kuomintang a bad name, and Borodin agreed to do his best.

Borodin found ready support for toning down Red activities in Editor Chen Tu-hsiu, Secretary General of the Communist Party. For some time Chen had been alarmed at the growing violence within his movement. He quailed at the anger incited by his young political cadres, and was shocked by the clashes between militant workers and the police. Editor Chen was by nature a man of peace and goodwill. He was a scholar and a liberal and only in theory an advocate of remorseless class struggle. He had once led a highly successful literary revolution but, as he was finding out, that had been no preparation for bloodshed on the streets. He readily agreed with Borodin that the time had come to call a halt.

Directives were issued that there was to be no more violence; demonstrations were to be conducted peaceably and clashes with the police were to be avoided. This led to angry questioning from within the ranks. Whose side was Editor Chen on anyway? Did he stand for bourgeois respectability or the triumph of the working masses? Answers weren't easy to supply and Chen's position was weakened. More than one subordinate came to doubt his ability to lead. Mao Tse-tung probably summed up a general feeling when he said: "I began to disagree with Chen's Right-opportunist policy at about this time."

One result of the changed policy was that Mao Tse-tung lost a job. Chiang Kai-shek, emboldened by his success in curbing radicalism, went a step further. At a meeting of the Central Executive Committee he proposed that all Communists working for the government declare their affiliation. Mao Tse-tung, back in his old seat as an alternate member, objected, pointing out that in many parts of the country disclosure of Communist membership would be an open invitation to execution by the landlords' min-tuans. The objection was noted and in due course Mao was relieved of his post in the Propaganda Department.

There seems to have been no personal venom in the firing. Chiang hardly knew Mao except as an outspoken radical and was merely taking advantage of his new prestige to carry out a mild purge. Interestingly, Chiang thought so little of Mao's work as head of the Peasant Institute that he was allowed to continue in that capacity. Mao himself later shifted his headquarters to Shanghai just to be on the safe side.

Though Chiang Kai-shek had grown in influence, he still desperately needed the weapons and money flowing in through the Russian alliance and went out of his way to prove that his solidarity with the proletariat was still unshaken. At a great rally in Canton he said: "The worker-peasant masses ... have swept away all the counterrevolutionaries and consolidated the basis of the national government." And he closed every speech with a raised fist and a shouted, "Long live the world revolution!"

Michael Borodin, Editor Chen, and workers and peasants may have been taken in by the rhetoric, but the conservatives of the Treaty Ports certainly were not. The Canton Coup had told them all they wanted to know: Chiang Kai-shek was their man—able, daring, and not to be dominated by radicals. The Western Hills Clique sent representatives to Canton to congratulate the general and take care of his needs, financial or otherwise. Among others came Chiang's old patron and relative by marriage, the financier and curio dealer Chang Ching-chiang. No opportunity was lost in impressing on the rising young general where the real power of China lay—among the compradors, bankers, and international traders allied with the taipans of the West.

There is no way of knowing how Chiang, busy with his final military preparations, reacted to the blandishments. His overriding concern was to begin the march from Canton to Peking, to crush the warlords combining against him, and to bring unity to China in fulfillment of Sun Yat-sen's dream. All other considerations had to wait on the success of the Northern Expedition.

9

The Aborted Crusade

THE NORTHERN EXPEDITION BEGAN AS AN AUTHENTIC crusade—a war to crush the infidel and establish a republic of light. And like any other idealistic enterprise it held together as long as the enemy was external and clearly identifiable as a force of darkness.

In 1926 the empire of the infidel warlords stretched from Manchuria in the north to the fringes of Canton in the south, a vast, loose conglomeration of conflicting jurisdictions and interests. The spiritual capital of this sprawling feudal system was at Peking, where the inheritors of Sun Yat-sen's first republic still kept up a debauched pretense of universal government. In normal times—which is to say times of habitual squabbling and contention—the provincial warlords paid little attention to Peking. But under the threat of an efficient army organizing at Canton with the intention of destroying them all, they drew together in a semblance of unity. Pledges were exchanged promising loyalty and support and individual militarists assembled troops in preparation for stout resistance.

Chiang Kai-shek never underestimated the forces arrayed against him. He knew that many of the tuchuns were tough and experienced generals who would fight stubbornly in defense of their territories. But he trusted in the discipline and modern weapons of his Whampoa-trained regiments and the superior quality of his allies. For Chiang too was supported by warlords, enlightened men like Li Tsung-jen of Kwangsi Province who realized that anarchy must end if China was to take its place among progressive nations.

Chiang Kai-shek left Canton on July 9, 1926 with 85,000 soldiers of the Republic, now retitled the National Government of China in anticipation of the unity the Northern Expedition was to bring about. The operational plan called for a two-pronged attack: one column under Li Tsung-jen was to fight its way north through Hunan Province to Changsha; while Chiang was to lead the second on a parallel course through Kiangsi to seize the provincial capital at Nanchang. Both campaigns were expected to be long and hard, consuming most of the summer.

The surprise came along Li Tsung-jen's route of march. Li was widely known as an expert strategist but no amount of military genius could account for the ease of his victories. Chief credit must go to Mao Tse-tung and his cadres from the Peasant Institute. They had worked overtime to convince rural populations that the revolutionary cause was their cause and, when General Li's forces advanced, the peasants rose against the local warlord armies. They sabotaged defense works or informed of troop locations, guiding Li's men by roundabout paths for flank attacks. They even attacked the enemy themselves, assaulting isolated units with antique swords and spears. And everywhere the Nationalist soldiers went they were greeted with smiles and flowers and libations of hot water, known in the countryside as "white tea."

Changsha was taken on August 12. The plan had been to wait until Nanchang fell; then the two columns were to advance together on Wuhan. But as Chiang Kai-shek's army had been held up by fierce fighting, Li Tsung-jen decided to move on alone.

Again astonishing things happened. The credit this time goes to the political cadres, Kuomintang and Communist, in the government's labor department. They had done a superb job of pre-selling the revolution. When Li Tsung-jen's army came in sight, the proletariat of Wuhan—some 600,000, the largest concentration of industrial workers in the nation—rose against the warlord garrisons and liberated the tri-cities.

Chiang Kai-shek, his own advance stalled before the trenches and concrete fortifications of an able militarist called Wu Pei-fu, was furious when he heard of General Li's successes. All his life he prided himself on his military talent and to be outdone by a subordinate commander was mortifying. Almost hysterically he pressed his attack, running from salient to salient along his battle line, demanding advance at whatever cost. In extremities he threatened to commit suicide, a trick he'd picked up from his admired hero Tseng Kuo-fan, conqueror of the Taiping Heavenly Kingdom, who had twice thrown himself into lakes, to be fished out by solicitous friends.

Finally in late September the Nationalists broke through and Nanchang was taken. Nanchang, Wuhan, Changhsa—together they traced an arrow pointing at the warlord capital of Peking, the ultimate target of the Northern Expedition. The original objective had been to march straight on to this conclusive conquest, ignoring Shanghai to the east until the nation was firmly under Nationalist control. Shanghai was fat and flabby and peripheral; it could wait.

But Shanghai refused to wait. The foreign residents had reacted with panic to the epic surge from Canton. They saw the victorious army of liberation in only one color—red. For hadn't the Soviet Union armed and supplied it? And wasn't it led by the notorious Chiang Kai-shek, called the Red general? Bloody revolution was approaching, and it could have only one meaning—the looting of Shanghai's wealth and the massacre of its foreign population.

Refugees pouring into the city—missionaries, traders, consular wives and children—added to the general atmosphere of fright. Frantic calls for protection were sent out to home governments and troops were rushed in—Gurkhas from India, marines from the United States, combat forces of one kind or another from

France, Japan, Belgium, Holland, and Spain. In all, 20,000 soldiers, backed by 125 warships, were assembled to safeguard the 25,000 civilians huddled in the foreign settlements.

The Chinese financial community was amused for a while by the panic of the Westerners. But when closing banks and canceled orders began to interfere with business, they called a conclave to restore sanity to the situation. A press conference was decided upon. If Western reporters could meet Chiang Kai-shek and see him as something other than an ogre dripping blood, fears might be allayed. Accordingly foreign correspondents and Shanghai journalists were invited to interview Chiang at his military headquarters in Nanchang.

The newsmen came crowding in, eager to meet the martial celebrity and judge for themselves. Some were disappointed. One described Chiang as radiating "nothing in his appearance to mark him as a leader of men." Another expressed doubts about his character: "Strong men have risen and fallen interminably since the [1911] revolution. Will Chiang go the way of the rest or is he a strong man come to stay?"

There was nothing weak in Chiang Kai-shek's stand on important issues. He spoke up boldly, telling his interviewers that the aim of the National revolution was to crush imperialism and restore freedom to China. Then he went on to denounce one by one the concessions wrung from the feeble Manchus since the Opium Wars of the 1840s. He called for the renegotiation of unequal treaties, the abolition of consular jurisdiction, and the end of extraterritoriality and special foreign rights.

Chiang was, of course, merely enunciating the programs and principles worked out by Sun Yat-sen and Borodin, but his forthright statements came as body blows to his conservative Chinese supporters who had promoted the interview. The "Red" general was supposed to dispel fears, not further frighten the Western taipans.

But Chiang Kai-shek would make no compromises. He was still in his own mind an active revolutionary, dedicated to the ideals of the Tsungli, and confident that, with Soviet help, a new era of independence for China could be achieved. He was to change in this attitude; circumstances were to force him in a new direction with different allies. But that time had not yet come.

One unexpected result of his interview with the foreign press at Nanchang was the reaction of the liberals in the government at Canton. This group, headed by the Tsungli's son and widow, along with Madame Sun's brother T. V. Soong, with Borodin's influence looming strong in the background, was outraged—not by Chiang Kai-shek's admirable presentation of Sun Yat-sen's ideas, but by his presumption in speaking up in public at all. He seemed to have forgotten that he was a mere soldier and had no authority to express the views of his government. Chiang's bold initiative at the time of the Canton Coup was suddenly remembered in a new light and it was decided to take immediate steps to curb this dangerous militarist who was obviously growing too big for his boots.

A sharp reprimand was sent to the general, ordering him to clear all future political statements through channels. Then, as a precautionary measure and to be nearer to the scene of action, the government left Canton and moved to newly liberated Wuhan on the Yangtze River. In addition a telegram was sent to Lefthand Wang Ching-wei in Paris, advising him of an impending split within the party, and urging him to hurry home to resume his rightful place as leader of the Kuomintang.

Actually another split was developing within the party of which few were yet aware. The Northern Expedition had encouraged an entirely unanticipated upheaval among the people. Peasants and workers, having helped free themselves from warlords and local tyrants, were adopting revolutionary attitudes of their own. Once released from feudal bonds, they refused to settle back into traditional ways while they waited for the promised reforms that the great crusade would bring. They wanted rewards and alleviation here and now. In the countryside they clamored for implementation of Sun Yat-sen's slogans—land for the tillers and reduction of rents and interest—and often took matters into their own hands when local officials proved unsympathetic. And in the cities militant workers demonstrated for better pay and shorter hours.

In Wuhan, the newly arrived National government was overwhelmed by demands and petitions and forced to deal with strikes and lockouts. And at his military headquarters in Nanchang, Chiang Kai-shek was finding that the efficiency of his army was being seriously threatened by the general unrest. Most of the Whampoa cadets, which comprised his officer corps, came from landlord families and the news of village uprisings and confiscated property played havoc with their morale.

Chiang Kai-shek, with his march to Peking only half completed, tried valiantly to hold his victorious army together. He extolled duty and loyalty as cardinal virtues and talked down the popular disturbances as matters that would soon adjust themselves. He refused leaves of absence to officers concerned about kith and kin, and treated resignations of commissions as mutinies. But as the unrest spread, even he knew there was a limit. Unless effective measures were taken to restore order in cities and countryside, his army would melt away.

Unexpectedly Chiang Kai-shek received help from an unlikely source—from Joseph Stalin in Moscow. By the winter of 1926–27 Stalin had all but won out in his intrabureaucratic struggle with Leon Trotsky and, in the course of his rise to power, had seized control of the Comintern.

The Comintern, created in 1919, had been Trotsky's main operational instrument in carrying out his policy of "permanent" revolution. Trotsky believed that the Soviet Union could not continue to exist in isolation; sooner or later a combination of capitalist powers was sure to crush it. Hence he put his faith in a series of socialist revolutions occurring successively throughout the world—his "permanent" revolution—which would destroy the foundations of capitalism itself. To accomplish this end, Comintern agents had been busy in both hemispheres fomenting political unrest wherever conditions warranted.

With Stalin's accession to power there was a change in ideology. Stalin believed in "socialism first in one country"—meaning the Soviet Union—so emphasis was taken off worldwide insurrections except where they might indirectly benefit the socialist motherland.

China was such a case. A promising revolution was underway and the victory of the Soviet-supported Nationalist government would guarantee Russia's Manchurian border for years to come.

Stalin had watched with satisfaction the first phase of the Northern Expedition, noting with approval the fighting spirit of Chiang Kai-shek's armies as they swept north from Canton. Then had come the disappointing loss of momentum, the stalling of troops at the Yangtze River instead of a continued triumphant march on to Peking. Stalin, kept informed by the Comintern advisers in the field, was indignant when he learned the reason—the Chinese worker and peasant masses had intervened.

Stalin, a solid Marxist, knew that the intervention was premature. Workers and peasants rose in their might only during a socialist revolution, not when a limited bourgeois movement, such as the Kuomintang's, was being carried out. And a bourgeois takeover must *always* precede a socialist upheaval; Marxist doctrine was rigid on that point. In the historical circumstances, the Chinese workers and peasants were acting as obstructionists if not actual saboteurs.

Stalin sent out directives—to Borodin and his political corps, to Editor Chen Tu-hsiu, secretary-general of the Chinese Communist Party. The worker and peasant movements must be damped down; the people must be made to understand that their demands must wait; the confidence of the bourgeoisie and its army must be restored; the march on Peking must be resumed and Sun Yat-sen's revolution carried out.

It was easier ordered than done. Liberation fervor had gained a momentum that was not to be easily checked. And considerations of justice were all too evidently on the people's side. In Wuhan, for instance, the Labor Federation was asking for an end to the twelve-hour work day, seven days a week, with unpaid "apprentices" (mostly women and children) depressing wages to below subsistence standards. Disciplined as the Communist cadres were, it went against the grain to carry out the new Comintern orders. They had taken pride in arousing militancy among the inert masses, and now they were being asked to reverse themselves, to advocate humility and surrender to the bosses.

And in the countryside it was worse. Peasants, incited to stand up for their rights, were not to be easily denied. Attempts by the political cadres to order an about-face were simply ignored.

In Shanghai, Mao Tse-tung was instructed to close down his Peasant Institute and convert his students into meek apostles of traditional ways. It was like ordering an arsonist to put out his own fires, as Editor Chen was to learn in due course.

In January 1927 Chiang Kai-shek went to Wuhan to discuss the general situation. He found the atmosphere in the tri-cities far from reassuring. Workers paraded in the streets, their right to demonstrate protected by Nationalist troops, lending legitimacy to scenes of social disorder always repellent to Chiang. He inspected the foreign concession, now cleared of Westerners since worker battalions had "won it back" for the nation during the siege of the city. British gunboats were drawn up on the river, ready to fire when their government decided what to do about confiscated goods and rights, thus adding another dimension to the already dangerous situation.

At a meeting of the Central Executive Committee, Chiang blamed the Communists for the disturbed state of affairs and proposed expelling them from the Kuomintang Party. The proposal was given short shrift by the dominant liberal group in the government. Chiang was sternly reminded of the Tsungli's Three Great Policies—alliance with the Soviet Union, cooperation with the Chinese Communists, and assistance to the workers and peasants. There were to be no departures from those guidelines. And besides the Communists, on orders from Stalin himself, were doing all in their power to damp down popular movements.

Chiang Kai-shek left Wuhan tight-lipped, only partially convinced by the arguments. And his doubts were reinforced when he returned to his headquarters at Nanchang. Distinguished visitors from Shanghai—"foreign and Chinese, diplomats and bankers," who no longer feared the "Red" general but saw Chiang now as the conservatives' best hope—brought disturbing news. The workers of that city, following the pattern set at Wuhan, were preparing to take over Shanghai and present it as a gift to the revolutionary armies.

Chiang Kai-shek wanted no more such gifts leading to license and disorder. But he was in a quandary as to how to cope with the impending insurrection. If he moved in troops to impose martial law, he was likely to incite mutiny among his own soldiers who would sympathize with the patriotic populations and refuse to suppress them.

Chiang suspected, despite the assurances he had received in Wuhan, that Communists were behind the planned Shanghai uprising. And in this he was right. Certain firebrands—including Chou En-lai—were ignoring the instructions of Stalin, Borodin, and Editor Chen and were staging the revolt pretty much on their own, convinced that the Marxist cause could best be served by proletarian upheavals.

Boldly now, Chiang Kai-shek took the step he had only suggested at Wuhan. He declared Communists "bad comrades," to be expelled from cooperation with the Kuomintang unless they learned to behave themselves better.

Urgent telegrams were dispatched from Communist headquarters in Wuhan ordering an immediate end to all subversive activity in Shanghai. But it was already too late. Preparations were far advanced and a test of strength was about to begin. A general strike was called and marchers filled the streets demanding the delivery of the city to "the heroic armies of the Northern Expedition."

Chiang Kai-shek was still in no hurry to act. He believed that the situation was about to be solved for him. The demonstrations must surely bring out the garrison of the local warlord to restore order to the city. When the disturbances were quelled, he meant to march in with his own troops, driving out the tuchun's forces and establishing Nationalist control over the population.

But events proceeded otherwise. Chiang's strategy backfired when the Shanghai workers raided the arsenals, seized weapons, and fought the local garrison to a standstill, finally driving it out of town. Then triumphantly in possession of the city—or at least the Chinese districts of it—the insurgents invited Chiang Kai-shek to enter, condescendingly offering to yield up the keys.

Chiang was faced by a dilemma, unquestionably the crucial decision of his career. He couldn't accept Shanghai on the insurgents' terms; neither could he trust his own troops to seize it from them, not while his soldiers were applauding the victorious workers as the heroes of the hour. Yet to save face he had to crush the uprising; he had to end Communist insolence once and forever.

But how was he to do it? Even if he could find the men to obey his orders without question—and he had a good idea of where they could be recruited—an open attack on the workers of Shanghai meant an end to the Soviet alliance. And it was Soviet arms and money and expert personnel that had propelled the revolution to its present success. Where could he turn for resources once Russian supplies were cut off?

There was an obvious answer, but Chiang must have pondered long in considering it. His Shanghai backers—the compradors, bankers, and international traders—had been holding out the lure of all the financial aid he might need in the future. But behind them loomed the foreigners, the all powerful taipans, the very imperialists Sun Yat-sen had sworn to expel from China. To enter into league with the Chinese financial community meant also to align himself with the Westerners on whom they depended, which meant in turn betraying the essential purpose of the revolution. The piper-payer calls the tune, and as long as the Westerners were paying, China would be for the Chinese only so far as it served foreign commercial interests.

In the end it was probably pride rather than questions of policies and principles that decided the matter. Chiang Kai-shek had traveled a long way from the diffident youth subservient to family and clan. He had learned to assert himself. He recognized his powers of leadership and, like most leaders, chose to act at a time of crisis rather than squander his prestige in uncertainty.

At any rate, on March 26, 1927 he secretly boarded a gunboat for Shanghai, beginning a journey from which there was to be no turning back.

In Wuhan, there was mixed concern and pride in Communist ranks at the developments in Shanghai. The concern centered mostly around Chiang Kai-shek. He hadn't been heard from since the workers' takeover and his silence was ominous. Chiang was little regarded as a political figure but his command of the armies made him dangerous. Borodin hurried to Shanghai to find out what was happening. Editor Chen remained in Wuhan on tenterhooks, urging ever greater disciplining of workers and suppression of agrarian movements.

Into this atmosphere of frayed nerves and short tempers wandered Mao Tse-tung in the early spring of 1927 glowing with the enthusiasm of a visionary. As ordered, he had been at work in the countryside since closing down his Peasant Institute, but hardly in the way Editor Chen had imagined. Instead of suppressing agrarian movements, he had been carried away by them. Rather than prohibiting peasant violence, he was a convert to what could be accomplished by a show of force. In answer to the cautious question "Are the rural populations going too far?" he had an apocalyptic answer: "In a very short time... several hundred million peasants will rise like a mighty storm, like a hurricane, a force so swift and violent that no power... will be able to hold it back."

Mao had incorporated these and other thoughts into an essay called "Report on the Investigation of the Peasant Movement in Hunan." For thirty-two days he had traveled from county to county, calling together "fact-finding conferences in villages and... towns" and watching aroused peasants at work. He had seen "local tyrants, evil gentry and lawless landlords... deprived of all right to speak," sweeping away "every bit of dignity" and Confucian authority they had "enjoyed for thousands of years." Humiliating landlords and enforcing crude justice had exerted a powerful appeal on the countryside: "[F]rom last October to January of this year... membership of the [peasant] associations jumped to two million and the masses directly under their leadership increased to ten million." Mao pointed out that "in a few months the peasants have accomplished what Dr. Sun Yat-sen wanted, but failed, to accomplish in... forty years"; they had solved the knotty problem of the people's livelihood—in rural districts at least—by the simple method of confiscation.

Of course, what was happening was all very illegal and "it is reported... that Chiang Kai-shek" and his friends "do not altogether approve of the activities of the Hunan peasants." But what of it? Rural insurrection was a fact and the Communist Party was faced with three alternatives: "To march at the [peasants'] head and lead them; to trail behind them, gesticulating and criticizing; or to stand in their way and oppose them."

Mao Tse-tung left no doubt as to where he stood on the issue. Carried away by his vision of the future, he went so far as to suggest that the peasants were the "vanguards of the revolution." This, of course, was sheer heresy; every Marxist knew that the proletariat, the industrial working class, was *always* in the vanguard. But the excited polemicist, no longer cared about orthodoxy. He had seen a revolution actually at work and believed that, with correct guidance, the rural populations could almost singlehandedly take over the sovereignty of the nation.

Mao's famous "Report on an Investigation of the Peasant Movement in Hunan," today solemnly studied in the People's Republic of China as a landmark document, was greeted with shock in Wuhan in March 1927. Apart from the glaring Marxist lapses, the whole tenor of the argument was not one that Editor Chen and his advisers wanted to hear. They found themselves uncomfortably in Mao's third category—standing in the peasants' way and opposing them—but they could see no alternative as long as Moscow ordered the conciliation of the Kuomintang conservatives at any cost. They reacted by criticizing Mao's report with contempt and scorn. The Central Committee rejected the conclusions, and publication of the text in *The Guide*, the party's weekly journal, was not permitted.

But Mao, with characteristic persistence, kept the issue alive. He copied out his report by hand for circulation and never lost an opportunity to speak up on the necessity for supporting the peasants, 80 percent of China's population.

Finally the leadership was goaded into taking notice. A land-survey committee was formed to look into the justice of peasant claims, and a ruling was eventually handed down that, in certain selected cases, expropriation might be permitted, provided that a landlord's holdings exceeded 500 mous (approximately 80 acres) and no Kuomintang officers were members of the family. Mao Tse-tung could hardly consider that he had won a victory. All rich landlords had relatives in the army, not to mention that holdings of that size were as scarce as grand pianos south of the Yangstze.

But the whole matter was rapidly becoming academic. It was now the end of March and, in Shanghai, Chiang Kai-shek was taking action that was irreversibly to transform the revolution. Soon enough the question was to be, not whom the Communists were to support, but who was to support them to save them from extinction.

10

Massacre at Shanghai

CHIANG KAI-SHEK, TRAVELING BY GUNBOAT FROM NANchang, arrived in Shanghai March 27, 1927. He was greeted on the Bund by a reception committee of admirers and swiftly conveyed by automobile through the International Settlement.

Looking out at the all-pervading evidence of foreign power—the flags of fourteen nations, the Victorian-Gothic architecture, the motor cars and Western-clad men and women conveyed by rickshaw, the foreign soldiers parading on the cobblestones or standing at sentry duty outside public buildings—Chiang may have reflected that this was not the way he had visualized his return to Shanghai. He had meant an entry of a different sort. With all of China under his military control and a Nationalist government firmly established at Nanking, he had meant to call the foreigners strictly to account for their eighty years of arrogant domination. Their imperial attitudes would be humbled, their rights and privileges taken from them, and they would be made to understand that their future presence in China would be tolerated only on good behavior.

That prospect was gone now, or at least postponed until some uncertain time in the future. Through unforeseen circumstances, Chiang currently needed the foreigners as much as they needed him. The old ways would continue, slowly eroding the China of the past without adding any new dynamic for constructive change.

Yet the general's arrival, hurriedly arranged as it had been, was not without drama. The fate of Shanghai rested squarely on his shoulders, though instead of imperialists he had come to punish his own countrymen. Word was out that the exterminator was in town to dispose of the Red rats that had closed down factories or in some cases had taken them over as workers' enterprises. No one knew how Chiang Kai-shek intended to do the job, but every facility was put at his disposal, including the use of an exclusive hotel in the French Concession never before opened to Orientals.

Conferences began. On the one side there was Chiang Kai-shek, on the other the wealth of Shanghai represented by both Chinese and Western financiers. The proposition was simple: in order to smash Communists and labor unions and restore the tranquility of the open shop and unchecked exploitation, money was needed in vast quantities. Money here and now, cash on the table.

The negotiators had come prepared. Fifteen million Chinese dollars were handed over with a further thirty million promised if results were satisfactory. The money was counted, the merchants were dismissed, and less respectable members of the community were called in for the practical business to be done.

Prominent among the newcomers were Doughty Dhu and Pock-marked Huang, gangster chieftains and old acquaintances from Chiang Kai-shek's former days in Shanghai. But Communist suppression was not left entirely to the more famous clans of the underworld. Any ambitious hoodlum who could muster a score of followers guaranteed to maim and kill without question as long as they were paid, was welcomed into the ranks. In this way, scraping the gutters of the city, a force of several thousand thugs were recruited. Chiang Kai-shek had found an alternative to his National army troops whose scruples prevented them from turning on populations they had marched to liberate. He had once led contingents of dare-to-dies; he was now ready to settle for killers-for-cash.

While preparations for the attack on the Chinese city were still progressing, Chairman Wang Ching-wei—traveling in the same leisurely style with which Sun Yat-sen had once responded to urgent messages to hurry home—arrived back in China. Chiang Kai-shek was at dockside in Shanghai when his ship pulled in on April 1. The men hadn't seen each other since Chiang's Canton Coup the previous spring and it is probable that their somewhat cool relationship hadn't changed. But it was important now for Chiang to win over the Tsungli's left-hand disciple, still the nominal leader of the Kuomintang, and he was eloquent in his arguments that the time had come to break with the Communists. As the most recent example of Red excesses, he could cite the Nanking "incident" that had taken place barely two weeks before. During the capture of the city, the foreign concession had been attacked, Westerners killed, and property damaged—outrages Chiang had no hesitation in attributing to undisciplined Communist troops. That was the final straw, as Chiang saw it. Unless the Kuomintang was purged by the expulsion of the Communists, the revolution was doomed.

Wang listened politely but wouldn't commit himself. He pointed out that he was on his way to Wuhan and must hear what the government had to say before coming to a decision. Chiang realized that this was a stall. He realized it more fully a few days later when Wang met with the Communist Secretary General, Editor Chen, who had hurried downriver to greet the returning chairman. Wang and Chen issued a joint statement proclaiming that the unity between the Kuomintang and Communist parties was as strong as ever and anything to the contrary was "malicious rumor."

The joint statement had an unfortunate effect on the workers' commune in control at Shanghai. As time had passed, as the invitation for Chiang Kai-skek to enter the city at the head of his troops had gone unregarded, suspicions had grown that a coup of some kind was in the making and defensive measures had been prepared. But with the joint statement, the insurrectionary leaders relaxed. For how long could Chiang be preparing hostile action when the head of his government declared that all was harmony within the revolution?

As for Chiang, the joint statement meant that the die was irrevocably cast. He had no alternative now but to strike out on his own, assuming leadership of the forces of reaction in a way he had never intended but that had been forced upon him by circumstances. And in the light of what he proposed to do, it meant an explosive rupture with the Wuhan government, with all the comrades who had served Sun Yat-sen long and faithfully and were now sure to regard him as a traitor to the Tsungli's ideals.

The attack began at four o'clock on the morning of April 12. Trucks fanning out from the foreign concessions rumbled into the Old Chinese City and the working class districts to the north and west. Each truck carried a contingent of seasoned Shanghai gangsters—later called "merchant volunteers" by the friendly press—concealing under their workmen's clothing knives, grenades, and handguns. Their primary objective was to seize the insurrectionists' widely scattered headquarters, but a second objective—the killing of anyone caught in the streets—soon became paramount.

The first victims were the pickets put out by the Labor Federation. These were quietly strangled to prevent their spreading the alarm; then the strongarmed gangs moved on to their main targets. Many of the revolutionary strongholds were still open as leaders worked through the night considering strategy if Chiang Kai-shek failed to move in troops to accept the city. They were so little aware of the true situation that they innocently welcomed into their midsts the underworld assassins posing as worker delegates from across town. They discovered their mistake only when guns were drawn and shooting began. Where access wasn't as easy and resistance was met, agile hoods climbed buildings and threw grenades through the windows, setting blocks of flimsy structures on fire.

By daylight the mobsters were able to report back to Chiang, masterminding operations from the Foreign Ministry Bureau, that all insurrectionary command posts as well as arsenals were in their hands. But Chiang, learning that barricades were being set up by determined workers, ordered the attacks to continue.

That was the signal for an orgy of slaughter. The gangsters were hardened to bloodletting as part of their profession, but always on the sly, always in danger of discovery and its penalties. Now they luxuriated in the sanction of authorized murder. They competed with each other in brutalities. When stubborn opposition was met, when desperate workers fired from behind improvised stockades or out of windows, fiendish ingenuity was shown in punishing the insolence. Gasoline was floated down the gutters and ignited, or women and children were dragged into the line of fire and executed one at a time until the defenders threw down their weapons and surrendered.

Even then the carnage continued. Prisoners remained prisoners only until they could be transformed into corpses—by throat slitting and garroting when ammunition ran out. The dead and wounded were piled into trucks and buried together. At the South Railway Station in the Old City a particularly barbarous method of dispatch was invented. Captives, tied by ropes, were fed alive into the fireboxes of locomotives.

It was a night and morning of horrors. Some seven hundred men, women, and children were said to have perished in the initial phase of the butchery. Later there would be more. And there were the usual narrow escapes. Editor Chen, attending a literary conference, was awakened from sleep by gunfire and barely smuggled out of his host's house before it burned. Chou En-lai was actually captured, but with his historic immunity somehow fought his way to freedom.

That afternoon, April 12, the surviving leaders of the insurrection, still not seeming to understand what was happening, hoping that it was all a mistake and that Chiang Kai-shek would undergo a change of heart if he understood the true loyalty of the Shanghai workers, organized a mass demonstration calling for justice and punishment of the criminals who had attacked them. By now Chiang had withdrawn his gangster hirelings from action. They had done their work of destroying effective opposition and the issue had turned to civil disobedience. Chiang was able to declare martial law, prohibiting further demonstrations.

Nationalist troops, screened for their dedication to their commander-in-chief, were brought on the scene. They blocked the streets and ordered the marchers to return home. But the unarmed workers refused to obey. In a magnificent if futile display of courage, they continued to march, chanting slogans and flourishing placards. The troops fired. The marchers wavered, broke, and fled, leaving behind scores of dead and wounded.

By the morning of April 13 Chiang Kai-shek was able to report the siuation in hand, though firing squads continued to mop up on insurgents, real or suspected. It was three weeks before what came to be known as the Shanghai Massacre was officially terminated and the city was safe for free enterprise again.

Repercussions in Wuhan were prompt and indignant. Chiang Kai-shek was denounced as a traitor and counterrevolutionary. At a meeting of the Central Executive Committee he was read out of the party, dismissed and expelled from all his posts in the Kuomintang. For good measure he was declared an outlaw; his arrest was ordered and a price put on his head, dead or alive.

Chiang, foreseeing this reaction, had already taken steps to counter it. He announced a new National Government of China which he installed in office at Nanking. It was an astute move. Nanking had always been Sun Yat-sen's choice for a capital and, moreover, the politicians around whom Chiang Kai-shek built his regime were all seasoned veterans of the Kuomintang. They constituted a majority of the original Central Executive Committee—twenty as against Wuhan's sixteen—and included the Tsungli's right-hand-man Hu Han-min, recalled from exile for the prestige of his name. The government was impressive enough to win immediate recognition from the Great Powers, by now thoroughly sold on Chiang as a champion of laissez faire as well as law and order. The Wuhan government might rage and scoff, but there was no denying that the general had worked himself into a strong position.

He had also, of course, worked China into a ludicrous position as far as ruling authority went. There were now in the nation three jurisdictions—the National Government at Nanking, the

National Government at Wuhan, and the warlord operated Republic of China at Peking—each claiming legitimacy in one way or another from Sun Yat-sen, and each insisting that it, and it alone, wielded sovereign power in the land. It was a situation that clearly couldn't last, but which of the claimants was to win out over the others?

In Wuhan, there was talk of settling matters at once by sending a punitive expedition against Chiang Kai-shek and his bogus Nanking government. But it never went beyond talk. Despite the deep division within the revolutionary armies, Chiang was still effectively commander-in-chief and, with the backing of the Shanghai foreigners, held too strong a hand. And as time passed, anger against the traitorous general subsided, absorbed by problems closer to home.

For anarchy still reigned in the tri-cities of Wuhan and in the surrounding countryside. Strikes, demonstrations, and rural upheavals were still daily events. Doggedly loyal to the writ of Sun Yat-sen who had spelled out in his Three Great Policies "assistance to the workers and peasants," and also persuaded to democratic tolerance by the Communists who sat on every important committee, the Wuhan regime allowed the disturbances to continue. But it was a trying time for Wang Ching-wei and his colleagues in the leadership. All were classically schooled and believed in the Confucian verities (with the possible exception of Sun Yat-sen's widow, the American educated Chingling Soong) and scenes of disorder were as painful to them as they ever had been to Chiang Kai-shek.

There must have been occasions when they envied the direct, if ruthless, measures the renegade general had taken. That he was still taking for that matter. The White Terror, as it was called, had spread south and west from Shanghai, encouraging landlords' min-tuans to murder at will in the countryside and provincial troops to quell unrest in the cities with bullets and bayonets. The Wuhan officials had observed these developments with a mixture of repugnance and fascination. The means were all wrong, of course—cruel and unconscionable. But perhaps the end justified them to some extent. Discipline and production had been restored in Chiang Kai-shek's territories, while in Wuhan industrial and agricultural strife and paralysis continued unabated.

Chiang seemed to have understood with canny accuracy the doubts that assailed the Wuhan government, for in May he came forth with a generous offer. If Wang Ching-wei and his officials cared to join the Nanking regime, they would be received with open arms. All would be seated on the Central Executive Committee, Wang would be made Premier, and the others appointed to posts of influence and opportunity.

The invitation so alarmed Borodin, Editor Chen, and the Communist cadres that Wang Ching-wei felt obliged to issue a statement spurning the attempt to suborn his government. But the yearning lingered on among the liberals. If only an honorable way could be found out of the mess, some dignified excuse to deliver men of goodwill from a chaotic situation.

Rescue came sooner than could have been anticipated. For Joseph Stalin in Moscow, astonished at the developments in China, decided to weigh in with a heavier hand. And as usual he made a botch of it.

Stalin had been stunned by Chiang Kai-shek's turnabout at Shanghai. He had never had a high opinion of the Kuomintang general. He boasted to cronies that when the time came, when Chiang had served his purpose, he would squeeze him out like a lemon and throw the rind away. The surprise at finding that Chiang had a will of his own and could stage such a counterrevolutionary coup as he had at Shanghai—in a sense, squeezing out Stalin and throwing him away like a useless rind—was both shocking and humiliating. But for a while, Stalin, caught in a rut, could only go on ordering his subordinates in Wuhan to make even greater efforts to subdue the workers so as not to risk breaching the united front with the liberal government of Wang Ching-wei.

Then a transformation took place in Stalin's thinking. And in a curious way it may have been Mao Tse-tung who influenced him. For Mao's "Report on an Investigation of the Peasant Movement in Hunan," neglected in Wuhan, was read and admired in Moscow. At a plenum of the Comintern, significant inferences were drawn from it. A report of proceedings stated that the Chinese agrarian problem—the struggle of peasants to rid themselves of feudal and military overlords—should receive a high priority in future. And apparently Stalin concurred in the analysis.

At any rate, in June 1927, he sent a confidential telegram to Borodin informing him that the time had come to "convert" the Chinese revolution. Little more could be expected from the "left" bourgeoisie—by which Stalin meant the Wuhan government—while the right wing had already started down the road of reaction under Chiang Kai-shek. Therefore there was no alternative but to break with the Kuomintang entirely and start developing the power of the workers and peasants under the leadership of the Communist Party.

The break was not to be immediate but was to proceed through a series of disguised stages. As a first step, pressure was to be put on the Wuhan government to authorize large-scale confiscation of land. To ensure success in this measure, a reorganization of the Central Executive Committee was to be demanded, with the Communists winning a voting majority. In case Wang Ching-wei and his fellow bureaucrats proved stubborn about this maneuvering, they were to be intimidated by a threat of force. To back up the threat, a contingent of 20,000 Wuhan workers along with 50,000 peasant auxiliaries were to be organized into shock troops in support of Communist policies.

Borodin must have been appalled when he read the telegram. He was a practical man, well weathered to the political realities in China by this time, and Stalin's simplistic analysis and dogmatic planning must have seemed to him fantasies of a pipedream. True, the masses were in revolt, but their insurgency was capricious, undisciplined, intent only on achieving immediate goals. And the infant Communist Party was certainly in no position to provide the control and leadership Stalin demanded. It was still undisciplined itself, as well as inexperienced and without prestige among the people. That it continued to exist and function at all was largely due to the indulgence of the Wuhan government. The fiasco at Shanghai had shown Communist weakness when acting on its own, cut off from the support of Kuomintang troops. But how to convince Stalin of all this? Or how to attempt to carry out the Kremlin's orders without inviting disaster?

Borodin wisely refrained from showing the telegram to Editor Chen, but he discussed it at length with the Comintern advisory group. Only one member, an Indian delegate called Manabendra Nath Roy, was confident on how to act. Roy was new to China, a recent appointee of Stalin in contrast to the others who were mostly holdovers from Trotsky's regime, and it may have been eagerness to score points with the Big Boss that influenced his judgment. At any rate he took the position that Stalin's message amounted to an ultimatum and should be treated as such, let the Wuhan government react how it might. He had the telegram translated into Chinese and took it to Chairman Wang Ching-wei.

Wang read the contents but he didn't collapse, if that is what Roy had expected him to do. For once in his enigmatic career he acted with precision and dispatch. He called a meeting of the Political Council, read the telegram and offered four proposals: that diplomatic relations with the Soviet Union be terminated because of unprecedented meddling in the nation's internal affairs; that the Comintern advisory group be dismissed and sent back to Russia; that Chinese Communists be expelled from the Kuomintang; and that the Communist Party be outlawed and its members prosecutd as enemies of the state.

The council adopted all the proposals with enthusiasm. An impeccable way out from the confusions and disorders of democracy had finally been found.

At the end of July the Comintern advisers left for home* but not before, in Chinese style, they had been fêted at a great banquet. Mme. Sun Yat-sen went to Russia with them, finding

---

*They didn't fare well when they got there. Of the men mentioned in these pages, Leo P. Karakhan, who issued the manifesto repudiating the Czarist treaties in 1919, died in Stalin's purge of 1938, as did Galen (Marshal Vassili K. Bluecher), chief military adviser at Whampoa. Adolfe A. Joffe, who negotiated the KMT-CCP coalition with Sun Yat-sen, committed suicide in 1927, apparently in despair at Trotsky's proscription and exile. Borodin edited an English-language newspaper in Moscow until the 1950s when he was sent to Siberia and death. Maring (Hendricus Sneevliet), original adviser to the CCP, was killed fighting for the Dutch underground against the Nazis in 1942. M. N. Roy, dismissed from the Comintern in 1929, wound up leading a Fascist organization in India during World War II.

no reason to stay on in China, now that her husband's legacy had been betrayed by blundering, opportunism, and treachery. She could have had few illusions about the Soviet Union she was to visit, but her faith in the eventual triumph of the revolution remained unshaken. She was to live to see its victory, though in an unexpected form, and to serve with honor as vice chairman of the People's Republic of China.

The outlawing of the Communist Party was the signal for reaction all along the middle Yangtze. Landlords' min-tuans were soon at work in the countryside restoring Confucian order with clubs and muskets, while in the cities, provincial troops, relieving friendly Kuomintang forces as guardians of the law, broke up demonstrations and drove the workers back to their machines. The White Terror, beginning in Wuhan three months later than Shanghai, made up for lost time by increased savagery. Few villages were without a picket of peasant heads on poles, and the firing squads of Wuhan and Changsha accounted for more "Reds" than had ever heard of the Communist Party. Some 330,000 men, women, and children are estimated to have died or disappeared during the bloodletting of 1927–28.

The gentlemen of the Wuhan government, liberals all, tolerated the suppressions with remarkable complacency, though their troubles were not yet over. Late in July the Kuomintang army of the west fragmented. Elements of the left—officers and enlisted men who were Communists or had become Communist sympathizers—were coming out in open revolt. The rebels had no program or defined objective. They were simply reacting with blind fury to the betrayal of the revolution. But in their ranks were some of the best fighting men of the Northern Expedition and their defection caused panic.

The mutineers decided to strike into Chiang Kai-shek's territory. They chose as their first target the city of Nanchang, until recently Chiang's military headquarters. Another reason for the choice was that Chiang had entrusted Nanchang's defense to an ex-opium smoking, concubine-collecting warlord called Chu Teh, unaware that Chu had been for years a secret Communist. Chu Teh was primed and ready to sabotage the defense when the attack on the city began.

Massacre at Shanghai

August 1, 1927—the day Nanchang was taken—is currently celebrated in the People's Republic of China as the founding date of the Red Army. It hardly seemed so at the time. The rebels were in Kuomintang uniforms, carrying Kuomintang banners and shouting Kuomintang slogans of liberation. They were hard put to it to explain to the people what their victory meant, how anything was different, or what the future held in the way of a new destiny. While these points were being debated, Chiang Kai-shek rushed relief troops to the scene and the conquerors of Nanchang, after a three-day tenure, were forced to beat a retreat. But a vital lesson had been learned: without political objectives, even the best armies are wasted. Or as the great V. I. Lenin had put it, "Without revolutionary theory, there can be no revolutionary movement."

Meanwhile in Wuhan the remnants of the Communist leadership were desperately arguing the same topic—a program for the future. The White Terror was gaining impetus and the party was in disarray—"in a chaotic state" Mao Tse-tung was to call it. Comrades were making themselves scarce. The luckier ones had left for Russia with the Comintern advisory group, while others had slipped downriver for refuge in the foreign settlements.

But Mao Tse-tung, always stubborn in a crisis, refused to run. He remained in Wuhan and was one of the ten last-ditch Central Committee members to convene at an emergency meeting on August 7. The first order of business was to get rid of Editor Chen. The Secretary General was roundly denounced as a right opportunist, a lickspittle of the bourgeoisie, and a traitor to the working class. It was a harsh judgment. The scholarly editor, trying to lead an insurgent movement and at the same time suppress it on Stalin's orders, had been caught in an impossible situation and could hardly be blamed for the confusion and rout that resulted. But since etiquette ruled out criticism of Moscow, a local scapegoat had to be found. And it was time that Chen Tu-hsiu moved on anyway. He was of another generation and the turbulent future belonged to men of sterner stuff.

A new Secretary General was elected, whose name needn't concern us since he was soon to be superseded by more dominant personalities. A strategy council followed during which objectives were discussed and assignments handed out. Then the meeting adjourned sine die as members prepared to escape Wuhan, each by his own resources.

Mao Tse-tung returned to his native province of Hunan charged with the "organization of a peasant-worker revolutionary army" though with only hazy instructions as to what to do with it after it was formed. He set about recruiting what he somewhat grandly called the First Peasant and Workers Army in the hills east of Changsha. He was well acquainted with the area through his political work and found peasants eager to enlist. All through August, with a towel wrapped around his head against the sun, he drilled his men in what he remembered from his days as a buck private in the revolutionary army of 1911–12. Weapons were a difficulty; all that could be mustered were pikes and staves. But Mao ran into luck when deserters from Kuomintang units joined him with modern rifles and ammunition.

As training progressed, Mao was troubled by the political imbalance of his forces—all peasants and no workers. He solved the problem by turning drill chores over to his brother Tse-tan while he hiked through the mountains to the coal mines of Kiangsi Province. The miners, suffering from inhuman conditions enforced by the White Terror, were ready for revolt and Mao set up a second training unit to accommodate them. From then on he commuted between his clandestine camps, making the trip through the mountains with a regularity that nearly cost him his life. For on one occasion, landlord min-tuans, getting wind that something was up, were lying in wait for him.

The details of Mao's capture and escape are exciting but they come down to us without suspense, almost with a feeling of déjà vu. In the light of history the outcome is so predictable. Though, of course, it didn't appear that way at the time. Ten years later, Mao still seems to be sweating as he remembers the experience:

> I was ordered to be taken to the *mintuan* headquarters where I was to be killed.... I therefore decided to attempt to escape, but had no opportunity to do so until I was within about two hundred yards of [our

destination]. At that point I broke loose and ran into the fields.

I reached a high place, above a pond, with some tall grass surrounding it, and there I hid until sunset. The soldiers pursued me, and forced some peasants to help them search. Many times they came very near, once or twice so close that I could almost have touched them, but somehow I escaped discovery, although half a dozen times I gave up hope, feeling certain I would be recaptured. At last, when it was dark, they abandoned the search. At once I set off across the mountains, traveling all night. I had no shoes [removed to prevent escape] and my feet were badly bruised.

The capricious nature of survival, the freakish illogicality that determined life or death, never ceased to puzzle Mao. In succeeding years, five members of his immediate family and scores of his closest friends were to die by execution or in battle. Yet he himself emerged from crisis after crisis unscathed. Once a bodyguard was felled by a bullet while leaning forward to light Mao's cigarette; and again he escaped unhurt though covered with the blood and entrails of comrades when a mortar shell exploded a few yards away. In old age, he developed a philosophy on the matter. He believed that for some reason death just hadn't wanted him and had always passed him by in preference for others.

By September the Communist leadership, now in hiding in Shanghai, had formed an operational plan—to attack cities with all available forces. Dutiful to the directive, Mao Tse-tung combined his contingents of peasants and workers and, on September 8, set out to assault Changsha.

It was a good time of year to gain support in the countryside. Rice crops were being gathered in, which meant that landlord and money-lender rapacity was at its height and so was peasant resentment. Mao's troops, as they advanced into the fertile valleys, were augmented by thousands of rustic volunteers in what came to be known as the Autumn Harvest Uprising.

The fighting caliber of Mao's little army and its hordes of auxiliaries was soon to be tested with depressing results. At the first clash with well-armed provincial troops, panic set in. "Discipline was poor, political training was at a low level, and many wavering elements were among the men and officers," Mao later explained, adding unnecessarily, "There were many desertions." So many, in fact, that he rapidly changed his mind about the objective of his campaign. Never mind Changsha; if he could preserve at least the core of his fighting force, it would be triumph enough for the first outing.

But even getting away from the enemy was no easy matter. The provincial troops pressed hard and more appeared to block the road south, the way to the mountains and safety. As Mao later remembered it, his disorganized army had to fight its way with heavy casualties through hordes of obstructing forces. Finally the hill country was reached and Mao herded his men up the slopes. Only about a thousand had survived to find sanctuary in a remote glen in the shadow of Chingkangshan, or Well-Ridge-Mountain.

The desolate spot was a last refuge, a valley of despair for defeated and exhausted men. But it turned out also to be a Valley Forge. For during that winter Mao Tse-tung started developing a new type of revolutionary army that, bit by bit, was to crack and shatter the Kuomintang, now the triumphant power in the land.

There were still, of course, two Kuomintangs with two capitals, one at Wuhan and one at Nanking, though with the disposal of the Communist issue, all real differences between them had disappeared. Nevertheless an elaborate game continued to be played out, each side standing on pride and prerogatives. Wuhan contended it was the sole legitimate government, with Nanking a secessionist group; therefore, unification talks, if any, must take place in Wuhan. Nanking said nonsense. Sun Yat-sen had always meant that city to be the capital of China, so it was the only possible location for a conference.

Chiang Kai-shek, suspecting that it was he who really stuck in the craw of the Wuhan government—after all, he had been proscribed as a traitor and there was still a price on his head—resigned to clear the way for a rapprochement. He yielded up his post as commander-in-chief of the armies and retired to his native Fenghua.

It was a handsome gesture and Left-hand Wang Ching-wei could do no less in noblesse oblige. He relinquished his chairmanship of the Wuhan government and sailed off to Europe again for rest and recuperation. After that the two sides got down to bargaining in earnest at a neutral city. They resolved their differences and made their deals and consolidated a congenial government at Nanking.

Chiang Kai-shek had withdrawn to Fenghua in a style different from his previous retirements. This time 400 bodyguards went with him. They were lodged in Chikow, Chiang's native village, while the general himself was carried 3,000 feet up a mountain to a Buddhist monastery prepared as a retreat.

There, on a sunny day in autumn, members of the foreign press corps were invited to share the matchless view of rocky crags, streams, waterfalls, and bamboo groves. Chiang greeted his guests in the long robe of a scholar and dispensed hospitality with seasonal fruits and nuts. He didn't look like a man who had resigned from the burdens of war and government at forty. Smiling, poised, relaxed, he gave the impression of being on top of things, if not actually manipulating them, confident that he would soon be called back to power.

And in the meantime what was he going to do? Well, he was thinking of a trip abroad to observe the customs of great nations among whom China must take her rightful place. He was particularly interested in the United States; he had heard so much about the industrial and economic development of that country and wanted to see it for himself. But the world was wide; his destination might be anywhere except Russia. Russia had betrayed China and was no longer a friend.

In fact, he did go abroad, but only to Japan. He went there not for education or recreation, but in pursuit of the wife he had picked to share his well-omened future.

11

Thunder on the Plains, Fire in the Mountains

IN THE CONFUCIAN CULTURE, MEN MARRIED FOR MANY REAsons—for wealth, for health, for property, for concupiscence, to satisfy elders or to reconcile clan feuds, sometimes even for love. But few sought a bride who was a personality in her own right and whose prestige in many ways outshone their own.

The Soong sisters of Shanghai were exceptions. History is replete with famous sets of sisters, from the Pleiades of Greek mythology through the Brontës of England and the Cushings of Boston, but the Soong girls hold a special niche. From their first appearance on the scene, their beauty, brightness, and American-educated ways exerted powerful appeals on progressive and enterprising Chinese men. The eldest, Ailing (Friendly Life), desired by Sun Yat-sen, had married H. H. Kung of the powerful financial family. The second daughter, Chingling (Glorious Life), had made the greatest coup of all by capturing the Tsungli on the rebound. And there was still a third daughter, Meiling (Beautiful Life). Meiling's name was currently connected with that of the mayor of Shanghai, but there was still time for a bold and resolute suitor to snatch her away in Lochinvar style.

Romantically disillusioning as it may be, Meiling had not been Chiang Kai-shek's first choice. We have Chingling's word for it that, after the Tsungli's death, Chiang tendered his widow a proposal through a marriage broker, an offer indignantly turned down. But by the fall of 1927, Chiang was firm in what he wanted. Meiling was at a Japanese health spa with her mother, so to Japan the general went.

He arrived in Tokyo with some éclat. Newspapers made much of the famous commander who had led his troops to victory over both warlords and Communists. Chiang responded with punctilious courtesy. Among other things, he sent his respects to the divisional and regimental commanders under whom he had served as a private in the Japanese artillery. This led to a certain amount of embarrassment since neither officer had any recollection of Chiang as a cadet. The best they could do was compliment him on "the great merit of being able to conceal his strength and not allowing others to appreciate his rare qualities." Reporters had better luck with Chiang's old sergeant. He recalled the fledgling soldier's "forbidding expression ... when ordered to clean out the stables."

Chiang moved on to Kobe where the Soongs, mother and daughter, were enjoying the spa. Meiling, after a ten-year education in the United States culminating with graduation from Wellesley College, was twenty-five years old. Her mother, Madame Soong, must have had the uneasy feeling that she was reliving an old nightmare when Chiang began his suit. It was the middleaged Sun Yat-sen, married, with children, asking for her youthful daughter's hand all over again. And this time worse, because Chiang didn't even profess to be a Christian. She no longer had the support of her deceased husband, but she knew exactly what to say: the match was impossible.

It was made possible because of Meiling's enthusiasm for it. It has been said that Ailing was the practical daughter, Chingling the romantic, and Meiling the ambitious one. If so, the prospect of uniting herself to the man destined to become leader of China must have had its attractions. At any rate she helped overcome

Madame Soong's scruples. Chiang undertook to clear himself of matrimonial entanglements and also to receive religious instructions in Christianity, though conversion was not guaranteed.

Chiang was prompt in his divorce arrangements. Within a month Chen Chieh-ju, his second wife, the bride of his Shanghai years, was on an ocean liner headed to the United States for "travel and study." This time the cliché had substance. Chen Chieh-ju did study, at Columbia University, where she is said to have taken a doctorate. Later she moved to San Francisco and in the 1960s wrote an autobiography. The manuscript was never published. It was rumored to have been bought up by Chiang Kai-shek's agents. We must applaud the enterprise of this remarkable woman in guaranteeing herself a comfortable annuity, while at the same time regretting the loss of a work that might have shed much light on Chiang's "mystery years" in Shanghai.

The Soong-Chiang nuptials took place in Shanghai on December 1, 1927. As a matter of fact they took place twice. The first version was a private, family ceremony at the Soong residence on Bubbling Well Road. The second was a more gala affair at the prestigious Hotel Majestic in the International Settlement with 1,300 guests, Chinese and Western, drinking the couple's health in champagne.

Chiang took his bride back to his hilltop monastery at Fenghua. No doubt it was a happy honeymoon. The pair had much in common. Besides ambition and energy, they shared Sun Yat-sen's vision of a modern China, Confucianism updated by tools and techniques of capitalism, the new grafted on the old.

But bliss was to be interrupted as telegrams and couriers poured in from Nanking. For the Communists were on the loose again, threatening Canton. Chiang Kai-shek was implored to resume command of the Nationalist forces and end the Red menace forever.

Joseph Stalin, thoroughly humiliated when his strategy at Wuhan had backfired, when his telegram designed to "convert" the revolution had resulted in the victory of reaction, had applied himself to redeem his errors. Reexamining the Chinese situation, he came to the conclusion that the setbacks were only temporary and there had been one important gain—the organization of an independent Red army. True, that army's first test of strength hadn't been impressive—capturing and holding Nanchang for only three days could hardly be called a triumph of arms. Nevertheless a revolutionary force had been brought into being that must not be allowed to dissipate. Accordingly he ordered the Red commanders to capture a city of their choosing and turn it into a permanent military base.

The commanders of the hodgepodge army—Chu Teh, Chou En-lai, and a promising newcomer called Lin Piao—did their best to oblige. In late September 1927 they attacked Swatow, a port in the province of Fukien. But weakened by dissension, discouragement, and disease, the Red forces barely took the city before they were driven out again. Thereafter the army fragmented and dispersed, disappearing into the hills under unit commanders. The diaspora may have been in imitation of Mao Tse-tung, who by this time had established a successful enclave in the mountains of Kiangsi, but it was more probably through sheer desperation as a means of survival.

Stalin, safe in the Kremlin, was furious at the collapse of an army on which he had built high hopes. Determined to salvage something from his disastrous China policy, he fell back on civilian insurrection. He ordered an uprising in Canton, always a militant city and now especially aggrieved because of heavy tax impositions put on it by the Nationalist government, the very regime it had nursed through infancy and sheltered during its rise to power.

Communist cadres in Canton, with whatever forebodings, obeyed Stalin's dictates. They organized the unions, smuggled in arms from Hong Kong, and on December 11 successfully launched a seizure of power that came to be known as the Canton Commune*.

The uprising was short-lived. By December 14 Chiang Kai-shek had hurried to the scene with a strong force of Nationalist

---

*A commune in this sense, the capture and administration of a city, is a specific exercise in the overall revolutionary objective of smashing the existing state machine and replacing it with a proletarian dictatorship.

troops. Street barricades were blown up, workers' battalions were annihilated and a suppression of the populace began that outdid anything perpetrated at Shanghai or Wuhan. For Chiang was as exasperated as Stalin, though for different reasons. Not only had his honeymoon been interrupted, but the persistence of the Communists, rising with Hydra heads after each decapitation, infuriated him. Firing squads were too slow to satisfy his wrath. Demonstrators were machine-gunned down as they paraded, and warehouses filled with captives were set on fire. When the White Terror finally ended, Canton, the city of rams, the cradle of revolutions, was reduced to spiritual impotence. And it was to remain so. Through twenty years of Kuomintang misrule, Japanese occupation and all-out civil war, Canton slumped in torpor, its vitality snuffed out.

Mao Tse-tung, locked away in his fastness at Chingkangshan, was far removed from these last convulsive efforts to resuscitate a failing revolution. But he was quietly at work on revival measures of his own, pursuing a strategy of limited objectives and small beginnings that were in the end to serve the cause far better.

By November 1927 Mao and his thousand-man army—augmented by the forces of two bandit chieftains who had thrown in their lot with the revolutionaries—had run short of provisions. So they ventured down the mountain slopes to the Hunan plains to liberate villages and establish food supplies.

Defeating the landlords' min-tuans proved easier than winning the confidence of the peasants. The district was isolated, untouched by the furor for rights and reforms that had swept the agricultural regions farther to the west during the Northern Expedition. Villagers listened skeptically to Mao Tse-tung's message that a new day had come, that landlord abuses need not be endured forever, and that property could and should be more equitably divided. But they were impressed by the good conduct of the Red soldiers, by their courteous and helpful behavior, and their restraint in matters of theft and rape traditional with the military.

Mao, a peasant himself and long experienced in peasant organization, was ready with the techniques to win the people over.

Meetings were called, grievances aired, landlords were accused of outrages face to face and were seen to tremble in fear for their lives. Soon enough Confucian bonds were broken through and the idea of village self-determination was adopted with enthusiasm. During the winter, self-governing communities were established in six counties of the foothills region.

Proof of the system, of course, lay in its ability to defend itself, and in January 1928 the first test came. Fleeing landlords had spread their stories of wrack and ruin and provincial troops were sent to stamp out the impertinent Red bandits.

Mao Tse-tung was ready for battle. He had been studying the works of Sun Tzu, the fifth century B.C. strategist of deceptive warfare, adapting Sun's principles to present times and conditions, and training his men in what amounted to guerrilla stratagems. The provincial troops, advancing carelessly through hill country, were set upon by surprise attacks; they were detoured from their line of march by flooded roads and lured into ambushes; they were harassed, chewed at, decimated, and finally put to rout by an enemy they never really saw but that seemed to surround them like swarms of lethal bees.

There were other novel features to the astonishing victory. Peasant partisans were employed to act as guides and intelligence agents and were also stationed in ditches and rice paddies to snipe at and distract the invading forces—a cooperation between the Red army and local militiamen that was to become a permanent characteristic of "people's" warfare. Also unprecedented was the Red army's generosity in dividing up captured arms and ammunition with the village partisans. And a final pattern for the future emerged when hundreds of prisoners taken in battle discovered, after intensive indoctrination, that they had been fighting on the wrong side and volunteered to join the revolutionary ranks.

The triumph was so complete, the villagers were so exhilarated at having participated in their own defense that Mao Tse-tung was encouraged to speed up political organization. Committees of all kinds were created—committees of workers, peasants, partisans, women, teachers, students, even committees of village elders and self-confessed loafers. Few occupations escaped the net and, of course, tucked into key roles everywhere were members of the Communist Party. Progress was so satisfactory that in February 1928 Mao took the bold step of proclaiming the jurisdictions under his control the first Chinese soviets.

Soviet is a Russian word meaning "a council." Soviets became important during the early convolutions of the Russian Revolution when factories, taken over by industrial workers, and baronial estates, confiscated by peasants, were run by councils of elected delegates. Soviets were, however, by no means confined to expropriated properties; they flourished within traditional organizations as well. During the stirring days of 1917, when both the Czar and a bourgeois government were toppled from power in rapid succession, soviets formed by soldiers, sailors, educators, and civil service employees played a significant part in the upheavals. Thus soviets were units of political opposition, islands of revolt that threatened the functioning of a constituted state.

When Mao Tse-tung proclaimed soviets in rural Hunan Province in 1928 he meant to challenge the authority of the Kuomintang. As it happened, the Kuomintang, busy with other things, hardly noticed what he was up to. It was the bureaucracy of the Chinese Communist Party that reacted with outrage and took prompt steps to curb the impudent revolutionary of Chingkangshan.

The party's Politburo, living precariously, constantly on the move in Shanghai's foreign concessions in order to escape the police, continued to arrogate to itself full and final authority over its shattered and scattered forces. Its policy, insofar as it had a policy, was an extension of Stalin's old line of using the Red army as a stick to beat the countryside, keeping the dust of revolution flying. Commanders were ordered to march up and down at random, killing landlords, burning their property and butchering "local bullies" wherever found. The intent was pure terrorism without real political or long-term purpose.

It was frustrating to the Politburo that few Red commanders were willing or able to carry out its directives. Most were apologetic, claiming that their forces were still too weak but that they would take to the field again as soon as strength had been regenerated. Mao Tse-tung distinguished himself by promising nothing. He ignored all instructions sent him from Shanghai while he went his own way, utilizing his army in what seemed to the Politburo indulgent and useless experiments among peasants.

For a while the leadership confined itself to criticism, accusing Mao of right opportunism, meaning that he was piddling with rural reforms when he should have been out killing, burning, and butchering. But when he had the gall to proclaim soviets—completely on his own hook without authorization of any kind—patience reached an end. Mao was denounced as an infantile leftist, dismissed from the party's Central Committee (for the second time) and deprived of all posts and offices. By March a substitute commander had been sent to take over from him at Chingkangshan.

Mao's career was again in eclipse and might have remained so during a critical period of the revolution but for a happy accident that intervened. He was to befriend a man whose prestige far surpassed his own and who was to be his ally in turning humiliation into triumph. Communists don't believe in fate, but it was something more than the inevitable process of history that sent Mao Tse-tung dashing down the mountainsides in April 1928 to rescue a hard-pressed band of Red troops led by the extraordinary commander called Chu Teh.*

Chu Teh was by all odds the most admired and accomplished soldier on the Communist side. Unlike Mao Tse-tung and other politicos turned warriors through necessity, Chu Teh was a professional militarist with impeccable credentials. Forty-two years old, a rugged and seasoned campaigner, his reputation for daring and imaginative leadership dated back to the 1911 revolution of Sun Yat-sen. But though he had known power and honors under the Republic and subsequent warlord regimes, he had remained true to his humble origins when the time came to stand up and be counted.

Chu Teh came from peasant stock in Szechwan Province, from

---

*His full name was Chu Chien-teh but like many revolutionaries he dropped his second, or generation, name. Sometimes the generation name came third, as with the sons of Chiang Kai-shek—Ching-kuo and Wei-kuo.

a family so poor that five of thirteen children were drowned at birth to remove their mouths from the rice bowl. It was early recognized that the boy was bright and the clan pooled its resources to see him through an education, hoping to benefit when he became an old-style, grafting official under the Manchu regime. Chu Teh fulfilled expectations by obtaining a *hsiu tsai* (the equivalent of a B.A. degree), but then dashed them by choosing a despised soldier's career because of the revolutionary currents in the air. He graduated from the Yunnan Military Academy just in time to participate in the uprisings that followed the bomb burst at Wuhan, distinguishing himself by the vigor of his assaults on Manchu garrisons, playing a vital part in liberating southwest China for the Republic.

Following Yuan Shih-kai's betrayal of Sun Yat-sen's ideals and the lapse of the Republic into warlord anarchy, Chu Teh too seems to have gone into a decline. He administered the territories under his control like any other tuchun, waxing rich on corruption, acquiring concubines and an opium habit.

Then had come the turmoil of 1919, the May Fourth Movement and the national protest against foreign imperialism, especially Japanese imperialism with its land-grabbing tactics. Chu Teh's conscience had reawakened; he sent his concubines home and destroyed his opium pipes. He went overseas in search of a faith which he found in communism in Germany. He was converted to the party and remained in Berlin for several years, studying and working at the strategy of revolution.

Chu Teh returned to China in 1926 during the Northern Expedition. He was welcomed by Chiang Kai-shek who, unaware of his recently acquired political affiliations, appointed him commander of the Nanchang garrison when he moved on to Shanghai. As we have seen, Chu honored his trust in the breach when he opened up Nanchang to the Red insurrectionists. Since August 1, 1927 is established as the foundation date of the Red Army, Chu Teh should be regarded as its patron saint because he made that first victory miraculously easy.

After the retreat from Nanchang and the epic disasters that followed at Swatow and Canton, Chu Teh almost alone attempted to carry out the dogmatic orders of the Politburo in

Shanghai. He was a professional soldier and he obeyed the commands of his technical superiors without question, ravaging the landlords of the countryside, killing, burning, and butchering for whatever good that did. Naturally he and his men became prime targets for provincial troops, and in time they were surrounded and pressed back against the mountains for final annihilation. It was at this juncture that Mao Tse-tung descended from Chingkangshan with relief forces to expedite the escape of Chu Teh and his battered warriors up to the Communist base camp.

There is today a commemorative stone marking the spot where the leaders met and Mao Tse-tung was "all smiles as he hugged Chu Teh." It's an appealing picture though not necessarily accurate. For it's possible that Chu Teh, politically orthodox and loyal to a fault to the dictates of the Politburo, might have been highly suspicious of his free-thinking rescuer whose views had won him dismissal from the Central Committee. While Mao, in turn, might have examined the tattered uniform, squat figure, and wrinkled peasant face of the celebrated general and wondered what on earth his military fame was based on.

But such first impressions, if they occurred, were rapidly dissolved as the men became better acquainted. They found a natural affinity for each other. Chu Teh, born to lead men in battle, had been wasting his talents and training in haphazard bandit warfare until he met Mao Tse-tung. Mao could provide the theory necessary to change formless skirmishing into meaningful campaigns. Chu, already familiar with the works of Sun Tzu, readily grasped Mao's application of ancient principles to modern conditions. Together the men went to work, developing tactics of mobility and surprise, building a concept of guerrilla warfare that could pit undermanned and undergunned forces against superior troops and still wring victory from the mismatch.

Meanwhile other developments helped the team of Mao-Chu, or Chu-Mao (the names were used interchangeably). That summer at the Sixth Congress of the Chinese Communist Party, held in Moscow for safety's sake, Mao's policy of rural sovietization was approved as a subsidiary measure for winning the masses, and the Politburo in Shanghai was forced, with whatever reluctance, to restore him to good standing and office. That was the signal for Mao and Chu to take off. Leaving Chingkangshan to Mao's successor, they moved north to set up a new base at the foot of the mountains in Kiangsi Province. The area, known as Maoping, offered a wider prospect for peasant organization and also a more favorable battleground for testing new techniques of guerrilla warfare.

At Maoping, Mao Tse-tung called a series of conferences, inviting leaders from other bases—there were about a dozen at the time—to debate with him on the current status of the revolution. Some of Mao's speeches have come down to us as pamphlets, among them the famous "Why is it that Red Political Power can exist in China?" and "The Struggle in the Chingkang Mountains."

Today, in China and elsewhere, students ponder these speeches as eloquent academic texts laying the foundations for peasant power in China. But there was nothing academic about them at the time they were delivered. They were polemics, desperate pleas for the Communist Party to open its eyes to the potential might of the peasantry which comprised 80 percent of the nation's population. Mao argued, often without tact, that Marxist should set aside, at least in the present crisis, the orthodox view that only industrial workers were fit to lead in the class struggle. There weren't enough industrial workers in China, four million at most, while militant peasants were everywhere awaiting organization. Alliance with them was essential if ever the masses were to be set in motion.

In the nature of things Mao's plea was doomed even before it was made. Other base commanders, dependent on authority and finding it in the Politburo as they had once found it in the heads of families and clans, had scant patience with his heretical notions. And in Shanghai the official leadership stiffened in its hostility toward the presumptuous voice crying in the wilderness. While at the Kremlin, Joseph Stalin, the man of steel, irritated by the paralysis that seemed to have gripped his Chinese comrades, was thinking up new ways to provoke them into dynamic action.

12

The Fat Days of the Kuomintang

CHIANG KAI-SHEK RETURNED TO NANKING IN JANUARY 1928 to announce the suppression of the Canton revolt and to request permission to resume his honeymoon. Permission was granted but not before Chiang had promised to complete the Northern Expedition at an early date by capturing Peking. The warlords above the Yellow River still imposed a threat which must be removed before Kuomintang officialdom could feel completely at ease to transact business.

Chiang's preparations for the resumed crusade were different from earlier days in Canton. He had learned a valuable lesson. This time there was to be no triumphant march through the countryside arousing the masses with the slogans of Sun Yat-sen. Chiang had arrived at his own interpretation of Napoleon's famous description of China as a sleeping giant that, when awakened, would shake the world. Like Mao Tse-tung, he had perceived that the giant was the peasantry and he had every intention of allowing it to slumber on undisturbed.

Chiang insured victory in the North by making deals with the warlords who opposed him. He made an ally of Feng Yu-hsiang, the Christian general, by assuring him of a free hand in the Northwest over which he claimed jurisdiction. And he guaranteed the cooperation of Chang Tso-lin, known as the Tiger of the North and the Emperor of Manchuria, by recognizing his unchallenged sovereignty beyond the Great Wall. Chiang Kai-shek was well aware that this was dickering and dealing in the old tuchun style. It was not what Sun Yat-sen had in mind when he organized an army to unite China by conquest. But he also knew, everybody knew, that the Tsungli's revolution was now dead except for face-saving gestures and that the unity of the nation was cheaper bought than fought for.

The sham crusade started out in April, the Nationalist troops advanced in two columns. Li Tsung-jen, the general who had beaten Chiang Kai-shek to the Yangtze in 1926, commanded the wing pushing up the central railroad, while Chiang undertook the more difficult route to the east. A third force under the Christian general also marched from the west. All three contingents timed their arrivals for a triumphant triple entry into Peking.

Despite the careful plans for a virtual holiday parade upcountry, Chiang Kai-shek's wing of the expedition unexpectedly became embroiled in a shooting war. For the Japanese, policing the city of Tsinan and fearful that a united China might threaten their interests on the Shantung pensinsula, invented an excuse to oppose Chiang's column. A pitched battle broke out, Japanese firepower inflicted severe casualties on the advancing Nationalists and the march was halted.

Chiang, alarmed at the development, disengaged as rapidly as possible. He had no wish to take on the Japanese and made whatever apologies were necessary, losing considerable face in the process. He hurried on to Peking by an alternate route but arrived too late for the triumphant entry. Li Tsung-jen and the Christian general, whose men marched to the tune of "Onward Christian Soldiers," had preceded him into the city.

Chang Tso-lin, Tiger of the North and self-proclaimed governor of Peking, made no attempt to defend the ancient capital. By prior arrangement, he withdrew his troops in good order as the Nationalists approached. This strategic maneuver cost him his life. For the Japanese, who had been secretly financing the Tiger for years, took the retreat as a betrayal, rightly sensing that they had been ditched because of a deal made with Chiang Kai-shek, and were quick with vengeance. As Chang Tso-lin's private train approached Mukden, his Manchurian capital, it was mysteriously blown up, the tuchun dying in the blast.

Late though his arrival, Chiang Kai-shek was accorded a hero's welcome in Peking. He visited the sepulcher of Sun Yat-sen at the Azure Cloud Temple to report on the fulfillment of the Tsungli's dream of a united republican China, and he promised that Sun's remains would be transported to Nanking as soon as a suitable mausoleum was constructed. And to prevent any further competition with Nanking as the national seat of government, Chiang ordered that the name Peking (Northern Capital) be changed to Peiping (Northern Peace) and the surrounding province altered from Chihli (Metropolitan District) to Hopei (North of the Yellow River).

Chiang Kai-shek, loaded with honors, his name now famous throughout the nation, returned to Nanking in July. With Confucian humility, he tendered his resignation as commander-in-chief and requested permission to retire permanently to Fenghua. Permission was refused on both counts. As he well knew, he had become China's indispensable man. He yielded to the inevitable and accepted appointment as President of the State Council, the highest political post the republic had to offer. He was also elected to the chairmanship of the Military Council, a status that carried the title Generalissimo, an honor that Chiang respectfully declined—though without much success—because it had once belonged to Sun Yat-sen. Concerning one name, however, he was adamant. No one was ever allowed to call him Tsungli, or supreme leader. The nearest admirers could come was Tsungtsai, or chief.

The first order of practical business was to reduce the army, which had ballooned to over 2 million men and was consuming 75 percent of the nation's revenue. Only some 400,000 of these troops were directly under the command of the Central Government; the rest were warlord and provincial forces, paid and supplied by Nanking. And therein lay a problem. For when

Chiang Kai-shek talked about a reduction, independent commanders suspected, not without reason, that he meant reducing *their* forces in proportion to his own.

Demobilization conferences dragged on without much result except for the conflicts that emerged. One by one the warlords left Nanking announcing their intention to retire from politics—which meant that they were going home to build up their armies. Tests of strength between the tuchuns and the government seemed inevitably to threaten, boding no good for the future.

To meet the danger, Chiang Kai-shek worked hard at improving the quality of Central Government troops. They were already the best trained and best equipped in the land, and now Chiang sought to further heighten their combat efficiency by importing German drillmasters. Among the distinguished corps of booted and monocled Prussian officers summoned to China were the generals Kreibel, Wetzell, von Seeckt, and von Falkenhausen. All were veterans of World War I idled by the Versailles Treaty, delighted to hone their skills abroad while they waited for a new spirit of militarism to revive the Wehrmacht at home.

The Germans worked hard and effectively at the Central Military Academy—the new name for Whampoa moved to Nanking—but there was one Chinese characteristic that baffled them. In spite of goads and incentives, cadets refused to show individual initiative in the field. Any good Confucian would have understood the syndrome even if the Germans couldn't. No right-thinking Chinese lad was going to risk acting on his own when it might seem to imply criticism of a superior.

On the political front, the Nanking administration settled into a pattern of departmental jealousies and intramural politicking. There was no great haste to produce national legislation because there was no great pressure to produce anything. All Kuomintang officials down to the level of county magistrate had been appointed—in effect had appointed each other—and were answerable to no constituency of voters. Attitudes of the old imperial regime of the Manchus were quickly revived. Obtaining office was the end-all and be-all of political existence. Once a man was in office, he owed loyalty only to his superiors; all below were fair game for exploitation and graft. Incumbency also offered wide opportunities for profit-making from the community at large and ingenious licensing and partnership arrangements were made as the cost of doing business. The old saying *"sheng-kuan fa-tse"* ("to become an official and spread benefits") rapidly developed into *"sheng-kuan fa-tsai"* ("to use officialdom to make a fortune") as the Kuomintang warmed to its work.

There was a vague feeling, especially among liberals, that the party, now in power, should do something about realizing Sun Yat-sen's Three Principles. The old objective of nationalism, or putting an end to foreign domination, was obviously no longer practical. But some thought headway could be made on the more blatant unequal treaties. So conferences were called with minor taipans and consular officials for extended talks over jasmine tea. But somehow the conversations always wound up in negotiations for foreign loans. The government's financial situation was continually in crisis, and the need for funds seemed always more pressing than the demands of national honor.

The Manchus had been able to administer China on an annual budget of some $75 million by paying their officials niggardly sums and trusting to individual chicanery to make up what additional income was needed for dignity of office. But such pinchbeck methods were no longer adequate for a modern nation with a large standing army, and strenuous efforts were resorted to in order to raise money. For example: when Chiang Kai-shek returned to Nanking after the Peking Expedition of 1928, he was in arrears in payment to his troops. So he called on the financiers of Shanghai to make good on the money pledged ($30 million) when he quelled the workers' insurrection in 1927. The merchants were reluctant to oblige—that was then and this was now. Chiang made short work of the recalcitrance. The mobsters of the Shanghai underworld were called into action again and, after a number of warehouses had been bombed and children of the wealthy kidnapped, the money was forthcoming.

But funds couldn't always be raised so dramatically. The government could count on a steady income from the customs service (liened to foreigners in 1900 and since then efficiently operated) and from the salt monopoly, but it had few other reliable resources. In the end the freight was always passed on for the rural districts to shoulder. New taxes were invented or old taxes were collected in advance—sometimes forty years in advance—and the peasants, squeezed by the pyramid on top of them, without allies or champions, were forced to pay.

Chiang Kai-shek, nominally the chief of government but actually a figurehead without real power, was concerned by what he saw going on around him. Financially incorruptible himself, he was disturbed by the greed everywhere evident in the Kuomintang. But he felt hemmed in by loyalties, limited in the action he could take. How, for instance, could he censure Hu Han-min, Sun Yat-sen's right-hand man and his senior in years of service to the revolution? Or Sun Fo, the Tsungli's only son? Or his brothers-in-law, H. H. Kung and T. V. Soong, both coining money hand over fist? Or for that matter, how at this late date could he change the characters of his own adopted nephews, the brothers Chen, Li-fu and Kuo-fu, who were peculating with the best of them? Family ties and party loyalties prevented public exposure of wrongdoing, so Chiang had to content himself with private lectures on virtue and accept at face value glib promises to reform.

Chiang could and did try to set a standard of moral rectitude by his own conduct. He had always lived abstemiously and now he accentuated his Spartan traits. He ate sparingly at banquets and gave up drinking altogether. He gave to charities, refused gifts, and made a public show of exercise, hiking vigorously about Nanking wearing out his bodyguards. Confucius had said to rulers, "When you yourself lead by the right example, who dares to go astray?" Chiang could only fulfill the scriptures and hope for the best.

A diversion from moral dilemmas was provided by the renovation of Nanking. Credit for the idea seems to go to Chiang's new bride; at any rate she took an active interest in converting the antiquated city into a capital fit for a great nation. Through the winter of 1928–29 the Chiangs worked together on the project, ordering slums torn down to make way for avenues, parks, and public buildings. American architects were imported at large salaries to help in the design. It was the period of art deco with Victorian influences hanging on, and the mingling of styles combined with local building techniques resulted in the erection of a kind of curly-roofed Chicago. The resemblance was enhanced by a loop roadway running around the city. This was the brainstorm of an American engineer who saved the civic wall, some sixty feet thick, by converting it to a new use.

A great mausoleum for Sun Yat-sen was hurried to completion and the Founder's remains were brought down from Peiping to lie in state on Purple Mountain besides the tombs of the Ming Dynasty. Brought down too was the foreign diplomatic corps, reluctantly exchanging beautiful compounds in Peiping for the cramped quarters and wretched climate of the Yangtze basin. At Chiang Kai-shek's insistence, all mission chiefs were raised from minister to ambassador in honor of China's new status. Chiang himself tried to fit into the cosmopolitan atmosphere by studying English under the tutelage of his wife. But his dead ear for languages led to a disaster. Greeting the British ambassador, Sir Miles Lampson, he attempted to say "Good day, Lampson" but the words came out "Kiss me, Lampson." After that he retreated once again behind interpreters.

The halcyon days of setting style and tone for the revived Republic couldn't and didn't last. Despite appearances, the nation had never really been unified. By buying off the tuchuns instead of destroying them, Chiang Kai-shek had mortgaged the future, and soon enough foreclosure threatened.

In the summer of 1929 a combination of southern warlords, known as the Kwangsi group, claiming unwarranted interference in the affairs of their province, rebelled against the Central Government. They took the field under their most distinguished general, Li Tsung-jen, who previously had been a loyal ally of the Kuomintang. An ally and also, as far as Chiang Kai-shek was concerned, a rival for military honors. For it had been Li who had fought his way first to the banks of the Yangtze in the Northern Expedition of 1926, and it was Li again who had spoiled Chiang's triumph at Peiping by preceding him into the city. Neither feat of arms sat well with the jealous commander-in-chief.

Chiang marched south to meet the challenge. In a long and costly campaign the superior firepower and discipline of his German trained troops proved decisive, though there was no clean-cut victory. Li Tsung-jen was too clever a strategist for that. He forced a stalemate and a truce and even collected an indemnity in return for quitting the country for a while. Kwangsi was gathered back into the Kuomintang domain but on a shaky lease.

The following year the same thing happened all over again in the Northwest. This time it was Feng Yu-hsiang, the Christian general, who revolted. And on the same grounds. He claimed autonomy for his region and resented Kuomintang attempts to administer it.

Again Chiang Kai-shek was forced into a punitive expedition to uphold the sovereignty of the Central Government. And it was while he was engaged in that campaign that he heard astonishing news. A Red army had attacked and seized Changsha. It had been able to hold the city for only a few days before being driven out. Nevertheless Chiang was profoundly shocked.

He had known for some time, of course, that Red bandits had been active in rural areas of Hunan and Kiangsi, but he had been willing to tolerate small-scale disturbances until he had disciplined the tuchuns. But taking a city was a different matter. Cities were always critical in Chiang's scale of military values. It meant the Red conspiracy was stronger than he had supposed, that it had gained momentum since he had last sought to exterminate it at Canton. As soon as possible he must concentrate all available forces for a final eradication of the menace.

It might have eased Chiang's mind to know that the attack on Changsha in July 1930 was an aberration, an opportunistic mistake, an unwarranted adventuristic putsch. At least that was Mao Tse-tung's later opinion and he should have known. He was there, on the spot. It was the last desperate gamble of a man called Li Li-san who was trying to prove himself worthy of the trust Joseph Stalin had put in him.

Li Li-san was among the lucky few who had escaped to Moscow after the Wuhan government broke with the Communists, unleashing the White Terror. Prior to that he had worked effectively as a labor organizer, among coal miners, mill hands, and longshoremen, and it was this background, along with the young man's forceful personality, that first attracted Stalin's attention. The Soviet leader sensed that in Li he had found the engineer who could put derailed Chinese Marxism back on the right track.

For Stalin was growing increasingly impatient with the inaction and excuses that were emerging from the Middle Kingdom. He could understand peasant power—he had made use of it himself in emergencies—and he could condone Mao Tse-tung's schemes for rural organization, but only on an auxiliary basis. The role of revolutionary leadership had been reserved by Marx, Engels, and Lenin for the proletariat, militant industrial workers led by the Communist Party. Stalin didn't care how few proletarians there were in China. Everything was secondary to rekindling their martial spirit and rededicating them to their historic duty. So in October 1928 he sent Li Li-san back to his homeland charged with "restoring a proletarian base" for the revolution.

In Shanghai Li Li-san assumed leadership of the Politburo, and went energetically to work. But he found that conditions had changed since last he had been in the country. The White Terror had wrecked the labor movements in the chief industrial centers, smashing their organizations and killing off all but a handful of militant leaders. And even the few that remained were without influence or followers. Workers, surfeited with sufferings, had no stomach left for political strikes and demonstrations with the inevitable aftermath of beatings and imprisonment. All they wanted was to be left alone. Many, in fact, had joined the Kuomintang yellow unions, paternalistic associations with a Confucian tinge. They joined partly for self-protection but also because membership sometimes led to better pay and working conditions—factors often ignored by Communist organizers.

Li Li-san saw that it was going to take time and money to revitalize the labor movement. Casting about for means of raising funds, he remembered a practice once successfully employed by his patron in Moscow. When Lenin, exiled in Switzerland, had needed cash to hold the party together, Stalin, at large in Russia and on the run from the police, had organized bank and train robberies to finance his chief. Li Li-san now ordered the Red commanders hiding out in the mountains of Hunan and Kiangsi to do likewise. Rather, since banks were scarce and railroads nonexistent in the impoverished South, he ordered fresh attacks on landlords with methods for extracting money left to individual ingenuity.

Li Li-san marked time during the year 1929 waiting for the funds to flow in. Conscientious Red commanders worked hard to carry out his rob the rich directive but results were disappointing. Landlords were canny about hiding their silver pieces, or they prudently moved them to the cities when they learned the objective of the new Red Terror.

Mao Tse-tung, independent as usual, refused to cooperate in what he considered an ill-advised policy. In a speech made at a party conference he argued that Red military forces should not be squandered on putschist missions by "roving rebel bands"; their true function was "to conduct propaganda among the masses, organize them, arm them, and help them to establish revolutionary power." Furious, Li Li-san accused Mao of "right opportunism" and a "peasant mentality."

By the spring of 1930 the heat was turned on from Moscow. Li Li-san, in command of the Politburo for eighteen months, had signally failed in resuscitating the workers' movement despite Stalin's optimistic estimate that a revolutionary tide was sweeping the cities.

Li Li-san grew frantic under the pressure. His mind seems to have been affected. "He is said to have told Chou En-lai [on the Politburo] that what China needed was a Lenin; and the next day to have remarked casually that he himself was probably China's Lenin." He devised a strategy to liberate the revolutionary fervor that Stalin said was seething in the industrial centers. He would collect a large army, with all Red bases contributing, and besiege cities. Even the threat of attack should be enough. It would be like Wuhan in 1926 during the Northern Expedition. The workers would stage an uprising on their own initiative and pour out to greet their liberators.

The idea became an obsession. And to make sure there would

be no resistance this time from Mao Tse-tung or Chu Teh, he appointed Chu commander-in-chief of the insurgent army and Mao political commissar.

The whole concept was a desperate, irrational gamble and everybody concerned knew it. Chou En-lai is supposed to have said, "Li Li-san has gone mad." But boxed in by party discipline and the implied suggestion that Stalin had ordered the undertaking, no one was able to protest effectively. Not even Mao Tse-tung at the beginning. Though later, at Changsha, it was a different story. And his revolt led to Li Li-san's downfall.

Much had happened to the Mao-Chu team since the autumn of 1928. For one thing, they had taken to the road again. Their new base at Maoping had turned out not to be as much of an improvement over Chingkangshan as they had hoped. Its situation in the foothills of Kiangsi offered easier access to the surrounding villages, but it was more difficult to defend and by winter the encampment was under more or less permanent blockade.

"Conditions . . . were becoming very bad," Mao recorded later. "The troops had no winter uniforms, and food was extremely scarce. For months we lived practically on squash. The soldiers shouted a slogan of their own: 'Down with capitalism, and eat squash!' "—a pun of sorts, since in Chinese "squash" sounds close to "landlords."

In January 1929 Mao and Chu decided to seek a new base. They broke through the blockade with their four thousand men and started trekking south. They clung to the fringes of the mountains as ancient sailors clung to the shore, ready to dash for safety if pirates or storms appeared. Along the way they made friends, the courtesy, honesty, and helpful consideration of the Red soldiers never failing to amaze the rural populations. They added to their fighting strength, too. In alcoves in the hills they found and rescued remnants of Communist contingents driven into hiding by the disaster of the earlier kill, burn, and butcher campaigns.

The small army progressed on south, dipped into Kwangtung Province and then turned back northeast into Kiangsi. Passage lay through the coal fields at Anyuan and here at least sparks of rebellion still flickered among industrial workers. Some seven hundred joined the Red ranks as volunteers. Mao Tse-tung was delighted to welcome them for ideological reasons if nothing else. His army was boldly billed as a Front of Workers and Peasants but there were few proletarians. In fact, in the entire Communist Party, less than 8 percent could trace their origins to the working class.

By this time the cross-country hegira was widely advertised and had drawn a crowd of provincial troops. Skirmishing was constant. Finally Mao and Chu decided to have it out in a full-scale battle, testing the strategy and tactics they had been developing for months. The result was a triumph of guerrilla warfare. The enemy was drawn into the center by an apparently easy target, then hit on the flanks by Reds who seemed to emanate from nowhere. Two regimental commanders, a thousand troops and eight hundred rifles were captured in a half-day's fighting.

With the pressure off, Mao and Chu moved north at a more leisurely pace, skirting the mountains that separated Kiangsi and Fukien provinces. And in May 1929, at a market town called Juichin, they found their promised citadel. All around was agricultural land, rich, productive and, most important, hilly—suitable for defensive maneuvering. The people were especially welcoming because a Kuomintang army had passed through shortly before leaving the usual bitter legacy of robbery, rape, and murder.

The Red forces, now numbering some ten thousand, unslung rifles and took on double duty, as propagandists among the peasants and minutemen prepared to act in their defense. In new territory, with new populations to win, Mao Tse-tung took pains to see that mistakes and excesses of the Chingkangshan period were not repeated. Only landlords and rich peasants were to be dispossessed, and even they were to be left with enough land to farm on the level of middle peasants. Reprisals for age-old wrongs and indiscriminate killings were kept firmly under control.

Already Mao was working his way toward building the largest

possible constituency within a given community. He could never make allies out of the possessing class, but he was careful not to drive them to ultimate desperation and vengeful flight. This forbearance, a reluctance to take Draconian measures when less strict would suffice—what came to be known as Mao's "forgiving" nature—was to be held against him when more violent men took over the leadership of the party. The compulsion to kill, burn, and butcher would take long to eradicate.

But meanwhile control was in Mao's hands. "[We] established soviets in all ... counties [of the area]," he recollected. "The existence of militant mass movements prior to the arrival of the Red army"—he's referring to the Peasant Association drives of 1926—"assured our success, and helped to consolidate soviet power on a stable basis very quickly." Very quickly because Mao, by confiscating land, was able to solve the problem of the people's livelihood that had always baffled Sun Yat-sen, just as, a half century earlier, Abraham Lincoln had ended the long debate on the economic feasibility of freeing the slaves by the single act of emancipation.

Up to this time, only district soviets had been organized. But in February 1930, at a conference of "the [local] Party, the army, and the [local] government," a long step forward was taken. All the Red bases in the province were consolidated into a single jurisdiction called the Kiangsi Provincial Soviet Government with its capital at Juichin.

It was from this promising and constructive work that Mao Tse-tung and Chu Teh were diverted in the spring of 1930 by Li Li-san's order to attack cities. At least it was something new in Marxist annals. Never before had a petit-bourgeois peasant army marched to liberate the proletariat, the militant vanguard of revolution.

Two armies were assembled, with forces drawn from the dozen or so Red bases north and south of the Yangtze River. Chu Teh was to head one unit, Peng Teh-huai, a tough, resourceful commander, the other, with Mao Tse-tung in overall political control. Li Li-san had already set the strategy of attack. Simultaneous assaults were to be made on Nanchang and Changsha; then the armies were to combine and march on Wuhan.

Chu and Mao, charged with taking Nanchang, reached it on July 29 with twenty thousand men and began what was more a propaganda barrage than a siege. They had no cannons to breach the walls so had to be content with rattling away with machineguns and rifles while they awaited the expected proletarian uprising from within, Nobody budged. The workers stayed put at their benches, earning an honest day's pay, indifferent to liberation.

To the west, Peng Teh-huai had better luck. His men battered down a gate and stormed into Changsha. But Peng, too, found little evidence of worker militancy. The people, if anything, seemed to resent the intrusion on their peaceful routines. They remembered vividly what had happened the last time they stood up for their rights and wanted no more of it.

At Nanchang, Mao Tse-tung soon became tired of the hopeless situation. The Red soldiers were trained for a very different type of warfare and were taking casualties without any chance of hitting back. He persuaded Chu Teh to abandon the siege and the troops marched west to join Peng Teh-huai at Changsha.

They met Peng coming out. After seven days of fruitless effort to organize Changsha's population, he had called it quits. The commanders consulted on what to do next. Their decision was helped by a frantic telegram from Li Li-san. He ordered the combined armies to reoccupy Changsha or, if that was impossible, to march immediately on Wuhan.

An attempt was made to reenter the city. But the defenders were back in place and resupplied. Also foreign gunboats had moved upriver to lend assistance. Caught between the fusillade from the walls and the shelling from the river, the Red forces were taking a mauling.

Suddenly Mao Tse-tung called a halt. On his own authority, but presumably with the concurrence of his commanders, he ordered a retreat from Changsha, back to home bases, all thought of moving on to Wuhan forgotten.

It was mutiny, of course. Worse still, it was a breach of Communist discipline and a repudiation of the party leadership, though Mao Tse-tung always maintained that he acted in the only way possible. Years later he was still asserting, "[We] saved the Red Army from what would probably have been a catastrophic attack on Wuhan."

Nevertheless someone had to pay, someone had to be the scapegoat. Fortunately for Mao it was Li Li-san. Moscow had been appalled by his unauthorized putschist policy against cities, and his humiliating failure drove the last nail into his coffin as Stalin's deputy in China. He was replaced by better indoctrinated leaders—twenty-eight of them, in fact—and by December Li was on his way back to Russia for reeducation and rehabilitation.

But the damage had been done. The capture of Changsha had refocused the Red menace in Chiang Kai-shek's mind, and the days of peaceful sovietization in the countryside were over.

Chiang Kai-shek began by underestimating his enemy. Back in Nanking in the winter of 1930–31, his campaign against the Christian general successfully concluded, he sent a combination of provincial warlords with a hundred thousand troops to clean out the Red bases in Kiangsi. The tuchuns, eager to oblige, rushed into action and into a series of traps, ambushes, and encirclements thoughtfully provided by Chu Teh's guerrilla forces. The tuchuns limped back to safety after a nightmare month, leaving behind twenty thousand men dead and captured, including a general.

Chiang returned to the attack in May 1931 with more thorough preparations. This time he sent 200,000 men, most of them Central Government troops, under the command of General Ho Ying-chin, his chief of staff and minister of defense. Like Chiang, Ho had studied at the Shinbo Gokyo Academy in Japan, where the principles of aggressive attack and relentless pursuit were taught. His campaign was an almost textbook model of these principles, except that it was Ho who was aggressively attacked when he walked into a trap and relentlessly pursued when he tried to get out of it. He was routed in two months, losing 30,000 men in casualties and prisoners to the Communists.

It was finally borne in on Chiang Kai-shek that bandit extermination required his personal attention. He mounted a third expedition—300,000 troops this time—and set up field headquarters for himself and his German staff at Nanchang, capital of Kiangsi Province. In July 1931 his men were sent into action, advancing cautiously.

The Red guerrillas gave way before them, marking time, avoiding battle. Every night the advance was studied by Mao Tse-tung and Chu Teh, huddled over maps like shortsighted chess players. When Chiang's strategy became evident—a dozen strikes at the center instead of a single drive—the counteroffensive began. Red contingents were set in motion, sliding in between Chiang's spearheads to converge in rear attacks. Night assaults, preceded by weird animal howls to unnerve the jittery Kuomintang soldiers, were particularly effective.

It was slow work, or comparatively slow measured against the previous campaigns. It took four months, or until October, before the Nationalists called a retreat after losing twenty thousand men and ten thousand firearms. It is only fair to add that Chiang Kai-shek was then no longer with his armies. He had been called back to Nanking by a more pressing crisis. In September the Japanese had attacked Manchuria.

13

Years of the Ram and the Rooster

J APAN HAD BEEN LATE IN ENTERING THE INDUSTRIAL AGE. Its rocky islands, jigsaw pieces floating off the Asian continent, had been left too long in isolation; its feudal population had been too fiercely protected from foreign influences that might threaten the internal regime. As a result, the machine revolution, getting up steam in eighteenth century England and running full throttle through the West by the mid-nineteenth, had passed Nippon by, stranding it in xenophobia.

Then in 1853 the black ships of the American Commodore Matthew Perry had sailed into Tokyo Bay to dump the backward nation out of sanctuary and force it to test its wits in the modern world.

Actually the enforced social and economic upheaval came to Japan not as an imposition but as a deliverance. For more than two hundred years the people had been existing in what seemed to Westerners a schizoid state, their loyalties split between a deified priest and a practical police authority. They had an emperor to worship, but he was locked away like a feeble-minded relative at a place called Kyoto, while the actual business of government was carried out by a despotic oligarchy, known as the Shogunate, headquartered in Tokyo.

This condition of affairs had come about through a baronial revolution against the monarchy—Japan's version of Runnymede and the Magna Carta though four hundred years later—to insure the domination of the landed gentry (the daimyos) and their armed retainers (the samurai) over the peasantry. Feudal power became absolute; the Shogunate, representative of the daimyos, saw to it that land and only land was to remain the basis of wealth and prestige. The emperor was banished to religious obscurity, serving as the spiritual emblem of the system.

But long before Commodore Perry's ships appeared, strains had shown up in the national economy. An expanding population needed other means of livelihood besides agriculture to survive. A lively handicrafts industry grew up and with it the beginnings of a mercantile commerce. Not only were goods traded within the country, but an illegal traffic also developed with Dutch and Portuguese merchant ships. This should have called for an instant crackdown by the Shogunate but it didn't because some of the best daimyo families were in on the racket.

Contradictions between principles and practice were solved by the liberating influence of Commodore Perry's visit. National pride was stirred as well as a desire to emulate the achievements of the West. The Shogunate was evicted and the emperor brought out of hiding to be installed in Tokyo as the actual head of government. Then, with its long schizophrenia ended, Japan turned to modernization with a will.

Daimyos, many already experienced in illicit commerce, stepped in to head trading corporations and industrial enterprises. Their sons, wearing strange-looking Western clothes, were sent overseas to learn the techniques of business, diplomacy, and parliamentary government. The sword-swinging samurai, haughty and truculent as ever, stepped into the shoes and uniforms of army and naval officers, while the disciplined, long-suffering peasants converted to factory hands without complaint. It was a thoroughgoing revolution, tight and orderly, run Japanese style from the top.

Industrial output flourished, especially in military hardware. Before the turn of the twentieth century, Japan was ready to flex its imperial muscles, and did. The annexation in 1895 of Korea and Taiwan from the feeble Manchu Dynasty in China only caused raised eyebrows, but the next feat of arms came as a shock. Between 1904 and 1905, Japan took on czarist Russia both by land and at sea and was overwhelmingly victorious. In a scant fifty years, starting from scratch, Japan had built herself into an industrial power that challenged the Western hegemony in the Orient.

Sun Yat-sen had been greatly impressed by Japan's achievement and had held it up as a model for China to emulate. Though later his admiration had cooled as he learned to distrust Japanese imperial ambitions. The seizure of German possessions in Shantung at the outbreak of World War I caused sober reappraisal; and even more the Twenty-one Demands of 1915 which sought to reduce China to a Japanese-administered colony. Intrusions and incidents, efforts to create trouble, had continued ever since. Warlords had been supplied with arms to perpetuate unrest, commercial privileges had been secured by bribes and, on the diplomatic front, Japan had never ceased to maintain that, because of propinquity and her need for raw materials, she was entitled to special rights in China not to be shared by other nations.

So far all this had been merely jockeying, an attempt to best the Great Powers in the "open door" policy of equal opportunities in trade. Japan's real objective had always been to seize physical possession of segments of China—especially coal- and iron-rich Manchuria—eliminating competition. But she hesitated to take the first step, afraid of international reactions. Afraid, that is, until she became obsessed by a greater fear—that China, united under a determined leader like Chiang Kai-shek, might find the strength to repel an invasion if too long delayed. Chiang's successful expedition to Peiping in 1928, nominally unifying the nation, was probably the deciding factor. As the Japanese General Staff saw it, they had only a limited time left in which to implement their master plan.

For they had a master plan, set forth in a document called the

Tanaka Memorial*. A year or so before, the prime minister, Baron Giichi Tanaka, had presented for the emperor's consideration a plan for world conquest. If the Yamato race wished to distinguish itself, the baron had said, it must strike at the Asian continent while China was still weak. It must seize Manchuria and Mongolia for their mineral resources; afterward an expansion into China Proper would drain off all other resources. Thus supplied and fortified, the imperial armies would be invincible. India could be conquered, then the Middle East, opening the way to Europe. All depended on the initial phase of the design—the subjugation of Manchuria.

There are authorities who claim that the Tanaka Memorial was pure fiction, that it never existed, that its published version was a Chinese fraud. The point is immaterial. The spirit of the document, real or apocryphal, was certainly alive and dominated Japanese military thinking for years to come—much as Alfred Mahan's concept of a two-ocean navy captivated American admirals, or von Schlieffen's scheme for outflanking the French armies obsessed the German Wehrmacht. Wars can sometimes be fought to vindicate plans on paper.

It took time for preparations. By 1931 imperial consent had been obtained, but then a new hitch developed. A worldwide depression was pinching the Japanese economy and parliamentary liberals called for a reduction in the military establishment to relieve the strain. That was a final spur to action; the army and navy must either be productively used or dwindle into discard.

Judicious assassinations in the Diet silenced or cowed civilian opposition. The powder keg was set, needing only a spark or, as the Japanese like to call it, an "incident" for ignition.

In mid-September a section of railroad track, patrolled by the Japanese on a treaty arrangement, mysteriously blew up. The location was near Mukden, the capital of Manchuria. Japanese screams were immediate; the outrage threatened their nationals in the country, not to mention the insult to the emperor. And on

---

*A memorial is a memorandum addressed to an emperor, with a distinction. A memorandum suggests the necessity for a reply, which is impertinent. A memorial simply brings a matter to the sovereign's attention, to be acted on or not as he pleases.

September 18, 1931—the Year of the Ram according to the Chinese calendar—Japanese marines, held ready in troopships, began to stream ashore.

News of the invasion caused Chiang Kai-shek to relinquish supervision of his Third Red Bandit Campaign and hurry back to Nanking. He found his government in turmoil, not knowing how to act. But worse from Chiang's standpoint was that the armies of Manchuria were preparing to act far too boldly. Their commander, Chang Hsueh-liang, son and heir of the late Chang Tso-lin, Tiger of the North, had ordered all-out resistance to the Japanese invasion—a serious mistake in Chiang's opinion.

Chiang Kai-shek had a respect that amounted to awe for the Japanese army. He had trained in it and he had tangled with it during his northern march in 1928, and he knew its efficiency and power. Certainly the wild hordes of Chang Hsueh-liang, also known as the Young Marshal, were no match for it. And there was always the danger that a war, started in Manchuria, would spill down across the Great Wall into China Proper.

He appealed to the Young Marshal to call off his plans for an aggressive defense in favor of a diplomatic settlement. He explained that he was lodging a protest with the League of Nations and was confident that league action would result in expelling the Japanese.

The Manchurian leader, loyal to an alliance he had made with Chiang, reluctantly allowed himself to be persuaded. He changed his order, instructing his troops to retreat—and they kept on retreating until they were squeezed out of their country. Methodically advancing, the Japanese took over the three provinces of the Northeast and began organizing them into a colony.

Throughout the months of the encroachment there had been a furious outcry in China. The Young Marshal was called a coward and Chiang Kai-shek was denounced for not sending troops to help stiffen his backbone. Students demonstrated. There had been few significant demonstrations since the May Fourth Movement of 1919 when the betrayal of China at the Versailles Treaty had heated emotions to a fever pitch, but the humiliation in Manchuria brought the students out again in force. Then the boycotts began; Japanese goods became anathema and Japanese shops had to close down. A National Salvation Association of some eight hundred thousand members was organized to enforce the boycotts with patriotic zeal.

Next came the strikes. In Shanghai, Wuhan, and Tientsin, workers in Japanese-owned factories walked off the job. And putting down tools became popular in other occupations. Even rickshaw coolies and prostitutes got into the act, refusing to service Japanese nationals.

The reprisals took the conquerors by surprise. They had invaded Manchuria to extract wealth, not to lose it as a consequence. They were alarmed when their share of the Chinese import market dropped from 25 percent to 14 percent in the months folllowing the Mukden Incident and they had the gall to complain to the Nanking government about unfair business practices. They also demanded an end to hostile demonstrations against them as insulting to both the Nippon nation and its emperor. Chiang Kai-shek, playing for time, desperate to keep the peace until the League of Nations could bail him out, obliged by prohibiting protest parades and, when necessary, sending in the police to break them up.

Predictably the outcries redoubled. Chiang Kai-shek became a prime target for domestic wrath. He was called a running dog of Japan and his resignation was demanded. But he hung on until the winter, or until delays and evasions from League of Nations headquarters at Geneva convinced him that he could expect no help from that direction.

The league, though it had done useful work in such matters as maritime law, was still an unknown quantity as an international peacekeeper. Manchuria was to be its first test, and the commission that finally arrived in China in March 1932 was impressively led by a British peer, Lord Lytton. The Lytton Commission held inquiries, took depositions, and traveled extensively, but in the end recommended no effective action. It was a performance that was to be repeated with the same result in later years when Mussolini attacked Ethiopia and Hitler marched into the Rhineland, leading to the bitter jest that the League of Nations was, like Westminster Abbey, a last resting place for defunct statesmen.

In December, disappointed in his hopes for an early international settlement and left high and dry to face the anger of his people, Chiang Kai-shek had no option but to resign. He may or may not have remembered the old Chinese adage that after a man has been in charge of his family's affairs for three years even his dog hates him, but the moral was relevant. It had been almost exactly three years since he had first risen to prominence in the government.

He retired to his Buddhist monastery in Fenghua on December 15, 1931, leaving behind a nation dismembered by the loss of Manchuria's 364,000 square miles of territory and a population of some 30 million. Actually the loss had been greater: the realm had been diminished by a further 19,000 square miles containing a population of 3 million, though Chiang Kai-shek might not have been aware of this. For in November 1931 Mao Tse-tung's Kiangsi Provincial Government had been retitled the Soviet Republic of China in defiance of and secession from the Nationalist regime at Nanking.

Mao Tse-tung himself had had little to do with this bold founding of an independent socialist nation. If he'd had his way, he would probably have been against it; he always resisted specious claims that outran reality. But by then Mao's views no longer carried weight. He was being phased out of authority, methodically downgraded by a new Communist leadership in Shanghai.

Li Li-san had departed China in disgrace but his "line"—rather Stalin's line—had remained behind. For the sage of the Kremlin was convinced that only the man, not the policies, had been at fault, and to implement them aggressively he sent to Shanghai a group of zealots known to history as the Twenty-eight Bolsheviks.

Not all of the twenty-eight have been identified and it is thought that wives, friends, and Comintern advisers may have been included in the number. But there is no doubt as to the leader. He was a young man called Wang Ming, already self-confident, commanding, and ideologically rigid at the age of twenty-four.

Wang Ming, son of a landlord, claimed to have been a radical by fifteen and a converted Communist by eighteen. Since then he had been studying at Sun Yat-sen University, the Comintern's training school in Moscow, where his gift for languages, especially Russian, brought him to Stalin's attention. With no interpreter intervening, the Soviet leader could tell the hard-crusted young man exactly what was wanted in China and send him back with confidence to do the job.

On arrival in Shanghai, Wang Ming went to work purging the personnel of his predecessor, Li Li-san—"capturing the apparatus" it was called. It was efficiently done. Any committeeman or bureau chief who hesitated in prompt loyalty was secretly informed on to the police, with arrest and execution as his probable fate. Next, future control of the party was insured by reducing the Central Committee from thirty members to sixteen. Chou En-lai, a Li Li-san holdover, retained his seat but Mao Tse-tung, already on the new leadership's suspicious list, lost out. Because of his chairmanship of the Kiangsi Provincial Soviet, Mao was retained as a "branch" committee member, subservient to the all-powerful board in Shanghai.

Ideological matters were then taken up. In February 1931 Wang Ming circulated a pamphlet titled "The Two Lines; or the Struggle for the Further Bolshevization of the Communist Party of China." Comrades in the countryside of Kiangsi had difficulty understanding what Bolshevization, or even Bolshevik, meant. They had become accustomed to thinking of themselves as soviets (*su wei-ai*) and even that term was difficult enough—too difficult, as it turned out, for uninitiated Kuomintang enemies who frequently offered rewards for the "Red bandit Su Wei-ai—dead or alive." The best that could be puzzled out by the rank and file faithful was that a Communist wasn't Communist enough unless he was a Bolshevik.

In "The Two Lines," addressed to the more sophisticated party leadership, Wang Ming undertook to correct past errors and lay down rules for the future. "Right opportunism" that had evolved from "coddling" peasants must cease. Rural populations must be made to understand that they were the auxiliaries, and only the auxiliaries, of the working class. From now on, first emphasis must be put on organizing and developing the mass power of the proletariat. The pamphlet was so evidently meant as an attack on Mao Tse-tung's ideas that he could only have studied it with foreboding.

Preliminaries out of the way, Wang Ming and his colleagues turned to vindicating Stalin's faith in them by restoring the proletarian base of the revolution. That task had brought about Li Li-san's downfall and all the problems that had plagued him still remained. There was high unemployment and a dearth of effective labor leaders. Workers remained passive, preferring semi-starvation wages to standing up for their rights and being dismissed to starve for sure.

Wang Ming's frustrations reached a peak after the Mukden Incident in September 1931 when all of China was stirred by wrath at the Japanese invasion of Manchuria. The workers, caught up in the general wave of patriotism, came to life. They struck, they demonstrated, they joined the National Salvation Association by the thousands—but under the leadership of the Kuomintang yellow unions while the Communists stood by helplessly.

Wang Ming's personal trials came to an end early in 1932 when he was recalled to Moscow to head the Eastern Section of the Comintern, but tribulations still remained for the other Twenty-eight Bolsheviks. In fact they increased when Po Ku, a twenty-three-year-old hardhead, aping Wang Ming's personality, succeeded to the leadership. The tricky practice of betraying unwanted "obstructionist" comrades to the Shanghai police boomeranged when the authorities began scouring the foreign concessions for Communist cells. Shanghai became distinctly unsafe for revolutionaries. Almost daily arrests were made of party members, and there were some narrow escapes. Chou En-lai once tested his historic invulnerability when he returned to his lodgings to find the police in waiting. He barely managed to squeeze out through a back door.

The time had come to beat a retreat and Mao Tse-tung's domain—elevated to the status of the Soviet Republic of China by Moscow's orders the previous November—offered the only safe refuge. During the spring of 1932 what was left of the

Shanghai leadership filtered down to Mao's capital at Juichin, traveling by foot or boat or, in one case, under a load of chickens in a peasant's wheelbarrow.

Once ensconced, the refugees pulled rank and began reorganizing the government along Bolshevik lines. Land policies were changed. Mao Tse-tung's leniency toward landlords and rich peasants was branded a dilution of the class struggle and the well-to-do were stripped of all possessions. Landlords, goaded to revolt, were killed; the less militant were driven away to starve or, more likely, cross the mountains to prepare for a vengeful return.

Procedures in the Red army also came under review. Soldiers' congresses and committees, organized by Mao to boost morale, were abolished. Officers and enlisted men were to wear different insignia and saluting was introduced. A start was made in training troops in trench and positional warfare, modern methods based on the drillbook of the Russian army. Guerrilla tactics were out. They were dubbed "peasant fighting methods" belonging to an earlier stage of military primitivism.

It is probable that Mao Tse-tung protested these changes, though party records are loyally silent on the point. If so, he was shouldered aside as Bolshevization of all phases of political and military life continued.

The question arises, how could it have happened? How could a group of outsiders—hard-nosed, immature know-nothings—take over a smooth-running, finely meshed going concern and start it down the road to ruin without meeting vigorous oppositon? Mao Tse-tung was not alone among the managers who had made the Kiangsi Provincial Government, later the Soviet Republic, a success. At least a half dozen base commanders had shared in the enterprise and now held high official posts in the jurisdiction. Why didn't they speak up? Why didn't they join with Mao in resisting the crass, doctrinaire newcomers?

Party discipline is one answer. By now it was recognized by all that strength could come only from unity, and that unity traced back to unquestioning obedience to the party leadership. Also Po Ku, acting chairman of the Central Committee, and his Bolshevik colleagues were vested with powers straight from Moscow, from the Comintern, from Stalin himself. It would have been a bold provincial who set himself up against such authority.

But in the end there was probably a more significant reason for the complacency with which the new regime was accepted—hostility toward Mao Tse-tung. Mao might be loved by the peasants and the common soldiers, but he was not popular among the base commanders. For Mao, apart from his unorthodox ideas, had made enemies by his independent will and arbitrary actions. His decision to abandon the attack on Changsha in 1930 was still held against him as a breach of discipline, and an even more damning display of dictatorial temperament had occurred shortly afterward.

This was known as the Futien Incident. Mao, angered at a public demonstration against him, had ordered the wholesale arrest of political opponents. When this was resisted, he sent troops to put down the uprising—the only case of internecine conflict, a civil war within a civil war, in the revolution's history and never to be repeated. Mao Tse-tung was thoroughly ashamed of the episode for the rest of his life.

Still, it had happened and it wasn't forgotten. The resentment remained long after. And it is probable that many base commanders secretly rejoiced when Mao was overridden and disciplined by the Twenty-eight Bolsheviks. He had grown too big for his boots and it was time he was cut down to size again.

Mao Tse-tung was learning, as Chiang Kai-shek had learned, that it wasn't enough for a leader to hold true to his own vision. He had to have luck as well. The luck of circumstances that made it clear in a crisis that he, and only he, could save the day and rescue his followers from the results of their own folly.

For Mao Tse-tung, slipping in prestige and influence, that time was still far off. But for Chiang Kai-shek in the spring of 1932 the wheel had already turned and stopped at his number. By popular demand, he was back in power.

Sun Fo, son of the Tsungli, had succeeded to the presidential chair when Chiang Kai-shek retired to Fenghua. Sun Fo was known as a genial, unpredictable politician whose ambitions could send him soaring in any direction. Behind his back he was sometimes called Sun Wu Kung in reference to the monkey of legend who could travel a thousand miles at a single leap. In his time he had been connected with both the right and left wings of the Kuomintang but now, in December 1931, he seemed to have settled down as a middle-of-the-roader.

The anti-Japanese demonstrations were still going strong and, in a bid for popularity, Sun Fo called off police interference and suppression. The Japanese protested and threatened retaliation, but the new chief of state felt safe in ignoring them. Even sword-rattling samurai weren't going to do anything foolish while the world still condemned them for their Manchurian invasion.

Sun Fo was wrong—it was a lifelong habit. Using the assassination of a couple of nationals as an excuse, the Japanese landed troops at Shanghai on January 28, 1932. Their motive has never been made quite clear. Possibly they wanted to intimidate the Great Powers with an overwhelming show of strength. Or it could be that, if all had gone well, they intended to implement stage two of Baron Tanaka's plan by moving on to an immediate conquest of China. At any rate they landed in force. Four divisions, or better than forty thousand men poured ashore to protect —or so the announcement proclaimed—the thirty thousand Japanese civilians in Shanghai.

Sun Fo, in a panic, appealed to Chiang Kai-shek to come back. But Chiang was in no hurry. He could only lose reputation by trying to defend a doomed city. Fortunately the troops of the Chinese 19th Route Army garrisoning Shanghai didn't see it that way. Patriotically motivated, led by an able general in Tsai Ting-kai, they began a stout defense. They erected barricades in the winding alleys of the Old City and the working class districts and made taking them costly.

Japanese warships on the Whangpoo estuary lobbed shells into the town, reducing vast areas to rubble. But the rubble served the defenders better than the attackers and Japanese bodies piled up. The fighting lasted for thirty-six days—until March 4 when a truce was arranged by the foreign powers. The Japanese withdrew in humiliation; if it wasn't a defeat, it wasn't the smashing victory they had anticipated either, and the slightly superior smiles of the Western taipans were galling.

General Tsai Ting-kai and his 19th Route Army were the toasts of China and the celebrations in the streets brought Chiang Kai-shek hurrying back to Nanking. It was too late to garner credit for the epic feat at Shanghai but Chiang saw to it that he wouldn't have to listen to Tsai Ting-kai's praises sung longer than was necessary; the military success of others always irritated him. As commander-in-chief, he ordered the 19th Route Army transferred to Fukien Province, ostensibly for rest and recuperation but actually to get it out of sight until adulation died down.

Chiang next turned to diplomacy with the somewhat chastened Japanese. He negotiated a treaty known as the Tangku Truce. The terms were hazy but they seemed to recognize the Japanese occupation of Manchuria on condition that there was no further territorial aggression. At least that's what the Japanese took the truce to mean because they began exploiting coal and iron mines and building steel plants as though confident of permanent possession.

The Tangku Truce drew fresh outcries from Chinese liberals, intellectuals, and students. They had tasted blood and triumph at Shanghai and were unwilling to settle for appeasement, no matter what Chiang Kai-shek said about the country's unpreparedness. They scoffed at Chiang's claim that he would defend the national boundaries with the last drop of his blood. They charged that he was hiding behind a shabby legalism. Manchuria was as much a part of China as the eighteen provinces south of the Great Wall. Every patriot knew that Manchuria—along with Sinkiang, Tibet, and the Mongolias—had always been a component of the Middle Kingdom, and it was not to be bartered away.

Chiang reacted to the pressure by turning again to an old project—his campaign against the Communists. A believer in action—he once said "the only failure is in failure to act"—he hoped that by vigorous eradication of internal enemies he could silence his critics. He invented slogans to rally the country behind him: "First internal unity, then external defense" and "The Japanese are an affliction of the skin, the Communists a disease of the heart." And to insure harmony in the government he

Years of the Ram and the Rooster

invited Wang Ching-wei to sit in the presidential chair while he concentrated on exterminating Red bandits.

For Left-hand Wang, recuperated and having traveled extensively in Europe, was back in China. Moreover he was in Peiping, causing trouble. Denouncing Chiang Kai-shek as a traitor who had sold out the revolution, he was apparently trying to promote a separatist government of his own.

Chiang Kai-shek chose to forgive and forget all this when he invited Wang to become head of state in Nanking. Close disciples of Sun Yat-sen were always sacrosanct as far as Chiang was concerned. He might lecture or admonish them but would never punish. Needless to say the erratic Wang accepted the invitation with alacrity and Chiang Kai-shek was free to begin his Fourth Suppression Campaign against the Communists.

He set up headquarters in Wuhan in April 1933, the Year of the Rooster. He had marshaled four hundred thousand men for the attack and his German advisers had worked out a brand new strategy. Isolated Red bases, such as those in Hupei, Anhwei, and Hunan provinces, were assaulted first and overrun, their survivors escaping to join the main rebel forces in Kiangsi. Then, methodically, the pressure of the Kuomintang armies was brought to bear on the plains below Nanchang.

To the delight of Chiang and his German staff, the Communists chose to resist the advance in set battles, stoutly defending trenches and fortified points. It seems as if the Kuomintang was fighting a different enemy, as indeed it was. Po Ku and the Twenty-eight Bolsheviks had been working effectively for over a year to knock guerrilla nonsense out of rebel heads. But they hadn't succeeded entirely. As the Kuomintang advance continued, exacting severe casualties, alarm set in among the Red field commanders. Mao Tse-tung was out of it, off the Military Council, and retired to piddling administrative duties, so he could no longer be appealed to for advice and strategy. But memories of the past revived in the able military minds of Chu Teh and such colleagues as Lin Piao of the light foot, who had trained his men to travel at a brisk trot all day, and the doughty Liu Po-cheng, the specialist in the hammer blow delivered from nowhere.

These men conspired together, ignoring doctrinaire directives from headquarters, to devise their own strategic plans. And they turned the tide of battle. The despised guerrilla tactics played havoc with Kuomintang forces grown careless by success, and inflicted what Mao Tse-tung was later to call "the most disastrous of [Chiang's] 'extermination campaigns'," and which Chiang himself confessed to be "the greatest humiliation" of his life.

During the final stages of the Fourth Campaign, with his division disappearing in enveloping Red tides, Chiang Kai-shek had ordered the 19th Route Army, conveniently located in Fukien Province, to attack the Communists from the east. Apparently he was unaware of what had been happening to Tsai Ting-kai and his heroes of Shanghai in the eighteen months since their historic resistance to the Japanese. Resentment, shared by officers and men, had swept the ranks; resentment at shabby treatment, at their banishment to the "sticks" which seemed more a punishment than a reward for duty courageously performed.

The mood of discontent had been exacerbated by contact with the Communists in neighboring Kiangsi Province. Few of the soldiers in the 19th Route Army had Communist sympathies, but many admired the stand the Reds had taken against the Kuomintang. And when Chiang Kai-shek ordered the attack on the Red bases, Tsai Ting-kai and his men decided that the time had come to make a stand themselves. They mutinied against the Nationalist government and declared an independent People's Republic of Fukien.

Chiang reacted quickly. He sent forces to attack the 19th Route Army by sea and also drove a column down the Fukien-Kiangsi border to cut off retreat into the interior. Tsai Ting-kai's rebellion was soon crushed, and Chiang found that another advantage had also accrued. Unexpectedly he had seized the Reds' eastern flank, holding a half-circle around their richest soviets, including their capital at Juichin. He rapidly capitalized on the situation. With the remnants of his Fourth Campaign armies, he rushed another column around the western edge of Kiangsi Province, completing the encirclement.

He now had his elusive enemies in a vise. He could tighten it slowly, squeezing them into the middle for slaughter; or he could starve them into submission if slaughter proved too expensive. Just to make sure there were no loopholes, he continually reinforced his perimeter. Eventually a million Kuomintang troops guarded the ring.

And so Chiang Kai-shek's Fifth Extermination Campaign began almost without pause as the Fourth ended. Inside the trap, Po Ku and his Bolshevik hardliners were undismayed by their predicament. In fact, confidence reigned. Opposing overwhelming odds offered a glorious opportunity to demonstrate Marxist invincibility. Slogans were advanced: "Pit one against ten, pit ten against a hundred—don't give up an inch of ground!" The Red army totaled only some two hundred thousand men, but it was supposed to beat off five times that number and counterattack victoriously.

Only Mao Tse-tung seems to have had grave doubts. "It was a serious mistake to meet the vastly superior Nanking forces in positional warfare," he was to say later. He probably said it then too—and repeatedly—but nobody was listening.

Even then, at the very nadir of his career, Mao Tse-tung was not entirely without official position. He had been elected chairman of the ill-fated Soviet Republic at its formation in November 1931, a title so meaningless to the Twenty-eight Bolsheviks who controlled all the machinery of government that he was permitted to keep it. So chairman of the shadowy regime he remained while stripped of all other influential posts—his seat on the Political Council, on the Military Council, and, for the third and last time, on the Central Committee—even the provincial branch.

It was as chairman of the Soviet Republic that Mao declared war on Japan during the attack on Shanghai in 1932. That was largely a symbolic gesture, but in December 1933 Mao tried to make realistic use of his office to gain allies for the hard-pressed soviets. When the 19th Route Army mutinied against Chiang Kai-shek, Mao proposed an alliance with Tsai Ting-kai that would have ranged seasoned troops on the Communist side. But the proposal was squelched. Po Ku would have nothing to do with a bourgeois militarist and Wang Ming wired from Moscow, "I'll shake [Tsai's] hand only if I can spit into his face."

To remove Mao Tse-tung from further political meddling, Po Ku sent him to the countryside to organize food supplies and recruit for the Red army. Mao soon found these objectives contradictory. Growing additional food required extra men, which recruiting drained off. He wrote pamphlets urging a balance between the needs of war and agriculture, but little attention was paid to his ideas. Po Ku was calling for an army of a million men to match Chiang's numbers, and where the food came from to feed them was beside the point.

By midsummer of 1934 a good deal else was beside the point. The situation was deteriorating and calls to arms and pamphlets on food production were of no immediate concern. Chiang Kai-shek's noose was pulling tighter, choking off rich farmlands and destroying the entrenched Reds who were trying to save them.

Chiang's German advisers had come into their own. They were finally fighting a war they understood. The parallels between the trenches of Kiangsi and the European holocaust of 1914–18 were too obvious to be missed. Tanks had proved the decisive weapon of World War I. Chiang Kai-shek had few tanks so the Germans improvised substitutes. They built concrete blockhouses at every advance, protecting the builders with strafing planes acquired on foreign loans. The blockhouses, impervious to Red machineguns and hand grenades, moved forward in thousands, slowly closing the ring around Communist territory.

Po Ku and his Bolshevik associates remained remarkably unperturbed by the tightening vise. They continued to formulate plans for ever stiffer Marxist resistance, supported in their strategy by their own foreign adviser—by coincidence another German, one Otto Braun.

Otto Braun's qualifications as a military expert were open to question. Prior to joining the Comintern, he had been a schoolteacher and journalist, though he had attended a course on infantry training in Moscow before his dispatch to China. He arrived in Kiangsi in 1933, smuggled in under a load of hay, to begin advising on martial matters with all the aplomb of a seasoned veteran. Otto Braun—his name was soon Sinocized to

Li Teh*—spoke no Chinese so his instructions had to filter through the interpretation of Po Ku, probably an arrangement satisfactory to both.

By August even the leadership began to realize that the situation was getting critical. The Kiangsi republic had shrunk to six counties and its population had been reduced to two million. Every day more men died uselessly and more villages fell to the Kuomintang. But Po Ku and Otto Braun, caught in a strategy of disaster, seemed unable to change it.

Mao Tse-tung, despite the gags imposed on him, found ways to make his views on the deteriorating situation known. He recommended relieving the pressures of encirclement by breaking through the ring at selected points in order to attack the Nationalist troops in the rear.

Breakthroughs were possible if planned with effective force and surprise. That had been proved earlier in the summer by a quixotic commander called Fang Chih-min. Fang had conceived the notion of leading an expedition into the North, rallying populations into a great crusade against the Japanese, and marching them on to Manchuria. He hoped thus to expose Chiang Kai-shek as a cowardly promoter of internal strife when the true enemy was Nipponese aggression. Fang had succeeded in penetrating the blockading ring, though afterward his small contingent had been overtaken by Kuomintang troops and Fang himself had been exhibited in a bamboo cage before being executed.

Mao Tse-tung's call for a new strategy in the critical situation of August was soon silenced. He was denounced as an "adventurist" and "military ignoramus" and was confined to house arrest in a village near Juichin. He was ill with malaria at the time, adding depression of body to mind. The wonder is the stoicism with which he held up. He still had friends in government. He might well have tried to stage a revolt, to seize power on the grounds of dire necessity. But apparently nothing of the sort occurred to him. He believed in centralized authority and party

---

*If this seems a distortion, consider what the West has done to the perfectly good Chinese name of Kung Fu-tze by translating it as Confucius.

discipline as much as anyone, and regretted only that incorrect policies presently prevailed. He was confident that circumstances and time, if there was time, must force a change. With incredible patience—"looking upon the interests of the revolution as his very life" as he was to say—he was willing to wait.

Sometime in late September Chou En-lai and Chu Teh called on Mao Tse-tung in his isolated, guarded village. Chou En-lai was still little more than an acquaintance, but there might have been embarassment on Chu Teh's part at seeing again a comrade with whom he had once worked like a brother and had for so long neglected.

The visitors brought news and wanted to know Mao's reaction. A breakout had been decided upon after all—not for the purpose of strategic maneuvering as Mao had advised, but to quit the country altogether, to move the Soviet Republic, lock, stock, and personnel out of Kiangsi and seek a new home elsewhere.

Mao Tse-tung agreed that under the circumstances it was probably a wise decision. There was still time to make careful preparations; in his view a retreat always called for as much logistic planning as an advance. Food supplies were low—rations were already down to twelve ounces of rice per person per day—and water was scarce owing to a dry summer, but there should be enough to hold out for three months while the military offensive was prepared.

Mao was told that there was to be no such luxury of time. The decision had been made to move in three weeks. Which brought up another matter: would Mao consent to serve again on the Military Council? Votes had been pledged to reseat him; a majority of members were looking back with nostalgia to the days of successfull guerrilla warfare.

Mao consented and was swept into the frantic preparations for departure. First there was the question of who should go. It was decided to limit the exodus to effective males except for the wives of higher officials. All other women, and the aged, infirm, and children were to be left behind. The announcement was stoically received, its necessity understood, and the heartbreaking farewells began. Families and clans were torn apart; wives, lovers, children, parents, and grandparents were separated, never to be united again.

Mao Tse-tung had been remarried in 1931 to a cadre worker called Ho Tzu-chen. His wife was to go with him, but not their children. The infants were left in the care of Mao's brother Tse-tan, who had volunteered to remain behind to help sustain the morale of the abandoned community. Mao Tse-tan's fate is known: he was executed when the landlords came back, protected by the bayonets of the Kuomintang. But the children disappeared without trace despite strenuous efforts to find them in later years when Mao Tse-tung's power extended to every corner of China. Mao's historic immunity to death was certainly not transferable to his immediate family. His other brother, Tse-min, was to die in revolutionary action in Outer Mongolia, and a son by his second wife, Yang Kai-hui, the professor's daughter, was killed in Korea, fighting against American forces in the 1950's. Yang Kai-hui herself had been executed in a Kuomintang pogrom in 1930.

The question never asked, or at least never answered, was *where* the soviet state and population were headed. Rumors circulated that they were on their way to complete Fang Chih-min's mission to fight the Japanese in Manchuria. But in the main, the prospect of getting away from Chiang Kai-shek's strafing planes, the sound of his artillery, and the sight of their own Red wounded straggling back in ever increasing numbers from the battlefronts was objective enough for movement. In an almost holiday spirit, the people packed their possessions. Everything that might be useful in establishing a new base was taken: spinning wheels, sewing machines, printing presses, even iron forges were slung on backs or loaded on donkeys and water buffaloes. Destination became unimportant in the excitement of getting away. In good time the leadership would tell them where they were going—if it knew.

The advance troops left base on October 16, 1934. Attacking at night in the southern sector of Chiang Kai-shek's perimeter, they blew up blockhouses, overran trenches, and cut their way through a maze of barbed wire, opening a breach five miles wide. Within two days the main body of the expedition poured through, a hundred thousand of them, including thirty-five women, each carrying a three-days' supply of rice and all the clothes they could crowd on their bodies. They tramped through the gap littered with torn wire and concrete rubble and kept on tramping. The Long March had begun.

14

Flight of the Hundred Thousand

THERE IS NO REAL HISTORIC PARALLEL TO THE LONG March, the Chinese *Chang Cheng*. Attempts have been made to compare it to the biblical exodus from Egypt, to Hannibal's crossing of the Alps, and to Napoleon's retreat from Moscow. But the resemblances are either superficial or misleading. Moses and his followers had divine intervention working for them, which more or less guaranteed arrival at their promised land. Hannibal, a canny general going after the Romans by an unexpected route, was unopposed on his Alpine crossing except by the elements, and suffering was mainly confined to elephants nipped by frostbite. Napoleon's retreat comes closer; its theme too was endurance and survival. But the outcome was predictable from the start and nothing could have happened to avert disaster. Whereas the Long March, though it began in confusion and never stopped being a rout, ended on a paradoxical note of triumph.

Perhaps the nearest equivalent is the Anabasis, Xenophon's victorious march with ten thousand Greek mercenaries from

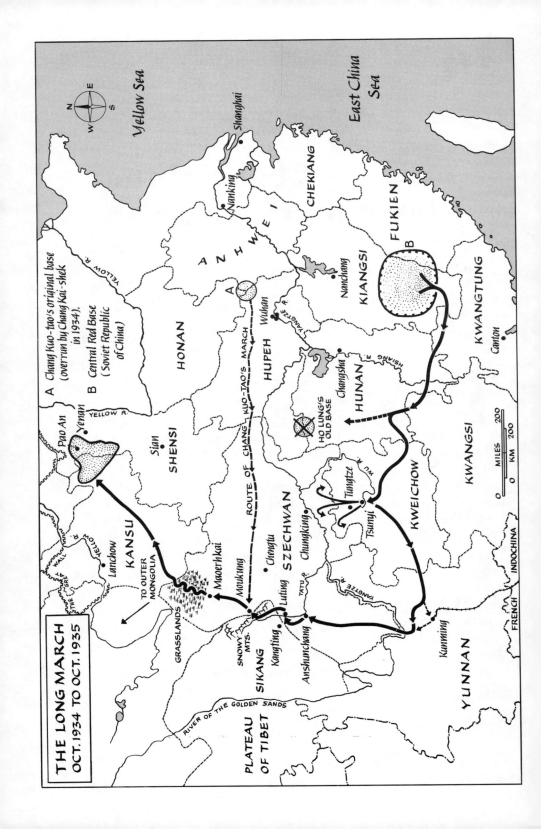

Flight of the Hundred Thousand

entrapment in Persia to the Aegean Sea, fighting off attackers every step of the way. But the scale was so small, the perils encountered and the feats of heroism performed were so routine compared with the Chinese experience, that the parallel breaks down.

Before the Long March was over, the survivors of the original hundred thousand refugees had trudged better than six thousand miles, or more than twice the breadth of the United States. They had crossed eighteen mountain ranges and twenty-four rivers, passing through ten provinces of China Proper with a detour through Tibet. They had taken by assault and abandoned sixty-two towns and cities and had fought their way past the armies of ten provincial warlords, not counting the pursuing and blockading Nationalist troops of Chiang Kai-shek—enemies totaling a million men in all. And they did all this and established a new base in the far Northwest as well in exactly one year and four days. It was the epic feat of the revolution.

The impetus of the first breakout, the surge through Chiang Kai-shek's perimeter in southern Kiangsi in mid-October 1934, propelled the expedition into Kwangtung Province, and it was a couple of days before order could be enforced and a route of march established. Columns were formed—fighting men on the flanks, and also acting as advance and rear guards—with officials, civilians, women, porters, and beasts of burden occupying the center. The motley caravan began moving in a westerly direction. Word was passed down the lines that they were headed for an encampment some two hundred miles away in Hunan Province. The destination made sense. A Red commander called Ho Lung had once occupied a flourishing base on the Hunan-Hupeh border and, though it was known he had been driven out during Chiang Kai-shek's Fourth Campaign, it was thought he had left guerrillas in the area who might combine with the marchers to establish a safe place of refuge.

To speed progress, the long columns traveled day and night, with rest halts to cook meals and catch naps. The exhilaration of that first leg of the journey before the reality of the Kuomintang pursuit caught up, lingered long in the recollections of veterans. There was a camaraderie and sense of adventure which expressed itself in constant singing, especially the refrain of the hour:

> The Red army fears not death;
> Who fears death is not a Red Army man...

At night the travelers lit torches fashioned from pine branches or frayed bamboo. The effect of the lighted procession was remembered as being like a fiery dragon coiling up the hills and down the farther slopes. The sight stimulated spirits and buoyed up hopes and inspired voices lifted in chants that rolled and echoed over the sleeping countryside.

Then the Kuomintang planes appeared; at first solo flights, picking up the target and gauging the direction of the march, but soon enough plummeting fighters strafed the road. Singing and exaltation ceased as wild dashes were made for the ditches. The wounded were a burden to be carried on litters, the dead often went unburied.

Chiang Kai-shek's ground troops were first encountered in strength at the Hsiang River. They were waiting, entrenched, guarding the fordable shallows. The alternatives were to search for another crossing or push straight in on the attack. Po Ku and Otto Braun, their Bolshevik ardor undiminished, ordered the head-on attack. The battle continued for the week it took the expedition to cross. The Red Army sustained thirty thousand casualties in dead and wounded. The dead were lucky. There were no longer enough living men to carry so many wounded and they had to be left behind.

The trek continued, headed up the highway in a direct line for Ho Lung's old base. There was no attempt at camouflage or deceptive maneuvering so that, even though the columns moved now only at night, Chiang's strafing planes had no trouble picking them up again the next morning. The singing, what was left of it, took an understandably sour turn. A new refrain had become a favorite:

> Today we walk and tomorrow we walk,
> And where do we walk to?

Flight of the Hundred Thousand

Certainly no longer toward Ho Lung's old base in Hunan. Chiang Kai-shek had guessed that destination and cut it off by massing troops in such numbers that even Po Ku and Otto Braun quailed at head-on battle. The columns veered to the west and kept marching, but without objective, with nowhere to go, the leadership bewildered and lost.

Battles continued to be fought on an almost daily basis at towns so small they are omitted from maps—Shen Yuan, Shih Ping, Huang Ping. These places had to be taken for food supplies. Sewing machines, donkeys, water buffaloes, and printing presses had long since been bartered for rice, and the Red army was reduced to feeding off the land. But it turned necessity to good account. Supplies plundered from the official yamens and landlords' storehouses were shared with the poor of the community. It was a quick lesson in socialist distribution and the Reds made full use of it in propagandizing their aims and programs.

During December the columns drifted north and west through Kweichow Province, living from hand to mouth, the mouths reduced 50 percent by death, disease, and desertions since the breakout in Kiangsi two and a half months before. In early January the expedition reached the river Wu, a fast-flowing tributary of the Yangtze, channeled deep between precipitous banks. Across it lay the market town of Tsunyi, of vital importance to an exhausted and hungry army.

For once Po Ku and Otto Braun were cautious. They had become sensitive to charges that they were butchers of men, so they advocated a roundabout approach to taking the town; perhaps there were easier crossings up or downriver. And for once—though opposition had been growing—the Military Council overruled them. The troops were too spent for delay, Mao Tse-tung said; Tsunyi had to be taken as quickly as possible.

A new imagination appeared in the strategy employed as Mao Tse-tung and Chu Teh began to work harmoniously together again. The assault on the town began at dusk. The attention of the defenders was distracted by attempts to seize the ferry while, under cover of the bluff, daredevil squads crossed the river on bamboo rafts, scaled the heights beyond, and subdued the garrison. For three days the soldiers feasted, rested, and hobnobbed with the citizenry while their leaders retired to parley. The compound where they met, the home of a minor warlord, is now a famous mecca for tourists and pilgrims. For at the Tsunyi Conference, held from January 6 to 8, 1935, events occurred that marked a new beginning for the Long March and elevated Mao Tse-tung to a position of authority he was never again to relinquish.

There was much to be discussed and reexamined at that critical meeting. The strategy of the disastrous Fifth Campaign was exhumed and worked over. Why had successful guerrilla tactics been abandoned for rigid positional warfare with its enormous cost in men? And since the breakout, why had there been nothing but head-on battles, decimating the Red army, feeding it piecemeal into Chiang Kai-shek's military machine? Commanders were angry at the destruction of their troops. So were civilian officials, though their anger was directed against Po Ku's increasingly dictatorial attitude as he sought by arrogance to escape criticism.

Po Ku, backed up by Otto Braun and other faithfuls, remained impervious to the blasts released against him. He claimed that he had been following Stalin's policies and censured his opponents for an insubordination that amounted to disloyalty to the Comintern and Kremlin. But the old shibboleths failed to work. Survival was more important to a majority of the comrades than ideological authority and, for the first time, Chinese Communists showed a willingness to make their own decisions, irrespective of what Moscow might think.

What came through chiefly from the raised voices and the heated arguments was an attitude toward Mao Tse-tung. From being denigrated and pushed aside, he was at last recognized by many as the man who had been right all along while the leadership stumbled from blunder to blunder. If he had been in charge during the Fifth Campaign there might have been a very different outcome. Of course, that was now past history, but there still was time to correct errors and misjudgments. Chou En-lai proposed forming a new Revolutionary Military Council with Mao as its chairman, and the resolution was carried.

Back in power, Mao Tse-tung called a meeting of all political and military cadres in the Tsunyi Catholic Church, the largest auditorium in town. He announced a program for the future march; it was to be turned into a crusade, educating and propagandizing the masses to prepare them for a people's government at some distant date. He also announced a destination for the marchers; they were going to the Northwest to build a new base, to regenerate strength and fight the Japanese.

The news was electric, stirring national patriotism, revitalizing spirits. Memories were revived of the old days when Red guerrillas ran provincial troops ragged and ground the Kuomintang to mincemeat. It could happen again, now that Mao Tse-tung was back in charge. The "spirit of Tsunyi," as it was called, proved infectious. The townspeople caught it and four thousand youths were recruited into the Red army.

There were twelve more days of work and excitement. The troops were reorganized; the long unwieldy columns were replaced by fast-acting combat squads. Saluting disappeared; officers and men put their heads together to remember tactics of surprise and deception. Chu Teh, back in his element, moved about tirelessly, praising, admonishing, exhorting. Finally the army was ready to move out. The Long March resumed—with a difference.

Chiang Kai-shek had moved his headquarters to Kunming, capital of Yunnan Province, to supervise the pursuit of the fleeing Reds. He had been furious when the rebel army had escaped from his Kiangsi trap in October. But as the situation developed, he decided that it was the best thing that could have happened. Once on the march, the Red bandits had no place to hide. He had already drubbed them unmercifully by air assaults and pitched battles and, as things were shaping up, he would eliminate them completely in a final series of encounters along the upper Yangtze River.

For as Chiang saw it, the Communists were headed straight upcountry to Outer Mongolia. It was an enormous journey of over a thousand miles, but where else could they be going? They could hardly hope to establish a base and settle down short of that goal, not with the Kuomintang armies in hot pursuit. So Outer Mongolia it had to be, perhaps with the expectation of linking up with Russian forces who had pushed their way to power in that region.

Another evidence of destination was the Reds' route of march—steadily northwest since leaving Kiangsi. Chiang had been somewhat puzzled by the reckless advance, always in straight lines, always along main roads where they were vulnerable to attack. The rigid dispositions were so different from earlier Communist methods, when cunning and deceptive tactics had caused serious problems, that Chiang wondered what had infected the Red high command. His German advisers supplied an answer: Communists were peasants and peasants were stupid. Guerrilla successes had gone to their heads and now they were trying to prove themselves real soldiers regardless of consequences. Chiang wasn't so sure. He had little regard for peasants, but Chu Teh, Chou En-lai, and some of the other commanders who had trained under him at Whampoa, were men to be respected. What had happened to change them?

The question, though, was academic. For whatever reasons, the rebels were steadily blundering north into a trap Chiang was preparing for them. At some point they had to cross the Yangtze River and Chiang was rushing into place a quarter of a million troops on a hundred-mile front to act as a reception committee.

Chiang knew exactly when the first Red contingents left Tsunyi. His intelligence was excellent; his elite armies were all equipped with the latest American field radios. As expected, the Communist movement was north. Red advance guards showed up at the Yangtze within a few days, noted the Kuomintang defensive arrangements, and fell back.

The Red probes continued for a month and then into a second month. Troops appeared along the hundred-mile front below Chungking, tested the defense with a flurry of shots, then disappeared again. It was borne in on Chiang and his staff that the Red bandits had lost their daring, that they were confused and disorganized on how to penetrate the blockade and cross the river that must be crossed.

It was too good an opportunity to be missed. Chiang ordered a sortie in strength—an advance on Tsunyi while the rebels were still torn by indecision. The advance got as far as a town called

Flight of the Hundred Thousand

Tungtze, located deep in a valley, before the Reds closed in from all sides. Twenty regiments were destroyed before the Nationalist troops extracted themselves.

In March there was even more exasperating news. The main body of the Communist army had left Tsunyi and was traveling south and west. But why in that direction unless—and it must have come as a shock—unless it meant to attack Chiang's headquarters at Kunming? Just in case, he ordered the city's defenses prepared, though there was no hurry about it; it would take at least a week for the Reds to appear. But in three days, there they were, outside the walls, lobbing in mortar shells.

Hurriedly Chiang Kai-shek and his wife (Madame had come along to share the excitement of Red hunting) were loaded on a train of the narrow-gauge railway that connected with Hanoi in Indo-China. Next day Chiang was informed—radio communications remained excellent—that the attackers had been driven off. They turned out to be only a small detachment, an advance unit of some kind that had been putting on a feint. Nobody would have believed that the fleet-footed corps under Lin Piao had literally run 125 miles in three days.

Chiang hurried back to Kunming. He learned that the main body of the Red army had been spotted to the west and had been tracked until it disappeared into the mountains. Where it was going, nobody knew.

But suddenly Chiang Kai-shek knew. It was an incredible idea but he acted on it. He ordered his troops blockading the Yangtze to hurry west as fast as possible. But their progress was slow. They were afraid to take chances after what had happened at Tungtze and moved cautiously, alert for ambushes.

Impatient, Chiang took a plane to scout the area for himself. But when he looked down on the upper reaches of the Yangtze—known in that region as the River of the Golden Sands—he was already too late. Thirty thousand Reds had crossed the river they had to cross and had disappeared into the forests on the other side.

Mao Tse-tung and his men had entered western Szechwan, a fringe territory claimed from time immemorial by China's rulers but rarely encroached upon by Chinese citizens. It was a heavily wooded jungle inhabited by the Yi tribe, a semiprimitive people noted for tall stature.

The Communists found the agricultural clearings and dwellings deserted, their owners having fled in fright. But friendly gestures and proffered gifts coaxed them out of hiding. They wore strange clothes and many carried gaudy feathered fowls. The soldiers' hopes for chicken dinners were to be disappointed, however; the birds were gamecocks, prized for fighting qualities in the ring. But presumably hens and eggs went with the cocks, because the Long Marchers carried away happy memories of travel through the Yi country.

Mao Tse-tung was particularly taken by the grave and courteous people, and they may have helped influence his ideas on minorities. He took pains in his future governments to curb Han chauvinism, an expression of the Chinese sense of cultural superiority, and stress the equality of all races on a human level. He was delighted when two hundred Yi youths volunteered to join the Red army, accepting them as symbols of ethnic unity.

The next hazard on the line of march was the crossing of the Tatu River, a tributary of the Yangtze. The river itself was not as threatening as the legends that surrounded it. For it was at the Tatu that the heroes of the *Three Kingdoms*, a venerated romance of ancient China, had met defeat. Also, in more recent times, it was there that the Taiping Heavenly Kingdom had finally flickered out in 1864. Shih Ta-kai, the Errant Prince of that rebellion, had led a crusade of a hundred thousand believers to spread the light in the West, but at the Tatu his relentless enemy Tseng Kuo-fan had caught up with him for an orgy of slaughter.

Both sides were aware of the historic omens and precedents. Chiang Kai-shek, who had recovered from his disappointment at the Yangtze crossing and was now in hot pursuit again, swore that he would drown the Red bandits in the Tatu as his idol Tseng Kuo-fan had the Taipings. Mao Tse-tung tried to alleviate the fears of his troops by promising that this time it would be different. They were, after all, Communists, and it was the business of communism to change history.

The Reds, traveling swiftly, reached the river opposite the

Flight of the Hundred Thousand

town of Anshunchang and ran into unexpected luck. Chiang Kai-shek had ordered all boats cleared from the south bank, but plain as day a fifty-passenger ferry was tied up at the nearside dock. The commander of the Anshunchang garrison, not dreaming that the Communists could be anywhere close, had ambled over to the south bank to feast with friends.

The ferry was quietly captured without exciting notice across the river, and Red soldiers dressed in Kuomintang uniforms plied back to the opposite shore. The subsequent surprise attack under the leadership of Lin Piao kept the garrison busy until reinforcements could be ferried over to take the town.

Then bad luck intervened. Heavy rains turned the river into a torrent, making traffic across increasingly difficult. Fewer than five thousand troops had negotiated the passage by the end of three days.

The lapse of time was ominous. The Errant Prince of the Taipings had also tarried for three days—in his case to celebrate the birth of a son—and the delay had given the imperial troops time to catch up with him. Mao Tse-tung decided not to tempt a repetition of history. He had heard of a bridge ninety miles upstream and elected to take the risk that it had not yet been destroyed.

The Red forces, dangerously split on opposite banks, began making their way north together. For a while Lin Piao's smaller contingent was visible from the west bank and the men shouted greetings and slogans across the water. Then the forests began and contact was lost.

Mao Tse-tung's troops arrived at the bridge at four o'clock one afternoon. Opposite them was the village to which the bridge had given its name—Luting, or "the bridge built by Lu," recalling some entrepreneur of the past who had seen an opportunity for turning a profit in tolls. The river was deep below its banks here, fully two hundred feet down and roaring in its channel. The bridge, a suspension affair, spanned the chasm—thirteen iron chains anchored in concrete, with planks serving as a roadbed. Only there were no planks when the Red army arrived except for a few on the farther side. They had been stripped off, leaving only the dangling chains. Chiang Kai-shek had ordered the chains cut, but the local authorities, ever considerate of private property, had judged it unnecessary. A force of provincial troops, dug in behind sandbags on the village side, made crossing impossible.

Mao Tse-tung and his commanders conferred on what to do. Reason dictated waiting for Lin Piao's contingent to catch up on the opposite bank to clean out the defenders. But who knew how long the wait might be? What if Lin Piao had run into opposition and was under attack? And what about Chiang Kai-shek's armies pursuing from the south? How long before they appeared to trap the main Red force between the forests and the river?

It was decided to force the crossing by "revolutionary" means. Volunteers were called for. Twenty-two stepped forward and the attempt began. The men jumped for the chains and, swinging hand over hand, propelled themselves across the chasm that yawned below. Their comrades tried to cover them with machine-gun fire across the gorge, but the defenders, well protected, concentrated on the swinging targets. One after another they went down. Bodies, wrenched from the chains, twisted and turned as they fell, their last cries lost in the roaring flood waters. Seventeen of the original twenty-two perished.

They were soon replaced. No more calls for volunteers were issued, but none was needed. Men rushed forward spontaneously to hurl themselves at the chains. They struggled to be next in line, urging those ahead to get a move on. Soon all thirteen chains were pulsing wildly from hands that clung and hands that weakened and let go.

Survivors of the Long March forever remembered the hysteria of those hours. The bank swarmed with men screaming their anger across the gorge. The defenders of the bridge shooting down their comrades had ceased to be simple peasants like themselves. They had become the embodiments of Chiang Kai-shek and the tyrants of the Kuomintang—or more likely, of former landlords, tax collectors, and usurers. The bitterness of two thousand years, the pent-up rage at beatings, cheatings, and hypocrisy found expression. And on the chains, the same hatred drove on the crazed men, narcotized to fear. The crossing of the Tatu River had long stopped being a military feat. It was an epiphany of vengeance.

The vanguard of the swinging lines reached the remaining planks at the village end and heaved up. The defenders, in a panic now, terrified by the specters that should have been corpses, tried to ward them off by throwing lighted kerosene on the boards. It was a futile gesture. The fires were doused by men flinging themselves on the flames. Their comrades hurled grenades over the sandbags, rocking the revetments. The defenders struggled to escape. Few succeeded.

The planks were replaced, the bridge was put back in commission. The Red army poured across singing. At the very end, the rearguard tangled with Kuomintang patrols arriving on the scene, then skipped across the bridge, lifting the planks as they went.

Next day the Communist forces were reunited, Lin Piao's contingent arriving without incident, and a memorial meeting was held to honor the dead. Chu Teh said in commemoration: "Heroism is an ancient concept. In the past, individual heroes ... arose among the masses [but] we create mass heroes of the revolution who ... are willing to die ... or live and fight until our people and country are liberated."

The men rested after battle, watching Kuomintang reconnaissance planes circling high overhead. The Red soldiers, imagining Chiang Kai-shek in each plane, shook their fists and yelled derision.

Chiang Kai-shek wasn't to be counted out yet. He had been frustrated again at the Tatu River but there was still a long way to go, with many opportunities left to engulf and annihilate the Red bandits. Anticipating their continued route of march to the north, he flooded western Szechwan Province with elite troops and moved his headquarters to its capital, Chengtu.

Chiang's preparations forced a critical decision on Mao Tsetung and his Military Council. A path had to be found around the Nationalist blockade, and the only way open was to leave China and find a passage across Sikang, a dependency of Tibet. It was terra incognita. Nothing was known of the area except its reputation for rugged mountains, inhospitable people, and a perpetual atmosphere of chill. But there was no alternative to attempting the route, and so the Long March entered a new and more difficult phase, where military tactics and correct ideology became irrelevant and heroism in battle gave place to sheer endurance.

It was late May and in the flatlands the weather was balmy, but on the high plateau of the Himalayas winter's grip never let up. The Red population clambered up what they were to immortalize as the Snowy Mountains—soldiers, officials, civilians, pack animals, and the surviving corps of women. Storms whipped around them. They sank in snow and slipped on ice as they negotiated the 16,000-foot passes. Most of the people had been born and raised in steamy South China and had never encountered such cold before. They were without the clothes to fend it off or the food to sustain inner heat. It was almost impossible to find fuel to cook meals, so food was eaten mostly raw. A gruel made from pounding rice kernels mixed with snow was the usual fare.

The misery went on for weeks. The cold affected minds, stirring strange aberrations. The guides became suspect; they were thought to be in collusion with the enemy—any enemy, Chiang Kai-shek or the Dalai Lama, it didn't matter. And attrition wore out bodies. By June, hundreds were falling in the snow never to get up again. The fortitude of many was remembered as they refused offers of help and urged their comrades on with revolutionary slogans. The marches by day were agonizing; breath came in gasps in that rarefied atmosphere. And nights were worse. There was no shelter. Snow was scraped away and the people huddled together in their cotton clothing trying to generate body warmth.

But somehow they survived. Or at least twenty thousand did, including a baby born during the worst of the going. In July the ragged cavalcade gratefully slithered down from what has been romantically called the Roof of the World into a northwest corner of Szechwan, the legions of the Kuomintang by-passed. At a town called Moukung a glad surprise awaited them: allies—fifty thousand Red troops under the command of Chang Kuo-tao.

Chang Kuo-tao and Mao Tse-tung were old acquaintances.

Flight of the Hundred Thousand

They had first met at the founding of the Chinese Communist Party in 1921 where they had begun to debate their differences. And they had continued to debate them ever since with growing heat. Chang Kuo-tao, a commanding personality of a somewhat rigid cast, had always adhered strictly to the Comintern line and considered Mao Tse-tung's unorthodoxy both undisciplined and dangerous.

After the Shanghai Massacre and the break-up with the Kuomintang, Chang Kuo-tao had established a revolutionary base at the junction of Honan, Hupei, and Anhwei provinces—elided with the Chinese love for contractions into the Oyuwan Base. He had been evicted during Chiang Kai-shek's Fourth Extermination Campaign but with considerable daring had marched the remnants of his army into Szechwan Province to found a new base and build strength again. Learning of the defeat of the Soviet Republic in Kiangsi and the subsequent trek to the north, Chang Kuo-tao had pulled up stakes and brought his troops west to join the emigrating Red government.

There was rejoicing in Moukung at the reunion. Chang Kuo-tao was congratulated on having anticipated the forced march through the Snowy Mountains and gauging the exact location at which the expedition must come out. Chang's fifty thousand troops, fresh and well equipped—some of the officers rode horses—were a welcome sight to Mao Tse-tung's bedraggled veterans. The combined forces were now of respectable size, capable of taking on the Kuomintang when next it struck.

But the harmony of reunion didn't last long. Soon quarreling broke out among the leaders. It seems incredible in that situation, with the enemy all around and survival depending on unity, that ideological scores had to be settled, but such was the case. Chang Kuo-tao was startled to learn of the changes made at the Tsunyi Conference in January. He was indignant to find that the discredited Mao Tse-tung had become chairman of the new Military Council, while Po Ku and Otto Braun, the Comintern's designates for leadership, had been reduced to ciphers. He refused to accept the decisions made at Tsunyi, claiming them illegal because the meeting had been called without the sanction of the Central Committee of which he was a charter member.

Further, he objected violently to the goal set for the Long March. The Northwest was a backwash and the notion of fighting the Japanese a utopian dream. He himself had a better solution. The combined forces must march west into Tibet to found a base impervious to Chiang Kai-shek's attacks. From that enclave they could expand slowly back into China, conquering the country.

The prospect of returning to the snow and ice of Tibet was anathema to most of Mao's group, but Chang had certified officials in his ranks and picked up further strength in Po Ku and other dissidents from Tsunyi. Besides he had an army that outnumbered the Long Marchers better than two to one, so matters had to be thrashed out.

The appearance of Kuomintang troops called a halt to debate. Rather, a suspension; for as Red forces fought off the Nationalist attacks, the leaders traveled farther north to a town called Maoerhkai to resume discussions.

At Maoerhkai Chang Kuo-tao surprisingly gave in—or appeared to. He agreed to the Northwest as a suitable destination and, in view of the critical military situation, urged an immediate departure. In the interests of amity, the Red armies were intermingled and split into two units—one under the command of the Tsunyi Military Council, the other under Chang Kuo-tao. For reasons never made entirely clear, Chu Teh was assigned to Chang's unit as commander-in-chief, with Chang acting as Chu's political commissar.

The troops moved out by different routes to split the pursuit, but with the intention of meeting again at the edge of the marshlands that lay ahead. Then something happened. The units lost contact, became irreparably separated. Chu Teh and Chang Kuo-tao's forces failed to show up at the designated rendezvous; in fact were never encountered again.

Once more party records are obscure on just what happened. Chang Kuo-tao later claimed a heavy Kuomintang attack had prevented the meeting. Chu Teh said a flooded river had caused him to turn back and had diverted his army off course. Mao Tse-tung always kept silent on the point, though he couldn't help but note that the reasons, whatever they were,

Flight of the Hundred Thousand

drove Chang Kuo-tao west into Tibet, the direction he had always wanted to go.

That at least was a fact. By the fall, Chang Kuo-tao and his army of thirty-five thousand men had moved west and south, reaching Kangting, capital of the Sikang dependency. There he established a regime he called the Szechwan-Sikang Base and Soviet of the National Minorities. He certainly seemed to be making his bid for leadership of the Red revolution, until events and circumstances brought him to grief.

But that was still in the future. Meanwhile in late August the second unit of the divided army under Mao Tse-tung and the Military Council began to cross the sink of China, known forever afterward to the Long Marchers as the Grasslands.

To many survivors of the epic journey, passage through the Grasslands was the worst leg of all. The bloody crossing of the Hsiang River, the terrifying hours at the Tatu, the misery in the Snowy Mountains, and the countless battles and hardships in between were only prelude. The Grasslands were bottomless pits, quicksand bogs, and nightmare mazes rolled into one. The area was a desolate swamp, stretching for scores of miles in every direction; a sump where water pouring off the ridge of Asia was collected and held as if by a giant sponge. In contrast, the swamps of the Nile were mudpuddles basking in a pleasant climate. Winds from the Himalayas screamed down over the Grasslands the year round, tormenting the landscape with chilling rains and hailstorms.

Even as the Red army started into the morass there was confusion. Word circulated that Chang Kuo-tao's contingent was headed west and his old retainers now attached to Mao's unit, not wanted to be separated from their comrades, revolted. Mao Tse-tung gave orders to let them go and twenty-two thousand departed. Mao was left with dangerously shrunken forces and the Grasslands were to take a further toll.

The men moved forward across the precarious footing. No marching here; it was every man for himself, feeling his way along the peninsulas that passed for terra firma—mats of organic matter built up through eons of rot. Grass of various kinds dominated the region. Sometimes it was short and meadowlike, more often it rose in canes above the soldiers' heads. Hacking a way through thickets, when the trail was lost, could be exhausting work.

Amazingly there were paths, though faint from scant traffic. Guides were necessary to steer the travelers along them and guides were hard to come by. The native population was sparse and primitive, living on roots and seeds and whatever rodents they could trap. Reclusion had turned them into fierce and bitter tribes, hostile to all outsiders. It was no use trying to make friends; the brotherhood of revolution had no relevance. Guides had to be caught and prodded forward at the point of bayonets. Resentment spread among the unseen denizens of the grass; Long Marchers who strayed from their groups were apt to be found later with their heads bludgeoned in.

Still, fear of the aborigines was second to fear of the mud. The mud wallowed all around, viscous, evil-smelling, waiting for missteps. It had a quicksand quality that sucked a victim down unless companions were prompt with ropes and poles. And once dunked, it was difficult to dry out again. The constant rain and absence of combustible wood defied fire-making. Pneumonia was a constant threat and chief cause of death.

Shelter at night was easier than it had been in the Snowy Mountains because canes could be cut to provide crude shacks. But food, the nemesis of the entire journey, continued a major problem. The travelers learned from their guides what roots and seeds were edible and consumed them raw. Many digestive systems, including that of Mao Tse-tung, were wrecked for years to come.

Finally the ordeal ended. The canebrakes thinned, the ground grew firmer under foot. In late September the Red army broke out into the steppes of Kansu Province. It was out in the open again, exposed to attack by Kuomintang forces drawn up and waiting for it.

Chiang Kai-shek had followed his enemy's progress through the Grasslands from observation planes and had prepared a hot reception. But he had miscalculated on one point. Still convinced that the Reds' objective was Outer Mongolia, he had massed his

Flight of the Hundred Thousand

best divisions against the Great Wall in order to block them off. Perhaps that error in judgment, and only that, saved Mao Tse-tung's forces from annihilation when almost in sight of their goal. Coming out of the swamp, they continued to march east instead of wheeling north as Chiang had anticipated, and so found only provincial troops obstructing their passage.

There was still a month of hard fighting ahead. The Red army, battered and wasted, had to contend with tough Moslem cavalrymen, descendants of invading hordes that had swept down on the Middle Kingdom centuries before. But the Long Marchers were not to be denied. They fought as they had to and died as they might, but they broke through—and incidentally captured hundreds of horses to carry their sick and wounded.

On October 7 they came in view of the loess hills of Shensi Province, built of soil blown down since time immemorial from the Gobi Desert. And they saw to their left the Great Wall of China, climbing and coiling over summits and valleys. It was an inspiring sight. Mao Tse-tung wrote a poem about it. But even more inspiring must have been the sight of five thousand Red troops under the command of Lui Chih-tan appearing over the horizon to greet them.

For it was at Liu Chih-tan's base that the Long March had been aimed. Liu's soviet, like all the others, had been established after the split with the Kuomintang in 1927, and for eight years he had defended it against warlord attacks. He had been lucky in his location. Because of its remoteness, the Shensi base had escaped Chiang Kai-shek's attention during his five extermination campaigns. So it had endured, an oupost of Red power, when all the others had collapsed, able now to offer refuge to a homeless government and army.

Liu Chih-tan guided Mao Tse-tung and his weary men through the treeless hills of his territory to the villages prepared to receive them. They arrived at twilight and one veteran vividly recalled the scene‘ "Suddenly there was the sound of gongs and drums and timbrels [and] a crowd to welcome us . . . Like a small sea they came up in the darkness, crying: 'Welcome, welcome . . . . Long live the Chinese Communist Party.' We wept."

That was on October 20, 1935—one year and four days after

the break-out in Kiangsi and the start of the 6,000 mile march. Of the original 100,000 men, some 7,000 finished the journey. The women fared better, 30 out of 35 surviving.

But numbers only begin to tell the story. What really survived was a commitment, a dedication to a purpose and a faith. The Long March was a liberation. It broke through both geographical and psychological barriers, freeing minds from age-old restrictions of village and district, opening up the vastness of a nation and a heritage. It forged a new people who within two decades were to overthrow a system of ethics and government which had hardly budged in twenty centuries. It was the dividing line, the cleft between the B.C. and the A.D. of the revolution. All that happened afterward was to be interpreted in the light of that single miracle.

Mao Tse-tung expressed something of the kind when he said:

> Let us ask, has history ever known a long march to equal ours? No, never. The Long March is a manifesto. It has proclaimed to the world that the Red Army is an army of heroes, while . . . Chiang Kai-shek and his like are impotent. It has proclaimed their utter failure to encircle, pursue, obstruct and intercept us. . . . In a word . . . the Chinese Communist Party, its leadership, its cadres and its army, have shattered the traitor Chiang Kai-shek . . . .

Brave words; hyperbolic perhaps, but justified by the genuine achievement. Mao Tse-tung's pride is evident, as is his bitter hatred of Chiang Kai-shek. And he had every reason to loathe and fear the man who for a decade had never stopped trying to exterminate him and his movement. Yet within a year, when by an incredible twist of fate Chiang Kai-shek was rendered helpless, captured, and yielded up for vengeance, Mao Tse-tung did everything in his power to help save his life.

15

Eve of a Great Change

THE TERMINATION OF THE LONG MARCH LEFT CHIANG Kai-shek as frustrated as a rabbit hunter who has driven his quarry from cover and chased it across miles of country without a kill. Though the animal is peppered with shot, its vitals have been missed, and it has escaped to sanctuary. For Chiang, the hunter, the weary work of flushing it out in the open again for the *coup de grâce* still remained.

He lost no time in testing the Reds' defenses. Within a month of their disappearance into the Shensi hills, he sent in an attacking force of sixty thousand men in the hope of a quick dislodgment. But the narrow valleys ending in abrupt cul-de-sacs were made to order for guerrilla maneuvering, and Chiang was forced to call off the raid after heavy losses. It was going to take another major effort, another massing of arms and forces, to surround and crush the rebels. So Chiang retreated to the city of Sian, capital of Shensi Province, to begin preparations for his Sixth Extermination Campaign.

Meanwhile he had been giving thought to the rise of communism, to the social and economic conditions that permitted rebellion to flourish in a nation committed to stability and order. He wasn't blind to the inequities of the countryside. He knew from his own boyhood experience in Fenghua that landlords could press too greedily on peasants, causing unrest from which Marxist agitators could benefit. As early as 1932 he had stated publicly that the Communist problem was "seventy percent political . . . and only thirty percent military. . . ." But his Confucian code prevented direct intervention in the existing order of things. And since he couldn't materially help the peasants, he was reduced to schemes for changing the landlords' hearts. But how?

He returned to an old obsession—moral leadership. He had never forgotten the charisma of Sun Yat-sen. And another of his heroes, Tseng Kuo-fan, conqueror of the Taiping Heavenly Kingdom rebels in the previous century, had also exercised his personal prestige and moral authority to return the nation to righteousness. Chiang Kai-shek longed for a similar force of character for himself. But as his abstemious living and high-minded conduct had done little to change the behavior of his contemporaries, he looked for better results by other methods.

He decided to promote himself by a public relations campaign. He first seems to have experimented with the idea during the winter of 1931–32. That was when his unpopularity after failing to resist the Japanese in Manchuria had brought about his retirement to Fenghua. He had called together his most devoted followers, the graduates of the first four classes at Whampoa whom Chiang had personally trained, distinguished by the name I-Chi, or chosen. He proposed that this group organize a movement of a new kind, based on hard work, Spartan living, and exalted spiritual values. Its purpose would be to regenerate the nation.

The I-Chi undertook the project with enthusiasm. They adopted the slogan of "Nationalize, Militarize, Productivize" and the guiding principle of unquestioned obedience to the leader. Just which leader was left a little vague, since Chiang's Confucian modesty wouldn't permit direct promotion. But later the identity became clear with the rallying cry of "Support Chiang Kai-shek as China's Hitler!"

The founding members of the movement called themselves the *shih-san tai pao* or Thirteen Princes, a name taken from historic legend. But they were soon referred to by cynics—who saw in them imitations of various redshirts, blackshirts, and brownshirts—as Chiang Kai-shek's Blueshirts. They were especially unpopular in the Kuomintang because it was within the government itself that the Blueshirts logically began their purification campaign. Quarrels broke out, disruptions threatened, and Chiang Kai-shek was forced to call off attempts to regenerate his officials.

Possibly Chiang questioned if he was on the right promotional track, but the Blueshirts had no such doubts. They developed a new project: regenerating rural areas as Chiang's extermination campaigns cleared them of Communists. Chiang, probably feeling that the grounds here were safe, gave his consent, though he was to rue the decision. For the Blueshirts, searching for a program to compete with the evicted Reds, resurrected Sun Yat-sen's old principle of "equalization of the land," or national purchase and redistribution of "excess" holdings. They approached the matter cautiously, advocating as a first step only the reduction of rents and interest that had been authorized during the Northern Expedition of 1926. But even that was too much. Howls from landlords were immediate. The Blueshirt cadres were branded as socialists—"redder than the Reds"—and once more Chiang had to end well-meant reforms*.

It wasn't until 1934 that the dedicated I-Chi found successful employment for themselves. And that was due to an accident, a brainstorm born of an annoying incident. In February, Chiang Kai-shek, burdened by the cares of his Fifth Red Bandit Extermination Campaign, was riding in his car when he saw a boy of ten smoking a cigarette. The car was stopped, the boy admon-

---

*He may have lived to regret this loss of nerve. Twenty years later on Taiwan, with the mainland gone and little more to lose, Chiang permitted experiments in "land equalization." They worked like charms. Landlords, flush with government purchase money and prohibited from reinvesting it in land or sending it overseas, put it into industry, thus stimulating the island's brisk economic development. Similar success in the 1930s might have taken the wind out of the Communists' sails and saved China for the Kuomintang.

ished, his parents brought on the scene and soundly lectured. The threat to health, the looseness of conduct, and the neglect of family discipline, all seemd to have outraged the general. Thinking about it later, he saw the incident as a reflection of all that was wrong with the nation as a whole. And thus was born the New Life Movement.

The New Life Movement was in essence the application of Confucian rules to modern times. Its program was to restore simplicity (in dress, food, and habits) and respect (for parents, clan, superiors, and the state) by observing the precepts of *li, yi, lien*, and *chih*. *Li* meant regard and courtesy, *yi* unselfish devotion to public welfare, *lien* purity of thought, and *chih* moral advancement. Later as the movement developed, practical applications of these ideas were spelled out in great detail—from rising early in the morning and rinsing the face with cold water, through waiting patiently in line for a bus without pushing or shoving, to fastening all buttons of clothes and standing respectfully when a funeral passed. There were strictures against spitting on the floor and sneezing in another's face, as well as calls to action in killing rats, swatting flies, and destroying body lice.

The Blueshirts were readymade administrators for the New Life Movement. They believed in the underlying principles and were zealous in promoting them. They organized New Life chapters in every important town and city, as well as schools and colleges—wherever footloose youth was to be found. The movement proved popular from the start, especially among the educated young. Not surprisingly they saw it as an avenue into Kuomintang officialdom, into government jobs from which they had been excluded since the imperial civil service examinations had been suspended three decades before. They might have reservations about the moral ideals of the program, but not about its practical side.

Chiang Kai-shek himself was too busy with his Fifth Campaign in 1934 to devote time to New Life supervision. But his wife, acting as his enthusiastic surrogate, brought to the task all her energy and flair for publicity. Throughout 1935, when

Chiang was chasing Communists around the perimeter of China, he was kept informed of the movement's success.

It was a success not confined solely to the Chinese. Unexpectedly the foreign missionaries took up the New Life Movement as their own. Treaty Port taipans might wax jocular about spitting on the floor and swatting flies, but not the missionaries. They found parallels between *li, yi, lien*, and *chih* and the four cardinal virtues of Christianity—prudence, justice, fortitude, and temperance—and never ceased praising the Methodist Chiangs (he had become one in 1930) as latter-day evangelists.

Chiang Kai-shek felt encouraged. At last he found himself moving toward the moral leadership he sought. In October 1935, partly to distract attention from his failure to wipe out the Red Long Marchers, but also as a further exercise in reform, he announced a bold program for the economic reconstruction of the nation.

He outlined an ambitious prospectus, initiating advances in agriculture, industry, labor, finance, and public welfare—especially putting the unemployed to work. In some ways the prospectus paralleled, and may have been inspired by, the social and economic changes Franklin D. Roosevelt was simultaneously trying to bring about in the depression-shocked United States. But whereas the American President was coaxing vast sums of money out of Congress and creating agencies to execute his New Deal, Chiang Kai-shek merely promulgated his proposals and left it to the benevolence of others to carry them out. In a radio address of January 1, 1936 he told his listeners that he expected the entire nation to cooperate in the programs he had set forth. He predicted that, if all would work in harmony, the vast reforms could be accomplished within a few years. His listeners—those who could afford radios—were entranced by the courageous vision and the impeccable classical phrasing of the speech; then went on with business as usual.

During 1936 Chiang spent much of his time in Sian engaged in preparations to root the Communists out of North Shensi. On second thought, he refused to dignify the coming expedition as his Sixth Extermination Campaign, preferring to consider it a mopping up operation. Hence he titled his Sian base "pacification" headquarters. But throughout the year his attention was constantly distracted by the Japanese who had become troublesome again beyond the Great Wall.

For it hadn't taken the Japanese long to breach the Tangku Truce of 1932 by which they had promised to limit their territorial ambitions to the three provinces of Manchuria. After a couple of years of organization and consolidation, they had started on the move again. The jursidictions of Jehol and Chahar in Inner Mongolia were absorbed and, to make it clear that they were on the continent to stay, the Japanese incorporated their possessions into an imperial puppet state they called Manchukuo. To add to Chiang Kai-shek's exasperation, they elevated to the throne of Manchukuo a ruler with some claim to legitimacy.

This was "Henry" Pu Yi*, the former boy emperor of China, the last of the Manchus, a dynasty that had originated in the Northeast. Henry Pu Yi had been smuggled out of abdicated retirement in the Forbidden City at Peking in 1927, to be groomed for future honors in the Japanese concession at Tientsin. Here he had held court and had learned to smoke opium while he awaited a return to power. His moment came in 1933 when his Japanese sponsors, having quit the League of Nations and thus cleared themselves of international restraints, elevated the dissipated young man of twenty-seven to the throne of Manchukuo as the Emperor Kang Te. His coronation ceremonies included a trip to Tokyo to visit with his fellow ruler, Hirohito of Japan.

By 1936 the Japanese had resumed their creeping expansion and were now threatening the Inner Mongolian province of Suiyuan. Chinese indignation, which had never ceased to simmer, came to a boil again. Demonstrators took to the streets demanding that Chiang Kai-shek lead his armies to stem the aggression. If he had suppressed the Communists as he officially claimed, what was stopping him?

Chiang, hard-pressed, playing for time, fell back on old routines. He ordered police to break up anti-Japanese demonstra-

---

*When the boy emperor had asked for a Western name to add to his imperial titles, his British tutor dubbed him Henry.

tions and arrest ringleaders—only to see his new, hard-won popularity evaporating rapidly.

A little desperate, looking around for some way to distract public attention, he hit upon a plan that many heads of state have found useful in emergencies—foreign travel. Though in Chiang's case, he didn't propose to leave the country. He confined his trips to the outback, the peripheral provinces, where few Chinese rulers had ventured before but which were now accessible through air travel. He persuaded his wife to accompany him. It promised to be an ordeal for Madame since she was subject to air sickness. But she was game. With her usual retinue of reporters, feature writers, and photographers trailing after her, she embarked on the goodwill mission.

The tour proved to be an unqualified success. It covered five thousand miles and included all the west and northern provinces of China Proper as well as disputed territories beyond. The Chiangs, dropping down from the skies, met with local governors, warlords, and dignitaries who had never hoped to see visitors from the distant capital at Nanking. And the Western missionaries in those remote regions were charmed within an inch of idolatry by Madame Chiang's unfailing graciousness.

Newspapers in the Treaty Ports and through the nation were filled with pictures and stories of the regal procession. Even the taipans were impressed. That fellow Chiang seemed finally to have established himself as the leader of his country. A modern leader at that; he took to the air with as much aplomb as that little chap with the mustache who was doing such remarkable things in Germany.

The impression on ordinary Chinese was even more profound. They followed the publicity blitz with rapture. They were stirred by mention of exotic peoples and places, and rejoiced in a leader who, by his mere presence on the scene, seemed to be expanding the national boundaries. In a sense, what was being lost to the Japanese in the East was made up for by what Chiang Kai-shek was spiritually winning in the West.

The change in attitude, the new acceptance and approval, was to be demonstrated on the occasion of Chiang's fiftieth* birth-

---
*Forty-ninth by Western count, but the Chinese give credit for a year in the womb.

day, October 31, 1936. A gift of seventy warplanes was purchased by public subscription—a gift that might also have carried the oblique hint that they could be usefully employed against the Japanese. A quarter of a million people turned up at the Nanking airport on the day of the presentation to listen to speeches and watch the new planes flying overhead in intricate formations spelling out in ideographs Chiang Kai-shek's name and age.

Confucian modesty prevented Chiang from being on hand to witness this display and listen to adulations in his honor. He found business to take him out of town for a couple of days. But on his return he made a radio address thanking the nation and giving credit for all he had become to his mother and Sun Yat-sen.

The speech, described as "in the best classical tradition, the language ... beautiful, and the tone ... modest and humble," was extravagantly admired, and much of the admiration passed on to Chiang himself. After all, he'd been around for a long time—a public figure for ten years, counting from the Northern Expedition of 1926—and in a land where age was venerated, where new goods were often sold as old to enhance their appeal, sheer longevity was in itself a reassurance. He'd passed through the period when even the family dog was bound to hate him and had emerged as an institution.

Not even the suppression of another anti-Japanese demostration in November and the arrests that followed dimmed Chiang Kai-shek's luster. He had arrived at a plateau where his faults were accepted along with his virtues. Without monument or proclamation to note the passage, he had transcended to the unchallenged leadership of his people. He had become the Generalissimo.

Mao Tse-tung too was to tread what he called a "tortuous road" during much of 1936. And as with Chiang Kai-shek, his problems centered on the question of leadership—or, more accurately, on establishing a correct policy line for the future. The Chinese Communist Party had achieved an epic triumph by completing the Long March. But once in Shensi, it seemed to falter and lose direction. It was as if Marxist ideology as an inspirational source had been exhausted by the trials of the journey.

Mao himself had made few contributions to socialist theory over the past few years. In the closing Kiangsi period his voice had been stilled by the Twenty-eight Bolsheviks, and during the Long March staying alive was the only thing that occupied minds. But now, with time for political analysis, mistakes of the past had to be repudiated and a more productive course of action worked out.

The Shensi base—the last stable enclave of Communist power in China—had become the national headquarters of the revolution. Dispossessed Red commanders and officials from other parts of the country kept drifting in, building the Central Committee and Politburo back up to plenary strength. This led to difficulties as far as Mao Tse-tung was concerned because the newcomers, out of touch with much that had happened since the Tsunyi Conference, tended to join ranks with the old hard-liners. A right wing emerged contending that what had gone wrong in Kiangsi was too much democracy, not too little, and demanding a return to an even stricter Bolshevik discipline.

Wang Ming, still active in Moscow, was continually pushing a "purist" line by radio, though his position had been weakened by a decision of the Comintern in the summer of 1935. For in August, at about the time the Long Marchers were approaching the Grasslands, Joseph Stalin had ordered a turnabout in Comintern policy. Alarmed by the growing threat of the dictators Hitler and Mussolini in Europe, Stalin had directed that Communist parties throughout the world join in anti-Fascist united fronts with their own bourgeoisie.

The right-wing Chinese comrades were unable to see how the directive could possibly apply to them. How could a united front be formed with the hangman? But Mao Tse-tung found it a liberating idea and went to work on it.

He had ample time for creative thinking during the winter of 1935–36. The veterans of the Long March had settled down comfortably in the Shensi villages assigned to them, digging barracks in the form of caves out of the hospitable hillsides. The consistency of the soil was such that cozy rooms, shaped like Nissen huts, could be hollowed out; quarters that were warm in winter and cool in summer and could even be quite elegant when the curving walls were plastered and decorated. Lin Piao of the light foot and Commander Liu Po-sheng, now called the One-eyed Dragon because of a bullet stopped along the way, kept the men busy on maneuvers which could be rapidly turned into guerrila warfare—as Chiang Kai-shek had learned to his discomfort when he tested the defenses in November 1935.

The combined Red forces—the Long Marchers plus the small army of base Commander Liu Chih-tan who administered the Shensi soviet from his capital at Pao An—now totaled some twenty thousand men, enough to stave off all but a full-scale campaign against the territory. This was demonstrated a number of times during the winter when heavy assaults were launched by local Nationalist authorities. In fact, the Reds chalked up a net gain of some three thousand officers and men who came over to them as a result of battle. The Red soldiers had devised a slogan—"Chinese must not fight Chinese; they must unite against Japan"—which proved effective in weakening enemy morale. And also proved that the rank and file were ahead of the party leaders in thinking up ways of forging a united front.

But Mao Tse-tung was not far behind. At a meeting of the Central Committee he made some startling proposals. He prefaced them by saying that revolution follows a tortuous road, so there was no need to be surprised by twists and detours. They were now on "the eve of a great change" and minds must be adjusted to the inevitable logic of facts.

One fact was that though the Red government had migrated to the Northwest to fight the Japanese, it was not strong enough to proceed without allies. And where were allies to be found? Mao answered firmly: within the ranks of the Kuomintang.

He hastened to clarify. He wasn't thinking of Chiang Kai-shek and the international bankers and compradors who supported him; such people were too far gone in corruption to be anything but enemies. But the "national bourgeoisie"—defined as small

Eve of a Great Change

industrialists, businessmen, and shopkeepers, harassed by foreign competition and neglected by Nanking—was a potential ally. As a class it was vacillating, but its patriotism had been proved by boycotts and demonstrations against the Japanese and it could be won over.

And how was it to be won over? First, its fears about communism must be allayed, and that could be done only by broadening the base of the Red government. Hitherto the soviets had represented workers and peasants exclusively, but the time had come to open up the gates. Mao proposed a constituency "to include . . . all . . . classes who are willing to take part in the national revolution."

If that wasn't bombshell enough, Mao had another explosive handy. He advocated changing the name of the Red government from the "workers' and peasants' republic" to a "people's republic." Why? So that "we [may] have the right to call ourselves the representatives of the whole nation." And he summarized his argument by stating: "This [winning of allies] provides a necessary condition for China's victory in the war against Japan and for victory in the Chinese revolution."

There was consternation and anger in the Central Committee. In the minds of many, Mao Tse-tung was advocating a surrender to the enemy, a sellout of Marxist doctrine. Charges of "right opportunist" and "revisionist" were hurled at him and his resolutions were voted down. Mao had probably anticipated the reaction. He was fond of saying that it took time for new ideas to penetrate, and much teaching and persuading too. So he waited patiently, educating and clarifying but never letting up through the spring and summer.

In the fall of 1936, the renegade Chang Kuo-tao, with a rather sheepish Chu Teh in tow, arrived in Shenshi almost exactly a year after the Long Marchers. His sojourn in Tibet had been a disaster. He had been unable to establish a base because of the poverty of the natives who had barely enough to feed themselves, let alone Chang's thirty-five thousand troops. In the end he had resorted to forced requisitioning, acting more like an oppressive warlord than a revolutionary liberator.

As soon as the spring of 1936 permitted, he had started west for Shensi with his depleted army. But disasters continued. He had fared far worse in the Grasslands than the Long Marchers, and afterward in battles with the Nationalists. He and Chu Teh arrived in camp with only scarecrow squads remaining from a once powerful army.

Chu Teh was absolved from blame because he had been throughout a virtual captive, but Chang Kuo-tao was put on trial for his crimes and conduct. Thanks to Mao Tse-tung's intervention he escaped with only a censuring. Mao always believed that a delinquent comrade could be rehabilitated by self-criticism and reeducation—he called it "cured of his sickness"—but in Chang Kuo-tao's case he was to be woefully wrong. Two years later Chang defected to the Kuomintang, turning informer for Chiang Kai-shek's secret police. His name still lives in party annals as one of the few arch traitors of the revolution.

Perhaps it was Chang Kuo-tao's experiences in Tibet that aroused Mao Tse-tung's curiosity as to whether the peasants of Shensi were suffering from the influx of his own troops. The government had moved to the capital at Pao An by this time—following the death in battle of the base Commander Liu Chih-tan—and Mao traveled through the countryside talking to villagers, drinking "white tea" and collecting impressions.

It was an impoverished area, short in rainfall and primitive in agriculture methods. The main crop was millet—to the sorrow of the rice-bred Red army—though legumes and sheep were raised where water could be scooped from the meandering Yellow River. But despite the general poverty and subsistence diets, Mao found the peasants cheerful about their lot. The former landlords seemed to have been a particularly vicious breed, and their eviction had given an emotional lift to the present freeholders. Far from resenting the Red army, the people thought of it as their friend; they had been astonished and delighted when uniformed volunteers had poured into the fields to help at sowing and harvest time. Every village youngsters wanted to be a Red army recruit and parents fanned enthusiasm by references to "our heroes" and "our protectors."

Mao Tse-tung was, at forty-four, friendly, relaxed, and gaining weight from his sedentary life. A peasant himself, he never ceased to learn from peasants. As he was to tell his cadres, "Take the ideas of the masses . . . hold fast to them and translate them into action." He believed that leadership consisted in finding and expressing the will of ordinary people, and he never failed in his regard for them.

The regard was mutual and reciprocated; ordinary people believed in and trusted Mao. Peasants began calling him Chairman Mao as a sign of respect and affection and soon the name was taken up by townspeople and soldiers.

Government officials scoffed. What was Mao chairman of anyway? The Military Council, perhaps, but nothing else—certainly not the Politburo or the Central Committee. But it did no good to object. As with Chiang Kai-shek, Mao Tse-tung had climbed without fuss or fanfare to a new plateau of esteem. Entitled or not, he had become The Chairman.

As Generalissimo, Chiang Kai-shek was fretting over unfinished business as the winter of 1936 closed in. The Red bandits were still at large, still holding out in the back hills of Shensi and nothing had been done to dislodge them.

Chiang had done his part. He had assembled three hundred thousand troops and mountains of equipment to move on order. But because of delays and excuses of one kind or another, the order was never given.

The fault lay with his commanding generals in Sian. Both were officers with impeccable records for energy and valor, but they seemed to have become strangely irresolute, disturbed by qualms the Generalissimo found both irrelevant and annoying. In October he had flown up to pacification headquarters to talk his commanders into a more aggressive attitude toward Communist eradication, and had come away with promises of obedience. But the excuses continued. Chiang waited and nothing happened.

In early December the Generalissimo flew to Sian for a showdown. His patience at an end, he was determined to force his recalcitrant generals into action by imposing an ultimatum. It was unfortunate timing because circumstances had been at work to reverse the situation and, in the end, it was the Generalissimo who had an ultimatum imposed on him.

This reversal of fortunes became known as the Sian Incident. It came about through a clash of wills and developed by impromptu stages into a national crisis. The spontaneous nature of the event reflected the character of its chief engineer, a young man of reckless daring called Chang Hsueh-liang, better known to history as the Young Marshal.

16

Collision in Sian

CHANG HSUEH-LIANG, THE YOUNG MARSHAL, WAS A character straight out of romantic fiction. He might have played the lead in a Chinese historical novel of derring-do, such as the *Three Kingdoms* or *Revolt Against the Tang*, but he could have fit just as easily into a border ballad by Sir Walter Scott. He was high-minded, idealistic, and patriotic, and when he believed that his nation might be saved by an act of unprecedented rashness he was willing to risk his life in the commitment.

Chang Hsueh-liang was born to the purple, the eldest son of Chang Tso-lin, the Tiger of the North and overlord of Manchuria. The boy showed an early aptitude for the martial arts and by the age of nineteen, dubbed the Young Marshal, was a divisional commander in his father's interminable wars.

Between campaigns the young man lived in some style in Mukden, combining a passion for fast cars with a taste for pretty women. He would tour the countryside with an eye out for an evening's pleasure and, having found a beauty, would speed her back to his palace. Next day the girl would be chauffeured home with expensive gifts for her parents, a line of conduct gratifying to both the lady and her elders.

The Young Marshal was thirty when he came into his inheritance. That was on the death of his father, blown up in his private train after evacuating Peking in 1928. The son couldn't get at the Japanese he knew to be responsible, but as an act of filial piety he rounded up and executed the Chinese who had actually set the bomb. He further made clear his hatred of Japan by declaring Manchuria a territory of China and swearing fealty to Chiang Kai-shek. The two men ceremoniously cut their wrists and drank from a common cup, the ultimate bond of friendship in the Confucian code.

Grief for his father may have led to the Young Marshal's opium addiction at about this time. A reporter, meeting "the world's youngest dictator" in 1929, described him as "thin . . . drawn . . . jaundiced-looking." Chiang Kai-shek, concerned for his blood brother's health, sent W. H. Donald to Mukden to see what he could do.

W. H. Donald—the Australian journalist, big, bluff, hearty, outspoken, the intimate of China's elite because of his un-Confucian habit of telling the truth—had been diplomatically unemployed since Sun Yat-sen's death. He now took on the rehabilitation of the Young Marshal with his usual gusto and optimism. A fresh-air enthusiast, he introduced the ailing ruler to golf. But though the patient may have healthily whacked balls during the day, he was still apparently hitting the pipe by night. At least his system steadily weakened and in the summer of 1931 he fell prey to typhoid. He was in a Peiping hospital on September 18 when the Japanese staged the Mukden Incident and the invasion of Manchuria began.

In no condition to take the field himself, the Young Marshal appealed to Chiang Kai-shek to oppose the invaders. Chiang refused to move. He explained that he had put the matter before the League of Nations and a verdict must be awaited. Bitter, but loyal to his commander-in-chief, the Young Marshal ordered his Tungpei (Northeastern) troops to withdraw before the Japanese. His bitterness was compounded when, during the general outcry at the retreat, he was accused of cowardice.

Collision in Sian

Two years later the Japanese invaded Inner Mongolia and again Chiang Kai-shek refused to allow the Young Marshal to go into action against them. Once more angry demonstrations erupted throughout China and once more the Young Marshal bore the brunt of the blame.

Realizing that he had become a political liability to his blood brother, the Young Marshal gallantly offered to make himself a scapegoat. In the tradition of defeated warlords, he announced that he was going abroad for travel and study. W. H. Donald went with him, but not before he had put his charge into a Shanghai hospital for a thorough drug sweat-out, and no nonsense.

The tour abroad lasted two years. In Italy the Young Marshal was delighted by the new high-speed motor roads. In Germany he was impressed, as were the most authoritarian rulers, by Hitler's one-man Fuhrer dictatorship. In France there were women, and in Britain golf.

He arrived back in China in glowing health. According to one observer: "He had put on weight and muscle, there was color in his cheeks, he looked ten years younger, and people saw in him traces of the brilliant leader of his youth.... It was a tribute to his popularity that, despite his errors of the past, his army enthusiastically welcomed him back."

The Tungpei troops had good reason to welcome their former chief. They had been stationed in Shensi Province as part of Chiang Kai-shek's build-up to attack the Communists, and had no stomach for the duty. They were within sight of the Great Wall. Beyond it lay Manchuria where the Japanese were abusing their kith and kin. That was where they wanted to fight, not against Communists with whom they had no quarrel. They wanted the Young Marshal to persuade the Generalissimo that he was taking on the wrong enemy.

The Young Marshal listened to the pleas to march back to his homeland with sympathy. But he wasn't in full charge of the situation. Chiang Kai-shek, always skillful at splitting authority, had appointed another general to joint command. This was Yang Hu-cheng, known as "Old Yang," a hard-bitten former warlord who had been a power in the Northwest before he had been brought to heel by Nanking. The Generalissimo hoped by this division of command to promote rivalry between the generals, spurring each to greater zeal in exterminating Communists.

But it didn't work out that way. The rivals soon struck up a friendship and found themselves united in their distaste for bandit campaigning. Old Yang had already tried some forays into the loess hills and had come out with a healthy respect for the Reds' fighting abilities. He had been even more impressed by their propaganda techniques. Their slogan "Chinese must not fight Chinese; they must unite against Japan" had lost him more men by desertions than he had suffered in casualties. What's more, it had all but won over Old Yang himself.

The Young Marshal was drawn into further investigations. He talked to officers and men who had been captured and released by the Reds, trying to gauge the Communists' sincerity. In the summer of 1936 he arranged a secret meeting with a Communist spokesman—Chou En-lai. After hours of discussion the Young Marshal became convinced of "the sanity and practicability of . . . a united front" against Japan.

Meanwhile pressure from Chiang Kai-shek was mounting. Why were his strategic plans for attacking the Reds' stronghold not being implemented? What was holding his generals back?

Getting no satisfactory answers, the Generalissimo flew up to Sian in October and finally learned what was on his commanders' minds. The Young Marshal argued that, with the Japanese menace growing, surely it was time to end the civil war and make an alliance with the Communist forces; also it would be wise to open up diplomatic relations with Russia again. Chiang Kai-shek put an abrupt end to this line of reasoning: "I will never talk about this until every Red soldier in China is exterminated, and every Communist is in prison. Only then would it be possible to cooperate with Russia."

When the meeting broke up, the Generalissimo evidently felt he'd had the last word since, as commander-in-chief, he had ordered obedience to his will. He returned to Nanking but still nothing happened in Sian, while in Shanghai more anti-Japanese demonstrations erupted and a group of distinguished intellectuals called the Seven Gentlemen were jailed.

These arrests brought forth an indignant plea from the Young Marshal. It was cruel, he said, to imprison patriots who had only been doing their duty in protesting the Japanese invasion; they should be released. The Generalissimo's answer was cold: "That is merely your viewpoint [while] I am the Government."

Apparently to humiliate his recalcitrant generals into taking action, Chiang sent a strong force of his own elite troops into the Shensi hills as an object lesson on how Communists should be attacked. But the moral point was somewhat lost when the contingent was ambushed and routed.

Furious now, determined to put an end to further shillyshallying, the Generalissimo flew to Sian for a final confrontation. He stepped from his plane on December 7, 1936 to begin a fortnight that was to convulse the nation and bewilder the world.

Chiang Kai-shek and his entourage were lodged at the hot springs resort called Lintung, fifteen miles from Sian. The hot springs are known as *hwa-ching-shih* which translates as "the bath of the Favorite," the Favorite being the courtesan of an 8th-century-A.D. Tang emperor at a time when Sian (Western Peace) was the capital of the Middle Kingdom. The city was very old, its culture flourishing when Nanking was nonexistent and Shanghai a mudflat on the edge of the Yangtze swamps. And it had remained important through the centuries. From Sian the silk caravans had started out for Samarkand and the barbarian shores of the Mediterranean Sea, and through Sian a handful of Europeans, Marco Polo among them, had ventured fearfully into Cathay. Sian was a book of history in itself, in which a new page was about to be turned.

The situation developed gradually. December 8 and 9 were passed in stormy conferences at Lintung—stormy because generals Chang and Yang hadn't changed position on the Red campaign that went against their consciences. On December 9 the Young Marshal had to take time out to cope with a demonstration. Hordes of students were gathering to march on Lintung to demand that the Generalissimo end the civil war. The Young Marshal couldn't permit such discourteous behavior toward his guest, and such was his popularity that when he promised to deliver the message personally to Chiang, the students disbanded and went home.

On the night of December 10—the last formal meeting—Chiang Kai-shek delivered an ultimatum. In two days he intended to make a radio address announcing the official start of Red bandit clean-up operations. Either the generals would speak publicly in support of the project, or they and their troops would be banished to the far corners of the nation, while loyal armies would be brought in to do their work for them.

December 11 was set aside for the generals to think things over, which was perhaps a mistake. Chang and Yang, conferring with their staffs, were infected by their officers' discontent and rebellious advice. A plot began to hatch. The scheme that evolved was so flimsy and improvised as to preclude thought of premeditation. Chiang's ultimatum had so narrowed down time that only action, any action, was important.

The Generalissimo spent the day (December 11) working on his radio address. Sometime during the evening the Young Marshal sent a message asking him to receive a caller named Sun Ming-chiu. It was explained that Sun was a promising officer in the Tungpei army who would be much encouraged by a meeting with China's leader.

Chiang seems to have suspected nothing. He put aside his work to receive the sturdy, sheepskin-helmeted captain. Sun Ming-chiu bowed nervously, hardly able to express his thanks because of the honor. The interview lasted only a few minutes, but long enough for the Generalissimo's face, figure, and movements to be photographed in the captain's alert mind.

The Generalissimo finished his speech, indulged in a hot bath from the thermal springs, and retired. Next morning, December 12, he was up early as usual. His schedule called for rinsing in cold water at 5:30 A.M., then for exercises before breakfast at six. But today there was to be no breakfast. At approximately 5:45 A.M. shots were heard. Aides rushed in with the news that the hostel was under attack and the Generalissimo must leave at once. A robe was thrown around his shoulders, but there was no time or memory for either his slippers or false teeth.

Chiang was guided through the compound and out into a

garden surrounded by a ten-foot wall. Nothing daunted, the Generalissimo asked for a hoist and scrambled to the top with commendable agility. Descent on the farther side was a different matter. In the predawn darkness he failed to see a drained moat, and bounced down some thirty feet of rocky ledge before reaching bottom.

He was momentarily stunned and lay helpless until his aides reached him. Once on his feet, he found he had wrenched his back. He was helped out of the moat and, though in considerable pain, continued gamely up the slope beyond. Meanwhile he was informed of as much of the story as was known. Some two hundred soldiers, identified as Tungpei troops because of their sheepskin helmets, had attacked the hostel. Continuing gunfire suggested that the defenders, mostly dedicated I-Chi, were still putting up a resistance. It was thought that the attackers must be Communist-inspired mutineers, and that the Young Marshal would soon send forces to suppress the revolt.

But then the shooting ended. Victorious yells were heard from the compound and there was still no sign of rescuers rushing to the scene. Chiang and his party continued to ascend the slope known as Black Horse Mountain. But finally the Generalissimo balked. How would it look for the leader of the nation to be found wandering around in a bathrobe? Besides, the rocks were cutting his bare feet. He sat down on a boulder and refused to budge. He would await rescue with dignity.

Shouts were heard close by. A search party had come up the hill. At its head was Captain Sun Ming-chiu, the diffident young officer of the night before, now needing no encouragement. Chiang Kai-shek may have realized for the first time that he was in the hands of no ordinary mutineers. The Young Marshal was deeply involved.

Captain Sun, identifying his quarry, stepped forward and apologetically asked the Generalissimo to accompany him down the hill. Chiang's answer was contemptuous and as clear as possible through missing teeth: "If you regard me as your prisoner, kill me, but don't subject me to indignities." Nevertheless he accepted a piggyback ride on the captain's broad back and the descent was made.

The Generalissimo was taken to a waiting automobile by a roundabout route in order to avoid the bloody scene inside the hostel where twenty of his devoted bodyguards had been killed in the exchange of fire. On the drive to Sian, Captain Sun Ming-shiu tried to allay his captive's fears but was sharply told: "Hold your tongue, you rebel! If you want to kill me, kill me right now!"

In Sian, the Generalissimo was lodged in a sparsely furnished suite in a government building—temporary quarters, he was assured. Here the Young Marshal came to see him. Viewing his commander-in-chief in sartorial disarray and without teeth seems to have been an unnerving experience. Or perhaps it was his guilt at his treatment of a blood brother, and an *elder* brother with all its Confucian connotations, that shook him. At any rate his courage failed and he began to deny that he had anything to do with the mutiny. The Generalissimo wasn't deceived. He cut through the pretense with impatient scorn: "Since I am in the hands of a rebel you had better shoot me dead. There is nothing else to say."

Chiang had found his line now—moral outrage combined with contemptuous defiance. It was a difficult defense to crack and certainly the Young Marshal had no luck. His apologies and protests were swept aside with such fulminations as: "I am armed with the principles of righteousness.... With these I must defend the honour of the people whom I represent and must be a faithful follower of our late leader (Dr. Sun Yat-sen)." That's the way he put it in his diary from which his dialogues with the Young Marshal are transcribed. "I shall not bring shame and dishonour to this world, to the memory of my parents and to the nation." And there was much more Finding it intolerable, the Young Marshal fled, sobbing.

Still in a lofty vein, Chiang drafted what would seem a far from reassuring telegram to his wife. He told her that he had always known he was to be a martyr of the revolution, implying that his time had probably come.

Next day the Young Marshal returned, buttressed by his coconspirator Old Yang and a group of civilian officials. The Generalissimo was looking better, in uniform again with his teeth restored, but he was still implacable. He had written earlier in his diary: "The courageous life as taught by the late Dr. Sun should be followed by us all . . . . Jesus Christ was tempted by Satan and withstood him for forty days . . . . I must maintain the same spirit which led Jesus Christ to the Cross." This stoic mood was still on him when he received his visitors. He refused to discuss anything that even smacked of negotiations. Let him return to Nanking and he would freely discuss any and all questions with an open mind.

Growing a bit desperate, the Young Marshal showed Chiang a lengthy telegram that had been dispatched to Nanking. It acknowledged that the Generalissimo had been captured—softened to "detained"—and outlined an Eight-Point program that was to be discussed prior to his return. The Eight Points called for ending the civil war and inviting all political factions into the National government, pardoning all political offenders and specifically releasing the Seven Gentlemen, guaranteeing rights of speech and assembly, implementing Sun Yat-sen's Three Principles by deeds rather than pious words, and preparing a national defense against Japanese aggression.

The Generalissimo read the telegram and dropped it on the floor. He was too furious to speak. His captors had moved past mutiny to insolence.

The telegram caused consternation in the Nanking government. For a couple of days rumors had circulated that something was amiss in Sian. But the Young Marshal's tight control of communications made accurate information impossible until the telegram arrived.

H.H. Kung, the Generalissimo's banker brother-in-law sitting in as acting president, was paralyzed as to what to do. So were General Ho Ying-chin, the Minister of War, and other high officials called together in a secret conference. It was decided that Madame Chiang must have a say in any decision and a plane was sent to fetch her from Shanghai where she was visiting. And just in case, a cable was dispatched to Left-hand Wang Ching-wei, traveling in Europe again, urging him to hurry home.

One thing Kuomintang officialdom could and did do was to clamp down a tight censorship. The Young Marshal had sent copies of his telegram to leading journals and news services, but their delivery was intercepted. Foreign correspondents managed to learn that the Generalissimo had been kidnapped but were left to speculate on how and why. A favorite theory cabled to home offices was that the Communists had pulled the coup of the century; another was that Chiang had been captured by warlords and was being held for ransom.*

The mystery was shamelessly exploited by some world capitals. Tokyo insinuated that a seditious uprising had been engineered by the Soviet Union. Moscow retorted that Chiang was the victim of a "Japanese plot." London preferred a droll, chauvinistic approach: "A strange affair," mused the *Times*, "a theme for a new Gilbert."

Actually Joseph Stalin was alarmed by the development. He saw chaos in China if anything happened to Chiang Kai-shek. He anticipated a power vacuum into which the Japanese would rush, extending their armies for another thousand miles across the Russian frontier. Almost in panic he radioed the Central Committee in Shensi threatening "publicly to disown the [Chinese Communists] unless they demanded Chiang's release unharmed."

The peremptory tone was resented by some on the Central Committee, especially by Mao Tse-tung. For once he seems to have forgotten the deference due the high priest of socialism. According to a witness, he "flew into a rage... swore and stamped his feet." What hurt was Stalin's attitude, his badgering invective, his refusal to believe that the Chinese party might have established a responsible government worthy of fraternal respect. And the insult was compounded because steps had already been taken to do what Stalin wanted.

It hadn't been an easy victory for Mao Tse-tung. Every man on the Central Committee had reason to hate Chiang Kai-shek. Memories of slain comrades and murdered relatives were still fresh, not to mention the savage pursuit during the Long March. When word was received that the Generalissimo had been cap-

---

*As late as 1945 J. B. Powell, a respected American journalist and editor in Shanghai, could write: "The size of the check... handed over in exchange for the release of [Chiang Kai-shek] has never been disclosed."

tured, there was jubilation at the Red base. The archvillain of China, the devil himself, had been delivered into —if not exactly Communist hands, at least into the hands of a quasi ally in the Young Marshal. A clamor went up for a public trial, with Chiang Kai-shek's execution assured for crimes against the nation.

But Mao Tse-tung, cool-headed, inexorably Marxist, had intervened. Applying concrete analysis to concrete conditions, he had seen as clearly as Stalin the chaos that would result. He had argued that there was no substitute for Chiang, with all his sins, as the country's leader. It was a contradiction of history that must be accepted; Chiang must be preserved until new forces could arise to supplant him.

After furious debate, Mao had prevailed. Animosities were shelved and unity restored as party discipline took over. It was decided to send Chou En-lai, already acquainted with the Young Marshal, to Sian. He was to function in dual capacity—as a united front lobbyist to help put pressure on the Generalissimo and as a security guard to preserve his life.

It was a difficult assignment for the thirty-eight-year-old official, then sporting a bushy black beard and just coming into his own as the party's diplomat. But he was to perform it brilliantly.

In Nanking, the arrival of Madame Chiang with her financier brother T. V. Soong, put new life into the debate on what to do about the Generalissimo. Ho Ying-chin, the Minister of War, had drawn up plans for an all-out air attack on Sian, but Madame strenuously objected. She had no wish to expose her husband to bombs unless absolutely necessary and suggested an interim approach. They really knew nothing about what was happening beyond what was contained in the Young Marshal's telegram. She proposed that W. H. Donald be sent to Sian to investigate the situation.

The proposal was happily adopted. W. H. Donald, a Westerner and neutral observer and also an intimate of the Young Marshal, was the ideal man. Donald, always ready for adventure, was dispatched to Sian in Madame's personal plane.

Meanwhile in Sian a discussion at cross purposes continued on a high moral level. The Generalissimo, hardening by the hour into an encrusted position, defied attempts to pry him loose. The Young Marshal complained that Chiang was despotic, arguing that "even as a simple citizen he [the Young Marshal] should have a chance to express his views about the affairs of the nation." The Generalissimo, according to his diary, came back with a crushing retort: "You are a military officer and cannot enjoy the same privileges as a common citizen.... Instead you have taken part in a mutiny [and] feel no remorse about your wrong-doing."

W. H. Donald arrived in Sian on December 14, the third day of Chiang's captivity. His hearty, matter-of-fact manner did much to alleviate tensions. The Generalissimo, feeling psychologically secure and physically better—the pains resulting from his fall into the moat diminishing—even agreed to move to more comfortable quarters which he had stubbornly refused before. Somehow during the bustle of transit he became separated from his personal papers, which were duly retrieved and handed over to his captors.

Next day the Young Marshal appeared before Chiang in a contrite mood. He confessed to an invasion of privacy: "We have read your diary and other documents and from them have learned the greatness of your personality." But his grievances hadn't abated: "[Your main fault is that] you always have in your head such men as Yo Fei, Wen Tien-hsiang and Sze Ko-fa* and are therefore behind the times in your mentality. Why do you insist upon sacrificing yourself for the sake of principles and not think of the possibility of achievement?" He received a sorrowful if mystic answer: "Sacrifice and achievement are one and the same thing."

The Young Marshal's situation was growing increasingly untenable. Whatever he had expected from Chiang Kai-shek, it had not been impenetrable stubbornness. How could concessions be wrung from a man who met every reasonable proposal with a moral lecture and acted toward his captors like a stoic father enduring the misbehavior of his children? Yet unless something was wrested out of that obdurate will, the whole enterprise would collapse in futility or worse. Worse because the Young Marshal's fellow conspirators, Old Yang and his senior officers, were already grumbling about the

---

*All patriots of Chinese history who gave their lives for the nation.

impasse and threatening to deal with the Generalissimo on terms other than talk.

W. H. Donald asked permission to return to Nanking and the Young Marshal couldn't very well detain him, though he recognized the danger. Once the report was in, once it was learned that the Generalissimo was safe and holding his captors at bay, an attempt might be made to rescue him by military means. Thus the civil war that the kidnap had been staged to end might explode again on a vastly expanded scale with the Tungpei armies treated as rebels.

To add to the pressure, bad news came from beyond the Great Wall. The Japanese, taking advantage of the crisis in China, advanced into the Inner Mongolian province of Suiyuan. The Young Marshal gloomily confessed to an unsympathetic Generalissimo that if the nation should suffer grievous hurt as a result of his coup, he would never be able to forgive himself. He would either commit suicide or take to the hills and become a bandit.

Though the Young Marshal didn't specifically say "Red" bandit, he may have been reminded of Chou En-lai waiting in the wings. So far he had been reluctant to allow the Communist emissary a private interview with Chiang Kai-shek but now, willing to try anything, he gave permission. The meeting was set up without prior arrangement since Chiang was sure to have refused if he had known. The Young Marshal simply introduced Chou En-lai as a "former subordinate," then left the room.

The Generalissimo had trouble recognizing Chou at first, perhaps because of the black beard. When he did, he turned away, jaws set. But the Red diplomat was prepared for the occasion. He clicked his heels, executed a military salute, and greeted Chiang as "Commandant," a form of address permitted only to the I-Chi.

For Chou En-lai was, of course, a genuine I-Chi, one of the chosen. He was not only from one of the first four classes at Whampoa, he was from all of them through service as a political commissar. Chiang made a fetish of his unconditional loyalty to his I-Chi and he couldn't make an exception in Chou's case even though he had lapsed into political rebellion. Slowly the Generalissimo's eyes came back and he returned the salute.

During their talk, Chou En-lai outlined what the Communists

were prepared to do in return for a cessation of the civil war and the formation of a united front against the Japanese. Sovietization would end, confiscation of landlords' property would end, and the Red regime would work in affiliation with the National government. Finally, but most important, the Communists would recognize Chiang Kai-shek as the leader of the nation and supreme commander of their armies.

The Generalissimo listened without answering. Chou En-lai persisted until he saw "a hint of reconciliation" in Chiang's eyes. Then he was ready to stop, but Chiang wasn't. He too had something on his mind.

Eleven years before, in 1925, he had sent his sixteen-year-old elder son Ching-kuo to be educated in Russia. He had acted on impulse, in support of Sun Yat-sen, to demonstrate his faith in the Kuomintang-Communist alliance of those days and in gratitude for Soviet help in the Chinese revolution. But he had regretted it ever since, especially since 1927 when he had changed his views about the local Communists and had turned on them at Shanghai. That action had made his name anathema to the Russians and also apparently to his son. At least the boy had denounced his father and said he would never return to China while Chiang was alive.

The filial split hung heavily on the Generalissimo's mind and he asked Chou En-lai's help in getting his son back. Chou said he would do what he could, promising to cable Moscow on the matter. This was satisfactory to Chiang and the interview ended.

That meeting was probably the turning point of the entire Sian captivity. When the men parted, the Generalissimo still had committed himself to nothing, but he had implied enough for Chou En-lai to reassure the Young Marshal and radio Mao Tse-tung that Chiang "would probably not go back on his [unspoken] word."

Curiously Chiang Kai-shek makes no mention of Chou En-lai in the voluminous diary of his Sian captivity. Perhaps he was unwilling to admit even in his private thoughts that a couple of hours' conversation with a bearded, polite-spoken rebel had succeeded in influencing him when all other efforts to breach his indomitable will had failed. Or possibly he was afraid of another implication—his own about-face. For Chiang too was at an impasse, with the consensus of the nation turning against him on the issues of civil war and Japanese aggression, and Chou En-lai's liberal terms for a united front offered an acceptable way out.

Neither did Madame Chiang, in her contribution to a book called *The Account of the Fortnight in Sian*, give credit to the persuasive Red diplomat, though she did concede that "quite contrary to outside beliefs [the Communists] were not interested in detaining the Generalissimo." But then she arrived late on the scene and may not even have known of the historic interview.

Madame Chiang flew into Sian at the Young Marshal's invitation on December 22 accompanied by T. V. Soong and the indispensable W.H. Donald, back on his second trip. The Generalissimo had been reading the Bible just before his wife stepped into the room and was impressed by the aptness of the verse he had reached: "Jehovah will now do a new thing, and that is, He will make a woman protect a man."*

Not that Chiang needed much protection at this stage. The Young Marshall's bargaining position had eroded to nothing. He made a last plea for a formal statement adopting at least half of his Eight-Point manifesto, but the Generalissimo wasn't listening. He had done too well with a stonewall defense to change his tactics now. Madame Chiang helped out by confiding in the Young Marshal that, though her husband was favorably inclined toward the Eight Points, it would be a mistake to force him to sign anything, thus leaving "a scar on his mind."

The Young Marshal had to take what reassurance he could from that. And apparently it was enough, because he issued an order for his prisoner's release on December 25—Christmas Day—and by so doing precipitated a crisis he hadn't counted on. Suddenly, at the eleventh hour, Chiang's life was threatened as never before during the weeks of his captivity.

For if the Young Marshal had made his peace with the situation, Old Yang had not. He was well aware that, unlike the ex-ruler of Manchuria, he was not a blood brother to the Generalissimo and he and his officers stood to suffer the punishment of mutineers if Chiang were allowed to escape to Nanking without commitment.

---

*Jeremiah, XXXI, 22, according to a Chinese translation.

What was needed and what he was determined to get was a guarantee of amnesty in return for Chiang Kai-shek's life.

On Christmas Eve a meeting of all officers of Yang's Hsipei (Northwestern) army was called. Fiery speeches were delivered by the light of bonfires to arouse ardor for a march on the Young Marshal's palace and the seizure of the Generalissimo. It was then that Chou En-lai stepped into his second role as guardian of Chiang's welfare. With considerable courage he addressed the angry men, appealing to their patriotism and trying to convince them that the salvation of the nation was at stake. He took considerable abuse but was finally able to calm down the assembly and abort the threatened action.

Christmas Day found the Generalissimo in a benevolent mood. Standing on the steps of his plane and addressing the generals Chang and Yang in farewell, he took upon himself the responsibility for all that had happened. He and he alone was to blame, he said, and he was returning to Nanking to ask for suitable punishment. The Young Marhsal was so overcome by this generosity of spirit and largeness of soul that he insisted on climbing aboard the aircraft in order to share the punishment.

The return to Nanking was a triumph. Enormous crowds jammed the airport, demonstrating their affection for the Generalissimo and their relief at his deliverance. His popularity had never been as great, nor would it ever be again.

Next day in the halls of government a veritable orgy of Confucian ritual was enacted. The Generalissimo reported on his captivity to a crowded plenum of the Executive Yuan. In conclusion he requested that he be relieved of all his posts because "due to my lack of virtue and defects in my training of subordinates [this]unprecedented revolt broke out." The Executive Yuan, playing right along with the charade, retired for a special session in camera at which it was decided that the punishment of such a "magnanimous personality" was unnecessary. Chiang persisted, tendering his resignation a second and third time, and each time it was unanimously rejected.

Then it was the Young Marshal's turn to participate in the theatrics. Accusing himself of being "crude, coarse, and wild," he made his confession. He wound up "blushing with shame" to demand the "punishment I deserve." The Executive Yuan took the second sinner more seriously than the first. The Young Marshal was turned over to a military tribunal, where he was given a sentence of ten years imprisonment with his blood brother Chiang Kai-shek appointed his jailer.

The sentence, in fact, turned out to be for life. The Young Marshal was consigned to a kind of house arrest—"soft detention" it was called. He was permitted to live luxuriously as befitted his station but always within confines of the capital. Chiang Kai-shek took him to Chungking during the Japanese invasion and afterward to Taiwan when the mainland was lost. He outlived his captor and is said to have become in his old age a research scholar specializing on the Ming period.

It fared worse for his coconspirator, Yang Hu-cheng, Old Yang. That tough ex-warlord had never expected much at Chiang Kai-shek's hands and he got even less. In due course he too was imprisoned, but behind bars. And he too was transferred to Chungking, but he never left it. The Generalissimo saw to that.

Yet neither man vanished into the shadows in vain. Of the fifty million Chinese who were to perish in the ensuing years of foreign and domestic conflict, they had more to show for their sacrifice than most. For in the end the Sian mutiny *did* accomplish what they had wanted: internal peace—for a critical decade anyway—and the military unification of the country which alone made resistance to the Japanese possible.

The names of Chang Hsueh-liang and Yang Hu-cheng deserve to go down in Chinese history along with Chiang Kai-shek's idols, Yo Fei, Sze Ko-fa, and the rest. But, of course, they never will because the China that the Young Marshal and Old Yang were trying to save was not that nation that emerged from the cataclysms yet to come.

17

The Devil Is Our Leader

THE EVENTS AT SIAN CAUGHT THE COMMUNISTS OFF balance. For years they had pushed against Chiang Kai-shek as the immovable force of evil, and his sudden give, his change of attitude, his willingness to at least listen to Chou En-lai's proposals for a united front, left the Red leadership spinning.

A dozen questions arose. Was collaboration with the Kuomintang reactionaries even imaginable? How could they be trusted after the betrayal of 1927 and all that had happened since? Could Lenin's famous locomotive of history, that took curves at such speed that all but the faithful were thrown off the train, have come full-circle—back to the days of 1924? Was detente with Chiang Kai-shek once again possible? Marxist soul-searching on the matter was stretched to the limit.

Even Mao Tse-tung took time to get his bearings. During the crisis he had been too concerned with saving the Generalissimo as a symbol of Chinese sovereignty to consider the political consequences. But now the new opportunity that offered must be analyzed and formulated into action before it slipped away.

A year earlier Mao had met rejection within his own party when he had suggested that the "national bourgeoisie" might be pried loose from the Kuomintang—a single limb, as it were, lopped from the tree. Now unexpectedly the central trunk, Chiang Kai-shek himself, had tumbled into the Communists' backyard. Or had he? Was Chiang's interest in ending the civil war genuine? Or was he merely trying to gull the Reds into letting down their defenses so as to hasten their destruction? Certainly the Generalissimo's departure for Nanking without committing himself on any of the Young Marshal's Eight Points left doubts about his true intentions.

Mao Tse-tung, always a believer in investigating before acting, began a cautious probe of Chiang's sincerity. On December 28, three days after the close of the Sian Incident, he issued a statement. First he congratulated the Generalissimo on an order withdrawing Nationalist troops from the Shensi border, a sign of peaceful intent. Then he made inquiries into what Chiang meant when he stated to the Young Marshal that "promises must be kept and actions must be resolute." Mao hoped this implied a "clean-up" of the Kuomintang's reactionary policies, and that Chiang intended to take the lead in forming an "anti-Japanese front uniting all parties and groups and really [taking] the military and political measures that can save the nation."

The Generalissimo made no response to this fishing expedition, so Mao Tse-tung proceeded with a more significant initiative. On February 10, 1937, with the concurrence of his Central Committee, he dispatched to Nanking a telegram outlining Four Pledges and Five Conditions.

The Four Pledges confirmed what Chou En-lai had offered Chiang Kai-shek at Sian: (1) a cessation of armed insurrection against the National government; (2) changing the name of the Workers' and Peasants' government to the Special Region of the Republic of China and putting its army under the direction of the Generalissimo; (3) instituting universal suffrage in the Special Region, including the enfranchising of Kuomintang Party members; (4) ending confiscation of landlords' property as an inducement for a common anti-Japanese united front.

The Five Conditions, on which the Four Pledges depended, were a truncated version of the Young Marshal's Eight Points: (1) ending civil wars and concentrating the country's strength to meet foreign aggression; (2) guarantees of freedom of speech, assembly and association, and the release of all political prisoners; (3) calling a conference of all political parties in a common endeavor to save the nation; (4) speedy preparations for resisting Japan; (5) improving the livelihood of the people.

It was now up to the Generalissimo to make a response, and respond he did with all the skill and dexterity that marked him as the politician par excellence of his convoluted era.

Chiang Kai-shek, recuperating at Fenghua from the bruised bones he had suffered from his fall into the moat at Lintung, had much to think over during January of 1937. His experiences at Sian had been salutary. Cut off from the sycophancy that surrounded him at Nanking, he had been exposed at first hand to popular feelings in regard to civil war and Japanese aggression, and had finally realized that changes in policy were essential if he was to remain the nation's leader.

He had implied promises at Sian, but how was he to keep them? Perhaps foolishly, he had made it a point of pride on his return to Nanking to insist that he had made no concessions while in captivity. How could he now institute a change of direction without making it appear he had been lying? Even to prepare armed resistance against Japanese aggression was a risky political venture. Many of his supporters in and out of government were allied with Japan. They were shareholders in Japanese companies or, for one reason or another, on the imperial payroll, and worked tirelessly for continued good relations. Whatever he did in allying with the Communists, opposing the Japanese, or promoting the economic betterment of the people, he was sure to be accused of divisiveness, of breaking the bonds of loyalty which held in place the oligarchy of grafting officials that passed as his government.

The Generalissimo returned to Nanking in early February for

a plenary session of the Kuomintang Central Executive Committee still unresolved on how to act. Then the Communist telegram arrived outlining the Four Pledges and the Five Conditions and Chiang Kai-shek began to see means of maneuvering.

He was as loud as anyone in denouncing the Red proposals. It was typical bandit insolence, a propaganda ploy not worth a moment's notice. And Chiang joined in the unanimous motion to reject the telegram without reply. Then he appeared to have a change of heart. He had been reading the classics, he said, and though the Central Executive Committee's action had been correct, it had perhaps been without benevolence. On February 21 he made a long speech excoriating the Communists, recapitulating his ten years of struggle to exterminate them, and utterly condemning the Red leaders for their crimes of treachery and violence. At the same time the recent telegram seemed to indicate possible repentance. Chiang proposed to put the Reds to the test, to find out if they were really sincere in wanting "to make a new start in life."

To offer them a last chance, he had perpared four peremptory demands. The Communists were to: (1) abolish the Red army and incorporate it in the National army; (2) dissolve their so-called soviet government; (3) cease propaganda that was opposed to the principles of Dr. Sun Yat-sen; (4) abandon the class struggle. Only on those terms could they be pardoned and received back into decent society.

The demands were, of course, essentially the same as the Communists' Four Pledges with the language reworked to make acceptance seem surrender to Kuomintang authority. The Central Executive Committee was a bit bewildered by the legerdemain, but the Generalissimo spoke with such vehemence—there were tears in his eyes when he spoke of repentance—that it approved the terms and ordered them sent to the Red capital.

There was more bewilderment in Shensi when the demands were received. But Mao Tse-tung, an old hand at seeing through the surface of things to the inner reality, urged provisional "capitulation"—provisional on how Chiang Kai-shek carried out the Five Conditions of the original Communist proposals.

And carry them out Chiang did—not always immediately or

directly but in time progress was made on all points, including those on the Young Marshal's program. The Seven Gentlemen, imprisoned for anti-Japanese leadership the previous November, were released one by one and all were out by July. The police were told to go easy on future patriotic demonstrations and the press was ordered to lay off such terms as "Red bandits" and "criminals" when referring to Communists. In government, the pro-Japanese Minister of Foreign Affairs was replaced, thus serving notice that an era of appeasement was ending. Negotiations were also begun to resume diplomatic relations with Soviet Russia after a ten-year break. And a date was set (November 12) for the convening of a People's Congress to inaugurate the stage of democratic government by popular vote as envisioned by Sun Yat-sen.

During that spring and summer of 1937 Chiang Kai-shek showed the beginnings of a new spirit that must have surprised even him. It was as if, in reestablishing cautious contact with the Communists, he was reviving the old days in Canton when Sun Yat-sen had been alive and the first united front had been established. He seemed to find stimulation in the development, perhaps because he sensed he was following at last in the footsteps of the Tsungli after so many years of unproductive detouring.

It was an interim of sincere intentions on both sides, and even some tangible results were obtained that might have paid dividends in a quasi-democratic united China if time had permitted. But time did not, and the moment of the possible was swept away in the storm that was about to break.

The Communists, the chief beneficiaries of the era of goodwill, were appreciative but also strangely schizoid in their reactions. The astonishing stroke of good fortune that had raised them overnight from rebel bandits hiding out in the hills of Shensi, to active partners in the legitimate government of China seemed to have increased inner party turmoil. Or so it appeared in the spring of 1937 when doctrinaire disputes rocked the Central Committee in the new Red capital of Yenan.

The seat of government had been changed in December 1936.

The Devil Is Our Leader

During the Sian crisis, at the Young Marshal's invitation, Mao Tse-tung had moved his regime from Pao An to more accessible headquarters. Yenan was a garrison town of some seven thousand inhabitants, but it was to grow. Mao brought with him in the first influx several hundred government officials, political cadres, and ranking military officers who went to work cutting cozy residences out of the hillsides. Ten years later, when Yenan had developed as the national center of Red culture, including universities, training schools, military academies, and industrial enterprises, the population exploded to one hundred thousand. After the founding of the People's Republic, habitation dropped back to fifty thousand—farmers, mechanics, townspeople, and squads of guides to the historic momuments and sanctuaries that today make Yenan, called the "Cradle of the Revolution," one of the prime tourist attractions of the nation.

It was from Yenan that the campaigns of the bitter Japanese resistance were directed and later the strategy that was to crush Chiang Kai-shek in the second civil war. From Yenan thousands of political cadres set out for the conquest of Chinese minds, spreading the thought of Mao Tse-tung who, in Yenan, delivered his most famous speeches and wrote his most influential tracts. And it was at Yenan that violent ideological battles were fought within the Central Committee, with none more momentous than the debate that raged in the spring of 1937 over the new alliance with the Kuomintang.

Now that the united front was a reality, sprung into being by the combustion of events, the opposing factions within the party polarized. Leading the anti-Mao forces was, as usual, Po Ku of the Twenty-eight Bolsheviks, backed by Chang Kuo-tao, again in good standing after a period of rehabilitation, with his ultimate fall from grace still a year off.

The attack of the hard-liners was based on "purist" dogma. What kind of Marxism was it to surrender confiscation of landlord's property and other socialist policies for a return to obsolete capitalist relationships? To adopt the Three Principles of Sun Yat-sen as a guiding philosophy for the Communist Party was a retrograde step. Perhaps some concessions had been necessary to bring about a united front but Mao Tse-tung, in his eagerness to placate the Kuomintang, had retreated into "right opportunism" and betrayed the revolution.

Mao saved his answers for a National Conference of the party early in May. There he told the assembly that there had been no ideological retreat; it was merely a question of changed perspectives. Before the Sian Incident the main contradiction had been seen as a conflict "between feudalism [the Kuomintang] and the masses of the people [the Communist Party]." Afterward a greater contradiction had emerged, "between China and Japan," submerging "internal contradictions...into a secondary and subordinate place." This was a concrete fact of history, and it had to be accommodated by "appropriate adjustments."

As for Sun Yat-sen's Three Principles, Mao contended that the Communist Party was not in basic conflict with them, even though its own socialist programs went much further. The main point was that "the people of the whole country [could] unite and fight for the Three Principles, a matter of the utmost importance in preparing to resist Japanese aggression."

Also, Mao pointed out, the Kuomintang had made concessions, too, abandoning with considerable loss of face its policies of one-party dictatorship, Communist suppression, and tolerance of Japanese encroachments. And Mao gave a fast brush to the charge that Marxist principles had been sacrificed by giving up the right to confiscate property. If and when war with Japan came, the issue would not be who owned the land as between landlords or peasants, but as between Chinese or Japanese.

Mao's arguments convinced the party conference and the opposition, abiding by the rules of democratic centralism—"unity, struggle, then unity again through struggle—" was forced into silence and the appearance of cooperation, at least for a while.

But Mao already had other matters to worry about. The missions sent to Nanking to iron out details of the united front were acting strangely. The political delegations under Chou En-lai seemed all too quickly to have fallen into Kuomintang habits of wining and dining, with negotiations conducted as a sideline. And the military commission under the leadership of Chu Teh was even more lackadaisical at getting down to business.

The Red commanders were, in fact, enjoying themselves thoroughly. They arrived in Nanking to find themselves famous. The public knew their caliber, despite ten years of maligning by the Kuomintang press and radio as despicable Red bandits. The indomitable Chu Teh, Lin Piao of the light foot, the One-eyed Dragon Liu Po-cheng and others were recognized as authentic folk heroes. Admired as the invincibles of the Kiangsi mountains and the Long March, they were followed everywhere by enthusiastic crowds.

And the adulation extended to higher echelons. The Red commanders in their shabby uniforms were back among their own kind, meeting and greeting spit-and-polish Kuomintang generals with perhaps just a touch of envy at their rivals' status and position. Many Red and Nationalist officers were old acquaintances, former comrades at Whampoa or on the Northern Expedition of 1926. There were welcoming feasts with toasts to the new entente. The visitors were taken to the Central Military Academy where smartly uniformed cadets paraded in their honor and German staff officers generously praised Red strategy and ingenuity in campaigns of the past. Under such circumstances who wanted to get down to the boring work of logistics and allocations of command?

Mao Tse-tung did. Almost alone he felt the urgency of events, the limitation of time remaining before Japan would be forced to act. As summer drew on, he became increasingly impatient, fretting at the snail's pace of the negotiations in Nanking. In due course, forgetting diplomatic niceties and perhaps attaching too much blame to one side, he let loose a blast at "the attempts of the Kuomintang to seduce Communist cadres"—he hesitated to spell out commanders and politicians—"with offers of fame and fortune and wine and women."

Mao may well have been a bit frantic at the time because, along with his irritations about Nanking, he was experiencing severe problems of morale in his home territory. He had won only half his battle by convincing the Central Committee that the measures taken to cement the united front had been correct. He still had to convince the rank and file of the Red Army, the political cadres, and the civilian populations, and that proved tougher going.

The people were dismayed by all that was happening around them. Their once proud soviet state had been renamed the Special Area of the Shensi-Kansu-Ninghsia Border Region or, to save breath, the Border Region. Their revered Red Army was now the Eighth Route Army of the National Government, marching no longer under a red flag but the official Kuomintang banner. Even the insignia on uniforms had changed. Red stars had disappeared from caps and blouses to be replaced by Kuomintang buttons—white stars on blue backgrounds.

But worse, infinitely worse and more bewildering, was the appearance of Chiang Kai-shek's portrait alongside the familiar faces of Marx and Lenin. It was to be seen everywhere—in mess halls, lecture rooms, and in the streets—the grim set mouth, squinty eyes, and stocky jaw of Chiang Kai-shek, commander-in-chief of the combined national armies.

Mao Tse-tung understood the shocked emotions and confused states of mind resulting, and did what he could to clarify the situation. "We are [still] fighting for socialism," he reassured his followers. "[I]f we lose sight of [that] goal, we cease to be Communists." But a revolution undergoes many stages and "[t]oday...an alliance [with the Kuomintang] is... a necessary bridge on the way to socialism."

The people wanted to believe him; they trusted Chairman Mao. But that portrait of Chiang Kai-shek kept getting in the way. How could a tiger change its stripes? How could a sinkhole rise to be a mountain? With peasant humor they devised a witticism that was only half a joke, "The devil is now our leader."

About the only bright spot for Mao Tse-tung that summer was the appearance of an unexpected Red army. It marched, ragged but proud, out of the mountains of Kiangsi and Fukien when word of the united front had penetrated the hinterland. The resurrected men were remnants of the Communist brigades which had stayed behind in 1934, the rearguards covering the breakout of the Long Marchers. Dispersed into the hills, they had been defending precarious bases against provincial troops ever since. In all they numbered some fifteen thousand. Chiang Kai-shek, in a benevolent mood, recognized the existence of these

The Devil Is Our Leader

irregulars and commissioned them as the New Fourth Army, entitled to draw the same pay and equipment as the already authorized Eighth Route Army.

Things were going well for the Generalissimo just then and he was disposed to be generous. He had reopened relations with Russia; a treaty of friendship and nonaggression was in negotiation; his son Ching-kuo was on his way back from Moscow with a Soviet wife and children; Britain and the United States, finally aroused to the Japanese threat, had advanced handsome credits for the purchase of military material; and from Japan itself, overtures had been forthcoming that might be interpreted as conciliatory. The Gernalissimo was beginning to believe that by astute diplomacy he had averted the danger of all-out conflict.

But Mao Tse-tung was not taken in. He cautioned from Yenan that the Japanese maneuvers were "preparations for a major war, and a major war confronts us." And he repeated a previous warning: "Japan is exerting every ounce of energy ... according to a definite plan, for the subjugation of China at a single stroke." But he might as well have been whistling into the wind. No one, not even in his own camp, was listening. That is until the night of July 7, 1937 when, with the shadow play over, the Japanese started on their conquest of the world, beginning with a clumsy ruse they were pleased to call the Marco Polo Bridge Incident.

18

Typhoon from the North

THE JAPANESE HIGH COMMAND WAS ALWAYS PARTIAL TO incidents. Declaring war was a final step, whereas incidents left room for maneuvering. If an incident was successfully brought off, as the Mukden Incident of 1931 had been, the situation could be exploited and expanded. If it failed, as the Shanghai Incident of 1932 had, claims could be made of achieved objectives, and retreat was possible without loss of face. The Japanese would have dearly loved to call the attack on Pearl Harbor in 1941 an incident. Unfortunately the American president and Congress wouldn't play along.

After the dramatics at Sian, the Japanese high command realized that a full-scale invasion of the Middle Kingdom could no longer be postponed. A united China meant eventually a strong China and Baron Tanaka's strategy had been predicated on striking while China was still weak. The sooner the attack began the better. Only time to organize and move up troops in paralyzing force was needed—a matter of six months at most.

The Japanese diplomatic corps went to work to lull Chiang

Kai-shek into a false sense of security while military preparations proceeded. The Tokyo Foreign Ministry suddenly found that certain regions of Inner Mongolia were not essential for Manchukuo's territorial integrity and set about forming them into an autonomous government which, it was hinted, might pledge allegiance to Nanking. Kuomintang hopes for peace were further aroused by a visit from a Japanese industrial magnate who came to offer aid in stimulating the Chinese economy. But early in July 1937 the charade ended; the Japanese war machine was ready.

On the night of July 7 Japanese troops, stationed in Peiping, began conducting maneuvers outside the city. There was nothing illegal about this; it was sanctioned by treaty rights. But the maneuvers that evening took an odd turn. Near a town called Lukouchiao, at a bridge named after Marco Polo because the Venetian traveler had once described the stone lions adorning it, Japanese squads went on a rampage.

A claim was later made that a soldier had been kidnapped* and his comrades were merely rousting villages and villagers in a search for him. But clearly the troops were acting on orders, creating disturbances, looking for trouble. They found it when a Chinese garrison, protecting government property, fired on them.

This was the Lukouchiao or Marco Polo Bridge Incident, and the Japanese wasted no time exploiting it. Howls of indignation echoed in the Nipponese press. Tokyo refused to listen when Chiang Kai-shek offered to set up a commission of inquiry. There was nothing to inquire about; the insult to the emperor was unpardonable and only thoroughgoing punitive measures could wipe out the disgrace. Japanese armored cars and motorized artillery began to roll.

For weeks Chiang Kai-shek temporized. He appealed to international opinion and sought the good offices of governments, hoping to find some diplomatic means of staving off war. But finally at the end of July, with Peiping and Tientsin already in Japanese hands, he spoke out in an address to the nation.

---

*He turned up a couple of weeks later in a brothel, an apparent deserter, but by that time his capture was irrelevant.

He explained that each time China had tried to compromise differences, the Japanese had taken it as a sign of weakness. Such arrogance was no longer to be borne. The time had arrived to avenge insults; the nation must arise as one man to take action against the bandits. And he ended with a special exhortation to the armed forces: "Soldiers! The supreme moment has come.... Never retreat! Drive out the invaders so that our nation may be born anew!"

Brave words—except for what was happening everywhere. Chinese garrisons and field forces were being bowled over by the might of Japanese armor, proving that it was going to take more than rhetoric to defend the nation.

Mao Tse-tung was quicker to speak out, but then he had foreseen the attack coming long in advance. Even so, it took time to argue out the party line, and it wasn't until July 23 that Mao delivered an address called "Policies, Measures and Perspectives for Resisting the Japanese Invasion."

Like Chiang Kai-shek, Mao called for the overthrow of Japanese imperialism. But unlike the Generalissimo he didn't limit himself to military measures. He foresaw a long struggle in which the morale of the civilian population would be of critical importance. To "mobilize the whole people," he called for freedom of speech and patriotic assembly, also for a reform of the National government by weeding out pro-Japanese traitors and replacing them with believers in democracy. He advocated an immediate program to improve the people's livelihood, and asked for wartime policies to regulate economics and finance. He advanced these and other proposals to "unite the entire Chinese people, the government and the armed forces" in a front as solid as the Great Wall.

The recommendations were lost on Chiang Kai-shek. However he viewed the war, it was certainly not as a crusade to liberalize his government and democratize the nation. The problem, as he saw it, was to steer the country through the Japanese infestation and deliver it at the end as little changed as possible from the Confucian ideal.

So early on the rift appeared, the conflict of objectives between left and right, between the Communists and the Kuomintang.

The chasm widened as the war progressed, though miraculously, through mutual need, the united front was to hold together until the smoke of foreign battle cleared.

The Japanese, sweeping all before them in the North, hardly paused to consolidate their gains before launching a second invasion. This was at Shanghai, a city that attracted them like moon-viewing in summertime. And with good reason; Shanghai controlled the Yangtze River, and possession of the Yangtze, navigable to the great gorges of the West, was tantamount to cutting China in two and pocketing the richer half. Besides, Shanghai was the international trade center of the Orient and it was good policy to put on an exhibition of shattering strength before the foreigners who were to be next on Baron Tanaka's list of conquests.

The Japanese well remembered their poor showing in 1932 and this time took no chances. Beginning on August 13, 1937 some one hundred thousand men were sent ashore, covered by the big guns of their newest battleships.

But the embarrassment was to be worse. In 1932 the defenders of Shanghai had held out for a month; in 1937 the resistance lasted for three months, with casualties said to be as high as 50 percent on both sides. The conditions were the same: the narrow streets, the deadly ricocheting fire, the house to house assaults, the buildings—toppled by dynamite or 16-inch shells from the harbor—dissolving into rubble across which men hunted each other like rats. The killing and maiming lasted into the fall, into the chill winds of November.

And this time the foreign concessions didn't escape. The Japanese battleships riding at anchor off the Bund proved too tempting a target for the inept Chinese air force. Several runs were made at them, the bombs missing by wide margins and falling into the International Settlement. Chinese civilians, crowding into the public squares for sanctuary, were masticated as the explosives plummeted among them. Blood ran in the gutters and long remembered was one grotesque tableau—a T-model Ford after a near hit, with its charred occupants sitting upright in death, the driver still gripping the wheel.

Chiang Kai-shek, directing operations from Nanking, was in

his element. Defending strong points against a relentlessly oncoming enemy was one of his specialties. He kept feeding in replacements to meet the Japanese reserves, deploying a total of seventy-eight Chinese divisions, or over a million troops. But in the end, the battle revealed an old Chiang weakness—lack of strategic foresight. The Japanese landed at Hangchow to the south, outflanking Shanghai and forcing the Generalissimo's withdrawal.

Lack of strategic planning was also fatal to Nanking, two hundred miles upriver. Inadequate defenses prompted the government to beat a hasty retreat. The Japanese, arriving a few days after evacuation, found the capital an easy prize.

What followed was one of the horror episodes of a war that was to be replete with them. The Japanese high command, stung by the long resistance at Shanghai and determined to evoke a terror of Japanese might that would serve them better in future, sacked the city. For two weeks imperial soldiers ravened in an orgy of killing, looting, and raping.

Practices that became commonplace in later campaigns were initiated at Nanking: torture to reveal hidden wealth; grave digging by those who would become corpses; bayonet practice with living dummies. The standard procedure of commandeering women and setting them up according to age and looks in officers' or enlisted mens' "comfort" homes was abandoned in favor of turning the entire city into a brothel, catch as catch can. Women were lucky to escape murder after rape because murder was on the brain. One hundred and fifty thousand were said to have perished before the holocaust was called off.

Savagery in war is an old story. After the Nazi record of concentration camp horrors and the United States atom bombing of Hiroshima and Nagasaki, not to mention such later outrages as the My Lai massacre, the sack of Nanking may seem a routine event. But what made the atrocity particularly ugly was the vindictive satisfaction that seemed to be derived from the pain inflicted.

The fact is that the Japanese had never really emerged from feudal barbarism; only the veneer had changed. The officers of the imperial army were still bound by the traditions of their samurai ancestors who tested swords on the necks of passing peasants, counting, it is said, the steps traveled before the head fell off. And the common soldiers, descended from those same peasants, were taking out on the Chinese a suppressed fury that might have been better vented against their own higher-ups. At Nanking, as elsewhere during the Pacific war, the Japanese feudal ethic was running true to type nearly a century after Commodore Perry's ships had opened the islands to Western civilization.

In the first phase of the invasion, the Japanese had sent a column below the Great Wall in a sweeping encirclement of the West. To the Communist Eighth Route Army fell the honor of helping the Kuomintang troops to check this drive. Chiang Kai-shek chose Taiyuan, capital of Shansi Province, as the focus for resistance. The city must be held at all cost.

The assignment was not welcomed by Mao Tse-tung. He never shared the Generalissimo's mania for defending strong points. Cities, even the most important of them, were expendable when compared to what he considered the main objective of warfare—the destruction of the enemy's forces at minimal cost to his own. But when the Military Council met to discuss the matter, he found himself in the minority. Chu Teh and other Red commanders, recently returned from Nanking, wanted to make a good showing in the eyes of the foreign-trained officers of the Kuomintang and insisted on carrying out Chiang Kai-shek's instructions.

So the joint responsibility for the defense of Taiyuan was undertaken. Though it soon turned out to be sole responsibility because the Nationalist commander, taking advantage of the Communists' willingness to fight, craftily withdrew his own troops, leaving the defense entirely up to the Reds.

The Eighth Route Army put on a gallant stand. It repelled two Japanese assaults on the city, fighting off tanks and motorized infantry with machineguns, grenades, and high-risk dynamite squads. But the third attack was too sustained, and the Communists were forced to retreat with heavy losses.

The Generalissimo was pleased by the creditable performance

and sent his congratulations. Mao Tse-tung, possibly suspecting that Chiang Kai-shek was trying to deplete the Eighth Route Army by attritional methods, was furious. He railed against the spirit of "heroism" that had taken hold of his commanders and called for a return to "independent, self-reliant guerrilla warfare."

At the next meeting of the Military Council, the commanders, sobered by the casualties at Taiyuan, were ready to listen to Mao Tse-tung and approved the strategies he proposed. The Eighth Route Army was to be broken up into small units, which were to reconnoiter the Japanese line of advance. No attack was to be attempted until a weakness was found; then the units were to converge for action.

The Red troops dispersed, fading into the countryside in a manner reminiscent of Kiangsi days. The Japanese pushed methodically on, passing from the province of Shansi into Shensi through difficult mountain terrain. And on September 24 Lin Piao of the light foot found an opportunity that might have been drawn from a guerrilla text book—two Nipponese divisions laboring through a mountain pass.

The Reds swept down the slopes in the old familiar style and before they had withdrawn left sixty-four hundred Japanese dead for the loss of only three hundred men. Mao Tse-tung was elated by the victory at Ping-hsin Pass; Chiang Kai-shek less so. He observed that guerrilla tactics were straws to stop a tiger, and his estimation of the eighth Route Army, never high, declined a notch or two.

And indeed the success at the Ping-hsin Pass was small compared to an authentic Chinese triumph of arms that was to occur six months later. In early April 1938 the Japanese eastern army of eighty thousand men, beating its way south through Shantung Province and perhaps grown careless because of the spongy resistance it had been meeting, found four hundred thousand Nationalist troops under the command of the redoubtable Li Tsung-jen waiting for it near the city of Suchow. Chiang Kai-shek, masterminding operations from Wuhan, where he had retreated with his government after the fall of Nanking, found the odds of five to one exactly suited to his theories of attack and ordered battle. Li Tsung-jen responded with vigor and, at a village called Taierhchuang, the Japanese were routed, leaving behind sixteen thousand dead, forty tanks, seventy armored cars, and mountains of weapons and equipment as trophies.

The victory at Taierhchuang should have been even greater. General von Falkenhausen, chief of Chiang Kai-shek's German advisory staff, called for an immediate follow-up, and stamped his boots in frustration when the Generalissimo refused to issue the orders. To a foreigner, the lapse in orthodox strategy may have seemed unpardonable, but those close to Chiang understood completely. Li Tsung-jen was his greatest military rival. He had beaten Chiang to the Yangtze during the Northern Expedition of 1926 and to Peking in 1928, and it was perfectly comprehensible that the Generalissimo had no wish to offer him further opportunities for glory.

Still, however incomplete, the battle was a notable triumph. All China rejoiced and hoped for more victories to come. But, in fact, Taierhchuang turned out to be the last large-scale clash of armies in a war that was to drag on for another seven years.

That summer Chiang Kai-shek's plans for the future took shape. Though the Japanese were still some four hundred miles from Wuhan and there was plenty of time to fortify the tri-cities, he gave little thought to defenses. Instead he spent his time supervising the dismantling of factories in the Pittsburgh of China. Machines, foundries, mill components, everything movable was loaded on flatboats or strapped on coolies' backs. A long trek lay ahead, a thousand miles upriver, up the fearsome Yangtze gorges to Chungking, the city deep in the mountains of Szechwan Province that the Generalissimo had chosen as his new capital. Chosen, apparently, without consulting his officials or military chiefs because, as he was to tell a journalist with superb self-assurance: "Wherever I go, there is the government, the Cabinet and the center of resistance."

How long had he had the move in mind? Possibly from the beginning, from the first attack at the Marco Polo Bridge; certainly after he tested Japanese power at Shanghai and learned Japanese intentions toward China at Nanking. Potent allies were needed to help resist the Japanese in the field, and at that milestone of history allies were in short supply. The League of Nations had proved itself a farce, yielding Abyssinia to Mussolini and Austria to Hitler with hardly a murmur. Appeasement was still going strong. Britain and France were about to barter away Czechoslovakia for a promise of peace at Munich, while Americans, sunk in their own economic depression, were indifferent to the woes of others. Chiang Kai-shek, left with no alternative but to defend China by himself, had decided that retreat to the hinterland was the better part of valor until the international situation blew up and propelled allies his way.

There were some who believed that Chiang was retreating too early, that the victories at Ping-hsin and Taierhchuang had proved that the Japanese could be defeated when the conditions were right. Among those who held this view was Chou En-lai, head of the liaison mission from Yenan. He believed Wuhan was a case in point. He knew the fighting potential of its industrial workers from past experiences and appealed to the Generalissimo to arm the people, turning Wuhan into another Madrid.

The Spanish civil war was then in its second year and the Fascist forces had not yet been able to conquer Madrid, vigorously defended by a civilian militia. The same thing could happen at Wuhan, Chou En-lai argued. All that was needed was arms and elementary training and the workers would make the tri-cities impregnable.

The Generalissimo had no intention of risking the experiment. He believed that war was for professionals, not for civilians who got wrong ideas once they had guns in hand. He continued with evacuation plans, publicly promising that the retreat to Chungking was only a strategic and temporary withdrawal. In the fastness of Szechwan Province he meant to rebuild the economy, train new armies, and regenerate the national spirit against the day of a mighty counterattack that would drive the invaders from Chinese soil. Meanwhile he was trading space for time. Nevertheless he lingered on in Wuhan until just before the Japanese arrival in October to keep a close watch on Chou En-lai's activities.

The phrases "regeneration in retreat" and "trading space for time" heartened the nation and won worldwide admiration among the democracies. But they thoroughly frightened the Japanese. Baron Tanaka's plans hadn't provided for a Chinese withdrawal into limbo and it posed serious problems.

The Japanese had begun their invasion in a holiday mood. They had expected an easy walkover as in Manchuria and had set a limit of three months to bring the nation to its knees. Yet by October 1938 sixteen months had passed. Nippon had committed over a million men to action and had lost a third of them to casualties and disease, and still the end was not in sight. Nor was the end likely to occur if Chiang Kai-shek and his government disappeared into the mountains where tanks and armored cars were reduced to parity with coolie soldiers shooting rifles and hurling grenades.

The Japanese, always politically elastic, changed their tone. The strident voice of conquest modulated to injured innocence as a peace offensive began. Press and radio poured forth the new doctrine: the Chinese had misunderstood the imperial intention, there was no need for hostility between the nations. The Japanese army would gladly sponsor Chiang Kai-shek's safe return to Nanking where he and his government would receive nothing but friendly cooperation in ruling the country.

Chiang Kai-shek, distant descendant of the Duke of Chou, disciple of Sun Yat-sen, and idolizer of historic patriots, was immune to such blandishments. But someone else was listening, and listening intently—the man the Tsungli had called his good left hand and had thought of as his heir apparent—Wang Ching-wei.

19

One Divides into Two

WANG CHING-WEI WAS A TYPE OF LOFTY CHINESE intellectual much admired by his fellow countrymen but exasperating to Westerners. Steeped in the culture of the centuries, he believed implicitly in Confucian values and dismissed the novelties of foreigners as gimcracks of no lasting importance. He thought of himself as a superior man, with a mind trained to meet any emergency and outthink any opponent. In morals, he went out of his way to raise himself above reproach; in manners, courtesy, and address, he cultivated a style that led to his being called "China's perfect gentleman." And along with his outer veneer, he had convictions and the courage to go with them. It was just his bad luck that he was born into an age when his type of man was obsolete.

Born in 1883, Wang Ching-wei was the son of a minor government official. He showed an early aptitude for classical learning and a brilliant career as a mandarin, or high imperial functionary, was predicted for him. Unfortunately the troubles of the Manchus and the suspension of the civil service system cut off these expectations. He did, however, obtain an appointment to study in Japan and in Tokyo met Sun Yat-sen. In 1905 he became a charter member and leading light of the Tsungli's Tung Meng Hui (United League).

Wang Ching-wei had physical courage. In 1909, at a low point in the league's fortunes and hoping to revive revolutionary ardor, he decided on an act of suicidal daring. Believing in Sun's theory of the "propaganda of the deed," he traveled to Peking with a group of dare-to-dies to assassinate the Prince Regent, ruling on behalf of the four-year-old emperor, Henry Pu-yi.

Dynamite was set under a bridge outside the Imperial Palace and the conspirators waited through the night for the Prince Regent's return from a banquet. Unfortunately they attracted the curiosity of a dog that began to bark. Other dogs took up the refrain and in due course the police were alerted. The conspirators were forced to flee. They might all have escaped if Wang Ching-wei had not betrayed himself by his famous courtesy. At the Peking railroad station, seeing a coconspirator off, Wang was impelled to lift his hat because she was a woman. This revealed his false queue, a sure sign of a revolutionary, which in turn led to his arrest.

At his trial, Wang took full responsibility for the discovered dynamite and proceeded to denounce the iniquities of the Manchu regime. His youth, his education, his courage and general deportment made such an impression on the court that instead of decapitation he was sentenced to life imprisonment. Within two years the Revolution of 1911 was to release him and turn him into a public hero. Wang celebrated by marrying the girl of the railway station whose charms had proved his undoing. Her name was Chen Pi-chun and she was the heiress of an immensely wealthy family. From then on Wang's political career, not to mention his frequent trips to Europe, were financed in style.

Wang Ching-wei had refused to accept a cabinet post during Sun Yat-sen's brief tenure as President of the Republic. He scorned the corruption and money-grubbing that office-holding implied. But later in Canton he acceded to a seat on the Central Executive Committee, though still refusing administrative responsibilities. By that time his puritanical streak had led him to organize the Six No Society—no smoking, no gambling, no drinking, no promiscuity, no corruption, no officialdom. Despite these strictures, however, he accepted the chairmanship of the Central Executive Committee when Sun Yat-sen died, leaping in one stride from political noninvolvement to head of government.

Unquestionably Wang Ching-wei detested the Communists from the start. Everything they stood for and their methods for achieving goals were repellent to his Confucian sensibilities. But since Sun Yat-sen had endorsed them, he stuck loyally by the united front alliance until Stalin's crass telegram of 1927 made a breach permissible.

Wang's attitude toward Chiang Kai-shek had also undergone changes. At first he had patronized the younger man, then quarreled with him because of his dictatorial methods in founding the Nanking government. Since then relations had blown hot and cold, Wang sometimes serving in the cabinet, sometimes not. Undoubtedly the men despised each other, but loyalty to the Tsungli's memory formed a bond that neither could rupture.

For Wang Ching-wei the outbreak of the Japanese war was more than a military disaster. It was a failure of diplomacy, the result of blundering by the Generalissimo. Wang, speaking perfect Japanese and oriented to the country by his years of residence there and the contacts he had maintained since, was sympathetic to Nippon's needs for expansion. On occasion—when he had headed the Nanking government during Chiang Kai-shek's Red bandit campaigns—he had helped appease the imperial claims by trade concessions and even gifts of outlying territories through ambiguously worded treaties. And there was considerably more disposable land outside the Great Wall, especially adjacent to the troublesome Communists, which could have been bartered away if Chiang had kept his head and played his cards right. Instead what had he done? He had made an alliance with the Reds, frightening the Japanese, and virtually guaranteeing an invasion.

It was too late to turn the clock back on that now. But when the Japanese began their peace overtures in the fall of 1938, Wang Ching-wei was alert to new possibilities. Why not let the invaders take over the country as long as the *form* of Chinese government was maintained? The nation had been overrun before in history but, by applying the formula of "surrender, appease, survive," had in the end triumphed over its conquerors. Why not again—this time with the advantage of a legitimate government in office from the start?

Wang Ching-wei, widely admired for his brilliance, didn't discount the difficulties of the undertaking, but his sense of superiority may have distorted his perspective. For he sincerely believed that the Chinese mind—rather *his* mind—could outthink and outwit and in the long run triumph over the harsh but unstable Japanese. He saw it as his mission in his fifty-fifth year to save his country further suffering by discontinuing the destructive element of war and traducing the invader from within.

He opened secret negotiations with his Japanese contacts before he left Wuhan. By the time he reached Chungking he had received encouraging replies. The authorities in Tokyo would indeed be interested in a Nanking government headed by Wang Ching-wei as premier. It was suggested that he leave China so that negotiations might be conducted in a more open, businesslike fashion elsewhere.

Wang made arrangements for a secret flight from Chungking. It turned out to be not so secret, because Chiang Kai-shek had an excellent intelligence service that kept him abreast of the details. But the Generalissimo made no effort to stop his old rival when he departed on the night of December 20, 1938. To imprison or even detain the Tsungli's left-hand man was unthinkable. Instead he planned to assassinate him.

The agent Chiang sent after the deserting Wang Ching-wei must surely qualify as one of the most persistent if inept hit men on record. He followed his mark to Hanoi in Indo-China, where Wang was to dicker and deal with the Japanese for more than a year. In Hanoi, though he failed in several attempts on Wang's life, he kept trying. He followed his target to Nanking where in March 1940 Wang was installed as premier of a puppet Chinese government, and peppered away at intervals thereafter. He finally got his man, though bungling to the end. For when Wang Ching-wei died in a Tokyo hospital in 1944, cause of death was given as belated complications arising from an assassin's bullet the year before.

Withdrawal to Chungking may have been a brilliant achievement in realpolitik for Chiang Kai-shek, but it put an extra strain on Mao Tse-tung's already difficult position. In 1937 he had seen in a united front with the Kuomintang two great advantages—an opportunity for peaceful and rapid development of his Border Region, and acquiring a powerful partner in a threatened war against Japan. Now, in the fall of 1938, the war was here and raging but the powerful partner had disappeared into the mountains of Szechwan. Mao had also been frustrated in the rapid development of the Border Region by unanticipated quirks and attitudes among his own people.

Perhaps Mao Tse-tung had done too good a job in selling the united front. Once the message sank home, once the alliance was recognized as a Marxist turn of history, a mood of relaxation settled in at Yenan. If the Kuomintang was to be a partner, let it be the principal partner. It was rich and backed by foreign powers; let it provide the guns and men to fight the Japanese. And on the political front, let it take the lead in fulfilling the principles of Sun Yat-sen. Why should Communists exert themselves for the people's livelihood until Chiang Kai-shek showed what he intended to do?

That was certainly the attitude of the hard-liners on the Central Committee, influenced through this critical period by Chang Kuo-tao who, though rehabilitated as to his previous errors, was as dogmatic and doctrinaire as ever in his present opinions. Chang, along with Po Ku, headed the opposition to Mao Tse-tung and they gained a valuable ally in the autumn of 1937 when Wang Ming, the original leader of the Twenty-eight Bolsheviks, returned in triumph from Moscow.

In actual fact, though naturally he didn't make much of it, Wang Ming had been more or less booted out of Russia. In August 1937 Joseph Stalin had signed a nonaggression pact with Chiang Kai-shek and, thus allied to the major power in China, he lost interest in the local Communists. He had long since lost interest in the Comintern, considering it an obsolete instrument of policy, and he regarded the Comintern's disciples in Moscow as vociferous nuisances who could better be employed at home. Hence Wang Ming's marching papers.

Nevertheless Wang Ming, always a showman, put the best face on his return from the Kremlin. He arrived in Yenan, according to one witness, as "an 'imperial envoy' from Moscow, holding high the Emperor's double-edged sword, his manner of speech... that of... transmitting an imperial decree." The news he brought was discomfiting. The Reds could expect no separate shipments of arms and supplies from the Soviet Union. Everything was going directly to Chiang Kai-shek for dispersal through the united front.

This information, of course, played directly into the hands of Chang Kuo-tao and his faction. Close cooperation with the Kuomintang was now more important than ever. The Red government was not only dependent on Chiang Kai-shek for political leadership, but for the weapons and equipment necessary for effective warfare against the Japanese. A slogan was adopted to convey the idea of total solidarity: "Everything through the United Front."

Both the slogan and the trend of thought were unacceptable to Mao Tse-tung. He remembered too well the first united front during Canton days when total reliance on the Kuomintang had led to the betrayals of 1927 and almost to the extinction of the Chinese Communist Party. That must not happen again, but how was the warning to be conveyed? He experimented with a slogan of his own: "Simultaneous alliance [with the Kuomintang] and struggle [against it]." But even he realized that the message was lost in the weasel wording.

Through the spring of 1938, while the Generalissimo and his Nationalist government were pushed west to Wuhan, and while Red army squads darted around advancing Japanese columns trying to find opportunities to strike, Mao Tse-tung studied the contradictions looking for a solution. And as time passed, the pressures mounted.

Party refugees, escaping from Shanghai, Peiping, and other Japanese-occupied cities, poured into Yenan. They were mostly intellectuals, staunch comrades but, from too long isolation, ideologically out of date. All had heard of the Long March but few knew abut the conference at Tsunyi where the Red leadership had changed and new policies had come into being. Many still adhered to the old line of the Twenty-eight Bolsheviks and, finding Wang Ming, the founder and chief theoretician of that group in Yenan, tended to fall under his influence.

Then there was the Red army, now retitled the Eighth Route Army. Its commanders were growing impatient with hit and run warfare—mostly run with little hit since the signal victory at the Ping-hsin Pass. They wanted to fight with field guns and automatic weapons in stand-up or "regular" battles that had some dignity to them. They wanted Russian arms and equipment and were ready to make almost any concessions to Chiang Kai-shek in order to get them.

In May 1938 Mao Tse-tung wrote a pamphlet to correct this dangerous line of thought. He called it "Problems of Strategy in Guerrilla War Against Japan." Its purpose was to argue that the basic approach was the same "both for regular and for guerrilla warfare" differing only in "degree and form." Though it was an indisputable fact that China was now on the strategic defensive, it was "possible and necessary to use tactical offensives within the strategic defensive, to fight campaigns and battles of quick decision [during a] protracted war . . ." By "initiative, flexibility and planning" and "the cumulative effect of many [small] victories," guerrilla action could weaken the enemy and finally change the momentum of the war.

Harking back to the old days in Kiangsi, Mao pressed the need to establish bases behind enemy lines 'in the mountains . . . on the plains and . . . in the river-lake-estuary regions." As yet he did not comprehend the full significance of the plan he was advancing because he wrote that "plains are less suitable than the mountains" since they were more exposed to enemy attack. The concept of disappearing headquarters that were everywhere and nowhere was yet to come. Though he did formulate the essential strategy of the future when he spoke of making "a front out of the enemy's rear." As a final carrot for his commanders, Mao promised that guerrilla warfare would be expanded into a more aggressive form he called "mobile" warfare and, as a last step, transformed into "regular" warfare when the time came to take the offensive and drive the Japanese out of China.

The Red commanders studied the pamphlet without enthusiasm. The prospect of returning to the hide-and-seek tactics of Kiangsi days held little appeal. Chiang Kai-shek had thought better of the Red army than that when he had praised its gallant stand at Taiyuan, and the Generalissimo was, after all, the supreme commander-in-chief. Perhaps it was Mao Tse-tung who had fallen behind, refusing to acknowledge that times had changed, still obsessed by the strategies of the past.

And so in all quarters—the army, the Central Committee, and among the political cadres—the mood of complacency and uncritical cooperation with the Kuomintang grew. Mao's warnings that class warfare hadn't ceased but was only in temporary suspension were smugly ignored.

And then an astonishing event occurred. Chang Kuo-tao, the loudest advocate of everything through the united front, defected to the Kuomintang. He renounced twenty years of dedication to the Marxist cause by marching back in time to Confucianism and traditional ways. In the summer of 1938 he slipped away from Yenan. Showing up in Wuhan a few weeks later, he publicly pledged allegiance to Chiang Kai-shek.

The apostasy can only be explained on psychological grounds. Chang Kuo-tao believed in authority. It made no difference whether the authority was wise or stupid as long as it was strong. He had served without criticism or complaint under Li Li-san and the Twenty-eight Bolsheviks when their iron-fisted policies were leading the Chinese revolution to ruin. Only after Mao Tse-tung had taken control at Tsunyi did he balk, and that was because he believed the line of authority sanctioned by the Kremlin had been broken. Later he attempted to set up as a dictator himself during his ill-fated adventure in Sikang during the winter of 1935–36. He seems never to have recovered from the humiliation of that failure, and Mao Tse-tung's tolerance toward him during his subsequent trial before the Military Council probably made matters worse. Chang Kuo-tao didn't want kindness or a chance to redeem himself. He could act with confidence only under tough leadership, the tougher the better. And when the united front gave him access to China's ultimate strong man, Generalissimo Chiang Kai-shek, he moved across the divide.

Whatever his motives, Chang Kuo-tao seized on the excuse of attending a rural celebration to leave Yenan. He kept on traveling until he reached Wuhan, where he surfaced with a job in Chiang Kai-shek's secret police apparently prearranged for him. He lost no time in issuing an open letter to his former comrades in Yenan, urging them to do as he had done if they were really sincere in their patriotism. In effect, he was calling for the abolition of the Chinese Communist Party.

Profound shock was felt in Yenan. Chang Kuo-tao's defection was not to be taken lightly. Along with Mao Tse-tung he had been a charter member of the party since its founding in 1921, and his betrayal seemed incomprehensible. Bewildering questions arose. How long had he been in secret negotiations with the Kuomintang? Had he been in Chiang Kai-shek's pay when he advocated Communist subservience to the united front? If so, where did that leave Wang Ming, Po Ku, and his other supporters? Were they tarred with the same brush of treacherous intent, or had they been merely dupes?

The atmosphere of suspicion and self-analysis was all-pervading. Only Mao Tse-tung appeared unperturbed. He saw in Chang Kuo-tao's desertion a case in point of what could happen when correct Marxist principles were abandoned. Chang's violent swing from ultra left to ultra right was a perfect illustration of the unity of opposites. There were conflicting sides latent in all men and all things, and only socialist thought and discipline could determine which would conquer. Or, put in another way, Chang Kuo-tao was living proof that one divides into two.

Mao Tse-tung helped clear Wang Ming and his cohorts from guilt by association and benefited by a strengthened consensus in the Central Committee. Soon afterward the army commanders swung into line. Chiang Kai-shek's decision in October to retreat to Chungking also caused them to revise ideas on military glory. Faced with fighting the Japanese with only their own resources, they had no option but guerrilla warfare.

Mao Tse-tung was to have another period of anxiety when the Japanese peace offensive got under way in the fall of 1938.

Perhaps he was at fault in misjudging Chiang Kai-shek's character, but the spirit of appeasement was in the air and Mao trusted no one. In September, Britain and France had signed the Munich Pact, bartering away Czechoslovakia to satisfy Hitler's territorial demands, and Mao was convinced that the same thing could happen in the Orient—a Far Eastern Munich, he called it. He already saw, or thought he saw, international diplomatic pressure being brought to bear on the Generalissimo to force him to give in to the Japanese, leaving the Communists isolated and vulnerable.

Then Left-hand Wang Ching-wei took flight from Chungking and Mao Tse-tung relaxed. He no longer feared a Kuomintang surrender. Pride, if nothing else, would lock the Generalissimo into place as a patriot, and Mao happily joined in the chorus of abuse hurled after the renegade Wang.

By the spring of 1939 Mao Tse-tung turned away from Chungking and facing north and east, was developing his own grand strategy. His guerrillas were infiltrating behind the Japanese lines and with them went his political cadres. No set pattern had emerged as yet, but Mao was confident that what had happened in Kiangsi would be repeated in the great plains above the Yangtze. He saw the dynamic of liberation, spreading from village to village, sweep across the land with combustible force.

That was his expectation, but the reality proved somewhat different. Mao Tse-tung, though of peasant origins, was unprepared for the peasants of North China. They resented intrusion and defied liberation. It was almost by accident that they were finally won over—not by what Mao and his cadres did, but because of an unanticipated reign of terror unleashed against them from another source.

20

Kill All, Burn All

THE FIRST PHASE OF MAO TSE-TUNG'S GRAND STRATEGY was carried out with dispatch. The Eighth Route Army, fragmented into guerrilla units, streamed out over the virtually unguarded northern plains. The Japanese had perhaps a million and a half men in China, most of them concentrated on the southern front, the rest dispersed in garrison duty in cities and towns or in patrolling the railroads. Internal pacification was left to puppet troops, the levies of provincial governors who had come to an understanding with the conquerors, and these were no match for the disciplined Red army regulars. By the summer of 1939 Communist contingents had fanned out over a vast area, north to the Great Wall and east to the Yellow Sea, establishing scores of bases along the way.

Following the guerrillas, or often traveling with them, came the political cadres, experienced in organizing villages from the earliest days on Chingkang Mountain to the latest in Shensi. But here the trouble started; the established techniques simply didn't work in North China.

The peasants of the plains were of a uniquely conservative breed. They were Confucian to the core, bending to authority, accepting the often harsh rule of their landlords with the same fatalism as they accepted the heat of summer and the storms of winter. Their indifference to improving their lot had been one of the chief causes for the failure of the Taiping uprising in the previous century. Peasants of South China had flocked in their millions to join the Heavenly Kingdom, but few converts had been made north of the Yangtze, thus providing the imperial forces with a stable base from which to crush insurrection.

The only anger these placid and obstinate people had demonstrated in recent times had been during the Boxer Rebellion in 1900. Then they had risen in righteous wrath against foreigners, whom they blamed for trying to change their traditional ways.

North China was infertile ground for Communist proselytizing and the Red cadres fared poorly. Proposals to hold village meetings in order to discuss rent reductions and expose the villainy of landlords were rejected. Appeals to patriotism and offers to train and arm defense corps to fight Japanese were ignored. All the people wanted was to be left alone.

Sometimes in desperation the cadres took over villages forcibly and imposed reforms, punishing landlords and others who objected. Mao Tse-tung might rail from Yenan that this was arrogant "commandism," but what else could the cadres do? How could they liberate people who preferred bondage except by force? For a long time it remained a vexing question.

To Chiang Kai-shek, settling down in Chungking in 1939 and looking out from his hilltop mansion known as *ying-wo* or the Eagle's Nest, the city below and the world beyond seemed dismal.

The city below was genuinely dismal, bereft of any charm or grace, utterly without distinction until it became the Generalissimo's capital. The beautiful city of Chengtu to the west had been Szechwan's provincial seat at least as far back as Marco Polo's time. Chungking, balanced on a rocky bluff between the Yangtze and Chialing rivers, had importance only because of its location. Piratical warlords had once extracted heavy tolls from traffic on the waterways and the place had continued to flourish as a market town. It had never possessed culture; not a notable temple or public building brightened its streets and its shabby, split-seam look had not been improved by the shacks that had sprung up everywhere to house the new influx of population. Close to a million refugees had crowded in from Japanese-occupied China to join the two hundred thousand original inhabitants.

The Generalissimo's prospect of the world beyond was no more cheerful than the immediate view. In September there had been a brief flurry of hope when Britain and France finally declared war on Germany over Hitler's invasion of Poland, but Chiang's expectations of relief from that direction were soon discouraged—first, by the long period of inactivity on the Western Front and then, in the spring of 1940, by the stunning collapse of France before the Nazi panzer divisions. Later the terror-bombing of England began, suggesting that Britain also was on its way to defeat.

By that time, though, Chungking knew all too well what bombings meant. Starting in 1939 the Japanese planes droned over, dropping racks of high explosives, sending the Generalissimo and his wife along with everybody else scurrying for the shelters carved from the rocky cliffs. It became a regular routine on moonlit nights, and havoc from the skies seemed likely to continue far into the future. For the Japanese had seized Canton and every other port up and down the coast through which military aid might be shipped in. They had even forced the British to close down the Burma Road for a while, cutting off China's last avenue of supply from the West.

There must have been nights when Chiang Kai-shek, huddled in his shelter, feeling the earth shake from products made in Japan, must have thought, not without envy, of the backsliding Wang Ching-wei, now installed as premier in Nanking. Wang was doing famously as a quisling head of state. He had formed a party he called the Kuomintang, claiming it was the true and original Kuomintang, alone faithful to the principles of Sun Yat-sen. His small army, recruited for him by the Japanese, marched in Kuomintang uniforms, under the Kuomintang flag and to the Kuomintang national anthem. It was as if there had never been an interruption in sovereignty, as if the Japanese had never come—a situation confusing to ordinary Chinese as, of course, it was intended to be.

And Wang Ching-wei was doing famously in another respect. He had bargained long and hard with the Nipponese conquerors and had come up with attractive allurements for his compatriots. Chinese businessmen, industrialists, and bankers were to be permitted to retain 51 percent, or controlling interest, in their enterprises, which guaranteed that substantial profits could still be made under the Japanese occupation. One by one the old Treaty Port compradors and tycoons slipped out of Chungking to make their way back to Shanghai or other bases. And soon they were discreetly followed by many of Chiang Kai-shek's senior officials, intent on paying court to Wang Ching-wei who now had lucrative jobs and favors to hand out. Twenty members of the Kuomintang Central Executive Committee are said to have left Chungking. The Generalissimo must have wondered as the drain continued whether he was to have any government or economic management left.

Through all this, Chiang Kai-shek had been keeping a wary eye on Communist activities in Yenan. He had watched with some bewilderment the Red expansion into North China, but when he grasped Mao Tse-tung's political objectives he took steps to put an end to them.

He began by ordering, as commander-in-chief, that the Eighth Route Army return to its Shensi-Kansu-Ninghsia base and confine its efforts in future to defending its own boundaries. When Mao Tse-tung protested that the objective of war was to fight the enemy and the enemy was to be found in North China, Chiang retorted that the Reds were doing no fighting but just moving around politicking in the Japanese rear. When he got no satisfactory reply to this charge, the Generalissimo cut off Central Government pay and supplies to the Communist armies. And when Red guerrillas continued to roam and agitate in the northern plains, Chiang moved two hundred thousand Kuomintang troops to blockade the Border Region to the west and south. He probably had no intention of threatening an invasion—as the Communists later claimed—but was simply making sure that the

Eighth Route Army didn't break out to proselytize areas under his jurisdiction.

He already had troubles enough in that regard from the Communist New Fourth Army. This unit, formed from the survivors of the old Kiangsi guerrilla forces, had been stationed south of the Yangtze River to help defend the Great Rear Area, as the territory governed by Chungking was called. Surrounded on all sides by Kuomintang contingents, the New Fourth had had to be circumspect in its political work. But by 1940 it was reducing rents and taxes in the villages under its control—legitimate policies as far as Sun Yat-sen's principles were concerned, but obnoxious to the Generalissimo.

Chiang by now regretted his generosity in commissioning the New Fourth Army and wondered how he could get rid of it. He hesitated to order it dissolved because that would risk an open break with Yenan. In spite of the irritations and conflicts that had arisen, the united front was still as important to the Generalissimo as to Mao Tse-tung, though for different reasons.

For Mao it meant security from internal attack while he pursued more important aims in North China. For Chiang it afforded evidence to the world that he continued to lead a unified nation, despite the antics of the quisling Wang Ching-wei. And appearances were all-important in the Generalissimo's mind. The dictators couldn't last forever. He rightly read the Berlin-Rome-Tokyo Axis Pact of 1940 as a sign of uncertainty rather than confidence, and knew, when the turn in the war came, that help from his allies would be greater the stronger China seemed.

So for more than a year Chiang Kai-shek held his hand on the pesky New Fourth Army until a serious Communist blunder on the plains of North China gave him his opportunity to slap it down.

By the winter of 1939 Mao Tse-tung was beginning to find correct methods for dealing with the hardheaded peasants north of the Yangtze. He began applying education by indirection, a technique he had developed to a fine art in the past. During the early days at Yenan he had tried to prohibit foot-binding. Finding the laws he enacted generally disregarded, he promoted job opportunities for nimble-footed girls. The results were gratifying: parents chose cash in hand over obsolete ideas of female beauty, and foot-binding stopped. Similarly, compulsory education for children fared better when time was alloted for the youngsters to labor in the family fields.

So now in the villages of North China the people's resentments were turned to profit. Cadres were instructed to keep a close watch for communities suffering from Japanese abuse. And there were many such close to towns and cities because the conquerors had a habit of sending out foraging parties to requisition grain. In the nature of things, along with the stolen foodstuffs went an assortment of other crimes—looting, rapes, and casual murders—leaving bitterness behind.

Red cadres were quick to move in on the affected communities, pointing out that the peasants' grain was always seized, not the landlords', and the peasants were the ones subjected to brutalities, not the gentry. The question was why?

The question could often lead to public meetings where the gentry's connections with the puppets in town could be traced, and the immunity purchased from Japanese looting denounced. If the expected anger erupted, the cadres were skilled at directing it toward positive goals—toward peasant councils that challenged the landlords' authority, toward demands for a reduction of rents and taxes, and all the other techniques of liberation.

Once liberated, a village served as an exhibit for the surrounding countryside. Peasants from miles around were invited in to inspect in the hope that they would catch the infection. At even a flicker of interest, Red cadres accompanied the visitors home to help change conditions in their own communities.

It was slow, stubborn work but Mao Tse-tung was content that progress was being made. Above everything he needed time for the development to continue at its creeping pace. So far the Japanese seemed either unconscious or unconcerned about what was happening a few miles from their strongholds, and Mao intended to keep them quiescent as long as possible.

He drew parallels with what had happened in Kiangsi. Rural organization had been proceeding apace in comparative calm until Li Li-san conceived his mad idea of attacking cities. That had drawn Chiang Kai-shek's attention and his subsequent extermination campaigns had put an end to political development.

Mao Tse-tung was determined that nothing like that should happen again. The Japanese must not be aroused to the rural organization going on under their noses. He cautioned Red commanders to limit their guerrilla attacks to expected objectives—railroad patrols and isolated movements of Japanese troops—keeping clear of the liberated areas unless their defense was absolutely necessary. As always, Mao put political development first; the power of armies grew from the cooperation of the people.

The Red commanders obeyed Mao's orders, though with some grumbling, until the summer of 1940. Then, en masse it seemed, they were seized by and old and insidious affliction— a desire for military glory. They were tired of cutting railroad lines and ambushing Japanese supply trucks. Many had been stung by Chiang Kai-shek's accusation that they were moving around behind the enemy's lines doing nothing. They led an army, proved and blooded, and they wanted to fight. They demanded that a meeting of the Military Council be called to work out new strategic plans.

Mao Tse-tung must have been appalled as he listened to the ambitious scheme advanced. His commanders proposed to employ some 150,000 Eighth Route Army regulars in a series of strikes against a dozen or more targets spread out over five provinces of North China. The stated purposes of the campaign were to disrupt Japanese supplies and facilities for months to come, to depress enemy morale and raise the hopes of Chinese patriots, but undoubtedly the true motive was to get in "some real fighting."

Mao Tse-tung argued long and strenuously against the concept. The "huge bonfire of attacks all over the place" not only threatened his policies in regard to village organization but was contrary to every military principle he believed in. Where were the basic guidelines he had so recently laid down in his treatise on anti-Japanese warfare? Where was the doctrine of concentrating a big force to strike at a smaller force? Or the caution to fight only battles of quick decision? Or to strike only when victory was certain? Everything had been thrown out in a fever to get at the enemy.

Party records are silent as usual on the stormy sessions that must have taken place. No doubt Mao Tse-tung inveighed against "adventurism" and—a new word in his vocabulary—"heroism." But his generals remained adamant and he was trapped by the party's system of democratic centralism with its rigid formula of "unity, struggle, then unity again through struggle." Outvoted in the council, he had no alternative but to endorse the campaign.

What was to be called the Hundred Regiments Offensive began on August 20, 1940. The strategy of attack developed in three phases. Phase one comprised assaults on mines, factories, munition plants, and other centers of Japanese war production. Phase two concentrated on railroads, highways, and canals, to destroy rolling stock and disrupt communications. Phase three was designed to ambush Japanese relief forces when they were rushed to the scenes of action.

The well-planned operations, lasting for three months, were successfully carried out. Extensive damage was done to the target objectives and a heavy toll in casualties was inflicted on the enemy—some 20,000 Japanese troops were killed along with 18,000 puppet forces. A particular achievement was the taking of 281 Japanese prisoners of war. For the first time Nipponese soldiers, trained to die rather than disgrace their emperor and ancestors by capture, demonstrated that the bushido code could be breached.

But in another respect the campaign failed in its purpose. There was no worldwide or even nationwide recognition of the daring feat. No foreign correspondents were on hand to observe and note. The Japanese passed off the attacks as Communist disturbances quickly suppressed, and it went without saying that, in Chungking, Chiang Kai-shek refused to give publicity to Red military successes when he had none to show of his own.

Yenan's claims of widespread victories were, of course, discounted in the foreign press. And even in Yenan a lid was kept on the people's enthusiasm. Mao Tse-tung remained wary, fearful for what his headstrong commanders might have precipitated. In the volume of his *Selected Works* that covers the period—works that he took a lively hand in editing—not a single mention is made of the Hundred Regiments Offensive. And with good reason. For when the Japanese recovered, when it was borne in on the imperial high command that it was not, as imagined, dealing with roving bands of Communist troublemakers but with a highly disciplined underground army capable of striking with stunning force, the measures taken to meet the threat resulted in a pogrom of unprecedented ferocity.

The man raised to supreme command in North China and given a free hand in Red suppression was General Yasuji Okamura. He was of samurai stock, steel tempered, shrewd and utterly ruthless. He was also thorough; he had a taste for his assignment and meant to hunt down and destroy every Communist hiding among the 200 million anonymous bodies north of the Yangtze River.

He began by tightening controls over county and district governments. He sternly warned puppet officials that they would be held responsible for future disturbances in their areas and ordered the roundup and delivery of all suspected Reds. As might have been anticipated, the bureaucrats consulted with village landlords, and scapegoats by the score were handed over to Japanese firing squads. It was an expedient but shortsighted policy; the hatred of the peasantry was aroused; the tenuous strands of patriarchal authority were stretched to the breaking point; and the liberating propaganda of the Communists, admired for their resistance to the Japanese, was more readily absorbed. And, of course, "disturbances" continued, squeezing the rural gentry between the growing patriotism of the people and the wrath of General Okamura.

Simultaneously the general had been moving on the military front. He shunned the Red bases in the mountains. Since he was a student of recent Chinese history, he knew the difficulties Chiang Kai-shek had experienced in that direction. But he spread a wide net for guerrilla strongholds on the plains. He planned encirclements of villages suspected of harboring Red contingents, advanced cautiously, and pounced when the ring was drawn tight. But continually he met with frustrations: no evidence of a military presence was found, no firearms, no ammunition, no uniforms. His prey had vanished like shadows at his coming and not even the hostages he took could tell him where.

Always resourceful, General Okamura changed his tactics. Reasoning that the guerrillas, wherever they were, depended on the villages for supplies, he developed a campaign to starve out the villagers. Foraging squads were sent in an organized pattern, district by district, to confiscate grain stores. No distinction was any longer made between the food stocks of peasants and their betters—everything was taken, which outraged the landlords and gentry, until then at least acquiescent to Japanese rule. But it wasn't angry words and damaged sensibilities that ended General Okamura's starve-out campaign. The Eighth Route Army, reverting to Mao Tse-tung's principles of warfare, became too adept at massing for attack on the wagon trains returning to town and repossessing the grain for the people.

Furious now, and under pressure from his superiors in Tokyo who were wondering why it was taking so long to eliminate ill-armed guerrillas, General Okamura staked everything on a new strategy. Convinced by this time that all villagers were either Communists or Communist sympathizers, he widened his target. Aware of the popular saying "the people are a pond and Red soldiers are fish swimming among them" he decided to drain the pond. He was prepared for mass genocide if necessary to carry out his mission.

He returned to encirclement, but on an expanded scale, enveloping entire counties containing a dozen villages. And he advanced in force, with automatic weapons and armored vehicles. The scope of operation was so wide that for the first time he began catching guerrilla contingents within his trap. And while armed men could usually fight their way out, the Red political cadres were not as lucky. Any villager who couldn't prove himself a resident through a long line of ancestry was summarily shot.

General Okamura was finally achieving results. But he needed time to work his way across the vast plains of North China and by December 1941 time was shortening. The imperial fleet had attacked Pearl Harbor, the United States was in the war, and the forces under Okamura's command—estimated at a million men—would soon be needed on other fronts.

The general responded to the pressure with a kind of frenzy. Exterminating Communists became an even greater obsession than it had been for Chiang Kai-shek. He accelerated operations, redoubled the troops involved, and added terror as a decisive weapon. To indoctrinate his soldiers in his own fanaticism he promulgated the policy of *Sanko Seisako* or the Three Alls—"kill all, burn all, destroy all."

And he meant it literally. As his troops advanced—in regiments now, closing in on a dozen counties at a time—they shot down peasants working in the fields and rendered the soil sterile by salt hauled in by the ton. Villages became slaughterhouses in the course of looting and raping; then funeral pyres as the torch was applied. The sack of Nanking was daily repeated in miniature everywhere in the land.

It was a terrible time to live through. Mao Tse-tung was later to say that the years 1941 and 1942 were the worst of the entire war.* There was little the Red army could do to protect the people. It was constantly in action, springing ambushes, attacking the Japanese flanks, taking heavy casualties in desperate battles. But for all its efforts it couldn't save the villagers or prevent destruction of their homes. Guerrillas helped the peasants dig tunnels, sometimes miles long. Such underground routes helped many to escape but they could also serve as charnel houses for the crippled, old, and infirm who at the point of Japanese bayonets were herded into them for gassing. Ablebodied adults and children who survived the ordeal of steel and fire were generally shipped off to Manchukuo as slave labor. It has been estimated that the population of the rich northern plain decreased from 44 to 25 million during General Okamura's reign of terror.

---

*Among other trials was Chiang Kai-shek's sudden attack on the New Fourth Army in January 1941, killing and capturing some four thousand Reds and driving the rest north of the Yangtze River. As the Generalissimo had calculated, Mao Tse-tung was too deeply involved with the Japanese to do more than vigorously protest the New Fourth Army incident, and the fiction of the united front was preserved, though the reality had long gone.

The worst was over by 1943 when Japanese troops were drained out of China to defend the empire in the Pacific, Burma, and the Philippines. Peace of a kind settled back on the land as the battered people tried to cope with famine, disease, and disarranged lives. General Yasuji Okamura had gone, passed into the pantheon of devils incarnate. And yet a word for the man. Almost singlehandedly he had done more for the Chinese revolution than any other figure in its history, excepting only Mao Tse-tung.

Consider the facts. When he had assumed command in North China he had, despite some Communist inroads, inherited a largely tractable population. The inhabitants of the villages, though not enthusiastic about Japanese rule, were willing to accept its reality as long as their institutions were not tampered with and they were left to work their fields in peace.

In just two years General Okamura changed all that. Successively he alienated both the peasants and gentry, and in the process he weakened the age-old feudal structure which had held communities together. And in his final rampage he destroyed the system completely, bringing about the worst possible calamities under the Confucian order—landlessness, rootlessness, and social chaos. He left the people no place to turn for authority but to the Communists who alone had tried to befriend them. And he had done all this in the name of eliminating Red guerrillas, another project in which he failed disastrously. In 1940 the Eighth Route Army numbered perhaps 250,000 regulars. Three years later it had doubled to 500,000, swollen by recruits who had but one object in mind—to kill Japanese. General Okamura had done his part in building an invincible force that within a decade was to conquer China.

Mao Tse-tung was to long ponder these strange dichotomies. Years later, as an aging patriarch in Peking, he corrected a Japanese delegation that was apologizing for wartime atrocities. On the contrary, he said, it was China that should thank Japan for teaching it so much. The occupation had offered great opportunities for learning in the northern plains and he wished that its influence could have extended south of the Yangtze. To Chungking, for instance. There had been a great need for education in Chungking.

But perhaps Mao was being unfair to Chiang Kai-shek. For the Generalissimo too had been learning hard lessons, and not only from the Japanese. From 1942 on, he had the Americans to contend with—a series of Americans who came to China to question his methods and belittle his ways. And by all odds his most formidable challenger was the man who came first—Lieutenant General Joseph W. Stilwell, sent by his president on an impossible mission.

21

The Will to Fight

FRANKLIN DELANO ROOSEVELT, THIRTY-SECOND President of the United States, was a China buff. Among the knickknacks on his desk in the Oval Office were curios brought back from Canton by a Delano uncle in the China trade. The President's famous smile, extending from chin to eyebrows, flashed as he recounted anecdotes of the old clipper-ship days.

Roosevelt, confident from the start of World War II that the United States would eventually be in it, had given a good deal of thought to the future of the Orient. He foresaw that, with Japan's defeat, a power vacuum would emerge which only a friendly democratic nation could be trusted to fill, and he had devoted effort to grooming China for that role. In speeches and press interviews, he never tired of praising China as a great democracy and Chiang Kai-shek as a selfless patriot, courageously leading the fight against Japanese aggression.

After Pearl Harbor he intensified his public admiration of Chiang and China. After all, it was good policy to substitute praise for the weapons and supplies Chiang was now demanding

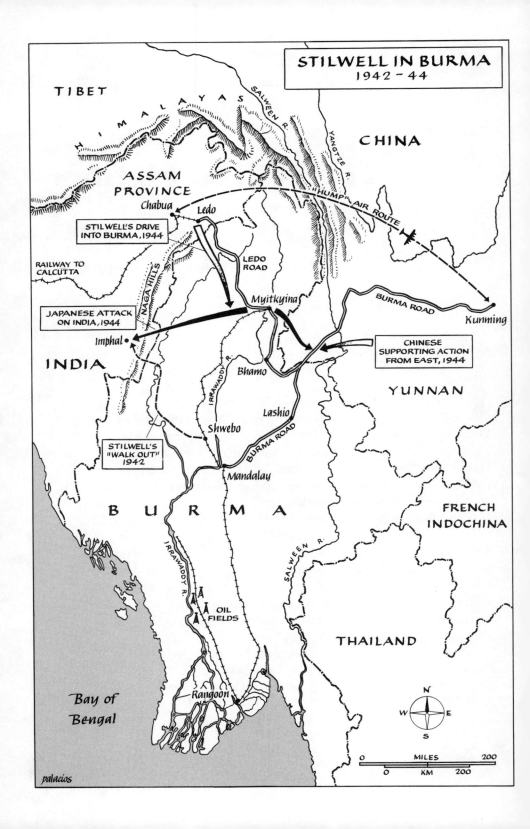

and which Roosevelt was in no position to give. But privately he was having doubts about the reliability of his ally. He was aware of Kuomintang corruption and the reports that reached him about the Generalissimo's armies were far from reassuring. In the two years since the retreat to Chungking, Nationalist forces had hardly fired a shot in defence of the homeland. And there was also the nagging suspicion that Chiang Kai-shek might yet surrender to the Japanese unless promptly propped up by American aid.

Material aid being out of the question—United States war production was just beginning to roll and first priority went to the European theater—Roosevelt improvised a characteristic solution. He sent a distinguished soldier to Chiang, to act as the Generalissimo's American chief of staff, for present help and as a symbol of greater assistance to come.

In some respects Lieutenant General Joseph W. Stilwell, the man chosen, was well qualified for his difficult assignment. He knew China, having served as a military attaché to the American embassy in both Peking and Nanking. He spoke the language, liked the country and its people, and had a high regard for the courage and ability of the average Chinese soldier. In other respects he was perhaps the most unlikely candidate that could have been selected. For Stilwell, a fearless, blunt, hyperenergetic West Pointer, a G.I. general admiringly called Uncle Joe, Galloping Joe, and Vinegar Joe by his men, was a go-getter and, as such, impatient of the stalling and polite evasions of Confucian finesse. He wanted to get a job done and he could be as stubborn as the Generalissimo when obstructed. The conflict between them began early and lasted for a stormy two years and eight months. And though, owing to their respective positions, Stilwell was finally vanquished, Chiang Kai-shek was the real loser because of what he might have gained.

To Joseph W. Stilwell, departing Washington D.C. for China in February 1942, President Roosevelt gave a single directive: "Keep Chiang in the war."

Oddly, Stilwell arrived in Chungking to find the Generalissimo fighting, or at least preparing to fight, not in China but in Burma. Chiang, responding to a British appeal for assistance in defending its colony, had sent two Chinese armies down through the Salween gorges to help close his own back door on invasion.

The Japanese, drunk with successes at Pearl Harbor, Manila, Hong Kong, and Singapore, had stormed ashore in Burma early in February. They had two main objectives: to seize the oil fields along the Irrawaddy River and cut off the Burma Road, China's last avenue of supply from the West now that all her ports were captured. By March, Nipponese spearheads were advancing up the railroad to Mandalay where the main Allied forces were digging in for a last-ditch defense.

The situation was growing tense when Stilwell arrived in Chungking. He had hardly presented his credentials before the Generalissimo courteously asked him if he would care to assume command of the Chinese forces in Burma during the coming campaign. Stilwell, flattered and eager to get into action, accepted the command and flew down to Mandalay to develop strategy.

As it happened, all the strategy developed during the next few weeks was by the Japanese. Their hard-driving commanders and agile, jungle-wise troops made short work of the Allied dispositions. First the British, or rather Indian sepoys officered by the British, were outmaneuvered and decimated. Then it was the turn of the Chinese to scatter under aerial strafings and retreat before the salvos of quick-moving artillery.

Stilwell's efforts to control the situation were hampered by a disconcerting discovery. He found that his authority as commander-in-chief was shadowy at best. In an old tradition of Chinese courtesy he had been given *yu ming wu shih*, or the title of power without the reality. His orders were ignored by theoretically subordinate generals who remained glued to their field radios to find out what the Generalissimo directed from Chungking. Under the circumstances, rout was inevitable, and it occurred when the Japanese mustered forces and attacked in strength.

Stilwell retreated to Shwebo with disorganized Chinese troops, knowing that his future in the theater depended on how he acted in the present emergency. He refused to board a plane flown in to evacuate him, and in the final panic of dispersion barely escaped capture. Then, when all that remained was survival, he led a band of followers on a famous "walk out." For weeks the fifty-nine-year-old general and an assortment of soldiers and civilians hacked their way through jungles, climbed mountains on goat paths, and crossed rivers on improvised rafts while fighting off insects, sickness, and hunger.

They reached Imphal on the outskirts of India on May 20, 1942. Stilwell was flown to New Delhi where, in a famous interview with the world press, he cut through the tired clichés and alibis of defeat with the blunt statement, "I claim we got a hell of a beating." The honest, pungent admission did much to relieve the gloom of continued disasters, especially when coupled with Vinegar Joe's promise to go back and wipe out the disgrace. And the general's own spirits were raised when he learned that some nine thousand Chinese troops had escaped the Japanese net and had straggled into India after him.

Stilwell had never wavered in his belief in the fighting qualities of Chinese soldiers. He held poor leadership responsible for their long history of defeats, and he proposed now to revitalize the refugees from Burma—to organize them into a modern army, with up-to-date training and equipment, inculcated with the will to give the Japanese a hell of a beating for a change.

Chiang Kai-shek reluctantly gave his consent to the proposal. Reluctantly because he was loath to give up any fraction of his command, especially to a foreigner. But he finally agreed because the men were marooned in India anyway and thus lost to him. So Stilwell set up a training camp at Ramgarh outside of Calcutta and turned his eager young staff loose to feed, clothe, drill, and inspire his Burma corps of the future.

Stilwell himself flew back to Chungking with even more ambitious plans. President Roosevelt had directed him to "keep Chiang in the war." In Stilwell's mind, always tuned to aggressive action, that translated into "make Chiang fight" and he set about selling the Generalissimo a new philosophy of warfare. He drew up charts and projections designed to turn Chiang Kai-shek's hibernating armies into active striking forces. He proposed among other recommendations to reduce the Central Government's three hundred undermanned divisions to approximately one hundred at full strength, also to weed out inefficient, time-serving officers and replace them with fighting generals. High on Stilwell's list of fighting generals was Li Tsung-jen, the hero of the victory at Taierhchuang. And singled out as an inefficient time server was Ho Ying-chin, the Generalissimo's Minister of War.

Stilwell, versed as he was in Chinese ways, seems to have been genuinely taken aback by the hostility his proposals aroused. What seemed to him necessary measures for cleaning house struck Chiang Kai-shek as threats to the house itself. Reducing the number of divisions would deprive many ex-warlords of lucrative berths through which their loyalty had been won, and dismissing inefficient officers meant doing I-Chis out of jobs. And the very idea of raising Li Tsung-jen, the Generalissimo's military rival, to a top command was unthinkable. As to Ho Ying-chin, though it might be said of him, in travesty of the tribute paid to the Duke of Marlborough, that he had never fought a battle he didn't lose or besieged a city he wasn't driven away from, still he was an old comrade-in-arms, a former instructor at Whampoa, and couldn't be dismissed.

Stilwell, strangely blind to these interlocked loyalties, kept plugging for his proposals. He took his case to Madame Chiang, hoping through her to influence the Generalissimo. He found the lady unsympathetic and failed to take warning from her hints—that it was necessary to be "realistic" and "heads cannot be lopped off; otherwise nothing would be left."

Vinegar Joe kept relentlessly at it. He had come to China to make Chiang fight and he wasn't going to be put off by circuitous evasions. And when evasions ended, when the Generalissimo told him bluntly that he had no intention of reorganizing his armies along the lines suggested, Stilwell was bitter. He had already formed an impression of Chiang as "a stubborn, ignorant, prejudiced, conceited despot" and the opinion grew.

Next it was the Generalissimo's turn to apply pressure. He told Stilwell that the present organization of his armies was not as important as their lack of supplies. President Roosevelt had promised China guns, tanks, and planes to be delivered, if not by the Burma Road, then by airlift from India. Where was this matériel that had been pledged? Why was Stilwell so "disobedient" as not to carry out his President's orders? And he demanded forthwith immediate delivery of at least five thousand tons a month.

Stilwell was exasperated by this attack. The airlift, organized by the U.S. Air Transport Command even before the Japanese had cut the Burma Road in the spring of 1942, was still struggling with enormous difficulties. Only twenty-five cargo planes were in use, delivering negligible tonnage. But it was achievement enough that a start had been made on the most horrendous freight route in the world.

The 550-mile flight between Assam in east India and Yunnan Province in southwest China crossed the towering mid-ribs of the Himalaya Mountains. Jagged peaks thrust up to 20,000 feet and more, usually cloaked in swirling clouds of mist. Winds howled across the barren rockscape, agitating thermal currents of sufficient force to disintegrate planes. And besides the elements, pilots flying the route had to contend with human enemies. For the Japanese had pushed into Burma to the town of Myitkyina (pronounced Mitchinaw) and, from its airfield, Zero fighter planes cruised the mountains looking for the lumbering American transports. Four hundred and sixty-eight were to be lost in the first three years of operation, shot down or sucked to earth by storms or mechanical failure. The fearsome stretch of contorted basalt was known to the G.I.s in the theatre as the Hump, and to the pilots that flew it as "clouds full of rocks" or the "aluminum trail."

In the fall of 1942 Stilwell, trying to explain the practical difficulties of air supply, found the Generalissimo totally uninterested. So again he tried an elliptical approach through Madame Chiang, then known in Chungking as the Madamissimo. She listened patiently to the logistics—in order to supply the 5,000 tons a month her husband was demanding, 304 cargo planes would be needed, requiring 275 pilots and 3,400 ground technicians, with 5 airfields at each end of the flight capable of handling 50 transports—and seemed impressed. But the Generalissimo remained obdurate, maintaining that "there are ways and means of doing things" which it was up to Stilwell, as his American chief of staff, to find.

So the rancor between the men grew, though in one area Chiang made concessions. He agreed to supply additional recruits for Stilwell's training program in India—some 44,000 were eventually flown across the Hump to the Ramgarh camp—and to provide a Chinese army to attack the Japanese from the east when the liberation of Burma began.

Getting ready for the Burma campaign occupied much of Stilwell's time during the winter of 1942–43, though again he was to meet with frustrations, this time from the British. His Majesty's government wasn't at all anxious to have a crown colony overrun by Chinese. Even though they came in the name of freedom, awkward questions might arise among the subjugated natives as to freedom from whom. So when Stilwell tried to set a date for the Burma invasion, British stalling began and continued at high echelon levels.

Vinegar Joe fumed and cussed and added the British to his list of those who didn't want to fight.

The Communists had kept abreast of Stilwell's difficulties with Chiang Kai-shek with vast amusement. Chou En-lai, leader of the Red liaison group in Chungking, publicly remarked that if the American general really wanted Chinese troops for training, he should apply to Yenan where any number would be given him without strings attached. And later Mao Tse-tung entered into the byplay. Reacting to a haughty speech in which the Generalissimo had claimed that the Kuomintang's "situation had never been so stable" and that "foreign criticism of our military and political affairs" was entirely due to "rumors and tricks," Mao Tse-tung retorted: "Curiously enough, such foreigners as Franklin D. Roosevelt . . . disbelieve the plausible explanation offered by Chiang Kai-shek."

But otherwise there was little to be lighthearted about in the Communist camp. The plains of North China were still devastated in the aftermath of General Okamura's Three All policy, and simply keeping the people alive became a major concern of the years 1942 to 1943.

Mao Tse-tung launched what came to be known as the Great Productive Drive. The entire effort of the areas under Communist control was devoted to growing food. In the Border Region new acreage was put into cultivation with irrigation systems devised to water crops. On the plains the Red army slung rifles to pitch in and help peasants restore fertility to fields. At guerrilla bases judged reasonably safe from enemy attack, the soldiers grew their own grains and vegetables to take the burden of support off the population.

The patriotic duty to till the soil extended to every level. Members of the Central Committee, the Politburo, and top army commanders all cultivated plots. Mao Tse-tung specialized in tobacco growing to support his nicotine habit, though later chroniclers have featured his cabbage patch as representing more respectable production. At the village level, among peasants and townspeople, women and children were organized into agricultural brigades. And jobs were found for the blind, halt, and elderly in tying, grading, and winnowing.

As the shortages eased, as the Great Production Drive—perhaps foreshadowing the Great Leap Forward of a later date—bore fruit and the threat of starvation was removed, Mao Tse-tung turned to another pressing matter, nothing less than the reeducation and revitalization of the entire Communist community. This was known as the Rectification Movement, and the need for it had been growing for some time.

The mushrooming of the party had led to confusions and disarray. In 1927, at the high tide of the first united front and before the Shanghai Massacre, party membership had numbered some 50,000. It had dropped to a handful during the trials of the early Kiangsi days, but had built back up after the Long March to 40,000 in 1937. Then came the deluge as intellectuals, students, and other patriots fleeing from the Japanese had poured into Yenan. By 1942 there were 800,000 registered party members with thousands more clamoring for admission.

The explosion had been far too abrupt. There hadn't been time to temper and condition the influx of newcomers. Mao Tse-tung wasn't overly concerned about the honest, serious-minded peasants and workers who had joined the party in droves, but the literate, vocal, and high-spirited intelligentsia threatened serious disruptions within Marxist ranks.

The trouble was not lack of goodwill, but lack of revolutionary standards and objectives. Many of the educated came from cities, from comfortable families and bourgeois settings. They were appalled by the primitive conditions in Yenan, by the differences in culture, and by the squalor and ignorance they met with on their first contact with peasants. And on a dietary level, important to Chinese, both the wheat eaters of the North and the rice eaters of the South found the millet meals of the Border Region repulsive.

Mao Tse-tung, a keen psychologist, noted the pattern of attitudes that developed. There was the enthusiasm of first arrival in Yenan, followed by disgust and depression, followed by a resurgent sense of superiority that Mao called "elitism." Intellectuals, banding together in the cadre schools, talked about raising the masses to their own level instead of stooping to the grass roots of peasant existence.

The Rectification Movement was designed to correct this perspective. And Mao Tse-tung, being a teacher, approached the problem in his own heuristic way. In one of his famous talks of the period, he told a class of cadres in training that:

> I began life as a student and at school acquired the ways of a student. . . . I felt that intellectuals were the only clean people in the world, while in comparison workers and peasants were dirty. . . . But after I became a revolutionary and lived with workers and peasants. . . I gradually . . . changed [and] came to feel that. . .in the last analysis, the workers and peasants were the cleanest people and, even though their hands were soiled and their feet smeared with cow-dung, they were really cleaner than the bourgeoisie and petty-bourgeois intellectuals. That is what is meant by a change of feeling, a change from one class to another.

He kept hammering away at what he called "rectifying the Party's style of work." Looking forward to the time when the cadres would be in the field dealing with the local peasantry, he anticipated derogatory attitudes with good humor. "Some people [say], 'What do these locals know? Clodhoppers!' " And to show that the clodhoppers know a good deal, he again used himself as an example: "Take me... Although I have been in northern Shensi five or six years, I am far behind the local comrades in understanding the local conditions and in links with the people here."

Patiently, in talk after talk, he made his points. Book learning wasn't enough. Marx, Engels, and Lenin could be quoted by the yard, but nothing would result unless objective conditions were studied with humility and problems solved by creative insight. He went so far as to call this attitude of concern and consideration love—"class love"—and emphasized that everything must spring from it.

By the end of 1943 Mao Tse-tung was satisfied that his indoctrination had taken hold, and the results certainly seemed to bear him out. Thousands of Red cadres—propaganda workers, agronomists, schoolteachers, even theatrical groups*—spread out over the countryside, changing the political face of North China. With the depleted Japanese forces quiescent in the cities, and puppet troops anxious to avoid encounters with the Eighth Route Army, the cadres had the field pretty much to themselves as they extended Communist control over a million square miles containing a population of 100 million people.

With success came unexpected developments. In the early days of difficult liberation, Mao Tse-tung, to prevent "commandism" and forcible conversions, had installed a "three-thirds" system. This meant that in any village or district council, only a third of the members could be Communists—the rest must be elected by popular vote without restrictions. It was later found on analyzing the "independent" two thirds holding office that 50 percent were peasants, 40 percent were intellectuals and merchants, and the remaining 10 percent came from the landlords and gentry. This was a significant 10 percent because it showed that many in the possessor class, far from being demoralized by the new order, had learned to make their way within it.

What was happening in North China was a vast revolution

---

*Among whom was an actress called Chiang Ching who became Mao Tse-tung's fourth wife.

that far outreached a strict interpretation of the class struggle. After two thousand years of a static society, people of all kinds were being shaken out of traditional ways and forced to adjust to change. It was both a frightening and exhilarating experience. For the change went further than alteration of habits and mental attitudes. It meant also transformations of souls and emotions, hopes and perspectives—a thoroughgoing psychological overhaul.

The Chinese have a term for the phenomenon—fan-shen. The literal meaning is "to turn over the body" but, by extension, there is the implication of turning over or changing almost anything—heart, mind, spirit, self. And in the end it means a change of personality, regeneration and rebirth.

Mao Tse-tung, consciously or unconsciously, had released the forces that were to change the character and nature of a people. He had seized vast populations by the scruffs of their necks to drag them, willing or unwilling, from feudal darkness into the light of the modern world.

Chiang Kai-shek, too, had been briefly dragged into the modern world in the fall of 1943. Franklin D. Roosevelt, still unable to supply the Generalissimo with much in the way of war matériel and so still, as a substitute, touting China as a great nation, had invited Chiang to a Big Three conference with himself and Winston Churchill at Cairo in November.

There was no real need for a meeting. The war objectives of all three nations were clear and nothing much could be expected in the way of expanding or expediting them. But Roosevelt and the British Prime Minister were on their way to meet Joseph Stalin at Teheran anyway, so the American President seized on the opportunity of a Cairo conference to bolster Chiang Kai-shek's status as a world leader, though Churchill thought the meeting a waste of time.

Perhaps another consideration motivated Roosevelt. Like most successful men, he had a profound belief in his own powers of persuasion and was convinced that he could "make Chiang fight"—he had taken up Stilwell's phrase—no matter who else had failed. He couldn't understand why the Generalissimo, with

The Will to Fight

his country's existence at stake, was hanging back like a weak sister while every other major power was fighting with all the manpower and dedication it had.

He was not to be enlightened during the Cairo Conference. Roosevelt and Churchill, both colorful personalities, were free and easy at the meetings, using banter and quips to ease the strains of diplomacy. In contrast Chiang Kai-shek sat stiff and humorless. He seemed impatient at the small talk—or as much of it as was translated to him by his English-speaking wife—and pressed hard to get down to business. Business, it turned out, was a demand for more and immediate aid, in weapons, supplies, and money, though he remained vague as to what he was prepared to do in return.

By prodigious efforts the U.S. Army Transport Command had fulfilled the Generalissimo's goal of five thousand tons a month across the Hump and was already on its way to doubling the figure. But that still wasn't good enough for Chiang. He now raised the ante to twenty thousand tons monthly, claiming that was the minimum needed to keep his armies in fighting trim. The Allied leaders were too polite to inquire—fighting trim for what? But later Roosevelt complained: "[That] fellow Chiang—I never could break through to him at all." And certainly he had begun to get some inkling of what Stilwell was up against.

Stilwell himself came back from Cairo with a fresh idea on how to make the Generalissimo fight. Rather, he had devised a plan that would permit Stilwell to do his fighting for him. Giving up on his proposal to reform the entire Chinese military establishment, Vinegar Joe now asked only for troops to be trained in American methods by American personnel along the lines of the Burma force currently in training in India. He requested an original assignment of thirty divisions—some 210,000 men—with another thirty to follow if the experiment proved successful.

In his own mind, he had reason to believe that the Generalissimo would agree to the project. As he saw it, he was offering to replace for Chiang, at American expense, the elite regiments formerly turned out at the Central Military Academy by General von Falkenhausen and his German staff before they had been recalled by Hitler in 1938. Most of those high-spirited, spit-and-polish cadets were gone now. Many had perished in the slaughterhouse at Shanghai; others had fallen unyielding at strongpoints as called for by the Generalissimo's heroic style of defense. As long as he had patriotically motivated men to stand and die, Chiang had sacrificed them remorselessly. But now he had few left.

In fact, he had few men of any quality left. Stilwell had investigated and been appalled at what he found. The Kuomintang armies were rotting away in idleness, eroded by desertions and disease. New recruits were conscripted by press gangs paid by the head for the men they brought in. Only peasants too poor to afford the immunity tax were caught. Roped together, they were marched to induction centers where beatings and starvation diets began. Conditions were so bad that only 56 percent of the inductees reached their assigned units, the rest deserting or dying on the way. Of the 1,670,000 men drafted in 1943, 735,000 simply disappeared, either as fugitivies or corpses.

In camp, conditions tended to grow worse. Recruits were flogged by non-coms and officers alike and diets were even sparser as those above profited from withheld rice. When a Kuomintang army moved, the roadside was littered with dead—victims of dysentery, smallpox, and typhus. Medical care was laughable. There were only two thousand doctors who could measure up to Western medical standards in the entire Nationalist army of some 5.7 million men. Hospitals, or the places that passed for hospitals, were body disposal dumps.

Stilwell was shocked by these revelations. As a result of them, he made one overriding qualification: he must have complete control of the troops under his command. Otherwise he knew that the morale he hoped to build would be lost in the crosscurrents of squeeze and graft. So on that basis he pressed for his thirty divisions—a Chinese army on Chinese soil, but with no interference from the Chinese government except in matters of policy.

To the surprise of no one except the blindly optimistic Stilwell, the Generalissimo was cool to the proposal. It was one thing for a foreigner to be in total command of Chinese forces in distant India, but it was quite another on Chiang's own soil. And it wasn't only the slight to his authority that piqued him. He saw difficulties in the plan that had never occurred to the blunt Stilwell. First of all there were the Nationalist generals, many of them Chiang's rivals. They were bound to be jealous of an elite Central Government army trained and equipped by Americans. They would suspect the Generalissimo of trying to enhance his own power vis-à-vis theirs, as he had attempted to do in the past. Then the practical matter of lost revenue resulting from Stilwell's foolish ideas about honesty would cause an outcry in and out of government. And finally there was the dangerous military expectation that would be aroused. With a potent army, Chiang would be required to fight the Japanese. And why should he waste resources in that project when his allies were so much better equipped to do the fighting for him?

Naturally none of this could be admitted openly. Nor, as long as Stilwell controlled lend-lease supplies, which were now beginning to flow across the Hump in encouraging quantities, could Chiang afford to antagonize the Americans. After all, Washington D.C. and the critical Franklin D. Roosevelt were only a radio message away. So the Generalissimo backed and filled, telling Stilwell that he was studying the thirty division program from all angles, and hoping that time would in some way bail him out. Meanwhile he stalled and the fuse on Stilwell's patience, always short, grew shorter.

22

Squatting on Mount Omei

IN DECEMBER 1943 STILWELL, TIRED OF WAITING FOR Chiang Kai-shek's decision on the thirty-division program, left Chungking for India. The long-postponed Burma campaign was weighing on his mind and he had decided that, failing help from his allies, he must go it alone before time ran out on him.

The British were still being evasive about committing forces for the liberation of their colony. In fact, Lord Louis Mountbatten, the British commander-in-chief in southeast Asia, was doing his best to talk Stilwell out of the invasion. He not too subtly hinted that the American was being motivated by personal pride, by his determination to settle accounts for that "hell of a beating," and that inconsequential jungle battles would have no bearing on the outcome of the war.

Stilwell disagreed. For him the retaking of North Burma meant reopening the Burma Road—or rather the Ledo Road, as he was now calling it. For he meant to build a new route from Ledo in India, connecting with the railhead from Calcutta, thus bypassing the old approach from the sea currently in Japanese hands. Furthermore, success in Burma would prove to the stubborn Chiang Kai-shek what Chinese troops could do under American leadership and thus hasten his decision on the thirty-division program. To Stilwell's mind the campaign was essential and there was no more time to waste. It would be fatal to be caught in the Burmese jungles when the monsoon rains started in April.

The Chinese troops trained at Ramgarh now totaled some forty-five thousand men and Stilwell had besides a contingent of three thousand American commandos, recruited from various theaters for unspecified hazardous duty. It was a small enough invasion force but Stilwell felt he had to risk it. In January 1944 the little army was unobtrusively trucked and railed to Ledo and the order issued to cross the border. Stilwell hoped to make up by surprise what he lacked in strength in overcoming the undermanned Japanese garrisons he understood to be policing North Burma.

The surprise turned out to be on Stilwell. For what his ground intelligence and air reconnaissance had failed to spot was a concentration of five heavily armed enemy divisions with three more coming up in support. Totally unsuspected was that the Japanese too had invasion plans. In a desperate gamble to confound the British and distract the Americans creeping up the Pacific islands, they had prepared an assault on India and their advance columns were already approaching Imphal, the gateway through the Naga hills. Stilwell's men blundered on the scene like picnickers into a hornet's nest.

There was nothing for Stilwell to do but to dig in and hold tight. The Japanese too were disconcerted by the unexpected situation, but decided to continue with their original invasion plans while holding off Stilwell's threat to their right flank. In the end it turned out to be one of the luckiest foul-ups of the war from the Allied point of view. The British, warned by Stilwell of what was impending, were able to concentrate forces and roll back the Japanese thrust at Imphal. And that solved another problem: the British, like it or not, were now involved in the Burma campaign. And soon Chiang Kai-shek was participating. With his allies heavily engaged, he honored his promise to send a Chinese army to attack the Japanese from the east.

Stilwell didn't stay dug in against his stronger opponent for long; it wasn't in his nature or philosophy of attack. Taking advantage of the extended Nipponese lines, he sent units probing over the ridges, herding the enemy into valleys where his artillery could get at them. His Chinese troops, heartened by effective weapons, fed by air supply, and getting immediate medical attention when wounded, fought valiantly. In fact, stimulated by the experience of actually beating Japanese for the first time, they out-performed Stilwell's expectations of them.

Even though the rains came early that year, spreading mud and misery, the Chinese brigades and the American commandos pressed on with the slow attritional work. The airfield at Myitkyina was captured on May 17. There were to be seventy-eight more days of bloody fighting before the town itself was taken but the airfield, from which the Zeros had been operating, was the big prize. Increase in traffic across the Hump was immediate and dramatic. Pilots, able to fly a lower and more direct route to China, delivered 25,000 tons in July, up 18,000 from June. By October tonnage had risen to 35,000, and in December was over 40,000. The eventual opening of the Ledo Road came almost as an anticlimax. For the rest of the war, more matériel was delivered to China by air than was ever trucked through the dust and grades of the Salween gorges.

In midsummer 1944 Stilwell returned to Chungking. Winston Churchill had hailed the Burma campaign as an "unprecedented feat of arms" and the foreign press was working overtime to adulate Vinegar Joe as a hero. But Chiang Kau-shek was not enthusiastic about his return. He foresaw new pressures for the thirty-division program, though in fact Stilwell's ambitions now went further. He had devised a new title for himself—Field Commander of the Chinese Armies. The idea was that the Generalissimo remain passive on a policy level while Stilwell, reverting to his original concept of overall command, regenerated his entire military establishment for him. Chiang Kai-shek braced himself against still another effort to make him fight.

As the Generalissimo saw it, there was no reason for him to fight—at least against the Japanese. Wherever he looked that summer, the Allied cause was victorious. In Europe, the Soviets

Squatting on Mount Omei

were smashing Nazi armies from the east, while to the west the Second Front had been opened up and American tanks were rampaging through the German defenses in France. In the Pacific, the Japanese homeland was coming under bombardment from newly captured islands, while at sea events were already shaping up for the Battle of Leyte Gulf that would spell the end for the imperial navy.

The Generalissimo had had nothing to do with all these resounding achievements. Yet in a peculiar and very Chinese way he couldn't help but feel that he had scored an even greater triumph. For hadn't Sun Tzu, the ancient philosopher on the art of war, said: "To win a hundred victories in a hundred battles is not the acme of skill: rather it is to subdue the enemy without fighting at all." And that is exactly what Chiang had done. He had kept himself on the side of victory without wasting his strength contributing to it. Through all the trials that had beset him, he had steered a judicious course, holding together his government, appeasing his rivals, and keeping his armies intact against the day when they would be needed for a more important purpose. For then as always, exterminating the Communists held first priority in the Generalissimo's mind. When the international war was over, when the foreigners had packed up and gone home, he would go to work to clear China of Reds.

He never doubted his ability to do the job. He had all but destroyed them in Kiangsi in the 1930s and he could do it again. But until the time came he had to move cautiously. He couldn't afford an open break with Stilwell or risk wearing out the patience of Franklin D. Roosevelt. Rather he must turn their incessant pressures to make him fight into arguments for acquiring more tanks, planes, and guns—weapons to be stored away until they could be deployed against the Red bandits.

So he continued to temporize with Vinegar Joe, listening gravely to his impudent proposals and pretending to study them with time-consuming deliberation, postponing indefinitely the need to commit himself.

As for Roosevelt, Chiang found he could make the President nervous by any suggestion of dealing with the Japanese. He never went so far as to threaten surrender, but he didn't have to. A mere hint that his government was faced with "collapse" or "liquidation" and that circumstances might force "other arrangements" was usually enough. It seems incredible that at this late stage in the war Roosevelt could have been taken in by such blackmail, but apparently he was. Promises of increased lend-lease or gold to stabilize the shaky Nationalist currency were usually forthcoming from the apprehensive President.

We have a record of Chiang Kai-shek's daily routine in Chungking at about this time. It is enlightening to compare his schedule with that of other Allied leaders during that 1944 summer of stress. Roosevelt was tied to his desk in the Oval Office from dawn to dark. Churchill and Stalin, with different temperaments, wrestled with decisions through the night in Whitehall or the Kremlin. In contrast, the Generalissimo's ordered life in his hilltop home, the Eagle's Nest, seems remarkably serene.

5:30 A.M.   Rises, washes with cold water, exercises.
6:00 A.M.   Breakfast (dumplings or noodles).
6:30 A.M.   Writes up previous day in diary, including thoughts, reflections, and self-examinations.
7:45 A.M.   Meditates for 15 minutes, developing poise and serenity.
8-10 A.M.   Paper work in office.
10-12 A.M. Conferences and meetings.
12-1 P.M.   Lunches with Madame and members of the family.
1-4 P.M.   Naps.
4-6 P.M.   Receives official guests.
6-8 P.M.   Has a drive and walk with Madame or some dignitary.
8-11 P.M.   Dines with guests; conversations on national problems.
11:00 P.M. To bed.

It is not to be supposed that the atmosphere was always as calm and Olympian as the schedule suggests. Despite his confidence in ultimate victory over the Communists, Chiang was worried by their activities in North China and kept close track of developments. Learning of the ease with which Red cadres were organizing villages, he dispatched political teams of his own to compete with them. The experiment was a failure. Villagers, discovering that administration under the "legitimate government" meant a perpetuation of landlord regimes, drove out the Kuomintang organizers and invited in the Communists.

The Generalissimo next conceived a more ambitious scheme to recapture what he called his "lost territories." He sent armies north to surrender by pre-arrangement to the Japanese. These troops, converted to puppet police units, were dispersed throughout the Red "liberated" areas—in position to link up with Chiang's main forces when he launched his anticipated Communist extermination campaign after the Japanese war was over. In all, some 800,000 Kuomintang troops were said to have been located in situ by this method. Mao Tse-tung, well aware of what was happening, exposed and loudly denounced the ruse, calling it treachery. Chiang Kai-shek called it "saving the nation by a devious path."

But there was another issue that summer that concerned the Generalissimo even more than the Communists. This was the parlous state of Chungking's economy. Many of the 10 to 12 A.M. "conferences and meetings" must have been devoted to the subject, not to mention the 8 to 11 P.M. dinner periods when national problems were discussed. Six years of unchecked profiteering and corruption had taken their toll. Inflation was rampant, hoarding endemic. Manufacturing production had all but stopped and there was a shortage of everything. The threatened "collapse" of government with which Chiang kept Franklin D. Roosevelt on tenterhooks was nearer to reality than Kuomintang officialdom cared to think about.

In 1938 Chiang Kai-shek had pledged that he was leading the nation into the safety of the interior in order to regenerate it—to build up its industries and revitalize its economy. Nothing of the sort had happened. Ineptitude, bungling, and graft had negated the bright hopes. The million refugees that had crowded into Chungking, along with millions of others spread out through the Great Rear Area, were living for the most part in neglect and destitution.

The industries that were to have provided jobs had turned out to be chimeras. Of the factories that had been trekked piece by piece up the Yangtze gorges, only a handful were still in operation because the government had allotted no priorities in raw materials. On the contrary: high-placed officials had connived to withhold the essential ores, chemicals, and yarns in order to drive up the prices. Many a golden egg had been extracted as long as the goose lasted.

Profiteers next turned to the necessities of life—food, clothing, shelter. Prices rose and kept rising until only the very rich could live above standards of beggary. The government tried price controls. They worked after a fashion for salaries but not for commodities, which disappeared into the black market. In 1939 a clerk in a government bureau was paid $60 a month when a pair of shoes cost $80. In 1941 he was still getting $60 but the shoes had moved up to $900. Clearly for the clerk and his family to survive he had to find and exploit some avenue of graft, and he did.

Graft, squeeze, corruption became a necessary way of life. Everybody was in on it. Army officers depleted their muster rolls and drew pay for a full complement. Merchants laced rice with white sand. Servants, stealing from their masters, kept the black market supplied. Crime became the great equalizer. And for those who may have been troubled by conscience, there was always the justification that their peculations were small compared to the wholesale robbery of the really high-ups.

Take H. H. Kung, Minister of Finance, as an example. In January 1942 the United States advanced China a loan of $500 million. H. H. Kung immediately used $200 million of it to buy goods smuggled in from Japanese-occupied areas. When asked for the rationale, considering that Chungking's industries were desperately in need of credit, Kung replied that he wanted to reward "patriotic merchants" under the Japanese yoke with a really good profit. He was never asked why a further $867,000 mysteriously turned up in his son's bank account, though the U.S. Treasury was interested when it found out about it. Nor did Kung ever explain how it was that, when he negotiated a purchase of planes from America, he included $16,000 per aircraft as his personal commission.

Other highly placed officials were equally rapacious. Many turned to that old gold mine of Confucian society—the land. Regulations were passed imposing heavy duties on choice holdings, and government loans were made prohibitive in cost except to insiders. By such rigging, 90 per cent of Szechwan's richest landlords were forced to sell. The new owners waxed fat on peasant rents and were in a commanding position to manipulate the food market.

Ruthless as the Kuomintang bigwigs were, some of their women were not far behind. Madame Kung, eldest of the glamorous Soong sisters, was a particularly blatant operator in currency juggling. By 1940 a witticism circulated in Chungking: "It's Madame Kung, not Japan, who is killing the Chinese dollar."

W. H. Donald, the Australian journalist and friend of China's great, went to the Madamissimo with this and other rumors he had heard about her sister. Donald was still in the employ of the Chiangs and was genuinely concerned for the family's reputation. More concerned, it turned out, than Madame Chiang because she told him sharply: "Donald, you may criticize the government or anything in China, but there are some persons even you cannot criticize." Donald, who prided himself on his honesty, felt that his usefulness as a confidant had come to an end and left China after a tour of thirty-seven years.

Of course, corruption is not a Chinese monopoly. There was plenty of it elsewhere, especially in wartime with its loosened economy. In the United States, trading influence for cash was a common enough practice and at least one congressman went to jail for it. And the very system under which American war production flourished—"cost-plus," where cost was anything the manufacturer said it was, with a healthy profit as the plus—invited fraud. But America had results to show; armaments poured from its factories and ships stuffed with goods sailed out to its allies. While in China nothing emerged from the frenzy of greed but the enrichment of the few. The pot was stirred but the soup wasn't thickened. And the substance of the nation continued to evaporate in the steam of inflation. The value of money was vanishing.

That was the aspect of the continuing economic crisis most

evident to the Generalissimo. His interest in fiscal matters was minimal, but he couldn't mistake the meaning of the falling exchange rate. Under his regime in Nanking the Chinese dollar had remained fairly stable in relation to the American dollar, declining in ten years from a ratio of 3-to-1 to 5-to-1. But since his withdrawal to Chungking, the loss of value had accelerated—from 20-to-1 in 1938 to 120-to-1 in 1943.

Chiang, seeming to regard the deterioration as an insult to the nation rather than a reflection on its stability, railed at his Minister of Finance—either H. H. Kung or his brother-in-law T. V. Soong, depending on who was in favor at the moment—demanding that something be done. Occasionally he took advice and tried to check inflation by decreeing severe penalties for profiteering. And sometimes merchants and minor officials were actually arrested and imprisoned, though never the gross offenders, never the people at the top. The hue and cry stopped well short of lèse majesté.

Eventually each ecomomic crisis was solved by the same resort—printing more money—thus adding coils to the inflationary spiral. Then the Generalissimo, satisfied for the moment, would subside again in his hilltop home where he watched the world with lofty detachment. Or, as Mao Tse-tung maliciously put it, where he squatted on Mount Omei with folded arms watching the tigers fight.

As far as serious fighting went, the Nationalists in the Great Rear Area and the Japanese in the other two-thirds of China had maintained a virtual truce since the Generalissimo's retirement to Chungking in the fall of 1938. But in that summer of 1944 the invaders unexpectedly turned belligerent again. They pushed down from Wuhan to besiege and capture Changsha, subduing at considerable cost a garrison that resisted with some of the old Whampoa spirit. Chiang Kai-shek was disturbed by the sudden activity. What did the Janapese have in mind? Where were they headed next?

Stilwell could have supplied the answer. But Stilwell had been issuing warnings for so long that the Generalissimo had stopped listening. Stilwell was, after all, an infantry officer, wedded to the philosophy of hard, slogging ground attack. He had little sympathy with newer theories of combat, particularly with air power. And in that he ran smack into conflict with Chiang Kai-shek's favorite American—Major General Claire Chennault.

Chennault was an accomplished soldier, a West Pointer who had resigned from the U.S. Army over the issue of air power. The army believed, and practised the belief, that air power was a tactical weapon, a subsidiary arm of offense. Chennault saw it as a major force, capable of independent strategic action.

In 1937 Chennault had come to China as the Generalissimo's air adviser. After the Japanese attacked, he got his opportunity to put his combat theories into practice. He organized a group of American volunteer pilots into a squadron that was to gain renown as the Flying Tigers.

Chennault, like Mao Tse-tung, had little use for romantic notions of warfare. He forbade his pilots to engage the enemy in solo combat. They must attack with odds of at least two against one, or not fight at all. This concentration of strength against weakness paid off handsomely. The toll that the Flying Tigers took of Japanese bombing planes eventually made the moonlight runs over Chungking too costly to continue.

Claire Chennault and his men became popular heroes. The Generalissimo led the chorus of praise and eagerly absorbed Chennault's theories on air power. The confident flyer believed that an air offensive, if adequately supported, could by itself drive the Japanese out of China. Chiang Kai-shek heartily approved of the principle, expressing as it did his fundamental policy—preserving his own troops while getting foreigners to do his fighting for him. Chennault was also an accomplished diplomat. Since Madame Chiang was the nominal commander-in-chief of the Chinese air force, he never failed to give her credit for helping his men down the enemy.

But all that had been before Pearl Harbor. When the United States entered the war, the Flying Tigers were incorporated into the U.S. Army as the Fourteenth Air Force, under control of the theater commander, Lieutenant General Joseph W. Stilwell. Chennault and Stilwell were different in personality, temperament, and outlook, and friction rapidly developed between them.

Chennault wanted a greater share in the tonnage across the Hump. Stilwell said he had no more to spare for what he called "fly boys." The Generalissimo was delighted at the growing feud. Always adept at manipulating his own rivals, he hoped that, with his help, the abrasion might lead to Stilwell's dismissal without loss of lend-lease.

Early in 1943 Chennault had taken a bold step. Chafing under Stilwell's restrictions and knowing he could expect no help from the War Department, where he would be forever suspect because of his zealotry for air power, he jumped channels and flew to Washington for a direct interview with the commander-in-chief, Franklin D. Roosevelt. He promised the President that, if given a free hand and sufficient operational supplies, he could sink a million tons a year of Japanese shipping. Furthermore, if provided with heavy bombers, he could devastate the Nipponese homeland itself.

Roosevelt, always a gambler, was impressed by the argument. He was also impressed by Chennault's forthright personality and emphatic presentation—a contrast to Stilwell's dour attitude and somewhat shambling way of speaking on important occasions. He was inclined to give Chennault what he wanted, but first he checked with Stilwell through the War Department.

Stilwell's reply was typically jaundiced. Chennault could sink ships only just so long. When it began to hurt, the Japanese would move in and put him out of business by capturing his airfields. Airfields could only be defended by ground troops, and as long as Chiang Kai-shek refused to allow adequate forces to be trained—Stilwell never faied to plug his ambitions for total command in China—defense was impossible.

That was the Generalissimo's cue to step stage center. He gave his personal guarantee to Roosevelt that the airfields would be defended; his present armies were powerful enough to hurl back anything the Japanese might throw at them. The President was sold. He issued orders for the Fourteenth Air Force to be separated from Stilwell's command, and Chennault was given permission to operate as he thought best.

It had been a great triumph for the Generalissimo and his favorite American commander. Moreover, Chennault had vindicated his promises to Roosevelt by vigorous assaults on Japanese shipping lanes. He had unquestionably hurt the enemy, and was still hurting it badly.

Now in the summer of 1944 the Japanese were reacting. Or were they? Changsha was a long way from any of Chennault's advanced bases. Besides, having taken the city, the Japanese seemed overcome by lethargy. They moved troops about, but there was no concerted drive in any direction.

Still, just to make sure, the Generalissimo dispatched additional divisions to protect Chennault's airfields. He had pledged his word to Roosevelt and nothing must go wrong. But despite precautions, he couldn't seem to dispel his uneasiness. A tension began to build that grew more acute the longer the Japanese stalled.

The American Vice President, Henry A. Wallace, saw no signs of apprehension when he visited Chungking that summer. To Wallace, as to other visiting celebrities, Chiang Kai-shek continued to give the impression of a poised and confident ruler. But Stilwell, more intimately attuned, noticed telltale indications. He described staff meetings at which Chinese generals sat with "ashen faces and trembling knees," apparently as the result of hysterical scenes before his arrival.

And there were more public demonstrations of overwrought nerves. One afternoon, driving in the countryside, the Generalissimo encountered a row of recruits roped together as they were marched to an induction center. It's naïve to believe that he had never seen the sight before, but he had never before reacted as he did then. He sprang from his car, ordered the ropes cut, and belabored the supervising officer with his cane. He followed this up with a visit to the induction center where he beat the commanding general, shouting: "You're destroying my armies!" Nor was that the end: the general was cashiered and later shot.

Then there was a curious incident which at least suggested an attempt to escape from stress. Rumors and gossip connecting Chiang with a young dancer had floated about Chungking for weeks before a press conference was suddenly called at the Eagle's Nest. Newsmen were startled to hear the fifty-seven-year-old head of state launch on a rambling, self-defensive speech interpreted by his wife. He was a Christian, he said, and as such it was against his moral scruples to take a concubine; the reports circulating were slanders. Madame Chiang's presence suggested her loyal support, though the impression was weakened when she left soon afterward for a trip abroad that was to keep her away for a year. A strong suspicion was left that lately the Generalissimo's daily naps from 1 to 4 P.M. hadn't been taken alone.

The summer passed; then in the fall apprehension was replaced by certainty. The Japanese were on the move, their objectives clear. As Stilwell had predicted, they were after Chennault's airfields. Those farthest east, in Chekiang Province, were wiped out in a matter of days, Chiang Kai-shek's defending troops battered and dispersed by shock attacks. Then the drive continued for the western bases, the most important located at Hengyang and Kweilin.

The Generalissimo ordered heroic resistance and stands to the last man. But orders did no good; his ill-equipped and half-starved men were bowled over and brushed aside. Chiang ordered commanding officers shot for cowardice. That did no good either; fear of consequences was wasted on generals whose troops had already disappeared. Hengyang was taken; then the Japanese closed in on Kweilin, with its concentration of machine shops and spare parts and stores of high-octane fuel.

Chennault, with his prized base on the verge of destruction and his dream of conquest by air power about to go up in smoke with it, was frantic, He called on Stilwell to airlift troops from Burma to help stiffen the defense. Stilwell refused. The Burma campaign was reaching a critical stage and he needed all available men.

Chennault appealed to the Generalissimo, asking him to countermand Stilwell and use his superior authority to recall the Burma brigades. But Chiang was in a predicament himself. He had promised Roosevelt that he could defend the air bases with his armies currently on hand, and to send for outside troops now would involve loss of face. So he kept crowding in more inept reserves, apparently hoping to ward off the Japanese advance by the sheer barrier of bodies. It was hopeless, of course. The bodies were blown aside and the enemy came rushing on. Stilwell was aboard the last plane out of Kweilin. He had stayed to the end doing the job Chennault couldn't bear to do—destroying installations.

In Washington D.C., Franklin Roosevelt was furious. He felt he had been taken in, both by Chennault's grandiose claims for air power and Chiang Kai-shek's bland assurances of ground support. The President had never been a complete admirer of Stilwell's blunt methods and abrasive personality, but now that the weakness of the Chinese armies had been fully exposed and Vinegar Joe had once again been proved right, his attitude changed. With an overreaction that amounted almost to venom, he swung in behind his dogged field commander to force on the reluctant Generalissimo the will to fight.

Thus far Roosevelt had been restrained in his dealings with Chiang by a convention he himself had created. As long as he had been promoting the Generalissimo as the leader of a great nation, he had been careful to observe the deference due a fellow ruler of equal status. He had been sharp at times, but always within diplomatic bounds and had been at pains to curb the impatience of the State Department and the Pentagon. On one occasion he had softened the tough wording in a note addressed to Chiang on the grounds that "one cannot speak sternly to a man like that or exact commitments from him as we might from the Sultan of Morocco."

But after the disaster of the Japanese advance, Roosevelt forgot deference due. He composed a message that even the Sultan of Morocco would hardly have stood for. He virtually ordered Chiang Kai-shek to hand over his armies to Stilwell for reorganization. And to emphasize his determination, he promoted Stilwell to the rank of four-star general to qualify him for supreme command.

The message was sent directly to Stilwell in Chungking in order to circumvent diplomatic channels that might seek to soften or distort the strict intent. Stilwell was, of course, elated. He finally had his government's full backing for the job he had come to China to do. He began work on a literal translation to read to the Generalissimo personally, though Patrick J. Hurley wasn't sure that was the best way to go about it.

Patrick J. Hurley was an emissary from Washington recently

arrived in Chungking. The Generalissimo, increasingly exasperated by Stilwell and looking for ways to bypass him, had asked Roosevelt for a diplomat of rank, not connected with the government, to act as a personal mediary in his communications with the President. Roosevelt, not yet hardened into position and still tolerant of Chiang's foibles, had sent him Patrick J. Hurley, a colorful Oklahoman and former Secretary of Defense under President Herbert Hoover. Hurley was still feeling his way through the intricacies of Chinese-American relations but he was a man of forceful opinions and, when Stilwell showed him Roosevelt's note, he spoke his mind.

Recognizing the dynamite in the message and guessing the Generalissimo's probable reaction, he urged Stilwell to go slow. He suggested that he, Hurley, or someone else deliver the President's ultimatum, and that Stilwell wait until Chiang had recovered from shock before seeking an interview. But Stilwell would have none of that. He had waited too long for his moment of satisfaction and was determined to be on hand to watch his hated adversary suffer.

Vindictiveness had taken over, in Stilwell as earlier in his president. The objectives of the war, all the carefully calculated diplomatic plans for the democratic future of the Orient and the balance of power in the Pacific, were lost in the sudden eruption of personal spleen and frustration. It was left for Chiang Kai-shek to restore statesmanship and perspective if anything was to be salvaged from the melange of bruised sensitivities and human failure.

But the Generalissimo proved unequal to the task. He listened silently while Stilwell, resplendent with the new stars on his shoulders, read what Roosevelt expected—demanded—of him. He tapped his fingers for a moment, then leaned forward to turn a tea cup on a table upside down. Stilwell, versed in Chinese ways, knew the interview was ended—as was also, though he may not immediately have recognized it, his career in China.

The Generalissimo's request for Stilwell's recall was couched in face-saving terms. It was simply a matter of personalities, Chiang said. He and Stilwell didn't get along and, besides, he had lost confidence in Stilwell's military judgment.

Roosevelt didn't resist the request. No doubt he had calmed down enough to realize the enormity of what he had demanded. Perhaps never before, short of actual conquest, had one head of state ordered another to yield up his army, the last sanction of power, to a foreign general.

Besides, the question of whether Chiang fought or didn't fight was by now academic. New decisions were being taken in Washington to bypass the Chinese mainland in the final assault on Japan. The Okinawa campaign, designed to provide a springboard from the South, was already in preparation, and negotiations had begun with Joseph Stalin to sweep down through Manchuria for a northern attack on the homeland. Chiang Kai-shek, reluctant for too long to do his share in furnishing the table, had lost his place at the feast. From now on he was to be provided with just enough lend-lease and financial support to keep his government from collapsing; otherwise he was to be left in the backwash of the victorious nations.

Stilwell left Chungking and China on October 21, 1944 never to return. There were ceremonies and exchanges of decorations before he boarded his plane, but the Generalissimo must have seen him disappear into the skies with a vast sense of relief, a feeling that a siege had lifted. If so, he was deluded because, with Stilwell's departure, American goodwill on many levels was irrevocably withdrawn from China.

For Stilwell was a type of scrappy, never-say-die fighter who had greater appeal to his countrymen than more celebrated generals. From the first, from the famous statement about taking a hell of a beating, Americans had gathered him to their hearts. Even while he struggled with insolvable problems, he had become a legend. And in the end it was widely recognized that he had done a heroic job. He had cleared North Burma of Japanese, turning the dirty jungle fighting into a major triumph of the Pacific when measured by the sorry body count of war—75,000 of the enemy killed, surpassed only by the 100,000 Japanese dead at Okinawa. Fighting with Chinese recruits and with little help from home, he had reopened from Ledo the old Burma Road—now called the Stilwell Road in his honor—and kept China in the war.

And what had been his reward for all this? The boot. He had been kicked out by the same Generalissimo whose nation he had saved.

The popular resentment was shared by the news media in the United States. After cautiously probing the White House and State Department and finding no resistance, press and radio opened windows to the new climate. Long-suppressed "inside" stories from Chungking were rushed into print and put on the air. The image of Chiang Kai-shek as the courageous leader of a democratic people—standard fare since Pearl Harbor—dissolved rapidly. Within months he had become a weak and vacillating political tyrant, presiding over a corrupt regime, supported in power by police bullies. The new picture was as much biased toward black as the former had been toward whitewash, but in the resulting bewilderment and confusion the Generalissimo was the loser.

Chiang Kai-shek bore it all stoically. He had always detested foreigners and he didn't much care what they thought about him as long as lend-lease kept coming in. Besides, he was confident that the alienation was only temporary. When the Japanese conflict was over and his real war against the Communists began, the Americans would be drawn back in spite of themselves. And they could work together in harmony then because his cause would be their cause.

23

Shall We Dare To Win?

MAO TSE-TUNG, STUDYING CHIANG KAI-SHEK'S DIFFIculties with the Americans through 1943 and 1944, saw room to maneuver. He hardly expected to wean United States support away from the Generalissimo in favor of his own regime, but at least there was the possibility of sharing in lend-lease and opening avenues of goodwill for the future. In any case it was high time that the Americans became acquainted with the Border Region, a nation within a nation, boasting control, according to Mao's current estimate, over a population of 80 million, with a regular army of 470,000, a supporting militia of 2,270,000 and a party membership of 900,000.

Invitations to visit the Communist capital at Yenan were issued to foreign correspondents through Chou En-lai's liaison office in Chungking. The correspondents were eager to go; the Kuomintang was not as eager to let them. Newsmen were blandly told by the official press bureau that the trip would be a waste of time because there were no Communists left in China; they had been eliminated during Chiang Kai-shek's extermination campaigns of the 1930s. The people going by that name in Yenan now were really nothing more than agrarian reformers, and so of little interest.

But the correspondents, appetites whetted, kept pressing through diplomatic channels and finally a junket was arranged. In May 1944 a planeload of reporters were flown to Yenan for a stay of several weeks. They brought back glowing accounts of a sober, hard-working community dedicated to public service, and where graft and corruption seemed to have disappeared from political life. One impressionable observer went so far as to describe Yenan as a "New Testament society." In general, contrasts with the greed and privilege of Chungking were not overlooked in the stories filed—though not necessarily passed through the official censorship.

Curiously, the correspondents found in Madame Chiang Kai-shek a rapt audience for the wonders they had seen. She invited a group of them to the Eagle's Nest and listened intently to what they told her: of the caves in which the Communist leaders lived; the community dining halls in which they shared meals with peasants and soldiers; the unskilled but hotly contested pingpong games through which they relaxed. She was particularly intrigued by descriptions of Mao Tse-tung squatting by the roadside to talk to villagers; breaking off from his studies to greet children pressing in at his door; or wandering around at night without a bodyguard. The Madamissimo listened to all of it, thought it over, then dismissed it with the cryptic remark: "Why those people have no idea what real power is!" The correspondents puzzled long over the statement, looking for a significance that went deeper than social snobbery, but found none.

The Generalissimo was less fascinated by accounts from Communist territory. He had feared from the first that the press visit would be used as an opening wedge and his suspicions were soon justified. The U.S. War Department asked permission for a military observer group to go to Yenan to gather intelligence on Japanese troop movements in North China. Chiang loathed the idea but it was July 1944, his troubles with Roosevelt were mounting, and he felt he had no option.

The observer group—called the Dixie Mission—spent some

seven months in the Border Region. Though the group reported regularly on the efficiency and morale of the Red armies, it is doubtful that its members ever saw them in action against the Japanese. We have the testimony of Chang Kuo-tao—now a Kuomintang agent—that by 1944 the Communists were exerting 70 percent of their effort in organizing the North China countryside, 20 percent in frustrating Nationalist attempts to stop them, and only 10 percent in fighting the Japanese. And though the source is tainted, there is no reason to question the figures. For by that time Mao Tse-tung's war against the Japanese was virtually won. What concerned him far more was the shape of the future within China itself—whether, through American or other good offices, a coalition government with the Kuomintang could be worked out, or there would be a return to the violent civil conflict of the past.

Coincidentally, that fall Patrick J. Hurley was debating the same problem. Hurley was still in Chungking, though in a sense Stilwell's departure in October had left him unemployed because Chiang Kai-shek no longer had need of a second mediary in communicating with Roosevelt. But by a fortuitous circumstance, Clarence E. Gauss, the American ambassador to Chungking, ailing and discouraged, had chosen the occasion to resign. The Generalissimo immediately recommended Hurley as the successor to Gauss, and the vigorous Oklahoman was now awaiting confirmation from Washington. While he waited, he devoted thought to the political future of China—an impending exigency as the Pacific war pushed to its inevitable end.

The Generalissimo had been on his best behavior since Stilwell's exit. Not only had he shown his approval of Hurley, but he had also welcomed with courtesy and cooperation Lieutenant General Albert C. Wedemeyer, appointed his new American chief of staff. He had immediately turned over to Wedemeyer not thirty, but thirty-nine Chinese divisions for training in modern warfare, with the promise of many more to come. Chiang seemed to be going out of his way to impress on Roosevelt that it had been Stilwell, not he, who had been recalcitrant and unreasonable all along.

Of course, the conditions under which the Chinese divisions had been handed over for training were different from those that Stilwell had insisted upon. It was understood from the first that the newly refurbished troops were to be under Chiang's command, not Wedemeyer's; hence it seemed likely that the Generalissimo would be as reluctant as ever to squander them against the Japanese. In fact, the suspicion was strong that Chiang, humiliated by the sorry performance of his armies in defending Chennault's airfields, had decided to take advantage of American military efficiency at American expense to get his fighting forces in trim for his coming struggle with the Communists. Certainly he continued to hoard—with only vague suggestions as to their eventual use—the tanks, artillery pieces, and automatic weapons now reaching him in quantity across the Hump.

Patrick J. Hurley, attuned to the Generalissimo's fixed bent of mind by this time, was disturbed by the implication that a civil war was inevitable. A booster and optimist by nature, he was also a canny businessman who had acquired a reputation in both Mexico and the Middle East as an oil negotiator. Hurley subscribed to the very American belief that there were no differences that couldn't be settled by compromise. All it took was the right deal. From what he had heard about Yenan, the Communists seemed reasonable people. Perhaps there was room, working from their end, to set up a framework for negotiations that could save China. It could be only that an impartial, broad-minded arbitrator was lacking to bring the two sides together. And who was better qualified for the job than Patrick J. Hurley?

Hurley quickly put his idea into action. Coaxing a reluctant consent from Chiang Kai-shek, he took flight for Yenan, departing from Chungking in such a hurry that he forgot to inform the Communists he was coming. Mao Tse-tung and his fellow officials had to scramble out of a meeting and pile into the old bus that served them for transportation in order to get to the airfield on time.

Hurley, descending from the embassy C-47, greeted the Red reception committee with a piercing Comanche war whoop. Perhaps there was something about the desiccated scenery of Shensi that reminded him of his native Oklahoma, but his uninhibited

Shall We Dare To Win?

mood continued. On the drive back to Yenan he regaled the company with tall stories about the West, including the one about following fish upriver during the summer drought by the flight of dust. His hosts, suffering through the translation, seemed to get the point. In fact, though they had never met anyone like Hurley before, they seemed generally well disposed toward him. It was only later, much later when the anecdotes had ended and confidence had waned that Mao Tse-tung was to call him a clown.

On the next day, November 8, they got down to business. Hurley was delighted with the Communists' readiness to cooperate for future peace, and the moderation of their conditions. A five-point program was worked out, incorporating plans for (1) unifying Nationalist and Red armies for the remainder of the war against Japan; (2) forming a coalition government of all patriotic parties with Chiang Kai-shek as President; (3) following the principles of Sun Yat-sen as the guiding platform of the coalition, with guarantees of political freedoms; (4) supplying all parties pro rata with lend-lease aid from foreign powers; (5) recognizing the legality of all parties in the coalition, including the Communist Party.

Hurley was so pleased with the results quickly and amicably achieved that, after the Red officials had signed the document, he added his own signature as a witness to a historic event. Elated, he boarded his plane for the return flight to Chungking. Then disillusionment set in.

T.V. Soong, the Harvard-educated Minister of Finance, the first to read the five-point document, told Hurley point blank: "The Communists have sold you a bill of goods." And the Generalissimo wasn't much more complimentary. He balked at the very idea of a coalition government saying that, with Communists, it was like inviting foxes in among the chickens. He was ready to make some concessions but not that.

In due course Chiang came up with a counterproposal. Vaguely worded as to specific policies, it advocated that the Kuomintang and Communist parties might work together "jointly" to carry out the principles of Sun Yat-sen. But it was definite on one point: as a prior condition to any talks, the Red Army must be handed over to the Nationalist government. To Mao Tse-tung, who had once stated that "all things grow out of the barrel of a gun," the condition was unacceptable. The counterproposal was rejected so an end was put to an immediate rapprochement between the Kuomintang and the Communists.

Hurley had little time to recover from his disappointment and reflect on what to do next because, when his appointment as ambassador to China was confirmed, he was recalled to Washington for consultation and briefing. On his return flight to Chungking, he traveled via Europe and stopped off in Moscow. There on the night of April 15, 1945 he had an interview with Joseph Stalin and Soviet Foreign Minister V. M. Molotov that changed his orientation toward negotiations in China.

The previous year Molotov had told Hurley that "the Chinese Communists are not in fact Communists at all." Hurley, a Republican conservative, convinced that all Communists were joined together in an international conspiracy directed from the Kremlin, had paid little attention to the remark at the time. But now, a year later, Molotov repeated the opinion and Stalin went even further in denigrating the Yenan rebels by calling them "margarine" Communists. He also added that he was willing to cooperate with the Americans in bringing about a unified China under the leadership of Chiang Kai-shek, whom he praised as "selfless" and "a patriot" though disapproving of some of his officials as corrupt.

Hurley seems to have been astounded that there could be such divisions of esteem within the Communist camp and quickly adjusted to take advantage of them. He was, after all, a freewheeler who thought in terms of making a deal, of bringing to bear all influences and pressures necessary to force an agreement between contending parties, irrespective of rights and wrongs, of principles or idealistic considerations. As he saw it, the unification of China was the overriding issue and, since the Generalissimo had refused to accommodate to Mao Tse-tung, methods must be found to make Mao knuckle under to Chiang. A new strategy must be worked out. And basing his plans on Stalin's attitude, Hurley changed direction.

When he returned to Chungking he did two things. He persuaded Yenan to send a delegation to open up talks, no matter how unlikely an agreement with the Kuomintang seemed at the moment. Second, and more important, he helped Chiang Kai-shek conduct secret negotiations with the Soviet Union for a Treaty of Friendship and Alliance. The old Sino-Soviet Nonaggression Pact, dating from the beginning of the Japanese War in 1937, was still in effect, but Hurley wanted a more substantive commitment, tying Stalin and Chiang together in a public display of solidarity. As he enthusiastically wrote to the State Department: "The Chinese Communists do not believe that Stalin has agreed or will agree to support the National Government of China under the leadership of Chiang Kai-shek. [They] fully expect the Soviet to support [them] against the National Government.... When [they] are convinced that the Soviet is not supporting them, they will [have no option but to] settle with the National Government...." And then he gave his reason for inviting the Yenan delegates to Chungking—to have them on hand when the moment of truth came; "The negotiations between the National Government and the Communist Party at this time are merely marking time pending the result of the conference at Moscow."

It was all carefully calculated—the maneuvering, the preparations for the double shock to the Yenan Reds: first the discovery that Stalin had sold them out by an exclusive treaty with the Generalissimo; then the realization that, unless they capitulated to the Kuomintang, they faced the opposition of both the United States and the Soviet Union in the event of a civil war. Carefully calculated except that Hurley had forgotten, if he had ever taken into account, the skeptical mind of Mao Tse-tung.

Hurley's visit to Yenan in November 1944 had raised high hopes and expectations. It seemed to party officials and cadres that the Border Region's long isolation was over, that American recognition had been won and help was at hand for supporting Communist participation in China's future.

Hurley's sudden cave-in on his return to Chungking had caused dismay. It seemed inconceivable that the man who had so generously endorsed the five-point coalition terms could without protest have permitted Chiang Kai-shek to send back his insulting counterproposal. The best that could be made of it was that the Generalissimo had pulled some kind of trick on the American. And indeed this suspicion seemed confirmed to most Red officials in the spring of 1945 when Hurley, apparently forcing Chiang to toe the line, obtained his consent for delegates from Yenan to discuss peace with the Kuomintang in Chungking. From all appearances the United States ambassador was still an impartial friend, eager to bring about a reconciliation between the sides.

Mao Tse-tung alone remained unconvinced. There was something too cozy going on between Hurley and "His Majesty"—as he had taken to calling Chiang Kai-shek. Mao had submitted the American diplomat to class analysis and had come to the conclusion that, as an imperialist and reactionary, he was not to be trusted. He tried to promulgate this view at an address to the Seventh Congress of the Chinese Communist Party held in Yenan in April 1945. He titled his talk "On Coalition Government" but it might better have been called "Give up Hope of Coalition Government." He pointed out that there were two ways to negotiate a settlement: the "honest way," where parties met at a round table conference to discuss and resolve differences, and the "dishonest way" now taking place in Chungking, with the Kuomintang stalling and evading and "making a pretence of 'handing state power back to the people' while actually 'handing it back' to the selfsame reactionary clique" that had been clinging desperately to it all along. Nothing was going to change the nature of the Kuomintang which had "already proved its complete bankruptcy," not even American diplomatic help, if indeed it was honestly intended. So the Communist Party had better look to its own resources, stick to its own principles, and prepare for the worst.

It was not a popular exposition. Staunch comrades in both government and the military yearned for an alternative to a final armed showdown with the powerful Kuomintang and continued to invest hope in American good offices. By midsummer, with the Chungking talks still bogged down, Mao Tse-tung began acting forcibly to dispel illusions. In an article called "The Hurley-Chiang Duel is a Flop" he called the stalling at the conference table a deliberate maneuver "to sacrifice the interests of the Chinese people"—by which he meant the Communist populations—and "wreck their unity." And on July 12, in a personal attack on the American ambassador, he went further, defining Hurley's policy as "encouraging the Kuomintang government to be still more reactionary."

Mao Tse-tung, though he was almost the only Communist to hold the opinion that summer, seems to have sensed the inevitability of a civil war. He had been preparing himself for it for some time. The year before, faced with the hypothetical question "Shall we dare to win?," he had answered emphatically, "Yes, we shall dare to win. . . everything." And he was still firm in that conviction, though the time had not yet come to shout it from the rooftops. The Japanese war was still to be won and, as late as July 1945, few had any idea how quickly the end was to come.

It came in a series of shocks and tremors with incredible speed and violence. On August 6, the first atom bomb was dropped on Hiroshima. On August 8, the Soviet Union entered the Far Eastern war, invading Manchuria. On August 9, a second atom bomb exploded over Nagasaki. On August 10, the Japanese agreed to "unconditional surrender" on condition that the monarchy was preserved. On August 14, the Allies accepted the condition and it was all over—eight days that ended for China a war of eight years.

Chiang Kai-shek and Mao Tse-tung blinked in the sunlight but neither had time to savor the moment. On August 8, the day of the Soviet invasion, Mao Tse-tung sent regiments racing into Manchuria to disarm Japanese and puppet troops on the periphery of the Russian advance. Chiang Kai-shek reacted promptly. He sent a wire to Chu Teh, commander-in-chief of the Red armies, ordering him to hold position and cease and desist from accepting enemy surrenders. Chu Teh retorted that, under the united front, he had as much right as Chiang to disarm Japanese, and if the Generalissimo was so eager to get their weapons, why didn't he go after the Nipponese troops in his own territory?

Chiang appealed to the Americans for help. Franklin D. Roosevelt was no more; he had died in office on April 12, 1945, in advance of victory in Europe but knowing that the triumph of the great alliance he had helped create was inevitable everywhere. His successor, Harry S. Truman, was still feeling his way, still uncertain of his policies, especially in regard to China where dark dilemmas, shelved by Roosevelt, were emerging again for solution. Truman responded to the Generalissimo's appeal with the support he thought due a loyal ally. From Tokyo, General Douglas MacArthur, supreme commander for the occupation of Japan, ordered Japanese units in China to surrender only to Kuomintang forces. While in Chungking, General Wedemeyer made available American transport planes to ferry the Generalissimo's troops into Manchurian cities ahead of the Communists.

And so the pattern was set. Without forethought or clarified aims, U.S. diplomacy blundered into unquestioning support of Chiang Kai-shek, compromising its claims to impartiality in any future negotiations with Mao Tse-tung and his government. Such negotiations would soon be needed as another development inevitably erupted—clashes between Red and Kuomintang forces above the Great Wall. Again without premeditation or plan, touched off by a scramble for spoils, civil war had irretrievably begun.

In Chungking, Patrick J. Hurley was suffering the dyspepsia of frustration. He had in his hands what he thought was the key to civil peace—the Treaty of Friendship and Alliance between Stalin and the Generalissimo which he was convinced would bring the Chinese Reds to heel—but suddenly the lock had developed resistance and refused to turn. T. V. Soong, head negotiator for the Chungking side, had been in Moscow for months now. All the terms of the treaty had been worked out, expressions of goodwill continued, but still Stalin's signature was lacking.

Then Hurley discovered what was holding back the Russian dictator. He wanted more than friendship from the proposed pact; he wanted sanctification for a devious deal. For at Yalta in February 1945, President Roosevelt, no longer concerned with China's status as a great power, had bartered away Chinese rights and territories in return for Stalin's promise of an early entrance into the Japanese war. At the time, Roosevelt had undertaken to inform Chiang Kai-shek of what he had done, but he had died without breaking the news. Now Stalin wanted the situation confirmed; he wanted Chiang's agreement to the concessions made at Yalta as a condition of concluding the Treaty of Friendship and Alliance.

To Patrick J. Hurley fell the duty of informing the Generalissimo that, without his knowledge, an American president had leased to the Russians the city of Port Arthur at the tip of the Liaoning peninsula. He had also internationalized the nearby harbor of Dairen and pledged joint control of Manchurian railways to a Sino-Soviet commission. All things considered, Chiang took it well. During more than a century, China had become accustomed to Western doubledealing and this was only a further insult added to the others. The time would come, after the Communists were suppressed and the nation was strong again, when he would redeem all the outright thefts and fraudulent peculations with punitive interest. Meanwhile all he could do was to cope and endure.

He gave his consent to the Roosevelt-Stalin deal and activity immediately stepped up in Moscow as fresh clauses were briskly written into the pact. But the pace was not brisk enough to suit Hurley when the thundering days of August began, when Japan collapsed and the strains within China surfaced. However, on August 14—V-J Day by Western count—the treaty was finally signed and Hurley was ready to execute his grand strategy.

He asked the Generalissimo to invite Mao Tse-tung to Chungking. The terms of the Treaty of Friendship and Alliance had not yet been published and Hurley wanted the Communist leader in camp, away from his supporters in Yenan, when he learned that Stalin had deserted him by pledging full support to Chiang's government. That would be the time, in the ambassador's estimation, to force on the shaken and isolated Mao a settlement of differences favorable to the Kuomintang regime.

To Hurley's chagrin, the Generalissimo balked at issuing the invitation. Perhaps a sour aftertaste lingered from the Friendship Treaty or, more likely, Chiang's indignation was freshly aroused by further evidence of Western hypocrisy. For within days of the Japanese surrender, the British were back in Burma and Malaya, the French in Indo-China and the Dutch in the East Indies, and no one was asking *them* to come to terms with the "freedom fighters" that had sprung up during their absences. Since the suppression of rebels seemed to be the order of the day, why wasn't Chiang allowed a free hand with his? Better to get on with stamping out insurrection now and be done with it.

Hurley was taken aback but he had powerful arguments on his side. The U.S. government was committed to peace in China and, unless the Generalissimo cooperated in bringing it about, he would stand clearly as an aggressor, with a subsequent loss of American sympathy and support. A support, it was unnecessary to add, that was already transporting his best troops into Manchuria where they would be left isolated if policies changed.

So in the end an invitation was sent. The telegram, couched in Confucian phraseology, was addressed to "elder brother" Mao Tse-tung to whom "younger brother" Chiang Kai-shek wished to extend his poor hospitality should he care to visit Chungking. Mao replied with equal ceremony, regretting his inability to travel at this time. A second summons was also turned down. But after August 24, when the text of the Friendship Treaty was published, Hurley was confident that the third and, by custom, obligatory invitation would meet with a better response.

As it happens, he was right, though not for the reason he had anticipated nor with the results that he had intended.

The official Communist version is that "Mao Tse-tung [went] to Chungking... in order to make every possible effort for peace and also... to show U.S. imperialism and Chiang Kai-shek in their true colours..." But publicizing to a worldwide forum the intransigence of the Kuomintang, aided and abetted by American diplomacy, was only part of the story. Mao Tse-tung went to Chungking because the very life of the Chinese Communist Party depended on it. He had to prove two things: that the coalition government for which his followers yearned was impossible short of abject surrender; and that a stand had to be taken against Joseph Stalin who, at this juncture of history, had spoken up again with suicidal advice.

Contrary to what Patrick J. Hurley had expected, the text of the Treaty of Friendship and Alliance had not been read in

Yenan with shattering dismay. By this time branch parties had learned to accept unexpected twists of Kremlin policy with some equanimity, justifying them on the grounds that the fountainhead of Communism must serve its own interests first for the eventual benefit of all. But what had hurt were the private instructions Stalin had sent in the wake of his betrayal. Both through his peremptory tone and the messenger he had chosen to deliver his orders, he had caused doubt and confusion, shaking the Yenan community.

We have Stalin's own account of what happened. Years later, reminiscing about the situation in August 1945, he recollected: "We told [the Chinese Communist Party] bluntly that we considered [an] uprising in China had no prospect, and that the Chinese comrades should join the Chiang Kai-shek government and dissolve their army. The Chinese comrades agreed here [in Moscow] with the views of the Soviet comrades, but went home to China and acted otherwise."

The question arises: who were the agreeing Chinese comrades in Moscow in August 1945? They certainly had not been sent from Yenan. In all probability they were the last of the contingent held over from old Comintern* days, headed by Li Li-san. At all events, Li Li-san, the former hard-liner and "attack the cities" advocate of 1929 and 1930, now long out of touch with the realities of China, crossed the Manchurian border with the invading Soviet armies and was whisked off to Yenan carrying Stalin's instructions. Consternation followed his arrival. The ranks divided between those always ready to bow to the Kremlin and those who bristled with defiance.

Mao Tse-tung's reaction was immediate. He had now no option but to go to Chungking, though he carefully defined the parameters within which he would negotiate: "We... are prepared to make such concessions as are necessary [to] obtain... legal status for our Party and a state of peace. But there

---

*Stalin had dissolved the Comintern in 1943; partly because, as a builder of socialism in one country, he had no further use for exporting revolution, but partly no doubt to reassure his Western allies of World War II that they need no longer fear Soviet-incubated communism.

are limits"—including surrender of the Red army—to what concessions were negotiable. And he ended on an encouraging note: "[O]ur Party is powerful [and] we must never be cowed by the bluster of reactionaries." Perhaps there is just a hint here that he included J. Stalin among the reactionaries.

In any case, Mao Tse-tung went to Chungking not on the defensive but on the attack, to gain recognition for his party "in the eyes of the whole nation and the whole world." Or as he put it with Churchillian overtones: "[W]e must . . . win over the many, oppose the few and crush our enemies one by one."

Patrick J. Hurley was elated when he learned that Mao Tse-tung was coming to Chungking. With all his old flamboyance, he flew to Yenan to escort the Communist delegation to Chiang's capital, making a big show of personally guaranteeing its safety. He had been hurt by Mao's recent criticism of him, and now poured on the charm to reestablish cordial relations.

But it was a bit late for that. A bit late too for the high hopes Hurley had invested in the conference. To the ambassador's disappointment, Mao Tse-tung seemed entirely unintimidated by the significance of the Soviet Treaty of Friendship and Alliance which had been calculated to cut the ground out from under him. As the negotiations dragged on, with Mao stubbornly pressing for constitutional safeguards for a coalition government, and the Generalissimo just as stubbornly contending that surrender of the Red army must come first, Hurley's misgivings grew. He had constructed the machine so carefully, and now it was stuck, spinning its wheels.

He took to moving in and out behind the scenes, offering his services as mediator and arbiter, only to find that he was not wanted by either camp. The Generalissimo took the attitude that the conference had been foisted on him against his will, and that the sooner the meaningless show came to an end the better. And Mao Tse-tung still stood by his analysis of class enemies, and no amount of pleading by Hurley that "he was the best friend the Chinese Communists had in Chungking" could change the conviction.

It was a difficult time for the American ambassador. He was in the position of an impresario who had staged a production of world significance, only to find that the principals would neither acknowledge his achievement or even his presence. Hurley was in his sixties, with a distinguished record behind him in both business and diplomacy, and he had hoped to cap his career by the epic feat of averting civil war in China. It should have been worth a Nobel Prize, and certainly it was a subject for historians to study for years to come. But now his prestige and anticipated honors were slipping away from him. Civil war, only a threat when the talks began, was hastening on. News of clashes between Communist and Kuomintang troops drifted in on the wires from Manchuria. Hurley drooped in the September heat and lost spirit. He suddenly found medical reasons for returning home. Apparently he thought that, if he wasn't present to witness failure, he couldn't be blamed for it.

He was in Washington D.C. when the Chungking conference petered out and Mao Tse-tung returned to Yenan. Though he had been expecting the news, Hurley reacted with a show of anger. To account to his superiors for what had happened, he looked around for scapegoats, finding them in the American Embassy at Chungking. Thinking back, he decided that his subordinates, especially those who had visited Yenan and had returned "soft" on communism, had betrayed him by encouraging Mao Tse-tun's obstinate attitude at the conference table.

He wrote a letter to President Truman, charging both his Chungking staff and, for good measure, desk officers at the State Department, with sabotaging his efforts for peace in China. Since he could no longer work in the prevalent atmosphere of disloyalty and conspiracy, he was resigning his ambassadorship.

The President accepted the resignation without protest. Hurley was, after all, Roosevelt's appointee, not his. To clean up the incomprehensible mess in China, Truman had another man in mind—General George C. Marshall, U.S. chief-of-staff during World War II and perhaps the most capable soldier of his time. If George couldn't do it, nobody could.

24

Circles within Circles

GENERAL OF THE ARMY GEORGE C. MARSHALL REACHED Chungking in December 1945, accredited as Special Representative of the President with the rank of ambassador. The designation had been carefully chosen; it provided Marshall with necessary prestige while enabling him to bypass the State Department in his communications with the White House. His job was to bring peace to China by democratic means. To back up the good intentions, Truman pledged generous loans once a democratic coalition government came into being.

The new envoy found immediate work awaiting him. Mao Tse-tung had returned to Yenan in October, but he had left behind a rump delegation that met with the Kuomintang for desultory conversations. News from Manchuria, where aggressive action had stepped up considerably, constantly converted the talks into quarreling forums where each side accused the other of treachery and bad faith.

Into this atmosphere of hostility and suspicion stepped George C. Marshall. Exhibiting the character and wide vision that had

won the admiration of such world leaders as Roosevelt, Churchill, and Stalin, not to mention Harry S. Truman, the ex-artillery captain of World War I who virtually idolized him, Marshall persuaded the sides to declare a cease-fire. To enforce it, he organized truce teams, consisting of Kuomintang, Communist, and American members, to investigate and control further skirmishing. And he soon displayed diplomatic talents to go with his military know-how. When Chou En-lai complained that American planes were ferrying Nationalist troops into Manchuria while doing nothing for the Red forces, Marshall pointed out that, while each side had equal rights of access to the area, the Communists had shorter distances to travel, which put the Kuomintang at a disadvantage. Chou, apparently reconciled by the argument, agreed to shipment of a specified number of the Generalissimo's men before air freight shut down.

With tensions eased and tempers mollified, Marshall returned the delegates to the peace table for serious business. The deliberations changed character as the assembly adopted a new name for itself—a Political Consultative Conference. The aim was to settle and clear away matters of principle and procedure so that a representative National Assembly might be called in the spring of 1946. Other parties besides the Kuomintang and Communists participated. Chief among them was the Democratic League, an amalgam of intellectuals and liberals, a highly respected group, though without real political power, since it possessed no army.

By the end of January 1946 encouraging progress had been made. To the surprise of all, Chiang Kai-shek demonstrated obliging cooperation and goodwill, offering every assistance in helping stage a sucessful conference. With astonishing magnanimity he yielded on positions where he had stood firm for twenty years. He agreed to free elections for the forthcoming National Assembly and concurred in plans for an expansion of government that would inevitably threaten his one-party rule. He raised no objection to legalizing all organized patriotic groups and approved their powers of veto. In only one area did he prove adamant—the composition of a National army to be formed under a new Military Council. He insisted on a proportion of five-to-one: five Kuomintang divisions for each Red. But as this roughly represented the actual strength of the rival forces then in existence, the Communists accepted the proviso.

The concessions were so far-reaching and freely made that even Mao Tse-tung, perhaps ascribing a miracle to Marshall's powers of persuasion, seems to have been momentarily taken in. He told a Yenan assembly, "The world is progressing, the future is bright. . . ." Though he had previously cautioned: "Words on paper are not equivalent to reality. Facts have shown that a very great effort must still be made before they can be turned into reality."

George C. Marshall was certainly pleased with the way things were going. So much so that, in early March, he perhaps injudiciously flew back to Washington to report on the encouraging prospects and to recommend a $500 million loan to help put the new Chinese coalition government on its feet.

Only the Kuomintang old guard was left dazed and bewildered. What did the Generalissimo think he was doing? Why was he temporizing with Americans and Communists when his real job was to get on with the civil war and crush the Red menace as rapidly as possible? What had changed him?

The concerns were needless; Chiang hadn't changed. In terms of the proverb, he was simply riding the tiger until the time came to fight it. He needed breathing space to get his troops into position for the coming offensive against the only enemy that had ever mattered to him. And while the Political Consultive Conference lasted, the United States was moving his forces into strategic locations without asking questions. And there was an additional dividend: not only was he deceiving the Americans, but he was also gulling the Russians into performing police work on his behalf.

Since V-J Day, Soviet troops had lingered uneasily in Manchuria. Joseph Stalin, nervous about the atom bomb and wanting to avoid any possible incidents, had planned to withdraw immediately after gaining the objectives guaranteed him by the Yalta agreement—ice-free ports opening on the Yellow Sea and control of the Northeast railways. He had tried to pull out in December 1945, but that had been too soon to suit Chiang Kai-shek. Noting that the Soviets had been scrupulous about shunning contact with the Chinese Red guerrillas streaming into Manchuria, the Generalissimo asked Stalin to continue garrisoning the chief cities for a while longer. Stalin had obliged, and more than obliged—quelling dissidents and installing Kuomintang officials in office as they were shipped to him by air. But by the spring of 1946 he'd had enough and firmly set an April date for his pullout.

By then Chiang Kai-shek was ready. He had some 137,000 crack troops in Manchuria and North China, garrisoning a series of key cities that looped down like pearls on a string—Harbin, Mukden, Chinchow, Peiping. His attacking posture was established. All that remained was to pull the thread unraveling the work of the Political Consultative Conference in Chungking and the war could begin in earnest.

The consultative conference was then in temporary adjournment. The delegates had handed over to their respective principals the results of their long deliberations. All the ingredients were their for a valid coalition government and a democratic future for China; they needed only ratification.

In March, the Central Executive Committee of the Kuomintang settled down to study the resolutions. It was an unusually dignified occasion for that august body because for years it had been acting merely as the Generalissimo's rubber stamp, if indeed he bothered to consult it at all. But now the members were asked to deliberate and decide with all the gravity of statesmanship, though there could have been few who weren't aware of exactly what was expected of them.

To their credit, let it be said that they made it look good. They pondered and puzzled for seventeen days before they concluded not to adopt the resolutions. Rather, they did adopt them, but subject to revisions and amendments they knew to be unacceptable to the Communists, thus killing the resolutions as effectively as if they had been rejected outright. It was a triumph of craft. The pretense of democracy within the Kuomintang had been preserved and the Generalissimo's face had been saved. For surely President Truman could understand the bitterness of defeat by the vote of his own party.

George C. Marshall, shocked by the development, left Washington and hurried back to China. He'd had no difficulty seeing through Chiang Kai-shek's stratagem and accused him of bad faith. But the Generalissimo wasn't attentive, owing to recent troubles of his own. The Russians, withdrawing from Manchuria, had infuriated him by two actions: they had looted the industrial centers of heavy machinery and, worse from Chiang's viewpoint, had turned over to the Chinese Communists the enormous stockpile of weapons they had captured from the Japanese.

It's easier to understand the first Soviet action than the second. Stalin had, after all, been a bank robber in his time and purloining Japanese forges and foundries may have seemed to him a legitimate way of helping himself to war reparations. But handing over the weapons—an enormous cache, numbering some 300,000 rifles and 5,000 machine guns, along with cannons, motorized vehicles, and other ordnance—was a different matter. It is too much to believe that his conscience was belatedly stirred at his abandonment of the Chinese Reds and that he was trying to make up. More likely he hoped that, by strengthening the Communists, he might involve America on Chiang's side in a Chinese civil war, thus lessening danger of an atomic attack on Russia, a prospect that dominated his thinking at the time.

Chiang Kai-shek was soon to be agitated by a fresh outrage. As the Russians withdrew from Changchun, capital of the former Japanese State of Manchukuo, Chinese Red guerrillas moved in to occupy it. The Generalissimo, calling the action "intolerable insolence," flew north to recapture the city.

George C. Marshall, seeing the cornerstones of peace, standing so secure a month before, tumbling about him, hurried after the Generalissimo. He argued long and hard that the fate of Changchun must be settled by negotiation or all hope of averting war would be lost. But he found Chiang deaf to reason.

In desperation, Marshall wired Mao Tse-tung, suggesting that Changchun be turned into an Executive Headquarters city—an extension of the idea of a truce team whereby a triumvirate of Kuomintang, Communist, and American members would exercise joint control. Mao was agreeable, but wanted the same administration for Harbin, Mukden, and Chinchow—cities above the Great Wall now in Chiang's possession. Marshall accepted the plan, but the Generalissimo did not. He was hysterical at the very idea and continued to assemble forces for an assault on Changchun.

The situation was so hopeless that Marshall was forced to play what he fondly hoped was a trump card. He retired as a mediator. He retired temporarily, it is true, but he threatened to make the withdrawal permanent, with all that meant in the loss of American support, unless Chiang Kai-shek came to his senses.

Marshall returned to Nanking, once more the Nationalist capital. At leisure he had time to think about Chiang's erratic behavior and to study positional maps. Bit by bit he pieced together the Generalissimo's strategic plans for defeating the Communists and was appalled by their megalomania.

Chiang Kai-shek held an enormous arc of cities, stretching from Harbin in north Manchuria to Lanchow at the fringe of Inner Mongolia. His front followed the main railroad south to Peiping, then swept west along the Yellow River as far as Loyang, continuing on, as far as Marshall could determine, through Sian and Lanchow to the highlands of Outer Mongolia. The territory enclosed roughly a quarter of China Proper and its extension beyond the Great Wall tripled the area. In terms of the United States, it was as if he had drawn an attacking line starting at Boston in the Northeast, swinging south and west through St. Louis, Missouri, and Tulsa, Oklahoma, then continuing north to come out at the Canadian border somewhere in the neighborhood of Winnipeg, Manitoba. The Generalissimo clearly proposed to drive inward from this gigantic semicircle with some five million troops of indifferent quality, of whom less than two million could be engaged in actual fighting. Even Hitler, when he attacked Russia with all his Stukas and panzer divisions and maniacal sense of destiny, hadn't dared to plan on such a scale.

Now Marshall understood Chiang's hysteria at the thought of giving up Changchun. The city, astride the railroad between Mukden and Chinchow, was essential to his string of fortifications, to his basic strategic plan. He needed it as he might a missing tooth. When Chiang returned to Nanking in late May 1946 having recaptured Changchun—or rather, reoccupied it, since Mao Tse-tung, never one to waste casualties in the defense of cities, had ordered it evacuated—he had calmed down considerably and was ready to talk peace again while he consolidated his gains. Marshall found Yenan willing enough to go along with the charade and a truce was arranged for delegates from the opposing sides to meet for further talks.

Perhaps it was none of Marshall's business, but he let the Generalissimo know what he thought about his overambitious plan for encircling and crushing the Communists. Chiang was deeply hurt. He told Marshall he didn't understand the situation in China. There was no question of Kuomintang troops being stretched too thin because everywhere they went they would be among friends—friends of Dr. Sun Yat-sen and his revolution, friends of the old culture and traditions. Chiang's mission, as it had been Tseng Kuo-fan's before him during the time of the Taiping Heavenly Kingdom rebellion, was to rally the people and restore the principles of Confucian harmony. And just as Tseng Kuo-fan had succeeded, so would he.

Chiang admitted that the Communists had been clever with their propaganda. In some places, especially North China, they had converted ignorant peasants and caused disruptions. But in the showdown, when the people had to choose between foreign ideas and ancient ways of life, ties of clan and kinship would tell.

There is something ludicrous as well as pathetic about the scene. General of the Army George C. Marshall, U.S. Chief-of-Staff and supervisor of MacArthur, Eisenhower, Patton, and Stilwell, was a soldier versed in global strategy who had just successfully concluded a war on four continents. Now he was advising caution to Chiang Kai-shek—who, for all his training at the Shinbo Gokyo Military Academy in Japan and his courtesy title of Generalissimo, was essentially an old-line feudal warlord—and was being told by Chiang that he couldn't understand the military situation in China because he didn't understand the Confucian heart. Whatever Marshall's private reaction was, he retreated hastily from further advice on the conduct of a war which, after all, it was his business to terminate as rapidly as possible.

But prospects of peace were fading fast as the summer of 1946 drew on. The delegates debating in Nanking were clearly acting as screens to cover the fighting that still continued despite the declared truce. Chiang Kai-shek was busy trying to clean out Red guerrillas who had infiltrated behind his strategic line—notably in Manchuria and Shantung Province—and Mao Tse-tung was countering the attacks with vigor, intent on whittling down the disparity of forces between the two armies.

Chiang Kai-shek's sabotage of the Political Consultative Conference in the spring had at least clarified one issue at Yenan—the Generalissimo was not interested in peace in China through a democratic coalition government. So the sooner the Communists made up their minds to a protracted civil war, the better.

Mao Tse-tung's first task was to alleviate depression and energize the fainthearted. Brimming with confidence, he issued optimistic statements: "Although Chiang Kai-shek has U.S. aid, the feelings of the people are against him, the morale of his troops is low, and his economy is in difficulty.... [W]e can defeat Chiang Kai-shek. The whole Party should be fully confident of this."

To the Red army he issued what might be called a refresher course on how the fighting was to be done: "[C]oncentrate an absolutely superior force—six, five, four or at least three times the enemy strength—and pick an opportune moment to encircle and wipe out one enemy brigade (or regiment).... When this has been achieved, we should, according to circumstances, either wipe out ... more enemy brigades or return to rest and consolidate.... Using this method we shall win. Acting counter to it we shall lose."

These, of course, were the familiar maneuvers of Kiangsi days—with a difference. Mao had moved from old-style guerrilla warfare to what he called "mobile" warfare, the distinction being the size of forces to be employed and the number of enemy troops to be caught. He was no longer satisfied with cutting off and destroying squads and companies; he now wanted regiments and brigades. He had calculated Chiang Kai-shek's effective field strength at 190 brigades (some 1,330,000 men) as against his own 800,000 odd regulars, and he wanted the odds evened as soon as feasible. Until parity was achieved, he meant to pursue a policy of "wear and tear" or "of wearing the enemy down to complete exhaustion and then wiping him out." Afterward he promised what his commanders had so long yearned for—regulation, stand-up warfare, with the Red army (soon to be called the PLA or People's Liberation Army) going after the enemy on the offensive.

For his political cadres, Mao Tse-tung reintroduced a potent weapon in May 1946. He sanctioned again confiscation of landlords' property, a policy that had been in abeyance since the united front of 1936 in deference to Kuomintang sensibilities. The Red political workers fell to with a new enthusiasm. Confiscation and redistribution of the land had always been the ultimate prize to spur peasants on to self-determination and village revolution.

So that summer in Nanking, George C. Marshall watched over a conference at which the delegates did little besides stall and squabble. He read uneasily reports from the field where his truce teams could no longer keep pace with the continuing eruption of hostilities. And he listened somberly to the Generalissimo's charges that the Communists, by confiscating property in the countryside, had put themselves beyong the pale for further consideration. Marshall, trying to sit on the lid, was wondering where it was going to blow up next.

Unexpectedly, it blew up in the cities, and both sides were responsible. The Kuomintang old guard, eager to get on with the civil war and irritated by Marshall's restraining influence staged anti-American demonstrations in Shanghai, Wuhan, and Tientsin, hoping that he would take the hint and learn that his presence was no longer welcomed in China. By a coincidence, the Communists chose the same time to inspire rallies of their own, though their anger was caused by Marshall's supposed partiality to the Kuomintang. The marching mobs, edgy and irritable on their own account because of food shortages and rocketing inflation, met and battled in the streets with warlike casualties.

The violence made headlines in the American press and President Truman intervened. He wired Chiang Kai-shek his alarm at the military and economic situation and urged that renewed efforts be made to bring peace to China by democratic means.

Chiang cabled back, putting the blame on the Communists for all that had gone wrong. Dissatisfied, Truman sent another telegram, pleading for a prompt end to hostilities so that the United States might provide aid for economic recovery. That was on August 31 and this time the Generalissimo didn't even bother to answer.

Marshall, always resourceful, came up with a new plan: a State Council, Kuomintang and Communists participating, where disputes might be adjudicated at a high echelon level. Chiang Kai-shek seemed to agree; then suddenly in September his forces were attacking Kalgan, a garrison city south of the Great Wall, which had been in Communist possession since soon after V-J Day.

Marshall's patience had reached the breaking point. He threatened to end his efforts for peace and recommend to Washington his own recall unless the Generalissimo called off his attack on Kalgan at once. But communicating with Chiang, who had flown to the scene of action, proved difficult—his radios seemed to be out of order for some reason or another—and Marshall received no definitive answer until October 10 when Kalgan was captured and Chiang returned triumphantly to Nanking.

Far from being apologetic, the Generalissimo was in an expansive mood. He had decided, he told Marshall, to do what President Truman wanted—establish an immediate democratic government. To this end he had set a November date for a National Assembly and sent invitations to all parties to participate.

The Communists' reaction was predictable. Mao Tse-tung too was getting weary of Chiang Kai-shek's manipulations and he demanded conditions, both political and military, before agreeing to enter the National Assembly. Delegates to the convention must be freely elected in accordance with the guidelines recommended by the Political Consultative Conference in Chungking during the spring and, on the fighting fronts, both sides must withdraw their troops to the positions held at that time.

These terms were unacceptable to the Generalissimo. Nothing could induce him to give up his string of cities in Manchuria, not to mention his recent acquisition of Kalgan. And besides, the

National Assembly he had in mind was somewhat different from the freely elected convocation Mao Tse-tung envisioned. He doggedly announced that he had given the Communists their last chance, and that the National Assembly would meet as scheduled, with or without their participation.

George C. Marshall finally realized what had been evident all along, the reality he would have seen earlier had he been able to clear his mind of his soldierly sense of duty. He did not need Mao Tse-tung's blasts, released in September and October, that his efforts at mediation had been "a fraud," "a smoke-screen for strengthening Chiang Kai-shek in every way and suppressing the democratic forces . . . so as to reduce China virtually to a U.S. colony." He himself complained that he had been "used" by both sides in a bewildering game of blind man's buff. His mission had ended in failure.

But just for curiosity he stuck around for Chiang's National Assembly which convened in Nanking on November 15, 1946. The hand-picked body, overwhelmingly Kuomintang but with a few representatives of splinter groups slipped in for show, meekly endorsed the political program offered them. Actually it was an astonishingly liberal program, incorporating many of the resolutions of the Political Consultative Conference of the spring. But as Marshall noted, there were no provisions for enforcing the rights and liberties granted. Chiang Kai-shek was, of course, elected president of the new government, though a surprise developed in the voting for vice president. After bitter in-fighting and over the Generalissimo's objections, Li Tsung-jen, Chiang's old rival for military honors, was installed in office.

On November 16 Chou En-lai called on Marshall to ask for transportation back to Yenan. The Communist representatives in Nanking were being recalled because, as Chou En-lai put it, the door to further negotiations has been "slammed." A mutual respect seems to have developed between Marshall and the Red diplomat during the months of their somewhat strained relations. Marshall had also met Mao Tse-tung—he had flown to Yenan at one point to prove his impartiality—but it is doubtful that the intellectually remote and politically suspicious chairman of the Communist Party had exerted much appeal for the forthright

West Pointer. Chou En-lai, firm, persistent, and patient, was much more to the American's taste, and real rapport seems to have sprung up between them.

They talked about the future of the civil war which was now patently about to break out into the open. Chou En-lai expressed confidence in the eventual outcome, though he regretted the misery that would be caused as Kuomintang troops slashed out over the countryside in ambitious campaigns. He startled Marshall by predicting that, within six months, Chiang Kai-shek would attack Yenan. Marshall, to whom Yenan was a remote target and of no strategic relevance, offered his opinion that the Generalissimo would be out of his mind to try it. Chou En-lai merely smiled.

Before he left China, Marshall had a final interview with Chiang Kai-shek. Steering clear of Chiang's military strategy, which he had learned by now was incomprehensible to a foreigner, he concentrated on political and economic matters. He urged the Generalissimo to reform his government, to dismiss incompetent and corrupt officials, and to take thought for the financial crisis that was paralyzing his nation.

Chiang blandly replied that everything would be solved when the Communist question was solved. China was primarily an agricultural country and, though there was some suffering in the cities at present, the economy would hold out until the Red bandits were annihilated—a period he calculated, now that the wraps were off and he could begin fighting in earnest, would take from eight to ten months.

He proceeded to startle Marshall by thanking him for his previous military advice. Perhaps his original plan for enveloping Manchuria and Inner Mongolia as well as North China *had* been too ambitious. He had changed his strategy now; he was going to concentrate on North China alone. Kalgan was to be an important outpost for this development, hence the necessity for taking it. From Kalgan to the north and Loyang to the south, he could move in to encircle the main forces of the Red army.

The situation, the Generalissimo explained, was similar to his Fifth Extermination Campaign in 1934 when he had encircled the Communists in Kiangsi. He intended to employ the same methods again, though this time he was confident of conclusive results. He had tanks and planes now, and the flatlands of the North China plain to work on. There would be no breaking out of his perimeter this time, no Long March. He had learned by experience; he would close in from all sides for total destruction.

Marshall must have stared. It was a joke in military circles the world over that conservative generals were always thoroughly prepared to re-fight the last war, and in Chiang Kai-shek he saw the very embodiment of the philosophy. He could hardly have taken it as a compliment when the Generalissimo, regretting that Marshall's role as a mediator was over, offered him as substitute a job as his personal military adviser.

Marshall left China early in January 1947. He returned to Washington and an ever-admiring President to be appointed Secretary of State. He was to go on to win acclaim as architect of the Truman and Marshall Plans that, for a while at least, staved off communism in Europe. But as with Stilwell and Hurley before him, he had been unable to change in the slightest degree the manifest destiny of China, caught in a conflict between the past and the future, the matrix of the old and the unpredictable new.

25

Amid Fire and Thunder

MAO TSE-TUNG CERTAINLY DID NOT BELIEVE THAT HE was about to fight the old campaigns of Kiangsi, or anywhere else, all over again. For him warfare, and especially civil warfare, was Heraclitus's river into which no man stepped twice. Through concrete analysis of concrete fact he kept testing the flow of the constantly changing current and evolved strategies to deal with it. He remained flexible, adhering to few military principles beyond the great underlying one which, as he restated it in February 1947, was in effect largely political: "[T]he difficulties of the reactionar[ies] are insurmountable because they are forces on the verge of death and have no future [while] our difficulties can be overcome because we are new and rising forces and have a bright future."

When the civil war began in earnest in May 1946, Mao Tse-tung concentrated on cutting down the disparity in front-line forces between the Nationalists and the People's Liberation Army. By the turn of the year he was able to report good results. In seven months of fighting he estimated that some fifty-six brigades—better than 400,000 men—of Chiang Kai-shek's regulars had been disposed of, "not counting the numerous puppet troops and peace preservation corps which were wiped out and those of Chiang's regular forces which were routed." In Mao's precise bookkeeping, "wiped out" meant totally eliminated, the entire force killed or captured; "routed" meant inflicting severe casualties, though the main body might have escaped.

This was a considerable adjustment, though still far from decisive. Mao Tse-tung calculated that another fifty Kuomintang brigades must be lopped off to achieve parity, and thereafter relative strength must be maintained by intensive recruiting. Chiang Kai-shek had reinstituted compulsory conscription—in abeyance since V-J Day—and by this means was to add 2,440,000 men to his armies in the next two years. Mao Tse-tung responded by finding a readier recruiting pool closer at hand—in prisoners of war. Before the conflict was over, some 800,000 Kuomintang and provincial captives had changed sides and were fighting as loyal soldiers of the PLA.

The key to converting demoralized prisoners into enthusiasts for a new cause was found in the *su-ku* or "speaking bitterness" campaigns. Su-ku was a development of the fan-shen techniques which had proved so effective in liberating the villages of North China. Prisoners, recovering from their surprise at being well treated by the Reds instead of being put to torture and death as predicted by their officers, were encouraged to speak out at mass meetings. The resulting *tu ku-shui*, literally "vomiting bitterness," spewed up all the old familiar grievances against the Nationalist military establishment—the insults and beatings, the starvation diets and embezzled pay—working up emotions to the fever pitch. When the atmosphere was ripe, the Red political cadres took over. Succinctly but effectively they explained how such injustices came to be, and began simplified education in the class struggle. It took about six weeks for the indoctrination to take hold. Then the prisoners were offered the option of returning home, expenses paid or, if they so wished, enlisting in the People's Liberation Army. Few could resist the temptation to join new comrades and settle old scores with the Kuomintang.

There was efficiency to such recruiting. While Chiang Kai-shek's conscripts appeared in camp with the mud of the paddy fields still clinging to their sandals and the dreary work of drill still to be taught, Mao Tse-tung's converted prisoners came to him as readymade soldiers. And there were other assets. Turncoat recruits were often experienced in the use of American weapons now pouring into Red hands through capture. During the war of resistance against the Japanese, Mao Tse-tung had called the invaders his supply sergeants. Now it was the Americans who were indirectly providing ordnance, and the Kuomintang was yielding up instructors in its operation.

So the winter of 1946–47 passed in both surreptitious battles and open conquests. To the Western press and radio, relying on handouts supplied by Nanking, it seemed that Chiang Kai-shek was triumphant everywhere. He held all the major cities of Manchuria and North China and seemed capable of taking as many more as he chose with little effort. Few understood the real situation—that outside the cities, in the vast and decisive countryside, the Communists were dominant, fighting a shrewd war of attrition calculated to whittle the Nationalists down to size.

All that remained was for the Generalissimo's long prepared offensive to begin. If it failed—or in Mao Tse-tung's mind *when* it failed—the momentum would shift and the despised Red army, born in desperation some twenty years before, and ever since but a step away from disaster, could go on the attack.

Although George C. Marshall's departure in January had cleared the way, Chiang Kai-shek took his time about beginning operations in North China. It wasn't concern for the growing strength of the Communists that stayed his hand. To the end he continued to think of them as ragged mountain fighters who could be easily crushed once flushed out into the plains and forced to fight in traditional ways. His conviction was bolstered by his victories at Changchun and Kalgan, important strongpoints that a potent enemy would have defended to the last man. What delayed Chiang's military campaign in the late winter of 1947 was the increasing chaos of the national economy. Despite his airy assurances to Marshall that all would continue to be well until the Communists were disposed of, the Generalissimo could no longer ignore the inflation, starvation, and bankruptcies that were paralyzing the cities. There was no money left to run the government or, considerably worse, pay his troops. Not even the financial wizardry of his brothers-in-law, T. V. Soong and H. H. Kung, could conjure up funds, and both were advising that only a large American loan could stave off total collapse.

Chiang Kai-shek saw the difficulties of soliciting American money under the present circumstances. George C. Marshall had left China with a bad taste in his mouth, and Marshall was now the U.S. Secretary of State, in a key position to block a loan. Somehow the climate in Washington must be changed. Sympathy for the Generalissimo and his cause had to be resurrected swiftly in order to meet the emergency.

Chiang fell back on an old role that had never failed to charm Americans—the selfless patriot. He played it out this time for the benefit of John Leighton Stuart, the newly appointed ambassador to China. Stuart, born in China of missionary parents, spoke the language like a native so there was no need for clumsy interpretations when subtleties were reached. He was also an educator—the former president of Yenching University in Peiping—and versed in Confucian ethics. He could well appreciate the concessions to pride and principles the Generalissimo was making by calling in a foreigner to help him preserve the peace of the nation.

Chiang told the ambassador that, above everything, he wished to spare China the agonies of a civil war. He had no doubts about the outcome of the struggle—his estimate for total victory had now dropped to six months—but it had never been his intention to bring the Communists to heel by brute force. He had wanted and had worked hard for the democratic coalition government that President Truman had proposed, but all his efforts had been frustrated by the recalcitrance of the Reds. He was aware that matters now stood at the eleventh hour, but he still hoped that a way might be found to bring the camps together and avoid fratricidal bloodletting.

John Leighton Stuart jumped at the bait. As with a growing list of Americans in the past few years, he saw himself anointed to play a vital role in China's destiny. It is beside the point whether the idea of a conference originated with him or was put into his head by the Generalissimo. The important outcome was that he dispatched a telegram to Mao Tse-tung inviting Yenan representatives to a peace parlay in Nanking under American mediation.

Mao Tse-tung's replay was so hedged about by qualifications as to amount to a rejection. He agreed to a conference but only on condition that the recent National Assembly and all the measures it had enacted be declared "bogus"; furthermore, before the sides met, all troops must be withdrawn to positions held in January 1946, the time of the Political Consultative Conference in Chungking when resolutions had been passed that seemed to guarantee a peaceful future.

Naturally such terms were unacceptable to the Kuomintang. Ambassador Stuart may have been disappointed, but Chiang Kai-shek was not. The maneuver had gained him all he had hoped for. As the news went out to the world press, edited by Nanking, Chiang had shown himself again to be a statesman of goodwill, prepared to do almost anything for the salvation of his country, while the Communists had exposed themselves once more as wreckers and obstructers.

With his credit in Washington reestablished, the Generalissimo could safely leave it to others to push through the American loan while he returned to the more congenial task of eradicating Reds.

In mid-March 1947 Chiang Kai-shek launched a surprise attack on the Communist capital at Yenan. A surprise, that is, to everyone except the Communists who, as Chou En-lai had hinted to George C. Marshall months earlier, had been watching the Nationalist buildup at Loyang and had expected the development.

Mao Tse-tung elected not to defend his seat of government. Partly, no doubt, he was guided by his old reluctance to waste men in the defense of cities but, beyond that, he had come to the conclusion that Yenan had outlived its usefulness. For a dozen critical years it had stood as the bastion and Mecca of Chinese communism. But times had changed and Yenan, stuck off in a corner of nowhere, was now too much on the periphery of things.

Mao was content to abandon it ideologically as well as physically while he moved closer to the heart of the nation where transformations were, as he was to put it, to "come into being amid fire and thunder."

The city was evacuated as Chiang Kai-shek's 230,000-man army approached. Political and military headquarters and cadres were moved out well in advance, though Mao himself and a handful of top officials waited until the last day before boarding the rickety old party bus and heading out of town. When gas gave out, they transferred to mules to continue their journey. Destination was both known and unknown; it was to be everywhere that action demanded.

Chiang Kai-shek was disappointed at occupying virtually empty real estate, but he made the most of the propaganda aspects of his victory. When news of Yenan's capture hit the wire services—adding to the Western belief that Red resistance was all but over—somehow it appeared that a hundred thousand Communists had been routed in the city's defense. And there were other more legitimate publicity angles. General Hu Tsung-nan, commander of the attacking forces, had sworn that he would neither cut his hair nor marry until he had reduced the citadel of communism. Cameras had a field day while he was publicly tonsured, then married to a bride rushed to him with a government-supplied trousseau. He was permitted only a truncated honeymoon, however. There was to be no delay in marching his troops north and east where they were to make contact with a strong Nationalist force issuing from Kalgan, thus closing the ring below the Great Wall and trapping the Red Armies in North China.

There is a tradition that Mao Tse-tung played an active part in what happened next. He is supposed to have offered himself as a decoy, luring Nationalist troops in chases after him that ended up in devastating ambushes. The tradition, though appealing, is beyond doubt apocryphal. Mao Tse-tung, directing operations that extended from the Amur River in Manchuria to the Yangtze fifteen hundred miles to the south, had more important things to do than play will-o'-the-wisp.

Besides, the strategy of counterattack had long since been worked out. The loess hills of Shensi were familiar stamping grounds for the People's Liberation Army. No high echelon decoys were needed to help it ambush Nationalist troops advancing through the narrow valleys. General Hu Tsung-nan's progress was cut off and turned back at a dozen points, as were the Kuomintang forces advancing from Kalgan. The Reds even engineered an encirclement of their own when fifty thousand guerrillas under the command of Liu Po-cheng, the One-eyed Dragon, slipped behind the Kuomintang's Yenan expeditionary force to cut off its communications with its bases.

The Generalissimo's North China campaign ended in a fiasco. The two prongs of his attack, far from closing the ring, were wrenched farther and farther apart. When General Hu Tsung-nan and his mauled army finally fell back on the safety of Sian, it was he, not the Communists, who had lost a hundred thousand men in the rout.

Perhaps for the first time Chiang Kai-shek's confidence was shaken. He knew he must stay on the attack. He must keep his offensive going, if he was to prevent the Reds from waging the long and costly war of attrition which was apparently their objective. But with his encirclement strategy in shambles, where could he strike next? At what target? He had a million men tied up in the cities of Manchuria, but they were useless to him in the present situation. In fact, he was finding it increasingly difficult to supply them, owing to Red disruptions of communications. Already his American military adviser, General David Barr, was urging that Chiang withdraw all forces below the Great Wall while there was still time for an orderly retreat. But this the Generalissimo refused to do. He refused to admit that his ambition had outrun his grasp, or to lose face by relinquishing claims to all of Greater China.

So he desperately went to work to devise new strategies. The need for victories was particularly urgent because of an alarming development in the United States. President Harry S. Truman had turned sour on the loan to China and a collapse of the national economy again threatened.

President Truman was riding the horns of a dilemma. His admiration for Chiang Kai-shek, never high, had been further weakened by the Pentagon's estimation of him as a blundering general. Privately he subscribed to the liberal point of view, that Chiang was an unabashed dictator, presiding over a corrupt and feeble government, and that further financial or military aid to him was both useless and immoral. But he was opposed by powerful forces in and out of Congress—known as the China Lobby—that demanded unlimited support for the Nationalists, arguing that anything less was a betrayal of the Generalissimo's lifelong fight again communism.

Truman, apparently a lame-duck President simply serving out Roosevelt's final term and almost certain to go down to defeat in the elections of 1948, was in a quandary about what to do. He had lost faith in his former solution of a coalition government in China. What had happened in Yugoslavia, with Tito's Communist regime taking over from the democratic moderates, had taught him the dangers of inviting armed Marxists into collaboration with other parties. But what else was left in the way of an equitable solution to the present conflict?

To gain time, to prove that he was vitally concerned without committing himself to anything, Truman sent Lieutenant General Albert C. Wedemeyer to China on a fact-finding mission. The Generalissimo was well pleased by the appointment. He had gotten on splendidly with Wedemeyer when he had succeeded Vinegar Joe Stilwell as his American chief of staff in Chungking, and he depended on him for a report at least favorable enough to guarantee the American loan.

But he was to be disappointed. Wedemeyer, for all his diplomatic suavity, was a hard-eyed observer. When he returned to Washington in September 1947 he delivered a report to the President that was a damning indictment of the Kuomintang and all its works.

Corruption had begun as soon after V-J Day as Nationalist officials could fan out into formerly occupied China. The richest rewards, of course, were in the Treaty Ports. In the words of one critic, the Kuomintang arrived in Shanghai, Peiping, and Tientsin like conquerors, "confiscating money, automobiles, gold and women." Little distinction was made between Japanese property and the goods of patriotic Chinese who had suffered through eight years of wartime oppression—all alike were swept in. An OSS* officer, Colonel Harley C. Stevens, reported in September 1946 that government corporations were being formed at the rate of one or two a week in order to squeeze out everyday capitalists for the benefit of insiders. Concessions were sold to Westerners flocking in—to airline officials, construction companies, oil speculators, and manufacturers of all kinds.

When the cream was off the top, rackets were invented to keep the boom going. Artificial shortages were engineered to force up prices; goods were declared contraband, then seized and sold on the black market. High officials preempted distribution of UNRRA (United Nations Relief and Rehabilitation Agency) supplies and sold them at a profit. In one case, when a ship's captain was asked what had happened to his UNRRA cargo, he replied blandly that a great typhoon had blown it away.

Lesser bureaucrats invented permits and licenses for almost everything—for buying and selling, owning and renting, eating and drinking. And then there were the grafts, usually carried out with the cooperation of the police. A favorite ploy was to accuse a merchant of collaborating with the Japanese, and then to extort a fine to clear his name, as an alternative to imprisonment.

In Manchuria, where pickings were slimmer, even greater ingenuity was shown in turning a profit. Hardware and plumbing were stripped from public buildings for private sale. At the Fuhsan coal pit, where the Japanese had extracted twenty thousand tons daily, production under Kuomintang management dropped to two thousand tons, but a fortune was reaped when the pit hospital was raided for medicines and drugs for illicit sale.

This orgy of greed, this looting of the country's resources without replacement or reconstruction, inevitably brought on runaway inflation. The Chinese dollar (CNC), which had been pegged at $3,350 per $1 U.S. at the end of 1946, had by November 1947 deteriorated to CNC $73,000 for each $1 U.S. And worse was to come as business stagnated and confidence in the

---

*The Office of Strategic Services, the predecessor of today's CIA.

government was lost. By August 1948 CNC was to drop to an exchange rate of $11 million against the American dollar.

In a desperate measure to restore stability, Chiang Kai-shek introduced a gold yuan, which he valued at four-to-one on the U.S. dollar, and recalled all previous currency. But the effort was futile. Within five months the gold yuan had slipped to a million-to-one and continued to skid. All the Generalissimo had succeeded in doing was to virtually dispossess the middle class and reduce the poor to further destitution.

As Mao Tse-tung had long ago predicted, the Kuomintang's inability to cope with the economy finally drove out of its camp all but the big landlords, big compradors, and the international bourgeoisie. Other classes were pressed into the arms of the Communists—not necessarily by choice but because any new regime promised better than the old. Significantly, during Chiang Kai-shek's inflationary troubles, Border Region currency increased in value. Intended originally only as trade scrip in the Communist areas, it came to be sought as a national exchange medium. In 1947 a Border Region dollar was worth CNC $5; by August 1948 it brought CNC $1,500.

There was a certain madness to this last wild spree of the Kuomintang. It was as if from the end of the Japanese war the party of Sun Yat-sen had lost confidence in itself and its future. Carefully developed plans to rehabilitate the nation and restore prosperity—the Generalissimo himself had written a treatise on the subject titled "Chinese Economic Theory"—were tossed aside in the fevered competition to amass personal wealth.

Nor can Chiang Kai-shek be too severely criticized for failing to control what happened. He was caught by the limitations of the Confucian ethic. He could rail against greed and deliver sermons against corruption, both of which he did. But he was bound by old loyalties which prevented him from cracking down on relatives or other closely connected wrongdoers with fines, imprisonment, or, if necessary, execution. Confucian principles dictated that he could lead only by personal example, and he was beyond reproach in remaining aloof from the general contagion. Cynics, though, have pointed out that he hardly needed to exert himself for money while his wife and in-laws were piling up fortunes for him.

In dealing with his widening economic crisis, Chiang gives the impression of a man in a daze. Fiscally inept himself, he depended on the advice of others and was furious when nothing worked, when proposed solutions led only deeper into the morass. Politically, he remained astute, canny, and manipulative, though even there panic seemed to develop as time went on. As the situation deteriorated, he drew further and further into himself, pushing from his mind all considerations except military victory over the Reds. It was if he had come to believe that that one solution would solve all others, that once communism was banished from the land the hearts of men would be automatically changed and the Great Commonwealth of Confucius would come into being.

For Mao Tse-tung the development was exactly opposite. The better things went for his side, the more he worried about what might go wrong. By the fall of 1947 he was able to sense the turn of the tide and to announce: "The whole situation between the enemy and ourselves has fundamentally changed as compared with a year ago." But still he never ceased looking for chinks in the Communist armor that might yet prove fatal.

Mao Tse-tung was a creative Marxist, if that isn't a contradiction in terms. Certainly the compliment must be applied with caution because it smacks of change in fundamental doctrine or "revisionism," the worst crime in the Communist lexicon. The most his admirers in the party would ever allow him was that, like Lenin and Stalin before him, he had "developed" Marxism, adapting its basic tenets to the needs and conditions of his times and nation.

But Mao Tse-tung *was* creative in a way that Lenin and Stalin—even Karl Marx himself—were not. Marx, the philosopher of change, never completely escaped the mechanical age to which he belonged. It was an age begun by Sir Isaac Newton who believed that, in calculating gravitation, he had merely revealed the rotating machinery designed and set in motion by God. Similarly, Charles Darwin believed that in his theory of evolution he had done nothing more than explain the random selection scheme of nature, though *he* left God *out* of his equation. Karl Marx, a contemporary of Darwin, was equally dogmatic. He believed he had discovered the underlying law of social relationships in the class struggle and that nothing could alter its rigid application. In fact, late in life his cofounder, Engels, was indignant when he found that workers were alleviating their lot by combining into trade unions. He considered this a dangerous bourgeois trend; it was the workers' duty to go on suffering until they could overthrow capitalism by a single traumatic upheaval.

Vladimir Ilyich Lenin, a pragmatist by nature, often had trouble adapting himself to hard-and-fast Marxist formulas. Since it was axiomatic that a bourgeois capitalist regime must always precede socialism, he was hard put to it to justify seizing power in 1917 while Russia was still a czarist-ruled feudal country. Fortunately Aleksandr Kerensky, a bourgeois democrat, solved the problem for him by staging a successful revolution in February* of that year. Eight months later Lenin dispossessed Kerensky in the October* Revolution, but the intervening time was critical for Marxist peace of mind. Those eight months counted as the necessary period of bourgeois capitalist control as far as Lenin was concerned. Afterward he could establish a Soviet Republic with a clear conscience.

Mao Tse-tung, a close student of the USSR, was well aware of what had happened next. The pace of advance had been too swift. Backward Russia was not nearly ready for socialism and Lenin had been forced to restore a modified form of capitalism in order to avoid collapse. Mao was determined not to make the same mistake when and if his opportunity came, but how was it to be avoided? China, still semifeudal and semicolonial under the Kuomintang, was even further behind in its industrial development than czarist Russia had been. How could a nation run by Communists enjoy a period of bourgeois capitalist development without rewriting the entire Marxist book?

Mao Tse-tung hit upon a brilliant solution with a concept he

---

*The February and October Revolutions actually took place in March and November respectively. The czars were so behind the times that they couldn't even keep the calendar up to date.

called New Democracy. Under this formula, socialism and capitalism could advance into the future side by side, with neither necessarily taking precedence over the other. Socialism could assume the immediate form of state capitalism, controlling heavy industry and essential services, while the rest of the economy could be developed by private enterprise—under suitable government regulation, of course.

Mao Tse-tung's famous essay "On New Democracy," first issued in 1940, had an immediate impact in Yenan.* The formulation eased many problems that had pressed hard on the orthodox, including the paucity of proletarians in the Chinese revolutionary movement. In Kiangsi days, Mao had strained to fill this category, going so far as to classify boatmen, shop assistants, cobblers, and tinkers as industrial workers to offset the peasants flooding his ranks. After adopting New Democracy, he relaxed. He was content to gather under his wing anyone he could attract—peasants, intellectuals, local capitalists, and national bourgeoisie—confident that in time the proletariat, locked in the cities, would be delivered up to him. He continued to call his party the Party of Workers and Peasants, but that was largely to satisfy the formalities. It is significant that when he took over the nation in 1949 he proclaimed a People's Republic of China, with no mention of soviets or socialism.

Mao Tse-tung was unique in that he dared to found a revolution almost entirely on the militancy of peasants. Such an orthodox Marxist as Joseph Stalin sneered at the attempt almost to the last. But Mao, a better analyzer of concrete facts, turned orthodoxy around when he observed: "In the world revolution the backward countries will be victorious first." And as a corollary he predicted: "America will probably be last [to go]." He recognized a dynamic that had escaped his predecessors—the greater the industrial development, the more numerous the proletariat, but also the more powerful the ruling class.

---

*In Chungking, too, as it turned out. In 1943 Chiang Kai-shek published—apparently in rebuttal of "On New Democracy"—a curious book called *China's Destiny* in which he passionately argued that the nation had no political future except under the Kuomintang, the sanctified party of Sun Yat-sen.

Amid Fire and Thunder

In the autumn of 1947, with military parity reached and a Red counteroffensive under preparation, Mao Tse-tung kept checking and rechecking the solidarity of the classes gathered together in his great portmanteau of New Democracy. He could count on the loyalty of the peasants and intellectuals, and more and more of the national bourgeoisie were being driven into his camp by the Kuomintang's economic collapse. But holding together the "enlightened" gentry—liberal magistrates, administrators, and rural intelligentsia—caused him concern. Such people were from the landlord class and the accelerated liberation of the countryside was putting stresses on their allegiance.

Moving from one PLA base to another with his Politburo in tow, Mao Tse-tung, Chairman of the party in fact now as well as in sentiment, issued warnings to over-eager cadres. "Do not be impetuous.... Treatment must be different for those [landlords] who are local tyrants and those who are not...." And again: "[T]here should be no repetition of the wrong ultra-Left policy which was carried out in 1931-34." This was a reference to the Wang Ming line in Kiangsi, when landlords who were not killed were driven off their property to starve. Now Mao demanded that they be left with at least the holdings of a middle peasant. And he had a word to say about executions too: "Reactionaries must be suppressed, but killing without discrimination is strictly forbidden; the fewer killings, the better."

Mao Tse-tung was keenly aware of class contradictions that could occur in the countryside. A landlord might also be an entrepreneur, owner of a flour mill or a packing plant. As a landlord he was a class enemy, but as an entrepreneur, adding to productivity, he was a progressive force to be cherished and encouraged. Mao was kept busy during those anxious times passing on such distinctions to his followers.

Mao was not, and never pretended to be, an egalitarian. The clarion calls of the French Revolution—liberty, equality, fraternity—left him cold. He was completely practical about it: "Whoever advocates absolute equalitarianism is wrong. [This] is a kind of thinking... which undermines industry and commerce...." For him, revolutionary needs always came first; democratic rights must wait until later. When in April 1948 the

Reds captured Loyang, the first sizable city to fall into their hands, Mao was quick to issue directives. "[D]o not lightly advance slogans of raising wages and reducing working hours. . . . Do not be in a hurry to organize the people of the city to struggle for democratic reforms and improvements in livelihood. . . . Do not foster . . . the psychology of depending on the government for relief."

The capture of Loyang brought Mao a new concern—the administration of cities. The cadres' vast experience in organizing the countryside was of little help in meeting this different challenge, but Mao Tse-tung saw immediately where to look for the new type of functionary needed. "We should make use of large numbers of working personnel from the Kuomintang's economic, financial, cultural and educational institutions"—though, of course, "excluding the reactionary elements."

Mao Tse-tung knew how to put people to work, how to enlist loyalties by opening up new goals. He once said that it took from eight to ten years for a Communist to achieve a correct class outlook, so he was never unduly disturbed by backsliders and recidivists. He continued to be optimistic, continued to believe that the revolution could call into being a new type of man and woman committed to simple, honest living without corruption.

And slowly, over twenty years, he had been achieving his aim. He was impressing a new stamp on an entire people. True, it was the kind of development that not everyone could understand or see the point of. A couple of years before, Madame Chiang Kai-shek had listened to newsmen returning from Yenen and, when she heard of the Spartan life shared by people and leaders alike, had said derisively of Mao Tse-tung and his officials, "Why those people have no idea what real power is!"

Perhaps not, but consider the case of Henry Pu Yi, last of the Manchus, once boy emperor of China and later monarch of Manchukuo, brother ruler to Hirohito of Japan. Henry Pu Yi had been raised in circumstances of privilege and luxury that the Madamissimo could scarcely have dreamed of. When his Imperial Highness was hungry, he had only to clap his hands for three hundred steaming dishes to appear for his selection. When he cut up in the classroom, his cousin was flogged in his stead so that the imperial body should suffer no indignities. And when he was impelled to boyish mischief, he could and did order servants to eat dirt from the palace floor.

Yet Henry Pu Yi was to change. In August 1945, when the Russians overran the Manchukuoan capital at Changchun, Henry Pu Yi was captured and handed over to Communist guerrillas. At Mao Tse-tung's orders he was sent to a reform colony where, among other things, he was cured of a paralyzing drug addiction. His reeducation in other respects continued for several years before, remolded, rectified, and rehabilitated, he was returned to Peking. He was further tested both as a gardener and a curator, at the Royal Palace where once he had ruled in splendor, before he was judged worthy of full enfranchisement. And Henry Pu Yi, descended from a celestial line of emperors, counted it the proudest day of his life when, as a common citizen, he earned the right to drop a ballot in a municipal election.

Perhaps, after all, it was Madame who didn't know what real power was.

Lieutenant General Albert C. Wedemeyer, after laying bare the facts of Kuomintang misrule, recommended in his report to President Truman that Chiang Kai-shek be required to reform his government as a condition of any further American aid. The recommendation didn't sit well with the Generalissimo; it was all too reminiscent of Roosevelt and Stilwell's insolence on the same subject. He hit back in the only way open to him, by playing on the prejudices and fears of United States conservatives. His intentions became clear when he told a group of visiting congressmen that "the predicament in Manchuria [is] an American responsibility." He seemed to imply that if the Red peril were to be contained, the United States must share with him in the defense of his country.

Chiang Kai-shek knew he had powerful backing both in Washington and outside the administration. His China Lobby included the Scripps-Howard and Luce publications, with their batteries of newspapers, magazines, and radio stations, and he had influential supporters on Capitol Hill, his chief spokesman in the House of Representatives being a Dr. Walter Judd.

Dr. Judd had once served as a medical missionary in China. He had been stationed in Shensi when the Communist remnants limped into that province at the end of the Long March. He had watched with wonder the spread of the Red gospel in the next few years, and in 1938 had written: "Fully half the students in our missionary school have joined up with the 8th Route Army, several of our preachers have also joined. They have left $30 and $70 a month jobs to get $10 jobs and they are bursting with enthusiasm and devotion about it. I wonder why we can't succeed in capturing the imagination of Chinese for [our] work in the churches." Ten years later, now a Republican Congressman, he still hadn't found an answer to that question, but he had found a cause in fanatical support of the Generalissimo, a converted Christian who had always been kind to missionaries.

In the summer of 1948 Dr. Judd and other champions communicated a message of hope to Chiang Kai-shek. They told him that they could not at present muster the votes to push through an American loan, but by November the situation would be radically altered. Thomas E. Dewey, the former governor of New York, was a shoo-in to defeat Truman in the presidential election. With a Republican administration in office, all the financial and military help Nationalist China needed would be forthcoming—and perhaps the deployment of U.S. troops as well. All Chiang had to do was hold out until November.

The Generalissimo took heart. He was a past master on defense and it was hardly likely that the Reds could budge him from his prepared positions in the few months remaining. In fact, he undertook an offensive of his own, trying to clear out a salient of Communist guerrillas who were active behind his lines in Shantung Province.

But Chiang Kai-shek's timetable didn't coincide with Mao Tse-tung's. In late summer the Chairman had declared, "We are prepared to bring about the fundamental overthrow of the Kuomintang." And in September the great PLA counterattack began, targeted at Manchuria.

Three years before, following V-J Day, Kuomintang and Communist troops had entered Manchuria with equal chances. The vast territory beyond the Great Wall was unfamiliar to both. Neither army had been able to penetrate the efficient defense system by which the Japanese had held it.

But early on Chiang Kai-shek had made some serious blunders. The Manchurian people, staggering into the light after thirteen years of Japanese captivity, had needed leadership—some symbolic figure from the past around whom they might rally. The Generalissimo had just the man in Chang Hsueh-liang, the Young Marshal and former Prince Charming of the Northeast. But he had him under house arrest because of his mutiny at Sian, and under arrest he remained, since such a humiliation could never be forgiven. It was left for Mao Tse-tung to rush in Chang Hsueh-shih, the Young Marshal's younger brother. Hsueh-shih was not a Communist, he wasn't even a well-known general, but he bore a magic name that helped to hearten Manchurians.

Then there was Chiang Kai-shek's misjudgment in turning loose some three hundred thousand Manchurian puppet troops that had served under the Japanese. Mao Tse-tung didn't share the Generalissimo's contempt for them and recruited thousands, thus providing himself with "local boys" knowledgeable about the terrain and closely connected with the people.

Finally there was Chiang's selection of the troops he dispatched to garrison the Manchurian cities. They were southerners for the most part, his crack, American-trained brigades. Many were veterans of Stilwell's Burma campaign, that magnificent corps taught to attack and keep on attacking until ammunition ran out. Now in 1948, after three years of idleness in the North, baked by the dry winds of summer and frozen by the hurricanes of winter, they were despondent and homesick, their morale gone. When the PLA attacks began in September, they responded like automatons, more concerned with saving their skins than Nationalist honor.

Mao Tse-tung's offensive had been conceived on a grand scale: Chinchow, Changchun, and Mukden were simultaneously put under siege. Preparations had been long in the making. Red partisans had carried away railroad tracks, isolating the cities from each other, forcing the Generalissimo to supply his garrisons by air.

For lack of fuel, his tanks had been rendered useless. Many of them had been dug into the ground outside the city walls to act as pillboxes. Fourteen years earlier, during Chiang's Fifth Extermination Campaign in Kiangsi, his German staff had improvised blockhouses to be moved forward in lieu of tanks. Now tanks, robbed of all offensive potential, were being used as blockhouses.

Chinchow was taken on October 15 with one hundred thousand prisoners. Chiang Kai-shek, alarmed at the collapse that threatened his entire chain of garrisons in Manchuria, ordered Changchun and Mukden held to the last man while he won back Chinchow. But his counterattack was driven off, and by October 23 the Changchun garrison had had enough. It surrendered with three hundred thousand men. Nor did Mukden hold out much longer; it capitulated on November 2. November 2 was a day of double disaster for the Generalissimo because, on that date in the United States, Harry S. Truman won an election victory over the heavily favored Thomas E. Dewey.

Nationalist defeats continued. Peiping and Tientsin were put under siege. Both held out and were bypassed as the PLA continued to march steadily south along the Generalissimo's ambitious perimeter line of earlier days. From secret headquarters in Hopei Province, Mao Tse-tung revised a previous prediction. "The original estimate was that the reactionary Kuomintang government would be completely overthrown in about five years, beginning from July 1946. As we now see it, only another year or so may be needed."

In desperation Chiang Kai-shek sent feelers to Washington, suggesting that American officers join his army. Ostensibly they would act as advisers but actually they would be in command of troops. The newly elected Truman turned a deaf ear to the proposal. Then the Generalissimo, throwing pride to the winds, sent his wife on a begging mission to the U.S. capital. She was to ask for a loan of $3 billion, an American general to command the Nationalist forces, and a declaration by the American government that it meant to halt communism in Asia.

Madame's reception was different from her triumphant arrival in 1942 when China was being hailed as a fighting ally and the Chiangs as great democratic heroes. Then she had lodged at the

White House and had addressed a joint session of Congress, charming the legislators by her spirit, her impeccable English, and her famous open-toed shoes with the sprightly bows. Everywhere she had been fêted and showered with gifts for Chinese refugees and wounded soldiers. In 1948 there were few fêtes and fewer gifts. The Madame was not invited to stay at the White House nor to address Congress. She was an embarrassment to the State Department and was shunned by Washington officialdom except for the most devoted members of the China Lobby.

President Truman was incensed at the request for a $3 billion loan. The Truman who had won a miracle election victory against the odds was a very different man from the uncertain temporizer of a few months before. He spoke his mind to intimates about "grafters and crooks" in China who cared nothing about the welfare of the poeple, and wound up with the charge that, of the two and a half billion dollars that had gone to the Kuomintang thus far, "I'll bet you that a billion dollars of it is in New York [in private bank accounts] today."

With avenues of outside help cut off, Chiang Kai-shek was forced to think in terms of saving himself by a great defensive battle. Circumstances had caused him to revise his opinion of the Reds as ragged mountain fighters, but he still believed he could defeat them in open combat through superior generalship. Accordingly he set about choosing the time and place for a heroic engagement.

The location for the coming encounter was more or less dictated by precedents. It was a military axiom that in order to hold the Yangtze River the enemy must be stopped at the Hwai—no mean stream in itself, a hundred miles to the north. And there were good omens for Chiang's success. The Hwai River had formed the boundary of the legendary kingdom of Chou, ruled by a family from which the Generalissimo believed himself to be descended. More recently it had been at Taierhchuang, close to the Hwai, that Li Tsung-jen had won the only authentic victory of the Japanese war. Chiang Kai-shek had surreptitiously studied Li's strategy and meant to reproduce it in vital particulars. He had at his disposal some 555,000 men, including the last of his American-trained divisions, and he arranged them in the formation of a "T," the cross-stroke stretching some fifty miles, from the important railroad junction at Suchow to the town of Haichow at the mouth of the Hwai River.

Mao Tse-tung and his generals welcomed the opportunity for a decisive battle. Their troops coming down from the North through Shantung didn't match Chiang's in number, but they aimed to make up the deficiency by calling in the army of Liu Po-cheng, the One-eyed Dragon, from the West. Strategy conferences, which went on for days at Mao's headquarters, were once interrputed by a curious development.

A telegram was received from Joseph Stalin. After years of belittlement and neglect, the Soviet dictator stooped to ask a favor of the Chinese Reds. Stalin was then in the midst of his Cold War with the Western powers and was particularly hard-pressed by the stand he had taken on Berlin—his blockade was being penetrated by the unexpected success of the Allied airlift. He asked his Chinese comrades to stretch out their conflict with Chiang Kai-shek. He was afraid that if the Nationalists were too quickly and decisively defeated, the Western powers might be alarmed into a general crusade against communism.

The request was debated at length at Mao Tse-tung's headquarters. There is a legend that Mao himself, always an admirer of Stalin for obscure reasons, was inclined to accommodate the Kremlin leader, but Chou En-lai said "No." Chou En-lai said that history would never forgive such passive opportunism, or the failure to act when the time was ripe. And so it was decided. The People's Liberation Army, some six hundred thousand strong as both wings converged, marched on Suchow, standing up and in battle order, giving Chiang Kai-shek his long-sought opportunity to prove his superiority in regular warfare.

The battle of Hwai-Hai—named for the river and its seacoast town Haichow—has been called Chiang Kai-shek's Waterloo. This is a misnomer. In the original Waterloo the defending forces under Wellington were able to take all that Napoleon's attackers could give them, and then stage a victorious counterdrive of their own. Nothing like that happened at Hwai-Hai. The battle was won and lost before it started. Years of maltreatment and inept leadership had taken their toll on the defending Kuomintang forces, while the attacking PLA, fresh from a thousand miles of uninterrupted triumphs, was unstoppable.

Certainly Mao Tse-tung was in doubt about the outcome. Prior to the battle he laid down a hard-and-fast timetable for his commanders: "You are to complete the Hwai-Hai campaign in two months, November and December. [Then] rest and consolidate your forces." Concrete analysis of concrete facts could hardly have come up with a more arrogant conclusion.

In the first days of the engagement the inevitable started to happen. Four Kuomintang divisions at the center of the "T" mutinied and went over to the PLA. The Reds immediately drove into the gap, splitting Chiang's forces. Another Red contingent went racing around the coast, ending Nationalist hopes of reinforcement by sea. Then Liu Po-cheng's brigades, moving in from the West, completed a second encirclement. The entire Kuomintang army was clamped like two lenses into a pair of thick spectacle rims. The Generalissimo, directing operations from Nanking, sent a tank column under his younger son, Wei-kuo, to crack the rims. But the Reds had anticipated tanks and deep trenches impeded their progress.

Because of the number of men involved, the fighting went on for weeks. But by the turn of the year, what remained of Nationalist ardor was fading fast. Surrenders became endemic. Finally all was over except for one stout corps officered by Whampoa faithfuls who, though cut off and starving, refused to give in. Refused, that is, until the Generalissimo ordered an aerial bombardment of their position in order to prevent supplies and weapons from falling into Communist hands. That did it. Proof that their supreme commander thought more of hardware than the lives of his own men ended resistance. In all, more than 325,000 prisoners were taken in what was, from the standpoint of troops engaged, the greatest battle in Chinese history.

Chiang Kai-shek was stunned by the defeat. For a while he refused to believe what was happening, closing off his mind with disastrous results to his body. During the last weeks of the action he developed a hemorrhage that wouldn't stop. Trying to steady his nerves, he reverted to a prop of his youthful Shanghai days; he couldn't sleep until he had drunk himself unconscious. And there were other throwbacks. His temper, under control at calmer times, broke out in tantrums. He ordered underlings beaten and officers shot for all kinds of imagined insolence. But his grip on his party and his army remained firm. The Kuomintang still danced to the crack of his whip.

On January 1, 1949 he pulled himself together for his annual New Year's Day address. He said he was of a forgiving nature and was willing to discuss peace, even though "the strength of the [National] government . . . is several times or even tens of times greater than that of the Communist Party." This drew hoots of derision from Mao Tse-tung: "Oh! Ho! How can people not be scared to death by such immense strength!"

On January 8, two days before the final surrenders at Hwai-Hai, Chiang asked the United States, Britain, the USSR, and France to act as joint intermediaries in peace negotiations. All turned him down. On January 15 Tientsin fell. On February 3 the People's Liberation Army paraded in triumph in Peiping. Shanghai was under siege though, as always, it would prove a tough nut to crack. It was to hold out until May 25. Meanwhile the main body of the victorious Red army was recuperating and reorganizing for an assault on Nanking.

On January 21 Chiang Kai-shek resigned as President of Nationalist China. Years later he gave as his reason that slogans were circulating, such as, "Unless President Chiang goes, no more peace talks." So he stepped aside for the good of the nation, to be succeeded in office by his bitter rival Li Tsung-jen whom he hadn't been able to keep out of the vice presidency.

Li Tsung-jen was promptly greeted by a broadcast from Mao Tse-tung outlining the conditions for any future peace talks. Since the first item on Mao's list was handing over the "arch criminal" Chiang Kai-shek for trial and punishment, the situation didn't look promising. Nor was it meant to be; Mao, in effect, was demanding unconditional surrender. Still, to gain time and because he had no alternative, Li agreed to negotiate on Mao's terms and sent delegates to Communist headquarters. There, acting to the end in accordance with their Kuomintang natures, the delegates seized the opportunity to make deals for themselves, abandoning the Nationalist cause.

Li Tsung-jen also had other problems. Though Chiang Kai-shek had purported to retire, he was still actively manipulating from behind the scenes. Among other things, he ordered China's gold reserves to be transported to Taiwan, thus leaving his successor without money to pay the troops.

In desperation Li Tsung-jen went to the American ambassador, John Leighton Stuart, to plead for a U.S. loan. Time had passed and John Leighton Stuart was more cynical than he once had been. He pointed out to President Li that a few Chinese families had squirreled away millions of dollars in Swiss and American banks. Surely in this emergency it was the duty of these people to withdraw their funds and put them patriotically at their country's service. Li Tsung-jen went sorrowfully away; no one knew better than he the limits to Kuomintang patriotism.

Through all this Mao Tse-tung kept up a noisy propaganda barrage. Partly he was marking time while his armies reorganized, but beyond that he undoubtedly enjoyed the satisfaction of being listened to with world attention. After so many years of crying in the wilderness, he was now crowing like a strident rooster.

He howled with justified wrath when General Yasuji Okamura was cleared of wartime crimes. General Okamura, perpetrator of the infamous "kill-all, burn-all, loot-all" pogrom in North China, had been captured in Tokyo and sent for trial to Nanking where he was acquitted by a military tribunal. Mao Tse-tung, seething with fury, solemnly warned: "We tell you gentlemen of Nanking frankly: *you* are war criminals, *you* will be brought to trial." And he kept harping on this theme until April when the PLA, having assembled thousands of rafts and boats, was ready to cross the Yangtze and storm Nanking.

An odd event occurred when the huge flotilla had thrashed its way across the river and reached the southern bank. A British gunboat, the *Amethyst*, chugging upstream on a routine patrol, was fired upon and damaged by Red shore batteries. The vessel managed to get away, but not before drawing and returning more fire in what turned out to be a running battle.

The British were indignant and demanded indemnities, but from whom could they collect? The Nationalists were innocent and, besides, theirs was a fading authority, while the Communists were rebels, unrecognized and unrepresented in the chancelleries of the world.

In time the incident blew over but its significance was not lost on Westerners trading on Chinese soil. Notice had been served; the day of the foreigner was over.

26

Transformations Utterly Inconceivable

THE PRESIDENCY RESIGNED, CHIANG KAI-SHEK RE-treated to Fenghua, to his well-appointed Buddhist monastery high in the clouds. Like other dictators, he had a penchant for lofty residences. In Chungking there had been the Eagle's Nest and, though elevation on the mudflats of Nanking was harder to come by, he had made a practice of passing the summers at Kuling, a mountain resort several hundred miles upriver. There was a double satisfaction in heights: they enabled the superior man to look down on the world and forced lesser mortals to labor up to him.

The thought of Li Tsung-jen installed as President of the Republic rankled, so the Generalissimo set about undermining his long-time rival. He was untroubled that, out of office, he was technically out of power. He had something better going for him—*yu shih wu ming*, or authority without the name. He had been in charge of things for so long that it was universally assumed he was still in charge. His orders to transfer the nation's gold reserves to Taiwan had been obeyed without question. And when he summoned Sun Fo, the Tsungli's heir, for a private conference, Sun Fo came.

The Generalissimo, scornful of Li Tsung-jen's weakness in attempting to negotiate with the Communists, suggested that Sun Fo form a separatist government in Canton. Canton was where the Kuomintang had first risen to greatness under Sun Yat-sen, and it could rise again. Chiang calculated that there were still a million loyal troops south of the Yangtze, and promised he would rally them into a new Northern Expedition to overthrow the insolent Red bandits. Stimulated by the prospect, Sun Fo hurried down to Canton where he set up a secessionist government in February 1949. Kuomintang die-hards and irreconcilables lost no time in flocking to his standard.

The Generalissimo, having split the government at a time of crisis, bewildering foreigners and discouraging last-minute efforts at assistance, sent out telegrams summoning Nationalist commanders to a meeting. The response was poor. Many provincial generals preferred to remain loyal to Li Tsung-jen; others were making their own private deals with the Communists. Taking his cue from these negative attitudes, Chiang secretly ordered the evacuation to Taiwan of such Central Government troops as he still controlled.

He had already selected Taiwan as the temporary retreat where he would build up strength to return triumphantly to the mainland. He had successfully employed the strategy before by his withdrawal to Chungking, where allies had been found to carry him back to power on the wave of a changed world situation. The same cycle was bound to happen again, with communism instead of fascism as the common enemy. He had only to wait. Meanwhile he had no intention of marooning himself on an offshore redoubt, however attractive. Formosa, the early Portuguese traders had called Taiwan, or "the beautiful."

On April 23 the Generalissimo for the last time "swept the tombs of his ancestors," as paying homage to departed clan spirits was called, and moved up the coast to Shanghai. Again acting only with the authority of a man who has become an institution, he took command of the city's defenses. He said he had come to stay; he swore he would die with Shanghai. But in mid-May, when the Red attacks gathered momentum, he boarded a gunboat and steamed out to sea. He felt no shame at the desertion for, as Confucius himself had said, "The superior man keeps to the standard of right but does not necessarily keep his promise."

Chiang Kai-shek took a leisurely cruise south, stopping off to inspect pinpoint islands for their defensive possibilities. Then his ship delivered him to Taipei, the capital of Taiwan, and the Generalissimo disappeared into the mountains, where a residence had been prepared for him. He was back in a landscape of bamboo and falling waters. It may have reminded him of the village where he was born—Chikow. Chikow means "at the mouth of a brook."

A delegation from Canton found him in this hideaway. The Generalissimo was pressed with questions. When was he coming back to rally his troops? When would he resume power again? Sun Fo was perfectly willing to resign the presidency once Chiang returned to the mainland.

Chiang Kai-shek was evasive. He didn't want to admit yet that he saw no alternative to a retreat to Taiwan. So he turned legalistic. Sun Fo resigning wasn't the issue. Li Tsung-jen was the legitimate president of the nation and it would be improper for Chiang to usurp his office until Li had formally stepped aside. All were aware that Li Tsung-jen had left for America, stubbornly refusing to yield the title.

The delegation returned to Canton, promising to resolve the difficulty. Chiang Kai-shek lingered on in his mountain retreat, calculating ways to win back world opinion. American indignation at Russia was then at its height, owing to the Berlin blockade, and the Generalissimo found his solution in a cause that had never failed him before—anticommunism. In July he flew to the Philippines and joined President Elpidio Quirino in a declaration proposing an anticommunist front among all Southeast Asian nations. The declaration made headlines in the West and Chiang was once more hailed as a champion of democracy.

Invigorated by his new prestige, the Generalissimo flew to Canton to test old loyalties. The warmth of his reception seems to have overwhelmed him. At a great banquet staged in his honor he ran the gamut of Confucian emotions. He was humble at the beginning ("I am ashamed to be back in Canton under the present conditions of retreat and failure"), moralistic in the middle ("I am appalled at the existence of gambling and opium-smoking under the very nose of the government"), and heroic at the end ("We must hold Canton, our last port, the last place from which we can use both our navy and air force: I am ready to perish with the city"). The Kuomintang faithful might well feel that, with Chiang at the helm, all would be right again.

But the Generalissimo was soon off on fresh travels—this time to Korea for a joint anti-Communist statement with President Syngman Rhee. And again there was acclaim in the Western press. The campaign was going so well that Chiang began to hope for substantial military and financial aid sooner than he had expected. In which case, it might still be possible to establish an area of resistance on the mainland.

With this prospect in mind, he took a plane for Chungking to reestablish feudal ties and explore again defenses offered by Szechwan's rivers and mountains. He lodged once more at the Eagle's Nest and solemnly reviewed provincial troops trotted out for his inspection. He even sent emissaries to the Tibetan tribesmen and was hurt to discover that the chieftains wanted nothing to do with him.

Still, he was encouraged enough to travel down to Kunming to find out what was left of the air lift that, at its peak, had transported eighty thousand tons a month across the Hump. Nothing now remained of that vast operation except a few disabled planes, but the Generalissimo was confident that with American money and know-how service could be restored and his base secured.

He returned to Canton to sound out the government on another period of resistance above the Yangtze gorges. But he found few eager to risk the adventure. By this time it was known that Chiang had sent his best troops and the nation's gold reserves to Taiwan. And, with Nanking in Communist hands and the PLA steadily marching south, Taiwan looked like the place to go for safe refuge.

Chiang Kai-shek flew on ahead to make arrangements. Then

he was suddenly stricken with concern for the nation's art treasures. In 1938 the masterpieces of centuries had been laboriously ferried by coolie-back and riverboat up the Yangtze to save them from the Japanese. Now Chiang meant to save them from the Communists.

The Generalissimo returned to Chungking. Canton fell to the Red army on October 14, but Chiang was too busy cataloguing and supervising the packing of masterworks to pay much attention. He was still busily engaged as an art connoisseur in November 1949 when the PLA penetrated into Szechwan Province. Then he reverted to generalship, ordering trenches dug and directing the emplacement of cannon. He remained actively in command until Red gunfire was heard from across the river. Indignant that there was no response, he rushed to his military headquarters to find it deserted. There is a legend that he picked up a tactical map that had fallen to the floor and punctiliously burned it to keep it from falling into enemy hands.

He did one more thing before leaving the city. He remembered Yang Hu-cheng—"Old Yang," the warlord general who had been the Young Marshal's accomplice at Sian. The Young Marshal had been transported to Taiwan with the rest of the government, but Old Yang rated no similar courtesy. He had been languishing in a Chunking jail since 1938 and now, hours away from his liberation, Chiang Kai-shek ordered him shot.

The Generalissimo retreated to Chengtu, the provincial capital to the west. During the latter part of World War II the U.S. 20th Air Force had operated out of Chengtu, a location so remote that not a single Japanese bomber had penetrated it. Chiang seemed suddenly to have been sparked by a new hope: the region might be turned into a stronghold again, with the enemy kept at bay by air power alone. He worked energetically at recruiting forces until the Reds began shelling the city late in December. Then he took a plane for Taiwan, never to see the mainland again.

Chiang slipped back into his old posts and commands with easy assurance. The Kuomintang Central Executive Committee had paved the way for him by sending Li Tsung-jen an ultimatum—either return by a specific date or resign the presidency. When nothing was heard from America, the office was declared vacant and Chiang Kai-shek was reinstalled as President of the Republic. The Nationalist Republic of China, be it noted. No one on Taiwan ever gave up claims to the great Middle Kingdom on the continent, and no one has yet, openly at least.

Chiang was not held to blame for what had happened, nor was there any cause to blame him. He had kept the faith, he had fought the good Confucian fight and only circumstances had been against him.

Everywhere, at all times, most conservatives have genuinely believed that the quality of life was better under their forefathers, but few besides Chiang Kai-shek have actually attempted to turn the clock back. And in this, as in most other things, he had been trying to follow a precedent. He saw clear parallels between his own career and that of his special hero, Tseng Kuo-fang, the scholar-official turned soldier who had crushed the Taiping Heavenly Kingdom rebellion in the previous century. Both had grown to maturity at a time of peasant unrest and, in dealing with the Communists, Chiang had tried to duplicate the uncompromising methods Tseng had employed on the wildhaired Taipings.

But though he saw the resemblances, Chiang was strangely blind to the differences that the intervening years had brought. Tseng Kuo-fan, in the 1850s and 1860s, had behind him the vast authority of the emperor as well as the loyalty of imperial administrators and the universal belief in Confucian values. He could afford to sustain early defeats while, with rigid discipline, he mobilized peasants and the gentry and waited for the internal collapse of the unstable Taiping regime.

By Chiang Kai-shek's time the situation within China had altered radically. The emperor was gone, so were the imperial administrators, and Confucianism was fighting a losing battle against Western ideas and foreign commercial penetration. It was too late to go back. Change of some kind was inevitable—not necessarily the extremes of social reorganization the Communists were calling for, but certainly some reforms of an outworn system.

But Chiang Kai-shek, inflexible, unbending, was unable to see the needs or adapt to them. It was said of him that he met change with no change, and so was doomed from the start.

Chiang Kai-shek always claimed to be a devoted follower and disciple of Sun Yat-sen. It is curious, therefore, that he so promptly cast aside the Tsungli's policies when he succeeded him to power. Had Sun lived another ten or fifteen years, he would in all probability have maintained his alliance with the Communists, and might conceivably, by carrying out even minimal land reforms, have stolen the Reds' thunder and reduced Mao Tse-tung and his colleagues to a small and essentially powerless opposition party.

But Chiang Kai-shek refused to compromise, refused to see any merit in the Communists' championship of the peasants, and hurried into an open breach. Perhaps, after all, Mao Tse-tung was right; perhaps it was essentially a question of class character. Sun Yat-sen, calling himself the son of a coolie despite his wide education and world travels, remained innately humble and willing to experiment. While Chiang Kai-shek, a son of the gentry, was steeped in reactionary attitudes and never widened his parochial outlook. And in the end, for all his lip service to the Tsungli's ideals, he chose to model himself on the rigid and obsolete Tseng Kuo-fan whose temperament and background were closer to his own.

An admiring biographer has said of Chiang Kai-shek: "He is one of the most consistent men that ever lived. He is so consistent that I do not believe he had changed much in his basic conceptions since his adolescence." And in all probability it went further back than that. Chiang seems never to have forgotten his childhood walks through Chikow village with his distinguished grandfather, observing the obeisance paid his patriarchal relative, noting the depths of bows and degrees of respect as between peasants, merchants, and lesser landlords. That had been a time of social harmony when China—or Chiang's microscopic view of it—was in balance, when everyone knew his place and there was a place for everyone. Any subsequent changes had been for the worse.

Nor could the selfishness and corruption of the Kuomintang be blamed for the debacle that happened. Chiang Kai-shek frequently lamented his inability to change the hearts of his officials, but he held no grudge against them for their excesses. The fault, if any, was his own for not setting a high enough moral standard. For Confucianism had little to do with the market place. It was concerned with social ethics, manners, and ceremonies, and presumed, without insisting on it, that right conduct would carry over to all phases of life. In this respect it resembled nineteenth-century Christianity that condoned greedy self-interest during the week as long as the pieties were observed on Sunday, while always hoping that the Figure on the Cross would moderate rapacity.

And yet after years of soul searching in the isolation of Taiwan, Chiang Kai-shek succeeded in finding a scapegoat for the disasters that had befallen him. He discovered he had not been defeated by the Chinese Communists, but by a vast international conspiracy directed from Moscow.

In 1956 he published a curious book called *Soviet Russia in China* in which he gave chapter and verse for his theory, dating back to his visit to the USSR in 1923 as a military observer. He traced all his subsequent difficulties—with warlords, domestic Reds, Japanese, even the economy—to the machinations of the Kremlin. And he issued a warning to the West. He denounced the phrase "peaceful coexistence"—becoming popular as a replacement for "cold war"—as a snare and a delusion. What the Russians meant by it was: "They want you to accept their 'peace' so that they alone can 'exist.' " Having contributed this insight to his allies, the Generalissimo's conscience was clear.

To all appearances, Chiang and his Madame settled down to their remaining years on Taiwan in peace and contentment. There were even times of stirring drama. When the Korean conflict broke out in 1950, American arms and aid were rushed to bolster the Nationalist regime, and an American fleet protected its island from attack. The Generalissimo must have lived in hope that it was the beginning of the anticipated World War III that was to sweep him back to power on the mainland. The prospect passed, but as long as tension between East and West continued the dream remained.

Meanwhile the Kuomintang was generous to its eminent leader. Besides a sumptuous residence in Taipei, the Chiangs were presented with a mountain retreat overlooking a body of water romantically called Sun Moon Lake. The Generalissimo took up fishing again, a diversion of his boyhood. He was fishing when a telegram was rowed out to him announcing the end of all formal resistance to the Reds on the mainland. He crumpled the message, slipped it in his pocket, and went on fishing.

For Mao Tse-tung, victory meant only the start of a larger quest, the search for a way of government whereby a monolithic party could rule in response to the people's will. But though he experimented for the rest of his life, he never found the formula for the coexistence of the revolutionary spirit and bureaucratic control.

His immediate concern, however, was to protect his new regime, and he took prompt steps to safeguard it from internal enemies. There was to be no forgiving and forgetting the crimes of the Kuomintang now that hostilities were all but over. He specifically warned: "It must never be assumed that, once they yield to us, the counter-revolutionaries turn into revolutionaries, and that their counter-revolutionary ideas and designs cease to exist." And again: "With victory ... the bourgeoisie will come forward to flatter us.... There may be some Communists who were not conquered by enemies with guns ... but who cannot withstand sugar-coated bullets." Until "remolded," die-hard reactionaries were to be sifted out or suppressed.

Mao also foresaw the probability of a letdown in Communist ranks owing to the euphoria of victory. He was quick with warnings on that too: "Certain moods may grow within the Party—arrogance, the airs of a self-styled hero, inertia ... and distaste for continued hard living.... We must guard against such [tendencies]."

To prevent vainglory, he decreed that there were to be no public celebrations of the birthdays of party leaders, nor were streets, towns, or cities to be named after living heroes. In this, of course, he was merely extending an age-old tradition of Confucian modesty. There are no Leningrads, Alexandrias, or Washingtons in China. Cities and provinces are generally named for their geographic locations. Thus Hankow means the city at the mouth of the river Han, Shantung is the province east of the mountains, while Yunnan, more poetically, is south of the clouds.

The Russian exposure and censure of the "cult of personality" was still some years off, but already Mao Tse-tung was determined that nothing like it must occur in China. Could he have foreseen in 1949 that in the 1960s hordes of fanatical youths would be waving little Red Books digesting his thought and hailing him as the sole prophet and guru of the revolution, he would undoubtedly have shuddered. But realpolitik has a way of catching up with even the most idealistic leaders.

Mao Tse-tung's main opposition to the policies he was trying to set for the new nation came, not surprisingly, from inner party circles. With victory in sight, the bonds that had more or less held together the Central Committee and Politburo through the tensions of the civil war began to unravel, and quarreling broke out in earnest among the factions.

In March 1949 Mao Tse-tung called a plenary session of his government at his headquarters in Hopei Province. The agenda was to establish the economic priorities in the reconstruction to come. Mao advocated increasing the scope of state-controlled industries, reducing the opportunities for private enterprise and changing the nature of land reform. In newly conquered territory, he recommended that the policy of distributing land to the poor and dispossessed peasants be continued. But in the older liberated areas—in North China, for instance, where villagers had enjoyed private ownership for up to ten years—Mao Tse-tung believed a start should be made on collectivization.

The protest from the opposition was stormy. For a majority of the old-line Bolsheviks and rigid-minded bureaucrats, Mao Tse-tung was pushing too fast. Quotations from his own "On New Democracy" were thrown back at him. In that essay, written a decade before, he had anticipated many years of a mixed state-controlled and capitalist economy before socialism could begin. His critics claimed that he had arbitrarily changed the rules and was now rushing into socialism before the country was ready for it. As for land collectivization, the very concept was sure to lead to peasant antagonism and trouble.

Party records as always are mute on who led the opposition and the strength mustered against the Chairman. We only know that the controversy was fierce because of the telltale phrases in Mao's rebuttals. He hit out at "some muddle-headed comrades", and even made a pointed reference back to "incorrect attitude[s] ... during the War of Agrarian Revolution" which suggests that the old Wang Ming hard-liners of Kiangsi days were still as stubborn as ever.

What the conflict boiled down to was, in essence, a clash between the authoritarians of law and order and more free-minded spirits who refused to lock a framework around the nation's future. The authoritarians, on the verge of practical government, wanted formulas to go by. They wanted precedents—whether from the old imperial civil service or from Stalin's more modern type of closed bureaucracy mattered little as long as the rules were hard and fast. The freer spirits, headed by Mao Tse-tung, wanted to shape the Chinese revolution as it developed, encouraging initiative here, suppressing reaction there, prodding the people on to release their own energies in constructive ways.

For Mao Tse-tung never ceased to believe in a continuing revolution, a constant fan-shen of the people, a turning over of the body politic, no matter how disconcerting that might prove to officialdom at the top. He believed it would be fatal for the Chinese spirit, quickened and uplifted by the Japanese and civil wars, to slump back into a long sleep of inertia, and he constantly devised means to goad and prod it into finding expression. The Hundred Flowers campaign, the Great Leap Forward, and the Great Proletarian Cultural Revolution were all efforts in this direction. And if he never completely accomplished his aim, he at least established the principle that revolutions can be kept alive only by more revolutions. In this respect he was ideological brother to another revolutionary called Thomas Jefferson who had said: "The tree of liberty must be refreshed from time to time, with the blood of patriots and tyrants."

Due to his enormous prestige, Mao Tse-tung carried through his measures at that plenary session of March 1949, but splits were opened up that were never to be healed. The essential core of democratic centralism—"unity, struggle, then unity again through struggle"—remained, but the spirit had departed and, in the future, struggle was to be the rule and unity the exception.

The delegates left Hopei and traveled north to Peiping, newly liberated by the PLA. It must have been a strange and exhilarating experience for Red officials. They had lived for so long in peasant shacks, or scooped-out caves, or even in billets under the skies, that to wander through the corridors of the Forbidden City where they were to be lodged, with imperial treasures visible on all sides, must have seemed a fantasy. Karl Marx had no aphorism for the situation but the always reliable Confucius had: "The concentration of wealth is the way to scatter the people, and letting it be scattered among them is the way to collect the people."

The time was ripe to announce the Republic. Mao Tse-tung waited through the summer. He waited while Shanghai and Nanking were captured and the People's Liberation Army had penetrated deep into south China, carrying all before it. Then with Canton under siege and the Kuomintang government fleeing to Taiwan, he announced October 1, 1949 as the day of celebration.

A half million people packed into the great square of Tien An Men in Peking. For the city had been renamed; no longer was it Northern Peace, but again the Northern Capital, seat of government over a territory greater in extent than the Manchus had ever ruled. Buildings were hung with gigantic pictures of Marx, Engels, Lenin, and Stalin. No replicas of Mao Tse-tung, Chou En-lai, or Chu Teh were to be seen because Mao had decreed it an impertinence for Chinese to appear in the presence of the great Communist founders.

The people pressed forward, waving fists, shouting endlessly. On a platform stood Mao Tse-tung flanked by the Central Committee, the Politburo, and Red generals more famous now than any warriors of legend. They stood and looked down on a sea of faces and fists and listened to voices swelling in jubilant gales.

What passed through their minds? Specifically what passed through the mind of Mao Tse-tung? Probably nothing at all. It was enough for him to enjoy the moment, to bask in the adulation. He had deserved the right. But if his mind could have drifted back, he might have been startled by the element of chance, of sheer blind luck, that had brought him where he was today.

He was and he had been a brilliant Marxist, and he had remained steadfast to his principles. He had unjustly suffered humiliation and punishment from his own party, but had never wavered in his belief that time would eventually vindicate him. And when he had fought his way to leadership, he had almost literally dragged his contentious and doctrinaire-ridden followers after him to an incredible triumph. Just twenty-eight years had passed since a dozen callow youths met on a houseboat near Shanghai to found the Chinese Communist Party. Twenty-eight years for Mao Tse-tung, the sole remaining faithful from that meeting, to play a major role in overthrowing a system that had lasted for twenty centuries and devise a new one to replace it.

Yet when all is said in appreciation of Mao's qualities, the element of phenomenal luck remains. Time and again what should have been a fatal error turned out a fortunate circumstance, what should have been disaster translated into success. In retrospect, the dice of history seem to have been loaded for Mao Tse-tung. Constantly teetering on snake eyes, they came up elevens.

We have only to go back to the Kiangsi days for an example. Mao once claimed that if correct military policies had been pursued against Chiang Kai-shek in his Fifth Extermination Campaign, a base could have been established in southern China which could "never have been destroyed."

But it was a historic necessity for the Kiangsi base to be destroyed. The Long March was mandatory, not only for its morale factor but to propel the Communists into the North, into Shensi Province where their future lay. When the Japanese war broke out, they were correctly positioned and ready for action. For it was in fighting the Japanese, not the Kuomintang, that the Reds first won a devoted and patriotic following.

Then there was the Sian Incident. To a certain extent Mao Tse-tung may have paved the way by circulating the slogan, "Chinese must not fight Chinese." But neither he nor anyone else could have anticipated the Young Marshal's astonishing coup in capturing and detaining the Generalissimo. And yet Mao was the chief beneficiary of the incident. His tattered party was elevated to respectability by the subsequent united front with the Kuomintang, and he was permitted at least a show of legality in the unorthodox methods by which he "liberated" the villages of North China.

Add too the ill-fated Hundred Regiments Offensive. It turned out to be the fiasco Mao had anticipated but, in the aftermath of Japanese brutality, the loyalty of a third of the nation was won for the Communist cause.

Finally there was the personality of the man who was Mao Tse-tung's opponent during the long duel dating back to 1925. Had someone other than Chiang Kai-shek succeeded to the leadership of the Kuomintang Party after Sun Yat-sen's death, the results might have been different. But who were Chiang's rivals for power? Of the three men designated by the Tsungli as his successors, Hu Han-min turned out to be a weakling, Wang Ching-wei proved a traitor, and Liao Chung-kai, perhaps the best of the lot, failed to pass the test of history by falling to an assassin.

Both Stilwell and George C. Marshall thought highly of Li Tsung-jen, a capable administrator and undoubtedly the best military strategist in China. But Chiang Kai-shek's jealousy held Li down, and he never succeeded—until fruitlessly at the end—from struggling clear of the wraps the Generalissimo threw over him.

So Chiang Kai-chek proved himself against all comers as the best the Kuomintang had to offer, just as Mao Tse-tung emerged on top on the other side. And that again was the Chairman's luck. Because Chiang, for all his political shrewdness, his charisma, and his ability to manipulate men and governments of a traditional nature, was wedded to the past and, unchanging himself, failed to understand that China was changing in spite of him. All Mao Tse-tung, the apostle of the future, really had to do was tend his flock, waiting for the forests of the past to topple of their own weight and corrosion.

On October 1, 1949 the forests were down, leaving only hulks and stumps to rot or be cleared away. The land lay open, ready for new men and a new destiny. As Mao Tse-tung himself had put it, a transformation had taken place "utterly inconceivable to people of the older generation."

The time had come to proclaim the Republic and, on the platform in Tien An Men square in Peking, Mao Tse-tung stepped forward. The shouting stilled, fists dropped like leaves, ears strained to listen to the Chairman's voice on the echoing microphones.

Fellow Countrymen:

For over a century, the pioneers of the Chinese people, including such outstanding men as the great revolutionary Dr. Sun Yat-sen who led the Revolution of 1911, have guided the masses in their unceasing struggles to overthrow oppression by the imperialists and reactionary Chinese regimes; this goal has now been fully attained through their dauntless and persistent efforts....

A drama begins with a prologue, but the prologue is not the climax. The Chinese revolution is great, but the road after the revolution will be longer, the work greater and more arduous.... To win country-wide victory is only the first step in a long march.... Even if this step is worthy of pride, it is comparatively tiny; what will be more worthy of pride is yet to come....

We are [now] at a time when the Chinese people have triumphed over their enemies, changed the face of their country and founded the People's Republic of China.... Thus begins a new era....

The Chinese people, one quarter of humanity, have stood up.... From now on no one will insult us again.

Afterword

THIRTY YEARS AFTER THE EVENTS CHRONICLED IN THIS history, diplomatic relations have been established between the United States and the People's Republic of China. With embassies in Washington and Peking and consular services in the chief cities of each land, the avenues of commerce are open again. Coca-Cola has dreams of plastering the streets with billboards for the "people's drink." Perhaps McDonald's envisions its golden arches in countless villages and international hotel chains see their hostelries soaring above cities like concrete pagodas. Eight hundred million customers, or is it nine hundred million or a billion? No market like it has offered since Columbus set sail five hundred years ago to tap the riches of Far Cathay.

But will it work out as U.S. business expects? Are the tough bureaucrats who run the People's Republic willing to permit the Americanization of China as Europe has been Americanized since World War II? It seems hardly likely.

Yet what do the Chinese expect from the entente at which they

Afterword

have been working since President Nixon's first visit to Peking in 1972? And what would Mao Tse-tung, lying in his sarcophagus outside the Forbidden City, have thought of it all? And are Chiang Kai-shek's bones, prepared since 1975 for a triumphant return to the mainland, now turning?

We can safely guess at Chiang's reactions by the response of his son and successor, Chiang Ching-kuo, President of Taiwan. The yelling mobs in Taipei, the burning of American flags, and the egg-throwing at U.S. diplomats could only have been an organized expression of the Kuomintang's outrage at our recognition of a hated enemy.

During the twenty-five years that Chiang Kai-shek ruled as the Nationalist President of China in exile, he never gave up claims to the sovereignty of the mainland, which he considered to be only temporarily in the hands of bandits. But he was realistic enough to know that Taiwan, with a population of some seventeen million, supporting an army of less than half a million, was in no position to enforce his claims short of a world cataclysm of some kind. It would take powerful friends and a convulsion—perhaps World War III—to restore him to power. Much as he might delude himself that the population of the Middle Kingdom would rise to his support once he stepped ashore, he would still have an army of some four million Reds to contend with.

Chiang Ching-kuo, dutiful son, whose Confucian education became an obsession with his father when the boy returned from Russia in 1937, is bound by filial piety to remain steadfast to his parent's irredentist dream. But now that the United States has deserted, where is aid to come from? Only the Soviet Union offers the power that could possibly carry the Kuomintang home on bayonets, and an alliance with that godless nation is unthinkable. Chiang Kai-shek always hated Russia and always believed that the Chinese Reds were the Kremlin's puppets. That Mao Tse-tung and Moscow's leaders finally broke with each other made no impression on him. A falling out among bandits adds nothing to the virtue of either side.

Yet in a curious way, diplomatic abandonment by the United States might lead to Taiwan's salvation. The sooner the Kuomintang makes up its mind that it is not a world power, but presides over a small, energetic, and industrially successful nation of the Third World, the better. The change in attitude will not occur overnight. Almost certainly the old claims and fictions will last as long as Chiang Ching-kuo holds the reins of government. But he is now in his seventieth year and when he is removed from the scene—along with the last of the Kuomintang old guard—realpolitik may prevail.

Meanwhile it will do little harm for the Great Power delusion to continue for another generation or so. It is an exercise in *yu ming wu shih*, the claim without the reality, familiar to the Chinese throughout their history. But it is possible that subtle changes may begin almost immediately. In schoolrooms, the imperial destiny of the Kuomintang may be soft-pedaled and the emphasis taken off a purely Confucian education in order to prepare the young for the realistic present. While in politics, more practical democracy may be permitted than is now the case.

And in the end, when competition with the mainland in goods and services really begin to pinch, it is not beyond the bounds of possibility that a reunion between the nations will take place peacefully and profitably. "If you can't lick 'em, join 'em." The phrasing is American but the sentiment is 24-carat Chinese. Even the Generalissimo, detesting the Communists as he did, twice maintained a collaboration with them. And it could very well be that Taiwan, for sound commercial reasons, will one day work out a third collaboration, joining the People's Republic as the nineteenth province of China Proper, without too drastic a strain on the lifestyle of its inhabitants.

But what about Peking? Will Hua, Teng, and the Central Committee have the patience to allow Taiwan to make up its own mind and return to the fold in its own good time? There seems no reason why not. They have allowed the British to stay on in Hong Kong, an island almost within hailing distance of the mainland and about which it has been said it could be recaptured by a telephone call. Peking allowed them to stay on and made a good thing out of it, too. The Crown Colony serves the Communists as a listening post, a propaganda platform, and a market for food-

Afterword

stuffs and manufactured goods from which it draws a favorable balance of trade amounting to $1 billion annually. Why should Peking be overly disturbed about Taiwan, an island more than a hundred miles away, which can do it no harm beyond tweaking pride? And even that sting has now been removed by the change of policy which has turned the Kuomintang's faithful Uncle Sam into an indifferent relative.

Which brings us to our final question. We know what American businessmen and industrialists want from the rapprochement with the mainland, but what, in short- and long-range terms, does the People's Republic expect from us? There is, of course, the implicit warning to the Soviet Union, the implied threat that China can reach out to powerful friends if trouble breaks out along the four-thousand-mile Sino-Soviet border. But that diplomacy is old hat; it belongs back in Mao Tse-tung's time and undoubtedly the present regime is reaching for something beyond. After thirty years' isolation, the rulers in Peking seem to be preparing to break out on the world market on an unprecedented scale.

As far back as 1949 Mao Tse-tung had warned: "As for the . . . recognition of our country by the imperialist countries, we should not be in a hurry . . . As long as the imperialists do not change their hostile attitude, we shall not grant them legal status in China." But after two U.S. presidential visits to Peking—not to mention a third junket by an ex-president, disgraced as a head of state but with his credentials as a capitalist undefiled—the atmosphere has presumably warmed up enough to justify another Mao injunction: "Wherever there is business to do, we shall do it. . . ."

Of course, the People's Republic has already been doing business with capitalist countries for years—with Britain, with France, Japan, and Canada. It has also been doing business with the United States, though on a limited scale, while it waited for the diplomatic proprieties to be resolved. It would be impossible to prevent the Chinese from doing business. Trading is a passion built into their natures like sex.

The Chinese have always been among the smartest businessmen on earth. Since ancient times they have penetrated the markets of their neighbors, from the East Indies to Malaysia, prospering everywhere and often dominating the economy. Even in hostile environments far from home, such as Western Chinatowns, they have flourished and expanded. And there is no reason to believe that the shrewd Chinese head for commerce has become addled under the People's Republic.

What then do they expect from the rapprochement with the United States and the opportunities it will open up? First in importance is probably employment for their overpopulated cities. During Mao Tse-tung's lifetime the urban rush was checked. Millions of job seekers crowding into Shanghai, Wuhan, and Tientsin were sent back to the farms—along with university professors, writers, and assorted intellectuals to foster and direct the "continuing revolution" at a grassroots level.

Now that has changed. The professors are back, the universities are expanding, competitive examinations have been reintroduced to seek out first-class brains irrespective of class origins, and thousands of students are being sent abroad to learn the techniques of capitalist production. The Four Modernizations—improved agriculture, industry, technology, and defense—are the order of the day. They are programs designed to propel China on an industrial course. But what is the end objective—to raise the standard of living in the Middle Kingdom or capture the markets of the barbarians without?

For a while, no doubt, the balance of trade will be heavily in favor of the capitalists, especially the United States. China must stock up on oil rigs, computers, military hardware, harvesting equipment, and machines to make machines. It needs the products of the West just as it once needed the technology of the Soviet Union to show it how to extract coal and iron more efficiently and how to build bridges and hydroelectric plants. For a period of time American heavy industry may enjoy a bonanza, not to mention Coca-Cola, and a host of other peripheral enterprises which the Chinese will accept as the gnats that always blow in with a favoring wind.

For a further period, trade may continue at a more evenly balanced rate as the products of Chinese and foreign industry are distributed throughout the land. Fertilizers, tractors, telephones, television sets, better roads, and housing will all come within the calculations of the Politburo. Communications will be especially important in turning the nation into what Marshall McLuhan has described as a Global Village. But there will probably be a limit to internal distribution. The Marxist-minded men in Peking have no intention of converting China into a consumer-oriented society such as we are familiar with in the West.

After the period of adjustment—predictions as to its length are both hazardous and fruitless—the turnabout will almost inevitably occur. We have seen what countries like Japan and West Germany, devastated by war, starting from scratch, have been able to do in reviving industry and penetrating the markets of the world with superior and cheaper products. But it may well be that their notable achievements may pale in comparison once the Chinese get going with a combination of machine and hand-intensive manufacture. Hand-intensive because an object of policy will always be the full employment of a billion people.

Yet that combination—the power of the machine knitted to fine-fingered skills—has made possible such marvelous artifacts as the grand piano, the precision Swiss watch, the racing yacht, and the Rolls Royce car—products meant for the very rich. It may be left for the Chinese—disciplined, hard-working, motivated by an ideal—to revive an era of quality craftsmanship in which products are simultaneously beautiful, lasting, and reasonable in price. Historically they once had a corner on such a market, with porcelains and lacquers, and even an intricately tough woven cotton fabric, known to early traders as "nankeens" (from Nanking), but now familiar to the West as levis or jeans. The Chinese have always been prime inventors—they were first with gunpowder, the compass, and printing—and there's no reason why they shouldn't go on inventing, perhaps to the dismay of the capitalist world. It could very well be that the United States, which expects to grow rich at China's expense, may suffer from the law of unintended consequences and find itself inundated by better and cheaper products than it can produce itself, and by ingenious novelties as yet unimagined.

If these projections prove valid, how will we in this country react to the competition? Mao Tse-tung once confidently predicted that communism, with its planned and controlled economy, would sweep the world, though he generously conceded that the United States, in view of its industrial development, would probably be the last to go. How can we prove him wrong? How can we hope to preserve our own free system while the rest of society slips away?

Certainly not through tariff restrictions which have always proved counterproductive in their effects. Nor will totalitarianism from the Right—the obverse side of Red—solve the problem. Rather we must look for new ways to release unsuspected energies among our own people. We once fought a revolutionary war to free ourselves from foreign economic bondage and awakened a new national spirit wherein a person's work was both a satisfaction and a source of rewards. That spirit—the Spirit of '76—today exists only as an advertising slogan for an oil company. It must be given new life and meaning. It must be extended to cover the entire nation, especially the ghettos of the unemployed, the refuse dumps of our society. Our system must adjust itself to provide jobs and decent living standards for all.

Yet when that has been said, when we have admitted that we have as long a road to travel toward self-fulfillment as the Chinese, a critical question still remains. Is the Middle Kingdom simply to be an economic rival in the foreseeable future, or a military threat as well?

Ironically, China has already obliged us by solving one long-term objective of American foreign policy. It has filled the power vacuum in the Far East for which American presidents have yearned since the time of Woodrow Wilson. None of them visualized a Red government as the stabilizing force, but history works in its own mysterious ways. Certainly with the colossus of the People's Republic standing guard, Japanese-type dreams of world conquest should be stilled forever in the Orient.

But will the People's Republic itself adopt the dream? As its power grows, will it nurse imperial ambitions? Indications are against it. If anything, the trend seems in the opposite direction. Peking—apart from punishing attacks on its border to "teach lessons"—appears to be withdrawing, spiritually and materially, within its own boundaries. A new conservatism is in evidence,

Afterword

Confucianism is respectable again, and something like the old imperial civil service is once more in operation.

This does not mean that China intends to retreat to the xenophobic isolation of the emperors, confident that nothing worthwhile existed among barbarian strangers. As we have seen, the new China is reaching out for the science and technology of the West to build its country in a new image. But clearly that image is not ours. The Chinese intend to shape an industrial revolution in their own indigenous way, adapting modern methods to serve and, incidentally, employ their swarming population.

If we need further assurance of China's dedication to internal development combined with peaceful intentions toward the world outside, we have only to turn to the speeches of Mao Tse-tung. A prophetic Marxist if ever there was one, he spoke up strongly and often for military defense but never for action beyond China's borders. Perhaps holding the views he did—that capitalism was on the decline anyway—he considered it a waste of energy to prepare for an Armageddon between systems that was not likely to occur.

In fact, Mao, late in life, seemd in an inordinate hurry to learn from the capitalist nations before it was too late, before their contradictions had rendered them weak and sterile. This was especially true after China's breach with the Soviet Union. Russian technology was, after all, late on the scene and still unproved. When he was rid of the Kremlin, Mao lost no time in making overtures through Presidents Nixon and Ford to get at the fountainhead of industrial know-how—the mechanized, rationalized, and computerized United States.

Of all the honorific titles imposed on him, Mao Tse-tung enjoyed most Great Teacher, but it could just as appropriately have been Great Student. He never lost his zest for learning. Mao is dead now and his *Little Red Book* is no longer compulsory reading, but the present Politburo and every official in the land can only disregard his theories of education at their peril.

This is how Mao summed up the condition of the People's Republic before he died. His directions are clear as to the road the Chinese people must travel before they can become truly great:

China used to be stigmatized as a "decrepit empire," "the sick man of East Asia," a country with a backward economy and a backward culture, with no hygiene ... where the women had bound feet, the men wore pigtails and eunuchs could still be found, and where the moon was inferior and did not shine as brightly as in foreign lands.... But after [years of hard work] we have changed the face of China. No one can deny our achievements.

[O]ur revolution came late.... From the developmental point of view, this is not bad. The poor want revolution, whereas it is difficult for the rich.... Countries with a high scientific and technological level are overblown with arrogance. We are like a blank sheet of paper, which is good for writing on.

[But] even when one day our country becomes strong and prosperous, we must still adhere to the revolutionary stand, remain modest and prudent, learn from other countries and not allow ourselves to become swollen with conceit. We must ... go on [learning after] scores of five-year plans. We must be ready to learn even ten thousand years from now. Is there anything bad about that?

Posterity can only answer that there is nothing bad about it at all. Ten thousand years seems a reasonable time for nations, however diverse in systems, to learn to live together in harmony and respect.

Select Bibliography

ABEND, HALLETT, *Treaty Ports*: New York, Doubleday, Doran, 1944.
ALLEN, G. C. and DONNITHORNE, AUDREY G., *Western Enterprise in Far Eastern Economic Development*: London, George Allen and Unwin, 1954.
BEAL, JOHN ROBINSON, *Marshall in China*: Toronto, Doubleday Canada Ltd., 1970.
BELDEN, JACK, *China Shakes the World*: New York, Monthly Review Press, 1970.
BERTRAM, JAMES M., *First Act in China: The Story of the Sian Mutiny*: New York, Viking, 1938.
BISSON, T. A., *Japan in China*: New York, Macmillan, 1938.
BLAND, J. O. P. and BACKHOUSE, E., *China Under the Empress Dowager*: Philadelphia, J. B. Lippincott, 1910.
BLOODWORTH, DENNIS, *The Chinese Looking Glass*: New York, Farrar, Straus, Giroux, 1967.
BRANDT, CONRAD, *Stalin's Failure in China 1924–1927*: Cambridge, Harvard Univ. Press, 1958.
CAHILL, HOLGER, *A Yankee Adventurer: The Story of Ward and the Taiping Rebellion*: New York, Macauley, 1930.
CARLSON, EVANS FORDYCE, *Twin Stars of China*: New York, Dodd Mead, 1940.
CHANG, H. H., *Chiang Kai-shek: Asia's Man of Destiny*: New York, Doubleday, Doran, 1944.

CHANG KUO-TAO, *The Rise of the Chinese Communist Party: The Autobiography of Chang Kuo-Tao* (2 vols.): Lawrence, Univ. Press of Kansas, 1972.
CHEN, JEROME, *Yuan Shih-Kai (2nd edition)*: Palo Alto, Stanford Univ. Press, 1972.
CHESNEAUX, JEAN, *Peasant Revolts in China (1840–1949)*: New York, Norton, 1973.
CHIANG KAI-SHEK, *China's Destiny* (including *Chinese Economic Theory*), with notes and commentary by Philip Jaffe: New York, Roy, 1947.
⸺, *Resistance and Revolution: Wartime Speeches from July 12, 1937 to January 3, 1943*: New York, Harper, (undated).
⸺, *Soviet Russia in China: A Summing-up at Seventy* (revised, enlarged edition with maps): New York, Farrar, Straus & Cudahy, 1958.
⸺, General and Madame, *The Account of the Fortnight in Sian When the Fate of China Hung in the Balance*: New York, Doubleday, Doran, 1937.
CHOW TSE-TSUNG, *The May Fourth Movement: Intellectual Revolution in Modern China*: Cambridge, Harvard Univ. Press, 1960.
CLUBB, O. EDMUND, "Chiang Kai-shek's Waterloo: The Battle of Hwai-Hai," *Pacific Historical Review*, vol. XXV, November 1956, 389–399.
⸺, *China and Russia: The Great Game*: New York, Columbia Univ. Press, 1971.
⸺, *20th Century China* (2nd edition): New York, Columbia Univ. Press, 1972.
CRESSY, EARL HERBERT, *Understanding China*: New York, Nelson, 1957.
CROW, CARL, *Foreign Devils in the Flowery Kingdom*: New York, Harper, 1940.
CROZIER, BRYAN (with the collaboration of ERIC CHOU), *The Man Who Lost China: The First Full Biography of Chiang Kai-shek*: New York, Scribners, 1976.
DURANT, WILL, *Our Oriental Heritage*: New York, Simon and Schuster, 1954.
EASTMAN, LLOYD E., *The Abortive Revolution: China Under Nationalist Rule, 1927–1937*: Cambridge, Harvard Univ. Press, 1974.
EPSTEIN, ISRAEL, *The Unfinished Revolution in China*: Boston, Little, Brown, 1947.
FAIRBANK, JOHN KING, *The United States and China*: Cambridge, Harvard Univ. Press, 1949.
FEIS, HERBERT, *The China Tangle*: Princeton, Princeton Univ. Press, 1953.
FERRELL, ROBERT H., *George C. Marshall* (vol. XV in series *The American Secretaries of State and Their Diplomacy*): New York, Cooper Square Publishers, 1966.

Select Bibliography

FITZGERALD, C.P., *The Birth of Communist China*: Baltimore, Penguin, 1967. (First published as *Revolution in China* by Cresset Press, 1952.)

GLICK, CARL and HONG SHENG-HWA, *Swords of Silence*: New York, McGraw-Hill, 1947.

HAHN, EMILY, *Chiang Kai-shek: An Unauthorized Biography*: New York, Doubleday, 1955.

——, *The Soong Sisters*: New York, Doubleday, Doran, 1941.

HAIL, WILLIAM JAMES, *Tseng Kuo-Fan and the Taiping Rebellion*: New Haven, Yale Univ. Press, 1927.

HAN SUYIN, *The Morning Deluge: Mao Tsetung and the Chinese Revolution 1893–1954*: Boston, Little, Brown, 1972.

——, *Wind in the Tower: Mao Tsetung and the Chinese Revolution 1949–1975*: Boston, Little, Brown, 1976.

HAUSER, ERNEST O., *Shanghai: City for Sale*: New York, Harcourt, Brace, 1940.

HINTON, WILLIAM, *Fanshen: A Documentary of Revolution in a Chinese Village*: New York, Monthly Review Press, 1966.

HSIUNG, S. I., *The Life of Chiang Kai-shek*: London, Peter Davies, 1948.

ISAACS, HAROLD R., *The Tragedy of the Chinese Revolution*: New York, Atheneum, 1966.

JOHNSON, CHALMERS A., *Peasant Nationalism and Communist Power: The Emergence of Revolutionary China 1937–1945*: Stanford, Stanford Univ. Press, 1962.

KOCH, ADRIENNE and PEDEN, WILLIAM (Eds.), *The Life and Selected Writings of Thomas Jefferson*: New York, Modern Library, 1944.

KRAMER, PAUL (Ed.), *The Last Manchu: The Autobiography of Henry Pu Yi, Last Emperor of China*: New York, Putnam, 1967.

LEVENSON, JOSEPH, R., *Confucian China and its Modern Fate*: Berkeley, Univ. of California Press, 1958.

LEVY, HOWARD S., *Chinese Footbinding*: New York, Walton Rawls, 1968.

LIN YUTANG, *My Country and My People*: (Fifth printing, Dec. 1935) New York, John Day in assoc. with Reynal and Hitchcock, 1935.

——, (Ed.), *The Wisdom of China and India*: New York, Random House, 1942.

LINEBARGER, PAUL M. A., *The China of Chiang Kai-shek*: Boston, World Peace Foundation, 1941.

LIU CHAO-CHI, *How to be a Good Communist*: Peking, Foreign Language Press, 1965.

LIU, F. F., *A Military History of Modern China 1924–1949*: Princeton, Princeton Univ. Press, 1956.

LOHBECK, DON, *Patrick J. Hurley*: Chicago, Regnery, 1956.

MAO TSE-TUNG, *Selected Works of Mao Tse-tung* (5 vols.): Peking, Foreign

Language Press. Vol. I (2nd printing), 1967: Vol. II (2nd printing), 1967: Vol. III (2nd printing), 1967: Vol. IV (3rd printing), 1969: Vol. V (1st edition), 1977.
McLUHAN, HERBERT MARSHALL and FIORE, QUENTIN, *The Medium is the Massage*: New York, Random House, 1967.
MULLER, HERBERT J., *The Uses of the Past*: New York, Oxford Univ. Press, 1952.
NISH, IAN, *A Short History of Japan*: New York, Praeger, 1968.
NIVINSON, DAVID S. and WRIGHT, ARTHUR F. (Eds.) *Confucianism in Action*: Palo Alto, Stanford Univ. Press, 1959.
PAYNE, ROBERT, *Chiang Kai-shek*: New York, Weybright and Talley, 1969.
POWELL, JOHN B., *My Twenty-five Years in China*: New York, Macmillan, 1945.
POWELL, RALPH L., *The Rise of Chinese Military Power 1895-1912*: Princeton, Princeton Univ. Press, 1955.
REMER, C. F., *Foreign Investments in China*: New York, Macmillan, 1933.
———, *A Study of Chinese Boycotts*: Baltimore, Johns Hopkins Press, 1933.
ROY, M. N., *Revolution and Counter-Revolution in China*: Calcutta, Renaissance Publishers, 1946.
RUE, JOHN E., *Mao Tse-tung in Opposition 1927-1935*: Stanford, Stanford Univ. Press, 1966.
SCHIFFRIN, HAROLD Z., *Sun Yat-sen and the Origins of the Chinese Revolution*: Berkeley, Univ. of California Press, 1970.
SCHURMANN, FRANZ and SCHELL, ORVILLE (Eds.), *Republican China: Nationalism, War, and the Rise of Communism 1911-1949*: New York, Vintage Books, 1967.
SCHWARTZ, BENJAMIN I., *Chinese Communism and the Rise of Mao*: Cambridge, Harvard Univ. Press, 1951.
SELLE, EARL ALBERT, *Donald of China*: New York, Harper, 1948.
SHARMAN, LYON, *Sun Yat-sen: His Life and its Meaning*: New York, John Day, 1934.
SHUB, DAVID, *Lenin: A Biography* (special abridged edition, 3rd printing): New York, Mentor, 1952.
SIAO-YU, *Mao Tse-tung and I were Beggars*: London, Hutchinson, 1961.
SMEDLEY, AGNES, *Battle Hymn of China*: New York, Knopf, 1943.
———, *The Great Road: The Life and Times of Chu Teh*: New York, Monthly Review Press, 1956.
SNOW, EDGAR, *The Battle for Asia*: New York, Random House, 1941.
———, *Journey to the Beginning*: New York, Random House, 1958.
———, *The Long Revolution*: New York, Random House, 1972.
———, *The Other Side of the River: Red China Today*: New York, Random House, 1962.

Random Notes on Red China: Cambridge, Harvard Univ. Press, 1957.
——, *Red Star Over China* (first revised and enlarged edition): New York, Grove Press, 1973
SOLOMON, RICHARD H., *Mao's Revolution and the Chinese Political Culture*: Berkeley, Univ. of California Press, 1971.
STEVENS, HARLEY C., "Business and Politics in China": *Far Eastern Survey* (Institute of Pacific Relations), Vol XV, no. 19 (Sept. 25, 1946)
SUN TZU, *The Art of War* (translated by SAMUEL B. GRIFFITH): Oxford, Clarendon, 1963.
SUN YAT-SEN, *San Min Chu I: The Three Principles of the People* (translated by FRANK W. PRICE): Shangai, Commercial Press, 1929.
TAN, CHESTER C., *Chinese Political Thought in the Twentieth Century*: New York, Doubleday, 1971.
TANG LEANG-LI, *The Foundations of Modern China*: London, Noel Douglas, 1928.
——, *The Inner History of the Chinese Revolution*: London, George Rutledge & Sons, 1930.
TANG TSOU, *America's Failure in China, 1941–50*: Chicago, Univ. of Chicago Press, 1963.
TAWNEY, R. H., *Land and Labour in China*: London, Allen and Unwin, 1932.
TENG SSU-YÜ, *New Light on the History of the Taiping Rebellion*: Cambridge, Harvard Univ. Press, 1950
TIEN-YI LI, *Woodrow Wilson's China Policy 1913–1917*: New York, Univ. of Kansas City Press/Twayne Publishers, 1952.
TONG, HOLLINGTON K., *Chiang Kai-shek: Soldier and Statesman* (2 vols.): London, Hurst and Blackett, 1938.
TUCHMAN, BARBARA W., *Stilwell and the American Experience in China 1911–45*: New York, Macmillan, 1971.
U.S. DEPARTMENT OF STATE (FAR EASTERN SERIES 30), *United States Relations with China, 1944–49*. (White Paper): Washington D.C., Government Printing Office, 1949.
WAKEMAN, FREDERIC, JR., *Strangers at the Gate: Social Disorder in South China, 1839–1861*: Berkeley, Univ. of California Press, 1966.
WALES, NYM, *Inside Red China*: New York, Doubleday, Doran, 1939.
WEDEMEYER, ALBERT C., *Wedemeyer Reports!*: New York, Holt, 1958.
WHITE, THEODORE H., *In Search of History: A Personal Adventure*: New York, Harper & Row, 1978.
——, and JACOBY, ANNALEE, *Thunder out of China*: New York, William Sloane, 1946.
WILLIAMS, EDWARD THOMAS, *China Yesterday and Today*: New York, Crowell, 1927.

Abbreviations
(used in Notes and Index)

CC	Central Committee (Communist)
CCP	Chinese Communist Party
CEC	Central Executive Committee (Kuomintang)
KMT	Kuomintang Party
PCC	Political Consultative Conference (1946)
PLA	People's Liberation Army
SW	*Selected Works of Mao Tse-tung* (5 volumes)
V-J Day	Victory over Japan (August 14, 1945)
WP	White Paper. (U.S. Dept. of State, *United States Relations with China, 1944-49*)

Notes

1. Reunion in Chungking

6.	"plain man of the people...": Snow, *Battle*, 283
6-7.	Question on Mao's first plane ride: *Time* (Sept. 10, 1945), 42
7.	"the utmost urgency": *New York Times* (Aug. 29, 1945). p. 7, col. 1
7.	"Old Boy": Han, *Deluge*, 451
8.	"his every gesture...": *ibid.*, 455
9.	"Wherever I go, there goes the government": Snow, *Battle*, 116
9.	"stern, high-minded, unyielding...": Payne, 2
9.	"we can now go back...": *New York Times* (Aug. 31, 1945), p. 5
9.	"sole political remark": *ibid.*, 5
10.	"murderous intent...": SW II, 277
10.	Old Chinese tradition of generals before battle: Payne, 272
12 et seq.	For "Summary of Conversations" at Chungking, see SW IV, 60-63
13.	Mao's complaint of being treated like a peasant: Payne, 271
15.	"words on paper": SW IV, 53
15.	Mao's hopes for a coalition government prior to Chungking Negotiations: SW IV, 48-49

2. Son of the Tiger Gentry

22.	"Greater than my mother...": Chang, H. H., 18
22.	Anecdote of ghosts: *ibid.*, 29
24.	Chiang's exercise for willpower: *ibid.*, 45
28.	"Impressed not only by [his] fervor...": *ibid.*, 72-73
28.	"I am a coolie...": Sharman, 51
31.	"running wild without a bridle": Tan, 126
32.	Growth of United League in China: Tang L-1, *Inner History*, 57
32.	"of average height, thin and wiry...": Sharman, 51
33.	"that man will be the hero...": Chang, H. H., 68
34.	United League oath of membership: Hahn, *Chiang Kai-shek*, 35

3. The Rebel of Shaoshan

37. Definition of "rich peasant": SW I, 138
40. "There were two 'parties' in the family...": Snow, *Red Star*, 132
41. "I felt that there with the rebels...": *ibid.*, 135
42. "I thought the [marauding] villagers' method...": *ibid.*, 136
43. "In a book called *Great Heroes of the World*...": *ibid.*, 138
43. "I considered the Emperor...": *ibid.*, 138
44. "kindly eyes [looking out] from...": Carlson, 167
44. a lone monk...with a leaky umbrella.: Snow, *Long Revolution*, 168 *et seq.*
44. "my first expression of a political opinion": Snow, *Red Star*, 140

4. The Bungled Bomb at Wuhan

48-49. Li Yuan-hung found under wife's bed: Tang L-1, *Inner History*, 81
51. Sun's collection of $400,000: *ibid.*, 52
53-54. For Sun's chaotic administration in Nanking, see Selle, 123 *et seq.*
56. Sun's address at the Ming tombs: *ibid.*, 128

5. Revolutionaries in Limbo

57. "Not a sound was heard as the orator of the revolution...": Snow, *Red Star*, 140
58. "They were not bad men...": *ibid.*, 141
58. "their corpses lying in the street": *ibid.*, 141
59. "An advertisement for a police school...": ibid., 143
59. "Fate again intervened...": *ibid.*, 143
59. "I was very regular and conscientious...": *ibid.*, 144
60. "a curious mixture...of liberalism...": *ibid.*, 148-149
60. "Great Teacher, Great Leader...": Snow, *Long Revolution*, 168 *et seq.*
61. He had begun his adult life as a teacher...*ibid.*, 221
61-62. For Sun's railroading plans and experiences, see Selle, 133-136
62. Yuan Shih-kai's dealings for a foreign loan: Chen, 126-127
67. He even employed an American professor...: Sharman, 203
69. Statistics on Chinese sent overseas 1916-1919: Chow, 37-38
69. "I felt that I did not know enough about my own country...": Snow, *Red Star*, 151
69. "very expensive": *ibid.*, 151
70. Mao's contribution, on physical culture, appeared in *New Youth* April 1, 1917.
70. "I was still confused..." Snow, *Red Star*, 152
71. Japanese trade increase in China: Remer, *Boycotts*, 234
72. "I became more and more convinced..." Snow, *Red Star*, 155
72. "I organized workers politically...": *ibid.*, 155
72. "The philosophers have only interpreted...": Marx, *Theses on Feuerbach*

73.   "The success of the revolution . . . ": Chow, 195

6. Cross Currents

76.   "He would fly into storms of temper . . .": Hahn, *Chiang Kai-shek*, 63
77.   projectionist thrashed: Crozier, 8
77.   "a harlot who particularly captivated": *ibid.*, 58
77-78.   "an almost mythical character": Powell, J. B., 132
79.   married "to a member of his [patron's] household": Tang L-1, *Inner History*, 231 *et seq.*
81.   Paraphrase of Karakhan Declaration; Chow, 210n
82.   "In May of 1921 I went to Shanghai . . .": Snow, *Red Star*, 157
85.   Sun/Joffe joint statement: Tang L-1, *Inner History*, 156
85-86.   Sun's proposition to J. G. Schurman: Sharman, 250

7. The Tsungli Passes

88.   diets of newborn rats . . . : Wakeman, 57
89.   For a biography of Borodin, see Brandt, 195-196
90.   "with the natural dignity of a lion . . .": Chang, H. H., 159
90.   "a long view of history": Tuchman, 92
90.   The men had met . . . in America . . . : Clubb, *China and Russia*, 231
90.   "more akin to a clique . . .": Brandt, 41-42
93.   "more than twenty trade unions": Snow, *Red Star*, 158
93.   "This Mao . . . is dangerous . . .": Han, *Deluge*, 102
94.   For an account of Mao's switched vote at the 3rd CCP Congress, see Rue, 37-39
96.   "Tsarism by other names": Payne, 96
96-97.   "a beautiful position with vistas . . . ": Chang, H. H., 18
97.   Whampoa Academy opened on June 16, 1924: Crozier, 71
97.   "Do not fear death . . .": Chang, H. H., 128
97.   "If our . . . Russian comrades had not come . . . ": *ibid*, 128
99.   "First . . . Mao is a person who . . .": Siao-yo, 53-55
100.   "I returned to Hunan for a rest . . .": Snow, *Red Star*, 159
100.   "once I had accepted [Marxism] as the correct . . .": *ibid.*, 155
100.   "A Communist should have largeness of mind . . . ": SW II. 33
101.   "oil, called 'gas oil' . . . ": Sun Yat-sen, 89
101.   "increase and decrease of population . . . ": *ibid.*, 85
101-102. "all citizens have received military training . . . ": *ibid.*, 105
102.   "the sovereignty of the people": *ibid.*, 238
102.   "the center of government . . . ": *ibid.*, 407
102.   "a sheet of loose sand": *ibid.*, 113
102.   "born in a stupor . . . ": *ibid.*, 120
102.   "When the people share everything . . . ": *ibid.*, 444
103.   "Taking my leave of you, dear comrades . . . ": Sharman, 308-309
103.   "Peace . . . struggle . . . save China": Tang L-1, *Inner History*, 197

8. Claimants to the Mantle
- 106. 540,000 workers flocked ... : Han, *Deluge*, 122
- 106. Increase in CCP members in 1925: *ibid.*, 122
- 107. "Ally with Chiang ... ": Tang L-1, *Inner History*, 229-230
- 107. "We are taking you along the path ... ": *ibid.*, 214
- 107. "The National Revolution cannot ... ": *ibid.*, 231-232
- 108. "representatives of 21 different provinces ... ": Han, *Deluge*, 127
- 109-110. Borodin's negotiations with the Christian General: Chang, H. H., 164
- 112. "single act [he had] destroyed ... ": Tang L-1, *Inner History*, 246
- 113. "I began to disagree ... ": Snow, *Red Star*, 160
- 113. "The worker-peasant masses ... ": Han, *Deluge*, 135
- 113. "Long live the world revolution!": *ibid.*, 135

9. The Aborted Crusade
- 117-118. Concentration of foreign troops in "defense" of Shanghai: Hauser, 167-168
- 118. "nothing in his appearance ... ": Chang, H. H., 166
- 118. "Strong men have risen ... ": *ibid.*, 166-167
- 121. Labor conditions in Wuhan: Han, *Deluge*, 148
- 122. "foreign and Chinese ... ": *ibid.*, 148
- 123. "the heroic armies of the Northern Expedition": *ibid.*, 152
- 125. "In a very short time ... ": SW I, 23
- 125. "fact-finding conferences ... ": *ibid.*, 23
- 125. "local tyrants, evil gentry" and "every bit of dignity": *ibid.*, 25
- 125. "[F]rom last October to January ... ": *ibid.*, 24
- 125. "in a few months the peasants ... " *ibid.*, 27
- 125. "it is reported ... that Chiang Kai-shek ... ": *ibid.*, 56
- 125-126. To march at the [peasants'] head ... ": *ibid.*, 24
- 126. "vanguards of the revolution": *ibid.*, 30

10. Massacre at Shanghai
- 129. Funds received by Chiang for "delivering" Shanghai: Crozier, 106
- 130. Joint statement of Wang Ching-wei and Editor Chen: Han, *Deluge*, 153
- 136. Stalin's telegram "converting" the revolution: Tang L-1, *Inner History*, 280-281
- 138. Estimate of dead and missing during White Terror: Han, *Deluge*, 171
- 139. "without revolutionary theory ... ": Lenin, V. I. "What is to be done?" (see *Collected Works*).
- 139. "in a chaotic state": Snow, *Red Star*, 162
- 140. "organization of a peasant-worker ... army": *ibid.*, 165
- 140-141. "I was ordered to be taken ... ": *ibid.*, 165-166

Notes

141. Mao's philosophy on why death passed him by: Snow, *Long Revolution*, 81
142. "Discipline was poor . . . ": Snow, *Red Star*, 166
143. Chiang's interview with newsmen regarding future plans: Chang, H. H., 184-185

11. Thunder on the Plains, Fire in the Mountains

145. Chiang proposed to Sun's widow through a marriage broker: Snow, *Journey*, 85
145. "the great merit of being able to conceal . . . ": Chang, H. H., 64
145. "forbidding expression . . . ": Hsiung, 61
146. Chen Chieh-ju's divorce from Chiang and her subsequent career: Crozier, 58-59
151. butchering "local bullies" . . . : Han, *Deluge*, 186
154. "all smiles . . . ": *ibid.*, 195
154-155. Mao reinstated after 6th CCP Congress: *ibid.*, 209-210
155. Full texts of pamphlets cited: SW I, 63-70 and 73-102

12. The Fat Days of the Kuomintang

160. Manchus administered China on $75 million budget: Tang L-1, *Foundations*, 68
160. Shanghai gangsters called in to collect debt: Eastman, 228-229
162. Loop roadway in Nanking: Chang, H. H., 207-208
162. "Kiss me, Lampson": Hahn, *Chiang Kai-shek*, 138
164. "restoring a proletarian base": Rue, 137
165. "roving rebel bands": SW I, 114
165. "to conduct propaganda among the masses . . . ": *ibid.*, 106
165. "He is said to have told Chou En-lai . . . ": Han, *Deluge*, 226
166. "Li Li-san has gone mad": *ibid.*, 230
166. "Conditions . . . were becoming very bad": Snow, *Red Star*, 169
168. "[We] established soviets . . . ": *ibid.*, 170
168. Founding Kiangsi Provincial Soviet Government: *ibid.*, 170-171
170. "[We] saved the Red Army . . . ": *ibid.*, 175-176

13. Years of the Ram and the Rooster

175. For full text of Tanaka Memorial, see Schurmann and Schell, 180-185
177. For an account of National Salvation Association, see Remer, *Boycotts*, 161
177. Decline in Japanese imports: *ibid.*, 198-199
178. Founding of Soviet Republic of China: Han, *Deluge*, 241
179. Reward for "Red bandit Su Wei-ai . . . ": *ibid.*, 242
182. For a full account of the Futien Incident, see Schwartz, chapter XII

183. Japanese striking force at Shanghai: Nish, 160
184. "the only failure is in failure to act": Snow, *Battle*, 117
186. "the most disastrous...": Snow, *Red Star*, 179
186. "the greatest humiliation": *ibid.*, 179
187. "Pit one against ten...": Han, *Deluge*, 252
187. "It was a serious mistake...": Snow, *Red Star*, 180
188. "I'll shake [Tsai's] hand only if...": Han, *Deluge*, 259
190. "looking upon the interests of the revolution...": SW II, 33

14. Flight of the Hundred Thousand
196. "The Red Army fears not death...": Han, *Deluge*, 274
196. At night the travelers lit torches...: Smedley, *Great Road*, 311
196. "Today we walk...": Han, *Deluge*, 275
203-205. For crossing of Tatu River, see Snow, *Red Star*, 198-199
205. "Heroism is an ancient concept...": Smedley, *Great Road*, 323
211. "suddenly there was the sound of gongs..." Han, *Deluge*, 303
212. "Let us ask, has history ever known...?": SW I, 160

15. Eve of a Great Change
214. "seventy percent political...": Chang, H. H., 217
214. "Nationalize, Militarize, Productivize": Eastman, 48
214. "Support Chiang Kai-shek as China's Hitler!": *ibid.*, 172
215. Thirteen Princes: *ibid.*, 36
215. Blueshirts' failure with agrarian reforms: *ibid.*, 51-52
216. For friendly account of New Life Movement, see Chang, H. H., 226-230
220. "in the best classical tradition...": *ibid.*, 241
220. "tortuous road": SW I, 165
222. "the eve of a great change": *ibid.*, 161
223. "to include...all...classes...": *ibid.*, 165
223. "workers' and peasants' republic" into a "people's republic": *ibid.*, 167
223. "we [may] have the right to call ourselves...": *ibid.*, 168
223. "This [winning of allies] provides a necessary condition...": *ibid.*, 171
225. "take the ideas of the masses...": SW III, 119

16. Collision in Sian
227-228. The Young Marshal's romantic conquests: Smedley, *Battle Hymn*, 36-37
228. "thin...drawn...jaundiced-looking": Snow, *Red Star*, 48
229. "He had put on weight and muscle...": *ibid.*, 48-49
230. "the sanity and practicability...": *ibid.*, 51
230. "I will never talk about this until...": *ibid.*, 375
231. "That is merely your viewpoint...": *ibid.*, 377

233.	"If you regard me as your prisoner . . . ": Chiang, *The Account of the Fortnight in Sian* (henceforth *Fortnight*), 126
234.	"Hold your tongue, you rebels!": *ibid.*, 127
234.	"Since I am in the hands of a rebel . . . ": *ibid.*, 129
234.	"I am armed with the principles . . . ": *ibid.*, 132
234-235.	"The courageous life as taught by . . . ": *ibid.*, 143-144
236.	Rumor of ransom for Chiang: Powell, J. B., 276n
236.	Tokyo insinuated that a seditious . . . : Tong, vol. II, 479
236.	"Japanese plot": Han, *Deluge*, 329
236.	"A strange affair . . . ": Chang, H. H., 244
236.	"publicly to disown the [Chinese Communists] . . . ": Snow, *Red Star*, 438
236.	"flew into a rage . . . ": Snow, *Random Notes*, 2
238.	"even as a simple citizen . . . ": Chiang, *Fortnight*, 150
238.	"You are a military officer . . . ": *ibid.*, 150-151
238.	"We have read your diary . . . ": Chang, H. H., 252
238.	"you always have in your head . . . ": Chiang, *Fortnight*, 152
238.	"Sacrifice and achievement . . . ": *ibid.*, 152
239.	"former subordinate": Chang Kuo-tao, vol. II, 488
239.	"Commandant": *ibid.*, 488
240.	"a hint of reconciliation": *ibid.*, 488
240.	Chiang asks help for the return of his son: *ibid.*, 488
240.	"would probably not go back on his [unspoken] word": *ibid.*, 497
241.	"quite contrary to outside beliefs . . . ": Chiang, *Fortnight*, 104
241.	"Jehovah will now do a new thing . . . ": *ibid.*, 94
241.	"a scar on his mind": Chang Kuo-tao, vol. II, 487
242.	"due to my lack of virtue . . . ": Snow, *Red Star*, 391
	"magnanimous personality": Chang, H. H., 259
242.	"crude, coarse, and wild": *ibid.*, 259
242.	"blushing with shame": Snow, *Red Star*, 391
242.	"punishment I deserve": *ibid.*, 391

17. The Devil is Our Leader

245.	"promises must be kept . . . ": SW I, 255
245.	"clean up": *ibid.*, 257
245.	"anti-Japanese front uniting all parties . . . ": *ibid.*, 258
245-246.	Four Pledges and Five Conditions: *ibid.*, 281n[7]
247.	"to make a new start in life": Snow, *Red Star*, 394
247.	Chiang's four demands on CCP: *ibid.*, 394
250.	Mao contrasts contradictions that have developed: SW I, 263
250.	Mao's defense of the Three People's Principles: *ibid.*, 270
251.	"the attempts of the Kuomintang to seduce . . . ": SW II, 66
252.	"We are [still] fighting for socialism . . . ": SW I, 290
252.	"[t]oday . . . an alliance [with the Kuomintang] is . . . a necessary bridge. . . . ": *ibid.*, 291

252. "The devil is now our leader": told to author in China.
253. "preparations for a major war...": SW I, 289
253. "Japan is exerting every ounce of energy...": *ibid.*, 267

18. Typhoon from the North
256. "Soldiers! The supreme moment has come...": Chang, H. H., 274
256. To "mobilize the whole people": SW II, 17
256. "unite the entire Chinese people...: *ibid.*, 18
257. Military casualties at Shanghai: Crozier, 202
257. Civilian casualties at Shanghai: Powell, J. B., 301
258. Sack of Nanking: Payne, 230
260. "independent, self-reliant guerrilla warfare": Han, *Deluge*, 341
260. Casualties at Ping-hsin pass: Snow, *Battle*, 346
260-261. Battle of Taierhchuang: Johnson, 35-36
261. "Wherever I go...": Snow, *Battle*, 116
262. Details on Madrid resistance: SW II, 29n[4]

19. One Divides into Two
265. Wang's attempt to assassinate Prince Regent: Tang L-1, *Inner History*, 63-71
265. Wang's marriage: *ibid.*, 98-99
265-266. Six No Society: *ibid.*, 206
267. "surrender, appease, survive": Linebarger, 209
269. "an 'imperial envoy' from Moscow...": Chang Kuo-tao, vol II, 572
269. "Everything through the United Front": SW II, 83
269. "Simultaneous alliance [with the KMT] and struggle...": SW I, 328
270. "both for regular and for guerrilla warfare": SW II, 83
270. "possible and necessary to use tactical offensives...": *ibid.*, 83
270. "initiative, flexibility and planning": *ibid.*, 85
270. "in the mountains...on the plains...": *ibid.*, 94
270. "a front out of the enemy's rear": *ibid.*, 93
272. Text of Chang Kuo-tao's open letter: Chang Kuo-tao, vol. II, 588
273. Mao's fears of a Far Eastern Munich: SW II, 254n[2], 255n[3]

20. Kill all, Burn all
277. Japan's allurements for Chinese businessmen: SW II, 359
277. Twenty members of KMT CEC went over to Wang: SW III, 144
280. "Some real fighting": Han, *Deluge*, 374
280. "huge bonfire of attacks...": *ibid.*, cited 374n
281. Three phases of Hundred Regiments Offensive: Johnson, 57
281. Casualties and prisoners during offensive: Han, *Deluge*, 374
284. 1941-1942 were worst years of entire war for CCP: Johnson, 58
284. Estimate of toll on population of North China: *ibid.*, 58

285. Mao thanks Japanese for "education": Snow, *Long Revolution*, 198-199

21. The Will To Fight
291. "I claim we got a hell of a beating": Tuchman, 300
292. "heads cannot be lopped off . . . ": Tang Tsou, 77
292. "a stubborn, ignorant, prejudiced, conceited despot": Tuchman, 317
293. 468 planes lost over Hump in first 3 years: *ibid.*, 309
293. Logistics for supply of 5,000 tons a month: *ibid.*, 313
293. "there are ways and means of doing things": *ibid.*, 357
294. Chiang's claim that situation was never so stable and Mao's reply: SW III, 179-180
296. "I began life as a student . . . ": *ibid.*, 73
296. "Some people [say] . . . Clodhoppers!": *ibid.*, 45
297. "Although I have been in northern Shensi . . . ": *ibid.*, 45
297. "class love": *ibid.*, 74
297. Class structure under CCP three-thirds system: Belden, 80
298. Fan-shen defined: *ibid.*, 485 (For an account of fan-shen in detailed action, see bibliography under Hinton, William.)
299. "[That] fellow Chiang . . . ": Snow, *Journey*, 347
300. only 56 percent of the inductees reached . . . units: Liu, F. F., 137
300. the roadside was littered with dead: Tuchman, 265
300. 2,000 doctors for 5.7 million troops: Liu, F. F., 140

22. Squatting on Mount Omei
304. Increased tonnage across Hump, June to Dec. 1944: Tuchman, 484
304. "unprecedented feat of arms": *ibid.*, 448
305. "To win a hundred victories . . . ": Sun Tzu, 77
306. "collapse" . . . "liquidation" . . . "other arrangements": Tuchman, 303-312
306. Chiang's daily routine: see Chang H. H., 221-223
307. "saving the nation by a devious path": SW III, 219
308. Chungking inflation dramatized: Crozier, 244
308. H. H. Kung's concern for "patriotic merchants" in Occupied China: Epstein, 223
308. $867,000 turned over to young Kung: Tuchman, 411
308. H. H. Kung's commission on planes purchased in U.S.: Snow, *Journey*, 217
309. KMT insiders disposses Szechwan landlords: Belden, 151
309. "It's Madame Kung, not Japan . . . ": Snow, *Journey*, 218
309. "Donald, you may criticize . . . ": Selle, 349
310. Currency exchange rates in Chungking: Tuchman, 411
310. squatted on Mount Omei: see SW IV, 16 and 23n^3
313. "ashen faces and trembling knees": Tuchman, 405
313. Chiang's fury at mistreatment of conscripts: White and Jacoby, 128

313-314. Chiang refutes rumors of marital infidelity: Tuchman, 490
315. "one cannot speak sternly to a man like that...": *ibid.*, 360

23. Shall We Dare to Win?
319. Estimate of CCP population, Party and army: SW III, 169-170
320. "New Testament society": told to the author in China.
320. "Why those people have no idea...": told to the author in China.
321. Chang Kuo-tao's estimate of CCP effort in North China 1944: Liu, F. F., 206
323. Mao calls Hurley a clown: Smedley, *Great Road*, 424
323. Five-point program worked out at Yenan: WP, 74-75
323. "The Communists have sold you...": Lohbeck, 314-315
323. Chiang's counterproposal to CCP: WP, 75
324. "all things grow out of the barrel of a gun": SW II, 225
324. "the Chinese Communists are not in fact...": WP, 94
324. "margarine" Communists: Brandt, 174
324. Stalin's proposal to cooperate with the Americans: WP, 95
324. "selfless" and "a patriot": *ibid.*, 95
325. "The Chinese Communists do not believe...": *ibid.*, 99
326. "His Majesty": SW III, 283
326. "the honest way" and the "dishonest way" of "handing state power back to the people": *ibid.*, 240-241
326. "already proved its complete bankruptcy": *ibid.*, 229
327. "to sacrifice the interests of the Chinese people": *ibid.*, 282
327. "encouraging the KMT government to be...": *ibid.*, 286
327. "Shall we dare to win?": Han, *Deluge*, 420
327. Chiang's order to Chu Teh: SW IV, 33
327. Chu Teh's reply to Chiang: *ibid.*, 34
330. Chiang's invitation to Mao addressed in Confucian style: Payne, 271
330. Reasons why Mao went to Chungking: SW IV, 48n
331. "We told [the CCP] bluntly...": Tang Tsou, 325-326
331-332. "We... are prepared to make such concessions...": SW IV, 49
332. "[O]ur Party is powerful [and] we must never be cowed...": *ibid.*, 49
332. "[W]e must... win over the many...": *ibid.*, 49
332. "he was the best friend the Chinese Communists had...": WP, 103
333. For full text of Hurley's letter of resignation, see WP, Annex 50, 581-584

24. Circles Within Circles
337. "The world is progressing...": SW IV, 59
337. "Words on paper are not equivalent...": *ibid.*, 53
338. KMT's CEC sabotages the PCC's proposals: Tang Tsou, 417

339.   Weapons Russia handed over to CCP: *ibid.*, 331n
339-340. Marshall's attempt to make Changchun an Exec. Hq, city: WP, 154 *et seq.*
340-341. Chiang agrees to a truce after taking Changchun: *ibid.*, 158
341.   Marshall tries to convince Chiang of his over-ambitious strategy: *ibid.*, 150-151
342.   "Although Chiang Kai-shek has U.S. aid . . . ": SW IV, 89
342.   "[C]oncentrate an absolutely superior force . . . ": *ibid.*, 103
343.   "wear and tear": *ibid.*, 133-134
343.   Mao reinstitutes policy of land confiscation: Belden, 169
343.   Anti-U.S. demonstrations by both KMT and CCP: WP, 170
344.   Chiang attacks Kalgan: *ibid.*, 188
344.   CCP refuses to attend Chiang's National Assembly: *ibid.*, 207
345.   Marshall's mediation is "a fraud": SW IV, 117
345.   "a smoke-screen for strengthening . . . ": *ibid.*, 109
345.   Marshall's concern for weak elements of National Assembly: WP, 214-215
346.   Chou En-lai predicts attack on Yenan: *ibid.*, 208
346-347. Marshall's last interview with Chiang: *ibid.*, 211-212
347.   Chiang offers Marshall job as military adviser: *ibid.*, 213

25. Amid Fire and Thunder
348.   "[T]he difficulties of the reactionar[ies] are . . . ": SW IV, 125
349.   "not counting the numerous puppet troops . . . ": *ibid.*, 119
349.   Chiang drafts 2,440,000 troops by compulsory conscription: *ibid.*, 287
349.   800,000 KMT prisoners fighting for PLA: *ibid.*, 271
349.   *Su-ku* and *tu-ku-shui*: Solomon, 214
351-352. Ambassador Stuart invites CCP to peace parlay: WP, 230-231
352.   Mao's response to invitation: *ibid.*, 231
353.   "come into being amid fire and thunder": SW IV, 284
353.   100,000 Communists had been routed . . . : WP, 237-238
355.   "confiscating money, automobiles, gold and women": Chiang, *China's Destiny*, 317 (Editor's note)
356.   government corporations were being formed at the rate of . . . : Stevens, 296
356.   Extortion through charges of collaboration: Crozier, 278
356.   Hardware and plumbing stripped for sale: *ibid.*, 279
356.   Fuhsan coal pit and fortune in drugs: Belden, 377-378
356-357. Devaluation of National currency: Crozier, 278: Beal, 317: Fitzgerald, 179
357.   Increase in value of Border Region currency: Belden, 106-107
358.   "The whole situation between the enemy and ourselves . . . ": SW IV, 147
359.   Engels' indignation at unions: Muller, 320-321

360. "In the world revolution . . . ": Wales, 215
361. "Do not be impetuous . . . ": SW IV, 201
361. "[T]here should be no repetition of the wrong ultra-Left policy . . . ": *ibid.*, 164
361. "Reactionaries must be suppressed . . . ": *ibid.*, 202
361. "Whoever advocates absolute equalitarianism . . . ": *ibid.*, 236
362. "[D]o not lightly advance slogans of raising wages . . . ": *ibid.*, 248
362. "We should make use of large numbers of . . . ": *ibid.*, 274
362. eight to ten years for a Communist to achieve a correct class outlook: SW III, 78
363. "the predicament in Manchuria . . . ": WP, 264
364. "Fully half the students in our missionary school . . . ": Smedley, *Great Road*, 366-367
364. "We are prepared to bring about the fundamental overthrow . . . ": SW IV, 261
365. Chiang turned loose some 300,000 Manchurian puppet troops: Crozier, 342
366. For CCP account of Chinchow-Changchun-Mukden (Shenyang) campaign, see SW IV, 265n[1]
366. "The original estimate was . . . ": *ibid.*, 288
366-367. Mme. Chiang's mission to Washington: Tang Tsou, 491-492
367. Truman's opinions about "grafters and crooks": Ferrell, 213
368. Stalin's request before battle of Hwai-Hai: Fitzgerald, 106
368-369. For detailed account of Hwai-Hai, see Clubb, "Chiang Kai-shek's Waterloo".
369. "You are to complete the Hwai-Hai campaign . . . ": SW IV, 281
369. he developed a hemorrhage . . . : Belden, 419
369-370. Chiang's heavy drinking and tantrums: Payne, 281
370. Chiang's New Year's Day peace address: SW IV, 309
370. Mao's retort to Chiang's peace address: *ibid.*, 312
370. "Unless President Chiang goes . . . ": Chiang, *Soviet Russia*, 200
371. Chiang orders gold reserves transported to Taiwan: Payne, 282
371. Li Tsung-jen asks for U.S. loan: WP, 303-305
371. "We tell you gentlemen of Nanking . . . ": SW IV, 327
371-372. CCP account of *Amethyst* incident: *ibid.*, 403n[1]

26. Transformations Utterly Inconceivable
376. He was humble at the beginning ("I am ashamed . . . "): Payne, 284
376. Peak tonnage across Hump: White, *Search*, 221
377. Chiang orders "Old Yang" executed: Crozier, 188
379. "[H]e is one of the most consistent men . . . ": Chang, H. H., 278
380. "They want you to accept their 'peace' . . . ": Chiang, *Soviet Russia*, 9

381.	"It must never be assumed that . . . ": SW IV, 362
381.	"With victory . . . the bourgeoisie . . . ": *ibid.*, 374
381.	"[C]ertain moods may grow within the Party . . . " *ibid.*, 374
383.	"some muddle-headed comrades": *ibid.*, 364
383.	"incorrect attitude[s] . . . during the War of Agrarian Revolution . . . ": *ibid.*, 373
383.	"The tree of liberty must be refreshed . . . ": Koch and Peden, 436
385.	"never have been destroyed": Snow, *Red Star*, 164
387.	"utterly inconceivable to people of the older generation": SW IV, 284
387.	Fellow Countrymen . . .

As reported by the *New York Times*, Oct. 3, 1949, Mao Tse-tung confined himself during this address to a factual proclamation of the People's Republic of China, an announcement of the officials who would govern it, and an invitation for recognition by other nations.

In place of this formal announcement, it seems legitimate to substitute excerpts from speeches Mao made within a few days of the occasion—excerpts reflecting both pride in victory and warnings for the future.

Sources for the text given are as follows:
Par. 1: "For over a century . . . ": SW V, 19
Par. 2: "A drama begins with a prologue . . . ": SW IV, 374
Par. 3: "We are now at a time . . . ": SW V, 19 and 20
Par. 4: "The Chinese people . . . ": The gist of the statement will be found in SW V, 17, but a translation found in *Wind in the Tower* by Han Suyin (page 33) better sums up the feeling and so is given.

Afterword

391.	"As for the . . . recognition of our country . . . ": SW IV, 370-371
391.	"Wherever there is business to do . . . ": *ibid.*, 371
396.	"China used to be stigmatized as . . . ": SW V, 313
396.	"[O]ur revolution came late . . . ": *ibid.*, 305-306
396.	"[But] even when one day our country becomes strong . . . ": *ibid.*, 306

INDEX

Amethyst incident, 371

Barr, Gen. David G., 354
Bluecher, Gen. Vasili K. (*see* Galen)
Blueshirts (*see* I-Chi)
Border Region government (CCP), 252; population and army, 319
Borodin, Michael, biography, 89; organizes KMT, 90-92; mission to Christian general, 109; at Wuhan, 121, 136-137; death, 137n
Boxer Rebellion, 25, 275
Boycotts (against Japan), 176-177
Braun, Otto (Li Teh), biography, 188; 189, 196, 197, 198, 207
Buddhism (Chinese version), 38-39
Burma, Japan attacks, 289-290; captures Myitkyina, 293, and driven out, 304; Japan's casualties, 317
Burma Road, 276, 290, 292

C & C clique, 68
Cairo Conference, 298-299
Cantlie, Dr. James, 30
Canton, described, 87-88; KMT regimes at, 79-80, 82-85; Commune at, 147-148; secessionist government at, 374; PLA captures, 377
Canton Coup, 108, 111-112, 114, 119
Central Military Academy, 159, 251, 299
Chang Ching-chiang (curio dealer), described, 77; influence on Chiang, 78-79, 114
Chang Hsueh-liang (*see* Young Marshal)
Chang Hsueh-shih (Young Marshal's brother), 365
Chang Kuo-ta, background, 206-207; at Moukung and Maoerhkai, 207-208; establishes govt. in Tibet, 208-209; is put on trial in Shensi, 223; defects to KMT, and analysis of character, 271-272
Chang Tso-lin ("Tiger of the North"), 157; assassinated, 157-158; 227
Changchun, as capital of Manchukuo, 339; PLA occupies, 339; taken by Chiang, 340; PLA recaptures, 366
Changsha, Mao attends school at, 44, then teaches and organizes at, 70-72; exiled from, 92-93; returns to besiege, 169, 170
Chen brothers (Li-fu and Kuo-fu), 161
Chen Chi-mei (Chiang's "elder brother"), described, 26; befriends Chiang, 26, 33, 49, 63, 66, 76, 77, 79; assassinated, 68
Chen Chieh-ju (Chiang's second wife), 77, 79; divorces and final history, 146
Chen Chiung-ming (*see* Hakka General)
Chen Pi-chun (Mme. Wang Ching-wei), 265
Chen Tu-Hsiu (Editor Chen), founder of *New Youth*, 70; secretary-general of CCP, 83; dilemmas at Canton, 112-113, and at Wuhan, 125, 126, 130; dismissed from office, 139
Chennault, Gen. Claire L., biography, 311; organizes Flying Tigers, 311; in conflict with Stilwell and appeals to FDR, 312; during Japan (1944) advance, 314; fall from favor, 315
Chiang Ching (Mao's fourth wife), 297n
Chiang Ching-kuo (Chiang's older son), 63; sent to USSR for education, 107; returns to China, 253; President of Republic on Taiwan, 389
Chiang Kai-shek; birth and background, 17-18; grandfather's influence, 18-20; schooling, 20-21; role of mother, 21-22; marriages, 23, 79, 145-146; decides on military career, 24; in Japan, 25-27, 27-28, 33-35, 64-66, 145-146; influence of Sun Yat-sen, 33, 64, 77, and of Chen Chi-mei, 26, 68, 77; role in 1911 revolution, 49; "mystery" years, 73, 76-79, 146, goes to USSR and his reactions, 9, 64; at Whampoa, 97-98; stages Canton Coup (which *see*); on Northern Expedition, 116-119; proposes break with CCP, 122-124; plots to suppress CCP, 129-131; stages Shanghai massacre, 131-133; establishes capital at Nanking, 133-134; suppresses Canton Commune, 147-148; completes Northern Expedition, 156-158; becomes KMT head of state, 158; attempts moral reforms, 161; renovates

417

INDEX

Chiang Kai-shek (*cont*.)
Nanking, 161-162; tuchun wars, 162-163; Red bandit campaigns, 170-171, 185-187; Mukden Incident, 175-176, and resigns office, 178; retirements to Fenghua, 63-64, 80, 96, 142-143, 178, 373, 374; founds New Life Movement, 216-217; becomes "Generalissimo," 220; before and after Sian Incident, 230, 231-235, 237-242; forms united front with CCP, 247-248, and resumes relations with USSR, 253; reaction to Japan invasion, 255-256; defends Shanghai, 257; moves capital to Wuhan, 260, then to Chungking, 261; friction with CCP, 277-278, 306-307, and attack on New Fourth Army, 284n; conflicts with Stilwell, 292-293, 300-301, 304-305; at Cairo Conference, 298-299; problems at Chungking, 307-310, 313; relations with Chennault, 311-312, but fails to save his airfields, 314, and is descredited with FDR, 315-316; after V-J Day tries to prevent CCP from entering Manchuria, 327; agrees to Chungking talks, 330, and his actions during talks, 12-14; helps promote PCC, 336, then sabotages it, 337-339; relations with Marshall, 338-347; relations with Stuart, 351-352; attacks Yenan, 352-353; reacts to PLA counteroffensive and defeat at Hwai-Hai, 365-369; resigns presidency and selects Taiwan as refuge, 373-374; his last travels on mainland, 375-377; resumes presidency of Republic on Taiwan, 377-378; estimate of his career, 378-380

Chiang Kai-shek, Madame (*see* Soong, Meiling)
Chiang Wei-kuo (younger son), 369
Chiang Yu-piao (grandfather), 18-20
Chikow (village of), 17, 143, 375
China Lobby, 355; composition of, 363, 367
Chinese Communist Party (CCP), founding of, 82-84; after Sun's death, 105-106; increase in members, 106; after Wuhan betrayal, 139; statistics on growth (1927-1942), 295
Chou En-lai, background, 97; at Canton Coup, 111; in Shanghai, 123, 132, 179, 180; in Kiangsi, 190; at Tsunyi, 198; before and during Sian Incident, 230, 237, 239-240, 242; at Nanking (1937), 250; at Wuhan (1938), 262; at Chungking, 294-319; relations with Marshall, 336, 345-346; before battle of Hwai-hai, 368

Christian General (Feng Yu-hsiang), described, 110; his deal with Chiang, 156-157; conflict with Chiang, 163, 170

Chu Teh, 49, biography, 152-153; at CCP capture of Nanchang (1927), 138, and later, 147; forms Mao-Chu team, 154-155, 166, 167; attacks Changsha, 169; during Extermination campaigns, 170, 171, 185; reconciles with Mao, 190; during Long March, 197, 199, 200, 205, 208; returns from Tibet (1936), 223; as C.I.C. of Red Army, 251, 259, 327

Chunking, described, 275-276; bombed, 276; conditions in (1944), 307-310; Chiang returns to (1949), 376-377

Chungking Negotiations (1945), Mao's arrival and banquet, 5-10; pressures on talks, 11-12; Chiang's real views, 13-14; Hurley's dubious role, 13; talks break off, 15, and Mao returns to Yenan, 15

Churchill, Winston S., at Cairo Conference, 298, 299; quoted on Burma victory, 304

Clemenceau, Georges, 51
Comintern, founding and function, 81n; 89, 99, 110, 112, 120, 135, 137, 180, 181-182, 188, 198, 221, 268, dissolved, 331n

Communist Party (*see* Chinese Communist Party)

Confucianism, as evidenced in the superior man, 9; at village level, 18-19; in education, 21-23; as stifling initiative, 36; in setting moral example, 161; Chiang's defense of, 341; ethical concerns of, 379-380; in economic action, 357-358; other aspects of, 77, 82, 97, 102, 111, 144, 146, 158, 228, 242, 264, 275, 285, 330

Confucius, as antiquarian, 36; quoted, 41, 109, 161, 375, 384

Consular jurisdiction, defined, 75; 90, 118

Dare-to-dies, 49, 130, 265
Darwin, Charles, 59-60, 101; as mechanical thinker, 358

INDEX

Dewey, Thomas E., 364, 366
Donald, W. H., as adviser to Sun, 54, 62, and to Young Marshal, 228-229; during Sian Incident, 237-239, 241; quits China, 309
Doughty Dhu (Shanghai gangster), 78, 129

Empress Dowager (Tzu Hsi), 23, 27, 30, 52
Engels, Friedrich, 83, 297; indignant at unions, 359

Falkenhausen, Gen. Ludwig von, 159, 261, 299
Fan-shen, defined, 298; 349, 383
Fang Chin-min (Red commander), executed, 189; 191
Far Eastern Munich, 273
Feng Yu-hsiang (*see* Christian General)
Fenghua (*see* under Chiang Kai-shek for retirements to)
Flying Tigers, 311
Futien incident, 182

Galen (Gen. Vasili K. Bluecher), 97, 111; death, 137n
Gauss, Clarence E., 321
Graft and corruption (*see* Kuomintang)
Grant, Ulysses S., 20
Great Leap Forward, foreshadowed, 295
Great Rear Area, defined, 278; 307, 310

Hakka General (Chen Chiung-ming), relations with Sun, 79, 80; continuing conflicts with, 82, 98, 103, 108
Hangchow, 24; captured by Chiang (1911), 49, and by Japan (1937), 258
Hankow, location of city, 47n; meaning of name, 381
Hengyang, U.S. airfield at, 314
Hirohito, Japan Emperor, 218, 362
Hiroshima, 258, 327
Hitler, Adolf, 177, 214, 229, 262, 273, 276, 300, 340
Ho Lung (Red commander), 195, 196, 197
Ho Tzu-chen (Mao's third wife), 191
Ho Ying-chin (KMT War Minister), 170, 235, 237, 292; deficiency of, 292
Hsing Chung Hui (*see* Revive China Club)
Hu Han-min (Sun's "right hand"), 98; character, 98-99; 103, 104, 105; career compromised, 106; 133, 161, 386
Hu Tsung-nan (KMT general), captures Yenan, 353; harassed and retreats, 354
Hump air route, flight described, 293; increased traffic, 299, 304; peak tonnage, 376
Hundred Regiments Offensive (CCP), 281-282
Hung Hsiu-chuan (Taiping "Heavenly King"), 19
Hurley, Patrick J., his function in Chungking, 315-316; character, 322; visits Yenan, 322-323; appointed U.S. Ambassador, 324; visits Stalin, 324, and promotes Sino-Soviet Friendship Treaty, 325; promotes Chungking negotiations with CCP, 329-330, and his role at talks, 332-333; quits China and blames aides for failures, 333
Hwai-Hai (battle of), location and Chiang's strategy, 367; compared to Waterloo, 368; account of battle, 369

I-Chi ("chosen" graduates of Whampoa), ideals and Blueshirt name, 214-215; in government and agriculture, 215; in New Life Movement, 215-217; 233, 239
Inflation, in Chungking, 307-309; postwar, 356-357

Japan, historical sketch, 172-175; policy toward China (*see* Tanaka Memorial); incidents at Mukden, 175-176, at Shanghai, 183, 257-258, and at Marco Polo bridge, 255; "peace offensive", 263; in North China (*see* Okamura, Yasuji); in Burma (*see* Stilwell, Joseph W.); advance in south China (1944), 314; surrender, 327
Jefferson, Thomas, quoted, 383
Joffe, Adolph A., as diplomat, 84; joint declaration with Sun, 85; death, 137n
Judd, Dr. Walter, quoted 363-364; encourages Chiang, 364

Karakhan, Leo P., issues Karakhan Declaration, 81; USSR ambassador to Peking, 81; death, 137n
Kerensky, Aleksandr, 359
Korea, 191
Kung, H. H., account of as youth, 65; marries, 78; 161, 235; as grafting KMT finance minister, 308, 310, 351

419

INDEX

Kung, H. H., Madame (*see* Soong, Ai-ling)
Kunming (city of), 199, 201; Chiang returns to (1949), 376
Kuomintang (KMT), named as National Party, 61; first Congress, 94-95; split between right and left wings, 133, and reunification, 142-143; actions in power, 159-161; condition of armies (1944), 300; graft and corruption in Chungking, 308-310, and after V-J Day, 355-358; 8, 11, 12
Kweilin, U.S. airfield at, 315-315

Laotze (founder of Taoism), 7; quoted, 73
League of Nations, 176, 177, 228, 262
Ledo Road, 302, 304, 317
Lenin, V. I., 83, 95, 96; quoted, 139, 244; as a pragmatist, 359
Li Huan-hung, as reluctant commander of Wuhan uprising (1911), 48-49; as President of the Republic, 67-68
Li Li-san, background, 163-164; actions as CCP leader, 164-166, 168-170; recalled to Moscow, 170; return to China, 331; 178, 179, 180
Li Teh (*see* Braun, Otto)
Li Tsung-jen, during Northern Expedition, 116-117; at Peking (1928), 157; revolts against Chiang, 162-163; victor at Taierhchuang, 261; elected V.P. at National Assembly (1946), 345; as President, 370; applies for U.S. loan, 371; supplanted as President, 377; 367, 373, 374, 375, 386
Liao Chung-kai (KMT official), 104, 105; assassinated, 106; 386
Lin Piao (Red commander), during Extermination campaigns, 147, 185; during Long March, 201, 203, 204, 205; 221, 251, 260
Lincoln, Abraham, 31, 168
Lintung (hot springs), 231
Liu Chih-tan (Red commander), founded Shensi base, 211; 222; death, 224
Liu Po-cheng (Red commander, "One-eyed Dragon"), 185, 222, 251, 354, 369
Long March, comparisons to, 193-195; at Hsiang River, 196; at Tsunyi, 198-199; crossing upper Yangtze, 201; among Yi tribe, 201-202; at Tatu River, 202-205; in Snowy Mountains, 206; at Moukung and Maoerhkai, 207-209; in Grasslands, 209-210; across Kansu, 211; arrival in Shensi, 211; Mao in praise of, 212
Lukouchiao (*see* Marco Polo Bridge Incident)
Lytton Commission, 177

MacArthur, Gen. Douglas, 328
MacDonald, J. Ramsay, 95
Madrid, defense of and application to Wuhan, 262
Mahan, Alfred (U.S. admiral), 175
Manchukuo (Japan puppet state), 218
Manchuria, Japan invades, 171; 175-176; size and population, 178
Mao Jen-shen (Mao's father), rise from poor to rich peasant, 37-38; becomes Buddhist, 38
Mao Tse-min (youngest brother), 92, 191
Mao Tse-tan (youngest brother), 140; executed, 191
Mao Tse-tung, birth, 36; early schooling, 37, 39-40; conflicts with father, 40; marriages, 40-41, 72, 191, 297n; attends "modern" school, 42-43; then Changsha Middle School, 44; joins 1911 revolutionary army, 58; uncertain as to future, 59-60; trains as teacher, 60, and goes to Peking, 69; reacts to May Fourth Movement and becomes Marxist, 72; at founding of CCP, 82-84; expelled from Hunan as troublemaker, 93; switches vote at CCP Congress and is rewarded, 94; demoted by Comintern, 99-100; organizes peasants, 100; reinstated by CCP, edits journal, 107, and directs Peasant Institute, 108; writes famous tract in support of peasant revolts, 125-126; after Wuhan debacle, recruits revolutionary army, 140; captured but escapes, 140-141; leads Autumn Harvest Uprising, 141-142; at Chingkang-shan, 142, 148-150; declares soviets, 151; forms Mao-Chu team and moves to Maoping, 154-155, and then to Juichin, 166-168; abortive putsch on cities, 168-170; downgraded by Twenty-eight Bolsheviks, 181-182, 187-188, 189; under house arrest, 189; during Long March—elected to leadership at Tsunyi, 198-199, and later splits with Chang Kuo-tao, 207-209; his problems in Shensi, 220-223; becomes "Chairman," 225; reactions to

420

Sian Incident, 236-237; cements united front, 245-246; new capital at Yenan, 248-249; defends united front to CCP, 250, and to Yenan population, 252; reacts to Japan invasion, 256; problems after KMT retreat to Chungking, 268, 270, 272; experiments and failures in North China, 272-273, 278-280; Hundred Regiments Offensive, 280-282, and aftermath, 282-285; initiates Great Production Drive, 294, and Rectification movement, 295-296; relations with Americans—disappointment in Hurley, 325-327; rejection of Marshall, 345, distrust of Stuart, 352; preparations for civil war, 342-343; reintroduces land confiscation, 343; strategy to reduce KMT forces, 348, and recruit for PLA, 349-350; quits Yenan, 352-353; appraisal as a "creative" Marxist, 358-360; his New Democracy coalition, 360-361; begins PLA offensive, 365-368; actions after Hwai-Hai victory, 371; introduces new policies, 381-382, and meets inner Party opposition, 382-383; his concept of "continuing" revolution, 383; review of Mao's "luck", 384-386; proclaims founding of People's Republic, 387; his views on the future, 395-396
Maoerhkai, conference at, 208
Marco Polo, 49, 231, 255, 275
Marco Polo Bridge Incident (Lukouchiao), 253, 255, 261
Maring (Hendricus Sneevliet), contacts Sun, 81-82; at CCP founding, 83-84; deals with Sun, 85; manipulates Mao, 94, and aftermath, 100; recalled and quits Comintern, 100; death, 137n
Marlborough, Duke of, 292
Marshall, George C., 333, his mission and status, 334; character, 334-336; arranges PCC talks, 336-337; upbraids Chiang, 338-339; withdraws, 340; scoffs at Chiang's strategy, 341; relations with CCP leaders, 345-346; quits China, 347; 386
Marx, Karl, quoted, 72; as mechanical thinker, 358; 83, 297
Marxism, purity of doctrine supreme, 84; Mao's devotion to, 100; rigid rules of, 121, though Mao challenges orthodoxy, 155
May Fourth Movement (1919), demonstrations against Japan, 71, 176-177
Mencius (disciple of Confucius), quoted, 73
Molotov, V. M., views on CCP, 324
Moukung, conference at, 205-208
Mountbatten, Lord Louis, 302
Mukden, incident at, 175, 228; captured by PLA, 366; 227, 228, 338
Mussolini, Benito, 177, 221, 262
Myitkyina (Burma airfield), Japan captures, 293; Stilwell retakes, 304

Nagasaki, 258, 327
Nanchang, 116, 117; Chiang's Hq. at, 120; 122; taken by Reds, 138; 153; siege of, 168-169; 171, 185
Nanking, as capital of Taipings, 20; Treaty of, 74; as Sun's capital, 51, 54-55; incident at, 130; as Chiang's capital, 133, 158, 159; renovated, 161-162; sack of, 258-259; restored as KMT capital, 340
Napoleon Bonaparte, 43, 63, 156, 368
National (or Nationalist) Party, see Kuomintang
National bourgeoisie, defined, 222-223; 360
National Salvation Association, 177, 180
New Fourth Army (CCP), 252-253; actions, 278; Chiang's attack on, 284n
New Life Movement, 216-217
Newton, Isaac, as a mechanical thinker, 358
Northern Expedition, from Canton to the Yangtze, 115-117; completed to Peking, 156-158

October 10th Agreement (1945), 15
Okamura, Gen. Yasuji, description and tactics of, 282-283; tribute to, 285; KMT clears of war crimes, 371
Okinawa, 317; Japan casualties at, 317
Oyuwan (Red base), 207

Pao An, 222
Paoting Military Academy, 27
Pearl Harbor, attack on, 283
Peiping (see Peking)
Peking, name changed (1928) to Peiping, 158; restored as Peking, 384; 16, 117, 255, 338, 366, 370
Peng Teh-huit (Red commander), 168, 169

People's Republic of China, 139; proclaimed, 387
Perry, Com. Matthew C., 172, 173, 259
Ping-hsin Pass, Red victory at, 260
Po Ku, inherits CCP leadership, 180; in Kiangsi, 181, 185, 187, 188, 189; during Long March, 197, 198, 207; at Yenan, 249, 268, 272
Pock-marked Huang (gangster), 78, 129
Political Consultative Conference (1946), 336, 337, 338, 342, 344, 345
Powell, John B., 236n
Propaganda of the deed, defined, 30, 47, 56, 265
Pu Yi ("Henry"), as boy-emperor, 42, 52, 265; as emperor of Manchukuo, 218; rehabilitation of, 362-363

Quirino, Pres. Elpidio, 375

Ramgarh, 291, 294, 303
Red Army, founded, 139; 151, 170, 181; renamed Eighth Route army, 252; at Taiyuan, 259; at Ping-hsin Pass, 260; Hundred Regiments Offensive, 280-281; in defense of North China, 284; renamed PLA, 343
Revive China Club (Hsing Chung Hui), organized by Sun, 29-30; 31
Rhee, Pres. Syngman, 376
Roosevelt, Pres. Franklin D. (FDR), China policy, 287-289; at Cairo Conference, 298-299; relations with Chiang, 315, 317; relations with Chennault, 312, 315; relations with Stilwell, 315; at Yalta Conference, 328; dies, 327
Roy, M. N. (Comintern), 137, 137n

San Min Chu I (*see* Three People's Principles)
Sanko Seisako (*see* Three-alls)
Schlieffen, F. M. Alfred Graf von, 75
Schurman, J. G. (U.S. Minister), 85
Seven Gentlemen, 230, 235, 248
Shameen, 88
Shanghai, origins and description, 74-75; administration, 75; population (1919), 76; underworld, 78; Red Scare in, 117, 129; workers organize liberation, 122-123; workers massacred, 131-133; attacked by Japan (1932), 183, and again (1937), 257-258; anti-U.S. demonstrations, 343; captured by PLA, 370

Shih Ta-kai (Errant Prince of Taipings), 202, 203
Sian (city of), 213, 217, 225; history of, 231
Sian Incident, 15, 226; plot hatches, 232, and is executed, 232-233; Chiang's defiance, 234-235; reactions at Nanking and internationally, 235-236; actions of CCP, 236-237; Mme. Chiang goes to Sian, 241; Chiang released, 242
Six No Society, 265-266
Sneevliet (*see* Maring)
Snow, Edgar, 38n, 100
Soong, Ailing (Mme. H. H. Kung), 62, 65, 144, 145; manipulates currency, 309
Soong, Charlie (father), account of, 65
Soong, Chingling (Mme. Sun Yat-sen), marries, 65-66; at Canton, 119; at Wuhan and after, 134, 137-138, 144, 145
Soong, Meiling (Mme. Chiang Kai-shek), 145, marries, 146; 201, 216-217; on goodwill tour, 219; during Sian Incident, 237, 241; relations with Stilwell, 292, 293; dismisses Donald, 309; relations with Chennault, 311; domestic problems, 313-314; interest in Yenan, 320; visits U.S., 366-367; 362
Soong, T. V., at Canton, 119; 161; during Sian Incident, 237, 241; as Minister of Finance, 310, 323, 351; in Moscow, 328
Soviet Republic of China, 178, 180; declares war on Japan (1932), 187
Stalin, Joseph, conflict with Trotsky, 120; takes hand in Chinese revolution, 121; 135; telegram to Borodin, 136; efforts to direct CCP policies, 139, 146-147, 151, 155, 163, 164-165, 178; calls for united fronts, 221; during Sian Incident, 236; signs pact with Chiang, 268; pressures CCP to make terms with KMT, 11, 331; denigrates CCP, 324; attacks Japan, 327; signs treaty with Chiang, 329; loots Manchuria and turns over arms to CCP, 339; asks favor of CCP, 368
Stilwell, Gen. Joseph W., character and mission, 289; "walk-out" from Burma, 290-291; organizes Burma corps, 291; conflicts with Chiang, 291-294, 299-301; begins Burma campaign, 302-303, and meets difficulties, 303-304; conflicts with Chennault, 311-312, 314-315;

reads FDR's ultimatum to Chiang, 315, and is recalled, 316-317; his accomplishment, 317-318
Stuart, John Leighton, background, 351; attempts to arrange CCP-KMT talks, 351-352; refuses U.S. loan to Li Tsung-jen, 371
Sun Ah-mi (Sun's elder brother), 29
Sun Fo (Sun's son), as mayor of Canton, 89; as president in Nanking, 182-183; sets up secessionist government, 374; 375
Sun Ming-chiu (Young Marshal's protégé), actions at Sian Incident, 232, 233-234
Sun Tzu (early military theorist), 150, 154; quoted, 305
Sun Yat-sen, birth, background, schooling and practice as M.D., 28-29; societies organized, 29, 31, 61; travels and kidnap, 30-31; Three People's Principles, defined, 31-32, and redefined, 90-92; failed putsches, 30, 46-47; successful uprising (1911) while Sun in U.S., 50-51; as first President of the Republic, 51; problems with government, 53-54; yields presidency to Yuan Shih-kai, 54-55; as director of railroads, 61; "second revolution", 62-63; exiled in Japan, marries, 66; returns to China and forms abortive governments, 79-80; succeeds in Canton with help of USSR, 82-84; accepts CCP into KMT, 85; Borodin's influence on, 90-92; first National Congress of KMT, 94-95, 96, 97, 100; Three Great Policies, 101; as lecturer, 101-102; illness and death, 103-104; conjecture on policies had he lived, 379
Sun Yat-sen, Madame (see Soong, Ching-ling)
Sze Ko-fa (historic martyr), 238, 243

Taierhchuang, victory over Japan at, 260-261; 367
Taiping Heavenly Kingdom Rebellion, hostile account of, 19-20; friendly account of, 28-29; 202, 275
Tanaka Memorial, 175; 254, 263
Tankgu Truce, 184, 218
Taoism ("The Way"), defined, 39
Ten-ten Day, 49
Three-alls (*Sanko Seisako*), 284

Three Great Policies, defined, 101; 122
Three People's Principles (San Min Chu I), defined, 31-32, and redefined, 90-92; 101, 160, 249, 250
Three-thirds policy (CCP), defined, 297
Tientsin, boycotts at, 177; Henry Pu Yi held at by Japan, 218; besieged by PLA, 366, and captured, 370; 255
Trotsky, Leon, 96; his "permanent revolution" defined, 120; 137
Truman, Pres. Harry S., succeeds FDR, 328; demands peaceful solution in China, 11, 13, 14, 15; appoints Marshall as mediator, 333, 336; re-urges peace, 343-344; refuses loan to KMT, 354; his dilemma in China, 354-355; wins U.S. election, 366, and refuses further aid to Chiang, 367
Tsai Ting-kai (KMT general), heroic defense of Shanghai, 183, and banished to Fukien, 184; his revolt against Chiang crushed, 186; 187-188
Tseng Kuo-fan, suppresses Taiping Rebellion, 20; fakes suicides, 117; his significance to Chiang, 378-379; 202, 341
Tung Meng Hui (*see* United League)
Tungtze, battle of, 256, 257
Twenty-eight Bolsheviks, account of, 178; in Shanghai, 180; in Kiangsi, 182, 185, 187
Twenty-one Demands (Japan), 66, 174
Tzu Hsi (*see* Empress Dowager)

Unequal treaties, defined, 91; 118, 160
United League (Tung Meng Hui), founding in Tokyo, 26; oath of membership, 34; expansion in China, 47; 32, 33, 265

Wallace, Vice-Pres. Henry A., 313
Wang Ching-wei (Sun's "left hand"), background and character, 99; 264-265; youthful heroism, 265; marries, 265; relations with Sun, 98, 103, 104, 105; as chairman of CEC in Canton, 106, 107; reaction to Canton Coup, 111-112; at Wuhan, 130, 134-135; reaction to Stalin's telegram, 137; resigns from office, 143; relations with Chiang, 185, 266; relations with Japan, 266-267; flight from Chungking, 267; actions as puppet Premier at Nanking, 276-277, 386; dies, 267-268
Wang Jo-fei (CCP official), 6

INDEX

Wang Ming (leader of Twenty-eight Bolsheviks), background, 179; actions in Shanghai, 179-180; recalled to Moscow, 180, but influence continues, 188, 221; returns to China, 268-269; 270, 272, 361, 383

Waterloo, battle of, 368-369

Wedemeyer, Gen. Albert C., succeeds Stilwell, 321; relations with Chiang, 321-322, 328; on fact-finding mission, 355, and recommendations, 363

Wellington, Duke of, 368

Wen Tien-hsiang (historic martyr), 25, 238

Western Hills clique, 107, 114

Whampoa, Military Academy, opens, 97; 10, 89, 97, 98, 109, 292, 310

White Terror, 134, 138, 139, 140, 148, 164

Wu Pei-fu (warlord), 117

Wuhan, origin of name, 47n; bomb explodes at, 47, and resulting action, 48-49; capture during Northern Expedition, 116-117; labor conditions in, 121; as capital of "left" KMT (1927), 119, 142-143, and of National government (1938), 260

Yalta Conference, 328-329

Yang Hu-cheng ("Old Yang"), background, 229-230; before and during Sian Incident, 231-232, 234; threatens Chiang's life, 241-242, and punishment, 243; death, 377

Yang Kai-hui (Mao's second wife), 71, 191

Yenan, becomes CCP capital, 248-249; described, 249; foreign press visits, 319-320, and also U.S. military mission, 320-321; evacuated by CCP, 353

Yi tribe, 201-202

Yo Fei (historic martyr), 25, 238, 243

Young Marshal (Chang Hsueh-liang), biography, 227-229; during Mukden Incident, 176; before and during Sian Incident, 230-232, 234-235, 238-239; punishment, 242-243; 365, 377

Yuan Shih-kai, founds Paoting Military Academy, 27; persuades Manchus to abdicate, 52, and barters with Sun for presidency of Republic, 53-55; keeps capital at Peking, 55; dissolves parliament, 62; yields to Japan's Twenty-one Demands, 66; plans to become emperor, 67; ambitions thwarted and dies, 67; responsible for warlord era, 67-68